Yugoslavia in Transition

Choices and Constraints

Edited by John B. Allcock, John J. Horton and
Marko Milivojević

At a time when it is generally agreed that Yugoslavia is plunged into a
deep crisis, a stocktaking effort is required which goes beyond the
current conflict. The events and issues which make the headlines need to
be interpreted within their context. The contributors to this volume – all
established authorities on Yugoslav affairs from four countries, including
Yugoslavia – are agreed that the real possibilities for choice facing
Yugoslavia will only become clear in the light of a better understanding
of the complex of economic, political and cultural constraints which have
been created by Yugoslavia's past.

John B. Allcock, Chairman of the Research Unit in Yugoslav Studies,
University of Bradford;

John J. Horton, Deputy Librarian, University of Bradford;

Marko Milivojević, Honorary visiting Research Fellow in Yugoslav
Studies, University of Bradford.

Of related interest from BERG

Georges Sokoloff, *The Economy of Detente: The Soviet Union and Western Capital*

Pierre Kende and Zdenek Strmiska, *Equality and Inequality in Eastern Europe*

Hans-Joachim Veen (ed.), *From Brezhnev to Gorbachev: Domestic Affairs and Soviet Foreign Policy*

Dietrich Geyer, *The Russian Revolution: The Historical Problems and Perspectives*

Dietrich Geyer, *Russian Imperialism: The Interaction of Domestic and Foreign Policy*

Jadwiga Koralewicz, Ireneusz Blaleckl and Margaret Watson (eds), *Crisis and Transition: Polish Society in the 1980s*

Jerry Kwaśniewski, *Society and Deviance in Communist Poland: Attitudes to Social Control*

Jerry Kwaśniewski and Margaret Watson (eds), *Social Control and the Law in Poland*

Marko Milivojević, John B. Allcock and Pierre Maurer (eds), *Yugoslavia's Security Dilemmas: Armed Forces, National Defence and Foreign Policy*

Peter R. Weilemann, Georg Brunner and Rudolf L. Tökés (eds), *Upheaval Against the Plan: Eastern Europe on the Eve of the Storm*

Yugoslavia in Transition

Choices and Constraints

Essays in Honour of Fred Singleton

Edited by
John B. Allcock, John J. Horton and
Marko Milivojević

BERG
New York / Oxford
Distributed exclusively in the US and Canada by
St Martin's Press, New York

First published in 1992 by
Berg Publishers Limited
Editorial offices:
165 Taber Avenue, Providence, RI 02096, USA
150 Cowley Road, Oxford, OX4 1JJ, UK

Library of Congress Cataloging-in-Publication Data

Yugoslavia in transition : choices and constraints : essays in honour
  of Fred Singleton / edited by John B. Allcock, John J. Horton, and
  Marko Milivojević.
    p. cm.
    Includes bibliographical references and index.
    ISBN 0–85496–609–9
    1. Yugoslavia—Economic conditions—1945– 2. Yugoslavia—Politics
and government—1980– I. Singleton, Frederick Bernard.
II. Allcock, John B.   III. Horton, John J. (John Joseph), 1940–
IV. Milivojević, Marko, 1957–
HC407.Y823 1992
338.9497—dc20   90–2695
                                                                      CIP

British Library Cataloguing in Publication Data

Yugoslavia in transition : choices and constraints : essays
  in honour of Fred Singleton.
  1. Yugoslavia, history, 1945–
  I. Allcock, John B. II. Horton, John J. III.
Milivojević, Marko, *1957–* IV. Singleton, Fred *1926–1988*
949.7023

ISBN 0–85496–609–9

Printed in Great Britain by
Billing & Sons Ltd, Worcester

338.9497
Y9

Contents

Contents

Maps, Figures and Tables

Maps

Figures

Tables

Acknowledgements

The editors would like to record their gratitude to Mrs Elizabeth Singleton for permission to use two maps formerly drawn for her late husband, Fred Singleton.

Recognition is also due to the following for kindly granting permission to reproduce quotations from published copyright material: Victor Gollancz Ltd, London, for the extract from Nora Beloff, *Tito's Flawed Legacy*; Indiana University Press, Bloomington, Indiana, for the extract from Pedro Ramet, *Nationalism and Federalism in Yugoslavia, 1963–1983*; Lexington Books, Massachusetts, for the extract from John J. Dziak, *Chekitsy: a History of the KGB*, Lexington Books, Massachusetts, 1988.

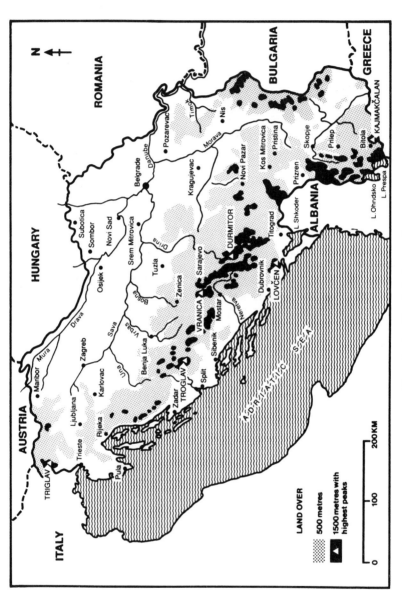

Yugoslavia: Physical Geography

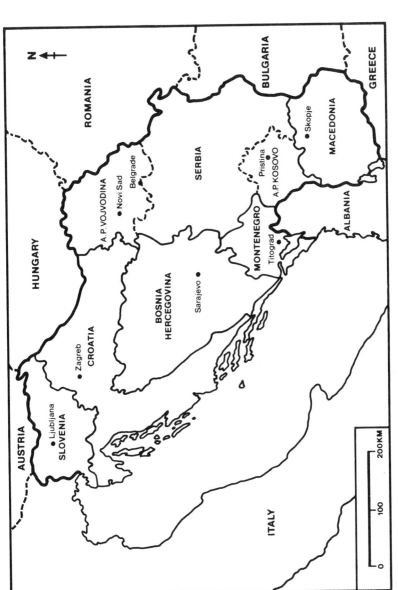

Yugoslavia: Present-day Administrative Boundaries

Introduction

John B. Allcock, John J. Horton and Marko Milivojević

Introduction

It is commonly agreed that 'Yugoslavia is in crisis'. Unfortunately, this diagnosis is of little help in providing an understanding of the nature of the country's current problems, or their causes. The term 'crisis' has no generally accepted use or definition in the social sciences, and its journalistic function appears to be to draw attention to the magnitude of problems without in any way explaining them. Contemporary discussion of Yugoslav affairs ranges over a variety of possible focal causes of 'crisis': attention has been drawn at various times over recent years to the scale of the country's international indebtedness, to high rates of inflation, the severity of inter-ethnic conflict, the prevalence of industrial disorder, and the general collapse of morale.

The solutions which have been offered are equally diverse, encompassing the discovery of a 'strong man' to lead the way (unspecified), the intervention of the military, the replacement of the current federal constitutional structure by a confederation, greater pluralism, the reassertion of party authority, and the adoption of a monetarist strategy in economic affairs. The only obvious point of agreement among these varied (and often contradictory) assessments is the affirmation that there is a 'crisis'.

'Crisis' or 'Transition'?

Without denying in any way the severity, and certainly not the existence, of the difficulties which beset Yugoslavia today, the

1

John B. Allcock, et al.

editors of this collection want to set debate about these questions in a
fresh context, leaving aside the rather unhelpful notion of 'crisis'.
Yugoslavia is without question in transition: important economic,
political and more broadly social changes are under way. Furthermore,
the current situation, for all its difficulties, does not offer the Yugoslavs
one possibility only. Their country is not heading down some deter-
ministic 'slippery slope' towards an end which is already ordained.
There are *choices* to be faced, which give alternative outcomes, and
which will be influenced by both policy and popular action. These
choices, however, are not free-floating opportunities: they are limited
in range, and each carries with it certain costs and risks. In other
words, choice takes place within a framework of *constraint*. Transition
– choice – constraint: a word is in order about each of these terms.

One of the limitations of the idea of 'crisis' is that it tends to
impose a false sense of immediacy on events. A 'crisis' is nothing if
not precipitate, sudden, and clearly defined in time. Within the haze
of connotation surrounding the term are at least two metaphors. On
the one hand, the crossroads offers us radically divergent possibilities;
totally different destinations in our journey. On the other, during
the course of a fever the disease reaches a point of intensity which
will either kill the patient, or, having been survived, will guarantee
recovery. Both of these images contain the idea of a critical point in
time at which the future is shaped in one way or another. Observers
of Yugoslav affairs both inside and outside the country no doubt
share the sense that a moment of this kind has been reached by
Yugoslavia. That may well be the case. But there is a danger that in
concentrating on the crossroads itself, one fails to see the journey as
a whole: the disease is not reducible to the single symptom of a
fever. In order to understand such critical moments, it is necessary
to place them back into the wider structures and processes which
gave rise to them. From this point of view, a 'crisis' is better
appreciated as a 'transition'.

The utility of the term 'crisis' becomes ever more doubtful as the
time during which Yugoslavia is supposed to have been 'in crisis'
steadily extends. David Dyker's recent magisterial examination of
the Yugoslav economy, roots the crisis in the economic reforms of
the mid-1960s. Harold Lydall prefers the period of economic and
constitutional change of a decade later. Even this more conservative
assessment spreads the crisis over a decade.[1] One can readily see the

1. See David Dyker, *Yugoslavia: Socialism, Development and Debt* (London,

2

force in Liliana Djeković's satirical comment with respect to the longevity of this supposedly critical moment – that 'In Yugoslavia, however, the reform of the reforms is already in preparation'![2]

An important characteristic of the work of the late Fred Singleton, to whom this volume is dedicated, was his capacity to see Yugoslav affairs as a complex whole. His writing about the country provided the reader with a broad sweep of events, or suggested a knotting together of spatial, historical, economic and political factors into a single configuration. The concern with 'transition' is appropriate to such an approach, and it is vital to our endeavours on this occasion. Yugoslavia, as it is today, is emerging from a highly particular set of historical circumstances which are more than a mere tenuous 'background' to the current situation. They continue to operate within that situation. What is more, serious as the problems of Yugoslavia are, they are not about to disappear.

The 'collapse' of Yugoslavia is heralded in several places. Two remarks are in order in relation to this possibility. First, the complete collapse of a social system is a relatively rare phenomenon, and one for which there are well-documented historical preconditions. Such a catastrophe requires either or both the active hostility of at least one very powerful external enemy, and the complete loss of resolution and cohesion on the part of its ruling stratum. Neither of these appears to hold at present. It is not unreasonable to assume, therefore, that Yugoslavia will continue into the future in one form or another.

Second, even if the frequently canvassed division of Yugoslavia were to come about, the problems which beset the country would in large measure remain, only to be resolved in another mode. The scenario which is often rehearsed in press and academic circles, whereby a 'Crovenia' composed of the former Habsburg and predominantly Catholic areas to the north and west separates from what would in effect be a 'Greater Serbia', would only create two states to confront the same problems of multi-ethnic composition, an economically marginal situation with respect to Western Europe, and the urgent need to modernize and relegitimate their state structures, which today beset Yugoslavia. *Plus ça change. . . .*

Routledge, 1990); Harold Lydall, *Yugoslavia in Crisis*, (Oxford, Clarendon Press, 1989).
    2. Liliana Djeković, 'Privredna kriza i privredna reforma u Jugoslaviji' (The Economic Crisis and Economic Reform in Yugoslavia), in Marijan Korošić (ed.), *Quo vadis, Jugoslavijo?* (Zagreb, Naprijed, 1989), pp. 23–40; see esp. p. 40.

John B. Allcock, et al.

The Dimensions of 'Transition'

One might legitimately ask, however, what kind of movement is being considered here. Without that addition of further content the notion of 'transition' is no more helpful than that of 'crisis'. Four processes come together in contemporary Yugoslavia, providing in their conjunction the terms of the equation which needs to be solved. These are: destalinization in politics, economic development, cultural modernization, decentralization.

It has been a curious feature of the past forty years that attempts to understand Yugoslavia have taken off, generally speaking ,from the points of contrast between it and the other countries of Eastern Europe. Several authors in this collection stress the uniqueness of the 'Yugoslav experiment'. This is as it should be, but an awareness of the dramatic quality of the former 'crisis', which in 1948 revealed the rift between the Communist Party of Yugoslavia and other members of the Cominform, can lead one to overlook the incompleteness of the process which was begun at that time.

The break with Stalin (as Zagorka Golubović points out forcefully) did not signal the end of Stalinism. In spite of the cosmetic change of title adopted by the former League of Communists of Yugoslavia and its several republican successors, it remains true that in Yugoslavia, Communist parties have fought more doggedly than almost anywhere else in Eastern and South-Eastern Europe to hang onto their 'leading role' in politics, *de facto* if not *de jure.*

The famous system of self-management continues to struggle uneasily and ambiguously between the status of a mere legitimating symbol and a truly distinctive political form. At the time of writing it is still unclear to what extent the 'marketization' of the economy sought by the Marković government has progressed beyond legislative prescription and has made any inroads into the culture of a politically managed (if not centrally planned) economy, in which the pole star is security of employment.

Recent events in Eastern Europe, now universally acknowledged under Mikhail Gorbachev's terms glasnost and perestroika, have served to make it very clear that in the struggle for destalinization Yugoslavia is in fact a type-case of political processes throughout the entire region, and not some kind of Balkan maverick. The study of Yugoslav affairs should no longer be the preserve of a few eccentric Yugophiles. An appreciation of what is happening in Yugoslavia has become a vital component of the comparative study which is necessary in order to grasp the general nature of the destalinization process. The relevance and interest of Yugoslavia's uniqueness lies in the special characteristics of the historical circumstances under which it has undertaken this particular transition, and not in the antiquarian curiosity of the fact of uniqueness itself.

If talk of destalinization in Yugoslavia may seem somewhat anachronistic, then reference to development may seem equally counter-intuitive. The frame of reference which treats countries in terms of 'development' and 'underdevelopment' calls to mind typically a 'Third World', which is by definition far from home. Yugoslavia is, after all, a European country.

Whereas this may indeed be an unfamiliar view of the nature of Yugoslav affairs it is far from unrealistic. Ljubomir Madžar indentifies Yugoslavia as lying within the 'upper middle' group of developing countries, measured by a number of economic indicators. Taking a longer-term historical view of the matter, at the end of the Second World War by all the classic indicators of underdevelopment there would have been no doubt that Yugoslavia merited that label. Poverty, illiteracy, ill health, low productivity, and low levels of urbanization, industrialization and capitalization were all the order of the day. Even if, as Thomas Poulsen's survey indicates, Yugoslavia has made noteworthy strides since the war in the development of its not inconsiderable human and material resources, so that today the country strikes the visitor as different from the images of starvation and squalor which are the stock-in-trade of the treatment of 'underdevelopment' in the mass media, this does not entitle us to regard the development process as in any way complete. This view is entirely consistent also with the changes in development theory over the past two decades, where concern has shifted from categories and indicators towards processes.

The development process *links* centre and periphery; it does not merely distinguish between them. In this respect Yugoslavia is still very much in a semi-peripheral position in relation to the major economic centres of Europe, regardless of its greater standard of living and economic performance in comparison with the immediately post-war years. The most visible and most hotly debated of the country's economic problems – international debt, inflation, regional inequality, industrial mislocation, and so on – are all typical perils of the development process and of semi-peripheral status.[3] It

3. It is a great pity that in this respect Nicos Mouzelis did not press through his

is only by a curious ethnocentrism that we are happy to recognize these as indicators of development problems in South America, but feel that it is somehow odd to apply them in Europe. Nevertheless, there is good reason to suggest that the entire problem of the economic dimension of the relationship of Eastern Europe to the Western part of the Continent can be illuminated by such a shift of perspective.

The significance of the development perspective in the understanding of Yugoslavia is not confined to the economic realm. A key component of the whole complex of problems which form 'underdevelopment' is the failure to develop appropriate institutions through which to handle the enhanced level and scope of both economic and political activity. The process of institutionalization, which encompasses the creation of accepted and taken-for-granted routines of action (and not just the enactment of formally constituted arrangements) is everywhere a slow and uneven process. Indeed, the search for institutional solutions can sometimes be very protracted indeed. Seen in this light, Yugoslavia's search throughout the post-war period for its own specific 'road to socialism' can be instructive as a contribution to the comparative study of the development process, and several components of the current 'crisis' are refocused as typical moments in this common transition.

'Culture' is a term which has yet to 'come in from the cold' in relation to the study of Yugoslavia. A concern with Balkan 'cultures' somehow places one in the ranks of anthropologists, and seems to suggest a preoccupation with a pre-industrial past and with local communities. Nevertheless, 'culture' is one of the continuing and fundamental concerns of social science, the general importance of which has recently been vigorously argued by Margaret Archer.[4] No appreciation of what is happening in Yugoslavia today can be anything like complete if it neglects the cultural level of analysis.

In this respect, the notion which most adequately serves to organize investigation is that of 'modernity'. This is, at the cultural level, the specific form which Yugoslavia's transition takes. Nevertheless, just as we have insisted that the political and economic standpoints from which the transition can be examined imply an

---

discussion of Yugoslavia into the post-war period. See Nicos P. Mouzelis, *Politics in the Semi-Periphery: Early Parliamentarism and Late Industrialisation in the Balkans and Latin America* (London, Macmillan, 1986).

4. Margaret S. Archer, *Culture and Agency: The Place of Culture in Social Theory* (Cambridge, Cambridge University Press, 1988).

awareness of conflict, so too the modernization process is fraught with contradictions. A multiplicity of models of modernity contend for recognition in Yugoslavia. Even within the matrix of self-management itself (and leaving aside for the moment all other elements historical and contemporary of the country's cultural diversity) there are deep differences between the sets of values which are said to be contained necessarily within the concept of self-management. Does one emphasize workers' control, or collective responsibility? Is participation fundamentally about the enhancement of security, or the raising of consumption? These and similar choices cannot be reduced to narrowly 'economic' or 'political' questions: they are located in broader moral perspectives and views about the nature of human beings and society. So much was recognized many years ago by Sharon Zukin, who characterized the basic cultural choice facing Yugoslavia as lying between 'equity' and 'efficiency'.[5] Dijana Pleština's essay at one level addresses the apparent contradiction between equity and efficiency, as this impinges specifically upon inter-ethnic and inter-regional problems in Yugoslav politics.

How else are we to understand the current struggles for national identity in Yugoslavia (at least at one level) if not in terms of a wrestling with issues relating to the creation of a modern collective identity? Similarly, the attempt to create a space for 'civil society' which lies between the state and the individual (which preoccupies many politically engaged people in Yugoslavia today) goes far beyond the search for political 'structures', and is better seen as an attempt to create a genuinely modern civic culture.

A concern with the process of decentralization, which is so centrally relevant to the chapter by Pleština emerges directly from a consideration of these other processes. At one level it can be looked at simply as a coincidental and accidental by-product of the other dimensions of transition; yet a case can be made for insisting that it has a character and momentum of its own. Whatever the political form which emerges from the attempt to ease aside the domination of the Communist Party; whatever the precise road of economic development which is followed; whatever the outcome of Yugoslavia's wrestling with modernity, one thing can be said with certainty: the viability of the result, in the Yugoslav case, will of necessity be

---

5. Sharon Zukin, *Beyond Marx and Tito: Theory and Practice in Yugoslav Socialism* (Cambridge, Cambridge University Press, 1975).

compelled to show a high degree of decentralization if it is to reflect adequately the complex structure of the country. The path of decentralization lies uneasily between various forms of centralism and fragmentation.

Pressures to lapse in both directions come from a variety of sources. The demand for greater centralization is made with bizarre unanimity both by those who represent, on the one hand, an extreme economic rationality (and who press the case for a unified Yugoslav market), and by those, on the other, who see Yugoslavia's salvation as preconditioned upon greater 'discipline'. The case for allowing greater independence to interests in politics, the economy and culture, to the point where fragmentation could be the only conceivable result, is similarly advanced from quite contradictory standpoints. To the extreme 'left' are the proponents of *oourizacija* ('boalization', as Madžar has termed it), and to the equally extreme 'right' are nationalists of various stripes.

To allow too great an influence in determining the direction of Yugoslavia's transition to any of these could be disastrous. In this respect, 'transition' must take the form of a movement towards a position of equilibrium – of stable decentralization, in which Yugoslavia's natural diversity is neither swamped by a mechanical or authoritarian centralism, nor allowed to collapse into a twentieth-century 'feudalism'.

All of these themes – destalinization, development, modernization and decentralization – are better managed within a more generous historical framework than that which is suggested by the term 'crisis'. Hence, in making them the connecting threads which bind together the various contributions to this collection of essays, the notion of 'transition' serves better to suggest the nature of their common concerns.

'Choice' and 'Constraint'

Academics are often regarded as if they are clairvoyants: their utility in relation to social events is supposed to lie in their superior ability to foresee the course of events in ways which are hidden from the lay mind. This misleading view of the character of the social sciences is in large measure kept in circulation by the fact that frequently we are tempted by this flattering image to play along with the game, especially under the seductive influence of the media of mass communication. A good deal of the expertise of social scientists, however, lies in our ability to disclose the complexity of situations and reveal the multiplicity of possible outcomes which are contained in any situation. It is the task of the entrepreneur or the politician to convince the public that what they have to offer is a bet on certainties. Social scientists, by way of contrast, should be ready to listen to the warning of Bob Dylan in 'The Times They are a Changing' (1963):

> Come writers and critics / who prophesize with your pen
> And keep your eyes wide / the chance won't come again;
> And don't speak too soon / for the wheel's still in spin,
> And there's no telling who / that it's naming.

Bearing in mind this point, the studies offered here do not set out to provide a prediction about the future of Yugoslavia. What the editors have been able to do, however, is to assemble contributions from fifteen experienced observers of the Yugoslav scene, some of them eminent Yugoslav academics, who are able to enhance the general appreciation of what might be the range of possible futures for the country and the nature of the forces and factors bearing on that choice. In other words, our concern is to indicate the choices available to Yugoslavia, and the constraints within which the direction of future development might be determined.

At the time at which these contributions are written, in common with all the other countries of Eastern and South-Eastern Europe, Yugoslavia is enmeshed in a complex series of changes. A number of potentially important legislative and constitutional proposals have been enacted, or are going through the parliamentary process, which will open up for the country specific avenues of development while closing off others. At the time of going to press also, although it is clear that the League of Communists effectively no longer exists (at least at the federal level) and a multitude of parties and groups aspiring to become parties have emerged, the form which political organization will take in the long run, replacing the League's forty-year monopoly, is by no means clear.

This degree of uncertainty does not mean that the authors whose work is collected here are prepared foolishly to rush into print where their angelic colleagues fear to tread. The enactment of a piece of legislation is no guarantee of its effectiveness; and the public launching of a political party gives no assurance whatever of its

9

longevity, and certainly not where multi-party politics is so novel and so insecurely established. Manifestos can give little if any indication of how newly-elected politicians will behave in practice. It is entirely possible that few of the expectations which they entertain about the future of their country will be realized in the future.

In addressing ourselves to the task of suggesting the nature of the choices and constraints which face contemporary Yugoslavia, the editors have tried to avoid any temptation to engage in a Russian roulette of prediction, or to extract the maximum possible significance from the fine detail of current affairs. Our aim has been to make intelligible both choice and constraint by displaying the underlying structures and processes which will shape events.

In this endeavour we have not sought to select only writers who share a single view about Yugoslavia, or to enforce an editorial assessment of events onto the contributors. A variety of views are both possible and legitimate regarding virtually every aspect of the country and its affairs tackled in this collection. To allow these possible contradictions to stand does not invalidate our task and is, in fact, directly relevant to our aim of emphasizing open historical possibility. It might be said to strengthen the reader's appreciation of the range of issues and the complexity of both the choices and constraints which will shape Yugoslavia's future.

To take only two examples of this diversity of views: Zagorka Golubović's conviction that the legacy of self-managing socialism will give a permanent cast to Yugoslav politics and society does not appear to be shared by Dijana Pleština. Evaluations of the past economic performance of Yugoslavia, and the reasons for its continuing economic difficulties, advanced by several of our authors, do not coincide.

The Contributions

The aims set out above are accomplished in two ways. Part I is composed of four long review-essays (by Poulsen, Golubović, Madžar and Pleština), which take a broad overview of the geography, and the social, economic and political development of Yugoslavia. (In their breadth of scope they might be said to provide an updating of Fred Singleton's own survey, *Twentieth Century Yugoslavia*, published a decade ago.) They are offered as a comprehensive framework within which to place more specific discussions of events or problems relating to contemporary Yugoslavia. It is important to note that two of the four are by prominent Yugoslav academics who are all engaged very actively in one form or another with issues of policy relating to their country. They are people who are intimately in contact with the material which they have to offer. Their contributions are not only of significance and interest for that reason, but also because there is far too little communication between Yugoslav scholars and the English-speaking world. In the normal course of events it is too easy to allow the definition of problems to be shaped by the projection of our own concerns. The future of Yugoslavia will be determined by the Yugoslavs themselves, however, and not by the prejudices and preferences (however well-informed) of outsiders. How Yugoslavs see their own future, therefore, is of particular relevance to our consideration of 'choices' and 'constraints'.

Possibly it is a consequence of this lack of communication with Yugoslav social scientists in the past that the task of attempting an understanding of Yugoslav affairs often has been undertaken on too narrow a front, allowing too much weight to too limited a range of factors. Thus, in the 1960s, one might have been forgiven for thinking that Yugoslav reality was exhausted by 'self-management'; in the 1970s, perhaps issues relating to the relations between the republics dominated discussion. In the 1980s the range of interests became wider, in that specifically economic problems such as debt and inflation competed for attention with the significance of nationalism. Nevertheless, even if we take all of these topics together, this still leaves unexplored a remarkably long list of important questions. These are of two kinds. In the first place we do not know anything like enough about the ways in which major trends and processes in Yugoslav society have consequences in practice for the detailed development of institutions or the way in which daily life unfolds for the ordinary people of the country. Furthermore, we do not devote enough attention to examining the ways in which those large-scale events and processes which attract the greatest attention from external observers of Yugoslavia are themselves rooted in lower levels of reality.

The intention of Part II, therefore – which includes the bulk of the contributions – confronts the problem of 'choice' and 'constraint' by beginning to redress this imbalance. Here authors have been invited to address themselves to a range of specific issues which have a direct bearing on the great problems which confront

Yugoslavia today. With only one exception, these essays are published here for the first time. In each case the author has been invited to participate in the project because of his or her ability to provide the reader with insights into aspects of the study of Yugoslav affairs, where the literature in English is either very thin or non-existent. This they have done in one of three ways.

Those in the first group provide the reader with a more-or-less systematic survey of an area of problem in which the material is either relatively scattered and fragmentary or poorly known in the English-speaking world. To this category belong Milan Mesić's treatment of the history of labour migration from Yugoslavia, and Marko Milivojević's survey of the Yugoslav intelligence community.

The second group deals with subject-areas which are probably better known, but they offer distinctive theoretical insights or angles of approach to the topic in question. Three essays are of this kind: Will Bartlett's econometric assessment of foreign trade and the stabilization policy in the labour-managed economy, Andrew Wood's review of Anglo-Yugoslav diplomatic relations (a rare venture into print by a serving diplomat), and John Allcock's treatment of Yugoslav nationalism in relation to the theory of political discourse.

The third and largest group, containing five contributions, consists of reports of original research projects into Yugoslav materials, either of a documentary or directly empirical character. Two papers deal particularly with issues relating to policy formation. Donna Parmelee examines the problems confronting the health services in Yugoslavia. Barbara Jančar reviews the gradual emergence of environmental policy. Four authors concern themselves with relatively under-researched aspects of the institutional structure of the Yugoslav economy. Patrick Artisien and Alan Brown evaluate the growth of investment by Yugoslav enterprises in foreign countries. John B. Allcock explores the role of the private sector in Yugoslavia with particular reference to the growth of tourism. Sabrina Ramet assesses the extent of the freedom of the Yugoslav press.

Two additional contributions lend a distinctive character to this volume. The intention of the editors in gathering this collection of essays has been to provide a memorial for the late Fred Singleton, our colleague at the University of Bradford for many years. Fred's contribution to the development and defence of Yugoslav studies has been considerable. Tony Topham, a longstanding friend and co-worker with Fred, has kindly agreed to provide in his introductory essay a personal view of his career which traces the inextricably interwoven components of academic and political commitment and of personality which provided the core of Fred's involvement with Yugoslavia. Topham's tribute conveys also the spirit of respect and affection with which the editors would like to present this book. John Horton has compiled also a comprehensive bibliography of Fred Singleton's writing about Yugoslavia, which both acknowledges his achievement in the field of Yugoslav studies, and constitutes a useful research tool for those who, along with the editors, wish to further the understanding of the remarkable country which is Yugoslavia.

April 1990

Fred Singleton: A Personal Memoir

Tony Topham

I first met Fred Singleton when we arrived concurrently at Leeds University as first-year undergraduates in 1947. He was already known to me by repute, as something of a legend in the radical youth politics of wartime Hull, our common home town. Being three years my senior, he had joined the Hull Youth Parliament in 1943, whilst a sixth-former at Hull Grammar School. (Youth Parliaments were sponsored by local education authorities, as an encouragement to young people to prepare for active roles in the post-war reconstruction of political society.) Fred also joined the local WEA branch, which was then a thriving centre for many political and cultural activities. But in 1944 he had been called up into the Navy, and had spent three years on active service in the Mediterranean.

This explains why we started University life at the same time, despite the age difference. It was not uncommon at that time: in my own faculty, a large majority of the male undergraduates were ex-servicemen. Fred was distinguished from most of them in not drawing attention either to his seniority or his naval service. He seemed no different in spirit from the school-leavers amongst us.

Fred's infectious, gregarious activism, which he sustained throughout his life, was evident already in the lively, debating, adolescent schoolboy. It was a quality remembered by his Hull friends of that period, several of whom retained that friendship to the end, and who came in numbers to his memorial party in Ilkley's Assembly Rooms in February 1988. Joyce Ramsay spoke to us on that occasion, recalling the teenage Fred conducting earnest political discourses with his fellow Youth-Parliamentarians, as he wheeled his bicycle home with them, after meetings, through the blitz-devastated and blacked-out streets of Hull.

In an article which he contributed to *Forum*, the journal of the

Hull Youth Parliament in October 1943, he chose to attack 'Vansittartism'. Lord Vansittart was a notorious Germanophobe, who had harassed the Chamberlain government for its pre-war appeasement of Hitler, from his post in the Foreign Office.[1] His politics might be thought to have expressed popular feeling in the midst of the war, but Fred showed that Vansittart represented a xenophobic and racist frenzy, which failed entirely to distinguish between Nazism and the German people. Against this the young writer inveighed, as carrying with it the vindictive seed of a new Versailles Treaty, and of future wars and atrocities. Fred, even at that early stage, had chosen an international, European theme, and one related to the question of nationality, and of unbridled chauvinistic prejudice.

Fred was born in 1926, and attended Hull Grammar School from 1937 to 1944. He wrote some autobiographical fragments towards the end of his life, in which he testifies to having had a happy childhood, which was rudely interrupted when he was sent as a war-evacuee at the age of twelve, to Thorne, a mining village near Goole, twenty-eight miles from Hull. This was such an unwelcome shock to him that he promptly ran away – back home! He was persuaded to return, and was billeted with mining families during his three-year stay, whilst German bombers were reducing much of his home town to rubble. His acute and humorous recollections of the life and characters of that earthy and bucolic community were part of Fred's anecdotal stock-in-trade ever after.

This was the Fred of whom I heard tell when I joined the Hull WEA branch, as I in turn reached sixth-form rank at Beverley Grammar School; he had by then joined the Navy. We were common products of the zealous, earnest, radical climate in which workers' education and left-wing politics flourished during and immediately following the war. I think we both responded to it with the same sense of revelation, since we both came from conservative, semi-detached, suburban, white-collar environments.

In Leeds, Fred was an outstanding student politician. In the student Socialist Society, his influence was extensive, and primarily directed towards the fostering of international links. He brought the first Chinese Communist student delegation to Britain and to Leeds; I recall only that they even *looked* like revolutionaries, with their standard black uniforms and serious demeanour.

1. A. J. P. Taylor, *English History, 1914–45* (London, Oxford University Press, 1965), p. 405.

Some of the scope of his work over these years is indicated by a brief and selective catalogue, which includes: Vice-President of the Student's Union in Leeds, Vice-President of the National Union of Students (NUS), Organizer of work camps and arts festivals, and a member of the NUS delegations to the International Union of Students' Conferences in Prague and Warsaw. He also made his first visits to the two countries which were to preoccupy him all his life, when he took part in road construction in British Youth Brigade camps in Yugoslavia in 1947, and in resettlement work for Karelian refugees in Finland, 1949.[2]

He found time to chair the Student Tuberculosis Foundation, to socialize energetically with a wide range of friends, and to graduate with a good honours degree in Geography. His degree dissertation was on 'The Historical Geography of Malta', chosen undoubtedly because of his first-hand knowledge of the island, from where he had sent back a long series of reports to Joyce Ramsay in Hull, during his naval service. This is another example of the remarkable continuity of Fred's concerns, for he retained an active interest in Maltese politics and the career of Dom Mintoff through the years.

His MA thesis concerned 'The Kalevala and the Historical Geography of Finland'.[3] Again we find the return to an already known

2. Fred gave a retrospective account of the Brigades at a seminar in Kragujevac in September 1987, which was published, posthumously, along with the other proceedings of the seminar, by the Institute for Contemporary History in Yugoslavia, in November 1988. Fred, together with the late Dr Branko Vuković, had been responsible for convening the seminar. His paper was singled out for attention at the launch of the publication, by Dr Venceslav Glišić, the Assistant Director of the Institute, saying that it was 'of particular interest, because it is a unique account and without his contribution we would have been less aware of one form of cooperation between young people of our two countries . . .'

Fred covers, in documented detail, including a wealth of statistics, the process of resettlement of refugees in Finland, in his *The Economy of Finland in the Twentieth Century* (Bradford, Bradford University Research, 1987), pp. 71–6. He shows that the sudden frontier changes between Russia and Finland, in 1940 and again in 1944, when Finland was twice forced to cede territory to the Russians, affected 11 per cent of the population – 420,000 people. 'Almost all the inhabitants of the ceded areas exercised their right to leave their homes, and to settle in Finland. . . The absorption of this large number of displaced persons . . . created many economic and social strains at a time when the Finns were grappling with the daunting problems of post-war reconstruction and of meeting their obligations under the reparations agreement. The fact that it was accomplished successfully in so short a time speaks volumes for the civic responsibility and social cohesion of the Finnish nation.' He adds, in a footnote, that 'some of the work of forest clearance and land reclamation was carried out by voluntary youth and student brigades. The present author was one of many British students who participated in this work during the summer of 1949.'

3. The Kalevala is the national folk epic of the Finns, a compilation of poems (runes), based on oral traditions which date back to the first millennium AD.

country, and one whose experience and sufferings called forth all of Fred's abundant capacity not only for enquiry and scholarship, but also for love.

By this time, Fred and I were, as postgraduate students, sharing a distinctly run-down flat in the vicinity of the university owned by a cheerfully rapacious landlady. In his warm-hearted and energetic company, I was able to observe and to share some of his concerns and enthusiasms. The flat, along with every house in that decrepit old street, has long been demolished, but the cobble-stones have been preserved, along with my memories of a man at war against injustice, whilst at peace with his chosen subject, the saga of a small people's struggle for national identity and independence.

Fred's affection for the people of small nations, engulfed throughout history by the predatory attentions of over-mighty neighbours and imperial conquerors – Finland and Yugoslavia having this theme in abundance and in common – is at the heart of his life's work and commitment. He was apt to say that Marxists, whilst properly concerned with class and with economic forces, underestimated nationalism as an influence in history and politics. His empathy with the subject, nation's nationalism, which was a liberating force, was matched by his hatred of xenophobia, imperialism, and racism.

The dual approach to an understanding of these forces, embodied in the titles of both the Maltese and the Finnish theses, was a consistent theme in Fred's teaching. In all his later studies, we find the same intersection of geography and history. It is an important truth to insist upon, as he did, that geography is historical and history is geographical, that time and space are the primary raw materials out of which economies, societies, cultures, nations and states are constructed. It is necessary to combine these disciplines for an understanding of the creations of these influences. What emerged in Fred's case were characteristically empirical geopolitical studies.

Whilst this research was in train, international student politics was exerting a profound effect upon Fred's whole outlook. He was involved in the great schism which rent European socialism in the early years of the Cold War, and as Eastern Europe fell under the dehumanizing control of Stalinist regimes. He struggled through conferences which were fraught with the machine-politics of the communist-dominated executive of the International Union of Students (IUS), witnessed and fought against the gerrymandering, the coercive pressures, and the abuse of procedure, which went with the Stalinist mode of conducting political conferences.

Fred has left us a sketch of what this was like, in the inaugural Olof Palme Memorial Lecture, which he gave at the University of Leeds in 1986.[4] (Fred himself was instrumental in founding this annual lecture, in honour of his old friend, so cruelly murdered in 1986.) Fred and Olof Palme, having helped to build Yugoslav roads together, became co-activists in the IUS in the early 1950s, and took part together in its Prague Congress of 1950. The Communist Party had embarked on the manipulation of student politics in the interests of Soviet foreign policy, in the previous year, as part of its demand that dissident Yugoslavia should be expelled, not only from the Cominform, but from everything else! Fred recalled the atmosphere:

> we were subject to the most appalling pressures from the official organizations in Prague. I can still recall those long appeals to Stalin which finished every speech made by an East European delegate, when the whole audience, except the Swedes, the Danes and the British, rose to their feet and rhythm-clapped for minutes on end: 'Stalin, Stalin, Stalin.' There was one girl in the East German delegation who, whenever this happened, produced a head and shoulders portrait of Stalin, almost life-sized, and waved it with the light of battle in her eye – 'Stalin, Stalin, Stalin'. That was the atmosphere of this Congress.

Olof Palme's reaction was to pull out of the IUS in disgust, and to help form COSEC, the Co-operative Secretariat of Students' Unions. Fred was for staying and fighting from the inside, as a democratic socialist opposition to the Stalinist take-over. He warned Palme that the United States Central Intelligence Agency

4. The lecture was published posthumously as *Olof Palme, Man of Peace, (1927–1986)*, by Michael McGowan, the Leeds Euro-MP, with the support of the Socialist Group of the European Parliament. Michael McGowan was a friend of Fred's, and they collaborated to found what is intended to become an annual lecture. The second lecture was, at Fred's suggestion, given by Martin Ennals, secretary of International Alert, in 1987. The third, in 1988, on the subject of apartheid in South Africa, was given by Lisbet Palme, Olof's widow. The occasion was an international one 'tinged with emotion for more than the obvious reasons'. ('Women', supplement of the *Yorkshire Evening Post*, 13 December 1988). As Lisbet Palme explained to the press: 'Fred Singleton met Olof even before I did, in the late forties, when they, as young people involved in politics, met at different places in Europe. Even then they found themselves in between the super powers in the struggle for domination . . . People like Olof and Fred could not be bought . . . I wanted very much to come here. I wanted really to come because Fred was such a good friend. They had so many common experiences.' The two widows, Lisbet and Elizabeth were able to meet and talk privately, too.

(CIA) would infiltrate COSEC in its turn, which is precisely what happened. When Palme recognized that COSEC was subject to this treatment he quickly dropped it, and the organization disappeared. The cold hands of the secret services in both camps operated in such a way as to close down and shut out any space between them, which might have been occupied by an independent socialist voice. This was no mere debating forum for a privileged student youth movement: whilst these struggles were taking place, show-trials in Prague were preparing the way for the judicial murder of old communist and socialist leaders, whilst less-renowned figures simply disappeared, throughout Eastern Europe. It was a fearful time, in which it was virtually impossible for independent socialists to get it right; possibly both the Palme and the Singleton decisions involved 'mistakes'.

In Britain too, the Labour movement faced its own problems of CIA infiltration. Whilst Arthur Deakin, General Secretary of the Transport and General Workers' Union, personified the bullying, witch-hunting mentality which went along with virulent anti-communism, the Bevanites struggled for that space, that third voice, in a hostile world. Ironically, Fred found himself, as Chairman of the Organising Committee of the 1951 National Students' Festival in Leeds, presiding over an event which was sponsored by, amongst others, the Congress for Cultural Freedom (CCF). Stephen Spender contributed a lecture at the Festival, on 'Students and National Culture'. The CCF and Spender were devoted to the anti-communist cause.

In these experiences lies a large part of the explanation for Fred's growing commitment to the independent road to socialism declared by Yugoslavia in 1948. It also entered into his assessment of Finland's struggle for a neutral independence, faced with the hegemonic Soviet Union as its next-door neighbour. In Fred's studies of the very specific geo-politics of that country, published over the years, he analysed the so-called phenomenon of 'Finlandisation', the craven accommodation to Russian interests of which Finland was accused by Western commentators and politicians. Fred defended the Finns, seeking to show how their skills and courage held the embrace of the Russians at increasingly tolerable arms' length. By 1982, he was dismissing 'Finlandisation' as a cold war propagandist device, used by right-wing writers such as Peregrine Worsthorne and West German politicians, to inhibit any attempt by the left in Western Europe to move out of the cold war strait-jacket towards a non-aligned and radical socialism and disarmament.[5] I believe that the trauma of his experiences in Prague and Warsaw led Fred thereafter to be extremely chary of committing himself to collective left-wing politics, or to any movement which looked remotely like a faction. He never wavered in his active membership of the Labour Party, but henceforth sought no office or personal influence. The parliamentary seat which he later contested was Harrogate, a no-hoper for any Labour candidate, fought as an educational campaign to hold out a socialist alternative.

After a short spell as a grammar school teacher in Bradford between 1953 and 1955, he joined the team of WEA organizing tutors in the Yorkshire North District. I had entered the same service one year previously and was delighted to welcome my old friend. We worked together in happiest association for the next seven years, even managing to synchronize our marriages and our parenthoods!

In the WEA, Fred concentrated on two main developments: the study and teaching of Yorkshire local history, and the organization of exchange visits, adult schools and research, between our WEA groups and tutors and the Workers' and People's Universities in Slovenia and Dalmatia. Working together with Fred Sedgwick, the doyen of WEA District Secretaries, he obtained the support of the United Nations Educational, Scientific and Cultural Organization (UNESCO) for those projects.[6] In this, and as a local historian, he made original contributions. He wrote, with Bill Tate, *A History of Yorkshire*.[7] He published, too, with me, a Fabian Research Series' study of *Workers' Control in Yugoslavia*.[8]

And here, as Titoism lost its appearance as a temporary and precarious aberration, and assumed its influential and permanent role as a founder of the non-aligned movement and as a new model

---

5. See, for example, F. Singleton, 'Finland, Comecon, and the EEC', *World Today*, February 1974, pp. 64–71; F. B. Singleton, 'Finland between East and West', *World Today*, August 1978, pp.321–32; and Fred Singleton, 'The Myth of "Finlandisation"', *International Affairs*, Journal of the Royal Institute of International Affairs, Spring 1981, pp.271-85. In the last article, Fred quotes from an article in the *Sunday Telegraph* (21 October 1979) by Worsthorne, 'When the New Soviet Men Take Over', which warned 'of a Left wing Labour government coming to power that would be prepared actually to cooperate with the Kremlin's plans for European "Finlandisation".'

6. See *Adult Education in Yugoslavia*, Report of a Delegation from the Yorkshire North District of the WEA (Leeds, Workers' Educational Association, 1960).

7. Fred Singleton and Bill Tate, *A History of Yorkshire* (Darwen Finlayson, 1960; reprinted Chichester, Phillimore Press, 1975).

8. Frederick Singleton and Anthony Topham, *Workers' Control in Yugoslavia*, London, Fabian Society, Fabian Research Series, no. 233, February 1963.

of market and self-managing socialism, the space which Fred had sought began to emerge. The New Left was born, and following it in the 1960s, the Workers' Control movement. Both were eager for news and views on the Yugoslav scene;[9] Fred's unique specialism was defining itself for him, as the 1950s became the 1960s. When he moved on from the WEA to take his first post as a lecturer in Geography at Bradford College of Advanced Technology, in 1963,[10] it took him just two years before he established the Research Unit in Yugoslav Studies, to coincide with the College's transition to university status. In 1972, the Unit became the Post-Graduate School of Yugoslav Studies, with Fred as its Chairman. In 1968 he became a Senior Lecturer, and in 1977 Reader, in Yugoslav Studies. After his retirement, he was made a Senior Visiting Fellow of the University, and was awarded an Honorary Doctorate of Letters. Some of his other multifarious duties and functions are listed below.[11]

Bradford's Vice-Chancellor Ted Edwards showed wisdom and courage in facilitating a centre of Yugoslav studies, and in enabling Fred, from this base, to become Britain's most distinguished expert on that country. He proceeded to produce a steady stream of his own writings, and supervised an impressive flow of postgraduate theses, which ranged widely over Yugoslav economic, geographical and political topics. He was constantly called upon, by editors of journals, encyclopaedias and annual surveys, and by the BBC, for definitive commentaries on Yugoslav current affairs. The present

9. See, for example, Fred Singleton and Tony Topham, 'Yugoslav Self-Management', in *New Left Review*, Vol. 18, Jan.–Feb. 1963, pp. 73–85, and Fred Singleton, 'Workers' Self-Management and the Role of Trade Unions in Yugoslavia', in Michael Barratt Brown, Ken Coates and Tony Topham (eds.), *Trade Union Register 1970* (London, Merlin Press, 1970).
10. In yet another coincidental and curious parallel in our careers, I had left the WEA for Hull University's Adult Education Department in 1962. But I did not lose touch with Fred, who visited his parents in Hull regularly, as well as taking part in joint political projects with me. Family holidays in the Yorkshire Dales made another happy point of contact.
11. Organizer of field courses for Geography students in Finland, Austria and Yugoslavia; external examiner for postgraduate theses on Yugoslav topics for the Universities of Sussex, Strathclyde, and Oxford (St Anthony's) and the London School of Economics; member of the Board of Studies in Social Sciences; staff member of the Students' Union Council; member of Senate sub-committees on student accommodation, extra-mural activities, and staff appointments; Chairman of the Bradford University World University Service Committee; Vice-President of the British-Yugoslav Society; Chairman of the National Association for Soviet and East European Studies; member of editorial or advisory Boards on *Soviet Studies*, the Abstracting Service for Soviet and East European Studies, Cambridge University Press Soviet and East European Studies; and Principal Investigator for the SSRC Project on Decentralization in Yugoslavia – an inter-university research project.

volume is of course a celebration of and testimony to the high esteem in which Fred's scholarship is held by specialists in this field, both in Britain and in Yugoslavia. The comprehensive bibliography, which John Horton has contributed here, demonstrates the wide range of his authorship, reaching well beyond the formal limits of his appointment in Yugoslav Studies at the University.

In his very first year at Bradford, the Skopje earthquake evoked from him an entirely characteristic response. He helped to organize a major programme of relief work for the stricken city, in the form of a student voluntary work-camp, which he led out, and in which 150 students participated for a three-month period. The project was awarded the United Nations International Co-operation Year Medal, and Bradford and Skopje became twinned towns.

Fred's tireless efforts at every opportunity to generate and improve contacts between socialists and humanists on the widest possible scale found a new expression in 1974, when he was one of the animators of the seminar on The Just Society, organized under the auspices of the Bertrand Russell Peace Foundation and Bradford University. This brought together Zhores Medvedev, and the work of his brother Roy, with representatives of the German and Austrian socialists, the Italian Communists, the British Labour Party, and a cross-section of Christian Socialists and East European 'Independents'.[12] Out of this seminar grew the discussion which led inexorably to the formation of the European Nuclear Disarmament Campaign.

Whilst this example shows that Fred retained all his commitment to the humanist-socialist project, his excursions into formal politics were now limited. He had last played a public role in the 1959 general election, which he fought for Labour in the Harrogate constituency. On that occasion – as in 1987 – Labour went down to a third successive defeat. And, as in the 1980s, there was much soul-searching and self-examination by the party in its aftermath. A fierce battle raged between left and right, as the party leader, Hugh Gaitskell, and his sympathizers, sought to attribute defeat to the party's commitment to public ownership, and argued from this assertion that the party should delete Clause 4, sub-section 4, of its constitution, which commits it to 'secure for the workers by hand or by brain the full fruits of their industry and the most equitable

---

12. The papers presented at this seminar were later published as Ken Coates and Fred Singleton (eds), *The Just Society* (Nottingham, Spokesman Books, 1977).

distribution thereof that may be possible upon the basis of the common ownership of the means of production, distribution and exchange, and the best obtainable system of popular administration and control of each industry or service'.

The resistance to Gaitskell's revisionism – which was more than cosmetic, since if successful it would have ended the socialist nature of the party – was led by the large trade unions and parliamentary left. Fred attended the party conference in Blackpool after the election, and contributed this speech to the debate on the causes of the defeat:

I do not know why most of you joined the Labour Party but I know why I did. I joined the Labour Party because I believed it was an instrument of social change that was going radically to alter the fundamental basis of our society. There are other instruments of change – social, even re-ligious, and in other forms, educational – which may bring about change; but I believed the Labour Party was the main political instrument for change. It seems to me that the people who wish to water down our socialism and to make small the differences between our kind of society, the way of life we represent, and that of the other political parties, are so blurring the image that this Party presents to the public that we are going to find that the average voter says: 'What is the difference between these parties except that one wants to put one set of faces in Downing Street and the other another set?'

This tendency to get away from the basic principles of our philosophy is one which is going to weaken our appeal to young people who are looking for a distinct and new approach in politics. I think there is a lot we can do within our philosophy of public ownership to win popularity. I do not think we should stick necessarily to the idea of the public monopoly of the existing nationalized service industries.

So far, we have not taken over any manufacturing industry. The methods to be used there may be quite different from those used in the public service industries. I should like to see a publicly-owned industry which is setting an example to the rest of industry in worker–manage-ment relations. I have not seen much of this in existing nationalization. We must set up some form of democracy in industry in which workers and consumers participate in the decisions about running the industry.[13]

13. Fred's advocacy of industrial democracy at the 1959 conference sprang of course from the Yugoslav model of self-management. It was to be another four years before the first Workers' Control Conference was held in Britain, eight years before the foundation of the Institute for Workers' Control, and fifteen years before a Labour Government with a manifesto commitment to legislate for industrial democ-racy was elected. In the event, the Prime Minister, Harold Wilson stalled on the project, then referred it to the Bullock Committee, whose recommendations were in

Then we might make some headway by giving a new image of national-ization to the public mind.

We lost the last election partly on our programme but mainly on what we were doing in the four or five years before the election took place. We had an ineffective parliamentary opposition because the image that they presented to the public mind was a blurred one. *It was not a clear picture of a new society*. . . . We did not present our philosophy of a Socialist Society which we are going to bring in, as contrasted to the philosophy of the capitalist society around us . . . We should do far more through the trade unions and our own Party organisation to educate our members in socialism, so that when we go to the country they will know what we are talking about and have a clear idea of the society we wish to create.[14]

There is here perhaps a hint of disillusion; Fred puts his belief in the party's radical intentions in the past tense. But he was not a dogmatic fundamentalist. Here, whilst he affirms the basic principles and the goal without compromise, his programmatic suggestions are modulated, attuned to the next possible steps – but steps in a purposeful march – towards a 'new society'.

By the end of the 1950s, when Fred made that speech, he had sustained some seventeen years of political activism. At the outset, he had battled through the onset of cold war politics internationally. The temporary relief initiated by Khrushchev, who actually visited Yugoslavia and shook the hand of the arch-deviator Tito, was short-lived, and it was Khrushchev who ordered the Russian tanks to crush the Hungarian rising in Budapest. At the end of the decade, Macmillanite complacency ruled Britain, and a Labour leadership, pusillanimous in its function as opposition, sought to dowse all flames of radical protest, such as the Campaign for Nuclear Disarmament, which arose in its own ranks.

Fred did not entirely abandon formal politics thereafter – he contested the European election for Labour in North Yorkshire in 1979 – but he now inclined to the 'long-haul' perspective. Some time in the 1970s, he said to me, as I too registered a degree of exhaustion from my work for the Workers' Control movement, 'socialism will not come in our lifetime'. This was not a desertion on his part, for socialism was not for him a career to be taken up or

---

turn diluted, frustrated, and abandoned, in the face of subversive threats from big business.

14. Labour Party *Annual Conference Report* (London, The Labour Party, 1959; my italics).

put down, but a moral imperative by which he lived his daily life, and ordered his priorities. He was not embittered, except perhaps momentarily towards old Stalinists, some of whom he still occasionally stumbled across in academic common rooms. Fred was a tolerant man, but he was prepared to make an exception in that case; Stalinism he did truly abhor.

But we should turn to reflect now with thankfulness on his decision to take early retirement in 1981, and of the rewarding and fruitful activities to which he then devoted himself. The output of his last years was prolific, as though he knew that he had a limited time ahead. He produced definitive texts on the economy of Finland,[15] on a new history of Yugoslavia,[16] and on environmental pollution in the Soviet Union and Eastern Europe.[17] His general knowledge of Eastern Europe, as of Scandinavia, was always wide-ranging and profound. He also revised his history of Yorkshire. In his studies of pollution in actually existing socialist countries, he broke new ground, and adopted an increasingly Green approach, asserting that industrialization brought natural havoc with it, whether practised in capitalist or socialized societies.[18] But this was more by way of challenging apologists who assumed that of course socialism was without sin, than an anti-communist rejection of any possibility of regeneration in Russia and Eastern Europe. He lived to see the first phases of Mikhail Gorbachev's new beginning, and warmly welcomed them.

In his 'retirement', he toured Europe freely, calling on old friends, both amongst the great and the good, such as Olof Palme, and amongst his purely private friends such as Petar Cvitković, the

15. Fred Singleton, *The Economy of Finland in the Twentieth Century* (Bradford, University of Bradford, 1987).

16. Fred Singleton, *A Short History of the Yugoslav Peoples* (Cambridge, Cambridge University Press, 1985).

17. Fred Singleton, 'Czechoslovakia: Greens versus Reds' and 'National Parks and Conservation of Nature in Yugoslavia', in Fred Singleton (ed.), *Environmental Problems in the Soviet Union and Eastern Europe* (Boulder, Colo., Lynne Rienner, 1987), pp. 169–82; 183–99.

18. Fred summarizes the situation in Eastern Europe as follows: 'The overall picture that one gleans from a study of the problems in the Soviet Union and Eastern Europe as a whole – and the material presented in this book represents a very small corner of a vast subject – is that, whilst old attitudes that refused to recognize that socialist societies are capable of committing ecological atrocities are being abandoned, a coherent new approach has not yet emerged. The Greens are no longer seen as enemies of socialism, but they are often regarded as irrelevancies, who may be ignored. Perhaps the Communist authorities should pay heed to Tito's statement that no country can call itself truly socialist that fails to protect its environment.' Ibid., p. 9.

carpenter from Split, whom he had first met in 1958 when that young, fine-minded man was working on an unfinished hotel which was scheduled to house a WEA study group in the town! Thirty years later, Petar now lives in Germany, with his German wife Ipse and a grown-up family. They all came to Fred's memorial party in 1988.

Amongst others on his itinerary, he told me that he always made a point of dropping in on Milovan Djilas, when he visited Belgrade. This might have been considered indiscreet, given Fred's status as a well-known friend of Yugoslavia, and a sympathetic scholar of its society. But, he explained, 'Djilas is old, lonely, and ostracised.' The instinct was humanitarian, rather than political. In the 1960s, he had observed and debated sympathetically with other dissidents in Yugoslavia, in the Praxis Group, despite their more than obvious unpopularity with the authorities there. It should be recorded that none of his minor 'indiscretions', whether committed out of compassion or because Fred loved to see authority challenged, prevented those authorities from awarding him, in 1981, the high distinction of the Order of the Yugoslav Flag, for his work in promoting relations between their country and Britain. This honour, I believe, he shares with only one other Briton, Fitzroy Maclean.

Those late tours of Europe were not, however, mere nostalgic pleasure trips by a retired academic. They comprised a series of exceedingly busy research and lecture tours, to Finland, Sweden, Germany and Yugoslavia. He even fitted in a lecture tour to the USA and Canada for good measure. Principally, he was collecting material for his studies of environmental pollution and the National Parks movement. But the scope of his engagements is astonishing. As late as September 1987, when he must surely have been carrying the disease which killed him only four months later, he was in Kragujevac, to present papers on 'Gladstone and the Eastern Question', and on 'The British Youth Brigades in Yugoslavia in 1947'.[19] It was by way of a bonus if, over these years, his studies took him across the paths of so many friends, or enabled him to climb his beloved Triglav, the Slovene peak which is Yugoslavia's highest, for the umpteenth time.[20] And, since his journeys usually brought him

19. See footnote 2.
20. He not only climbed it, he wrote about it. See Fred Singleton, 'The Triglav National Park', *Slovene Studies*, Vol. 10, No. 1, 1988, pp. 39–49. The journal's editor added a note: 'The untimely death of Fred Singleton prevented his completing the maps to accompany his article.'

twice through Hull, where he used the car-ferry to Rotterdam, why of course it was natural for him to call on me, and rapidly to make new and welcoming friends amongst the circle of trade unionists and socialists in Hull.

Another great source of happiness for him in his 'retirement' was the cottage which he acquired in Hebden-in-Craven. Whilst Fred loved company, he was also a self-sufficient person. In social life a vigorously gregarious man, in the process of composition he sought rural isolation. His cottage was the retreat to which he hurried after every material-gathering excursion into the world, and where he ordered the material into books, articles and lectures. This does not imply an inability to collaborate with others; the number of his publications written, and of conferences organized, in harness with colleagues, is evidence enough on that point. Furthermore, the village pub, the Clarendon, furnished him with enough convivial company in between chapters!

Indeed, Fred and friendship, Fred and compassion, Fred and conviviality, are a series of synonyms. Of these, his conviviality was evident and manifest. His friendship was open and uncomplicated. His compassion was profound, but expressed unobtrusively, with a northern reserve, in deeds rather than words. Beginning with his own family – his wife, Elizabeth, and his children, Anne, Kate, Andy and Jim, who were both family and friends combined – he cast his net wide and generously.

If you were one of his students, or his accountant, or someone he came to know in the local pub, you were highly likely to end up as another friend, invited to join him in climbing the 'Three Peaks' of his cherished Upper Wharfedale,[21] or to stay at his house, or to join him on one of his car-journeys across Europe. The accountant of

---

21. Fred was not, in any orthodox sense, an athlete. In fact he delighted to tease those of us who played serious cricket, and took such matters as Yorkshire cricket seriously, and then to reveal that, quietly, he had acquired a not inconsiderable knowledge of its characters. He even claimed that, as a child, he had obtained the autograph of old George Hirst – master Yorkshire cricketer – at the Scarborough Cricket Festival. But he could not resist any chance to deflate the solemnity with which devotees of organized games treat their obsession. At the same time, Fred was a dedicated walker and climber – though not a 'mountaineer'; that would have been too close to humourless athleticism. He had great stamina, as well as expertise in fell-walking, where his geological and geographical knowledge was used to extract the maximum interest from the experience. His feel for the influence of physical geography upon history was that of an 'outdoors' man. In his historical studies of Yugoslavia, for example, he not only identifies and describes the geological format of the mountain passes and the river valleys, but peoples them with the migrating tribes whose great movements came together to form nations.

whom I speak, David Verity, said to me at Fred's memorial party: 'Fred "gathered" people'. This struck me as a most apt metaphor. He made a prolific harvest of us – 280 people came to that memorial party, and Elizabeth still worries about those whom she could not contact in time – yet he did not gather us 'to him'; Fred's friendship was not clinging or demanding. He gave much and asked nothing in return.

He was very often the good samaritan; his unselfconscious and discreet compassion for those low in spirit or health, especially amongst young people, was one of his most endearing traits. Such people would be invited to share his family home, where Elizabeth and the children would give firm but unobtrusive support, and where Fred's company was available without stint.

His simple love of convivial company found another quirky expression when he joined in the new pastime of the general knowledge quiz, conducted between teams from local pubs. A league of such clubs was formed in the Bradford area, and Fred was an enthusiastic member of the Jacob's Well team. After he died, the league bought a new cup, and named it the Fred Singleton Memorial Cup, for which they now compete, and which Elizabeth has recently presented to its first winner.

‘   It is fitting to dwell on this, for Fred, most cosmopolitan of men, was full of quiet love for his native Yorkshire and its people.[22] 'Think locally, act globally', is an inspiring slogan, with more than one connotation. It seems entirely appropriate that, in his last months, Fred was working on his latest Finnish text, on the organization of the Fourth World Congress of Soviet and East European Studies, and signing the first author's copies of the new edition of his history of Yorkshire.

Finally, something must be said about the extraordinary humanism and serenity with which Fred faced his untimely death. When he knew that his cancer was terminal, he 'organized everything', 'he went into overdrive' (these are Elizabeth's words), and led his family and friends firmly but gently to accept and share with him the inevitability and the sadness, without guilt, concealment or embarrassment. He wrote to us all, and tried to see as many of us as possible. He talked wisely about the unnecessary anguish which is

---

22. Fred sometimes emphasized and deployed an authentic Yorkshire accent, either for comic purpose and gentle self-mockery or, mischievously and devastatingly, to puncture the academic pomposity which he disliked so much.

added to our natural grief in Western societies by their fear of death, and their revulsion when confronted with this most natural process. His death, which came on 10 January 1988, was deservedly peaceful.

It was Fred himself, in consultation with his family, who decreed that there should be a party, to follow a private family funeral after a decent interval, so that we could gather and renew old acquaintances, talk about our memories of him, and hear his favourite music and poetry. All to whom I spoke on that moving and cathartic occasion wondered at it, and were grateful to him both for the rationality of the process he had organized, and at its kind, didactic purpose. It was not the least thing he did to illuminate so many lives, gathered by him for the last time to talk, to eat and drink together, and to hear readings from Kalevala, Macedonian poetry and John Donne, and to listen to 'Falling in Love Again' sung by Marlene Dietrich and the Geordie children's song 'Dance to your Daddy' (these having special memorial resonance for his family), a movement from Sibelius' D minor string quartet, and finally Paul Robeson singing, from the Ninth Symphony, Beethoven's setting of Schiller's 'Ode to Joy'.

Postscript

The commitments and continuous concerns which guided Fred's life-work in a number of fields have marched quite dramatically towards centre-stage, even in the short time since his death. A check-list reveals how much he is missed, for the contributions he would have made, but more to the point, it shows that Fred stayed with the grain of the future, contributing to the long haul in seminal ways.

Consider how:

1. Perestroika and glasnost have transformed the socialist project in Russia and Eastern Europe. Whatever immediate and medium-term difficulties this movement faces, destalinization is now irreversible, and dialogue between the different world socialisms is now universal, where before, only the Yugoslavs, in settings such as the Cavtat conferences, sustained it. Fred always held out the prospect of that dialogue, in all his work.

2. In Western Europe, there is a new convergence, promoted by

independent socialists, upon the concept of a 'Europe of the Regions'. Fred's combination of internationalism and a strong sense of national, regional and county identity fits so well into this frame of thought.

3. In the field of environmental politics, his pioneering and original work is gathering significance daily. He combined geographical and political insights into the problem, from a socialist perspective. We shall need that model as a constant in the years ahead.

4. Yugoslavia's current severe crisis has many causes and facets. Fred's multidisciplinary method is strikingly appropriate to its analysis. His emphasis on nationalism in both its positive and negative aspects is particularly relevant, especially since quite the most damaging consequence of the politico-economic crisis is the stimulus it has unhappily given to a resurgence of xenophobic hysteria, as some elements amongst the Serbs, Albanians, Montenegrins, Croats, Macedonians and Slovenes invoke the conflicts of their pasts, as a frame of reference for their future conduct.

I wish to express my affectionate thanks for the help afforded me in preparing this chapter by Elizabeth and Ann Singleton, and Kate Hatton. In seeking to pay proper tribute herein to my friend, I hope that I have reflected a little of their love and respect too – and that of his sons Andy and Jim – for their husband and father. I alone, however, am responsible for the content, and for any errors that may appear.

PART I

Contemporary Yugoslavia in Transition: An Overview

1

Yugoslavia in Geographical Perspective
Thomas M. Poulsen

Introduction

Few states in the world exhibit as great a geographic diversity as the Socialist Federal Republic of Yugoslavia. It stands at the crossroads of many of Europe's most significant physical and cultural discontinuities. Through its territory run divides between mountain systems and plains, continental climates and Mediterranean subtropics, regions of economic development and those emerging from a rural subsistence way of life. Across its boundaries pass frontiers between Christians and Muslims, Magyars and Slavs, influences from Rome and those from Byzantium. It is a bridge between Central Europe and the Aegean world, between Western traditions and those of the East.

Yugoslavia ranks ninth in size among the countries of Europe, its 98,766 square miles approximating the area of the United Kingdom or the Federal Republic of Germany. On a North American scale, it is comparable to the area embraced by Oregon or Wyoming. Its population of some 23,000,000 is eighth among the European states, equivalent to that of the combined Benelux countries but representing less than half the numbers to be found in France, West Germany or Britain. Across the Atlantic, its total population ranks ahead of New York's, but is slightly less than numbers living in California or in Canada.

The diversity of population in Yugoslavia is the greatest to be found in any European state outside the Soviet Union. Past patterns of migrations, religious proselytizing, and external political control have left a legacy of cultural and economic differences that successfully have resisted the homogenization pressures that welded the peoples of other European states into unified nations. Only a tiny

33

minority of the population truly identifies itself as 'Yugoslav'. Most people see themselves – and are seen by others – as 'Serbs', 'Croats', 'Slovenes', 'Macedonians', 'Montenegrins', 'Bosnian Muslims', 'Albanians', or 'Hungarians'.

Each of these groups is a nation in its own right and, following the end of the Second World War, received a degree of political recognition of this status within the Socialist Federal Republic. Thus, each of the five principal Slavic-speaking groups had a 'people's republic' named for the group, while two 'autonomous regions' were established within the Serbian people's republic in areas of noteworthy concentrations of Albanians and Hungarians. A sixth republic, Bosnia and Hercegovina, was created in a historic region of mixed Croatian, Serbian and Muslim populations. The political distinctiveness of the republics and autonomous regions was reinforced after 1963 by an increasing economic self-sufficiency and coherence within each area, often to the detriment of the economy as a whole. The politically contentious nature of these arrangements is witnessed by the fact that the autonomous regions were fully reincorporated into the republic of Serbia in constitutional reforms forced through in 1989–90.

Patterns of Terrain

The varied terrain of Yugoslavia is perhaps best visualized in four distinctive parts: a region of hills and basins paralleling the Adriatic and covering up to 40 per cent of the country in the west, a small section of the Alps in the northwestern corner, a portion of the broad Danubian (or Pannonian) plain to the northeast, and a jumble of hills and mountains along the eastern and southern borders of the country.

The western zone consists primarily of limestone rock that originally lay in horizontal beds between sandstones, shales and other rocks made up from sediments in ancient seas. These beds were bent by tectonic forces of the earth's crust into a giant series of folds paralleling the present coast and extending from the Italian border to Greece. The areas dominated by limestone are collectively known as the 'karst' (*krs*), while areas of other sedimentary rocks are termed 'flysch' (*flis*). Over geologic time, erosion has removed most of the exposed flysch, but the limestone has tended to remain standing in the form of elongated ridges trending in a northwest–

southeast pattern. These so-called 'Dinaric Alps' generally reach 900 to 1,200 feet in elevation, with a few attaining heights of 4,500 feet or more.

Rain falling upon the limestone is most often diverted into cracks in the easily dissolved rock. It then forms underground rivers, rather than developing erosional surface channels as happens with other rock types. Yugoslavia's limestone is honeycombed with caves that often have fantastic internal forms. The Dinaric Alps are noted for their rich beds of bauxite, the raw material for aluminium. It is estimated that Yugoslavia contains 100 million tons of bauxite reserves.

The limestone ridges of the karst area stand above 'poljes' (flat-floored valleys) where the region's meagre cropland is concentrated. Poljes are mainly the result of stream erosion of flysch rock. Because they are mostly drained by streams that pass underground into channels in the limestone ridges, they frequently are flooded for extensive periods. The Adriatic sea has risen some 300 feet since the last Ice Age, drowning a number of former poljes and leaving the limestone ridges to form a number of elongated islands parallel to the coast, such as Brač and Hvar. Picturesque inlets and coastal lakes, including Kotor Bay, south of Dubrovnik and Lake Skadar on the Albanian border, were also formed by the flooding of poljes. In general, the coastline rises steeply from the sea. Only the Istrian Peninsula in the extreme north and a lowland area south of Zadar in the middle coast constitute plains adjacent to the sea.

The Dinaric region has progressively less limestone towards the east. Here surface streams rent the highlands across the grain, cutting deep gorges that often have spectacular waterfalls. It is difficult country to traverse, as invading Turks and Germans have found. There are within it a few basins and wider valleys suitable for concentrations of farming. The most notable is the Sarajevo Basin, containing the capital city of Bosnia–Hercegovina. Soils are much less depleted than in the karst zone, with forests dominating the landscape.

Yugoslavia's section of the high Alps is concentrated in the Slovenian Republic. It includes the Karawanken Alps, forming the border with Austria, and the Julian Alps further south, dominated by Mt. Triglav, Yugoslavia's highest peak (9,400 feet). This zone has some of Europe's most breathtaking scenery, particularly where mountain glaciers during the last Ice Age serrated the higher ridges or carved such picturesque features as Lake Bohinj. Within the

Alpine zone lie several lowlands where population is concentrated. These include the Ljubljana Basin, in which the Slovenian capital city is located, the Celje Basin to the east, and the upper Sava and Drava river valleys.

The Danubian plain is a region of Europe that has been sinking rather steadily into the earth's crust over geologic time. However, its surface has remained at a fairly constant level of some 500 feet above sea level, as materials washed out of the rising surrounding highlands have continuously filled it in. The surface tends to be very flat because currents of an ancient geologic sea that once occupied the region have spread such sediments evenly. In more recent time annual flooding of the Danube and its tributary Tisza, Sava, Drava and Morava rivers have continuously veneered the surface.

Not all of the Danubian region is flat terrain. Low hills stand on the margins of the plain, separating the broad valleys of the tributary streams as they enter the plain. Most notable in this regard are the Slavonian hills between the Drava and Sava rivers. Also, in the closing phase of the last Ice Age, the region was coated with thick layers of wind-blown dust (loess). Subsequent precipitation and flooding eroded much of this material, but pockets remain as fringing plateaus that rise 200 feet or more above the plain. These plateaus have excellent soils, but suffer from a lack of surface water. The sedimentary rock layers beneath the plain and adjacent stream valleys contain most of Yugoslavia's meagre resources of oil and gas.

The eastern mountains of Yugoslavia stretch from the Romanian border to Albania. In the north they are extensions of the 'reverse-S'-shaped Carpathian chain of young mountains, which are best viewed as an eastward extension of the Alps. They curve from eastern Czechoslovakia southward and westward through Romania, and then, after passing across eastern Serbia, lead eastward to the Black Sea, becoming the highland backbone of Bulgaria.

The mountain chain is broken by the famous ninety-mile long 'Iron Gates' (Djerdap) gorge of the Danube river, that serves as Yugoslavia's northeastern border. At its narrowest the mighty river was at one time only 600 feet across and very swift. The reservoir created behind the Djerdap dam has widened the narrowest parts and tamed the current. The Yugoslav section of the Carpathians is not high, the ridge tops reaching 2,000 to 3,000 feet of elevation. The area is noteworthy for its rich beds of copper ore at Majdanpek and Bor.

South of the Carpathians stretching to the border with Greece is the Rhodope system of mountains, one of the oldest rock masses exposed on the surface of Europe. Highland summits range from 2,000 to 6,000 feet. However, the area is blessed by a water-level north–south route along the Vardar and Morava rivers that since ancient times has seen the passage of armies and merchants between Mediterranean and Central Europe. The rivers link a series of basins, the largest of which includes the Macedonian capital Skopje. The Rhodope area is significant for metallic ores, particularly the lead and zinc of the Trepča area of Kosovo.

Along the Albanian border the mountains become higher and more spectacular. Ranges reach more than 8,000 feet in places. At the foot of these mountains are several noteworthy low areas, including the Kosovo basin and Yugoslavia's two largest lakes – Prespa and Okhrid – which lie on the international borders with Greece and Albania.

Climatic Patterns

As in so many other geographic elements, Yugoslavia occupies a medial position in Europe's climates. It finds itself subjected to the flows of moving air-masses that have acquired characteristics of temperature and moisture over northern seas, polar lands or tropical oceans. Giant storms formed along air-mass boundaries bring precipitation and often strong winds. The 'Bora' blowing southward down the Adriatic in winter is one of the most formidable of Europe's recurring wind patterns, at times literally pushing automobiles off roads.

It is useful to view the climatic pattern of Yugoslavia by a three-fold regional division: a Danubian plains zone in the northeast, a Mediterranean coastal zone in the southwest, and a highland zone in between.

The largest share of Yugoslavia's population lives in the northeastern plains region or on its periphery. Here the climate is similar to that of the western Soviet Union and of the other states of East Central Europe. In the summer, air, distant from the sea and warmed by sun-drenched land, reaches average July temperatures of 70° F or more. Evaporation and transpiration by plants is high, and the moisture-choked air is often provoked into rainfall by the development of local thunderstorms and by grander passing cyclonic storms.

In winter the air has often stagnated or passed for long periods over Russian and Ukranian snow fields. January average temperatures hover around the freezing mark, and the cooler air contains much less moisture. Precipitation is less than half that of summer months, with annual totals ranging from 45 inches in the western margins to less than 20 inches in the east.

The coastal zone has a quite different pattern. Despite its proximity to the sea, it can be quite warm in summer, reaching July averages of 80 ° F or more. The air most often has its origins aloft, spiralling out of the huge mass of high pressure that builds outward over Europe from the Azores Islands in the Atlantic. As it descends, it warms by compression. It is also very dry, since its trajectory over the sea is usually far too short to evaporate and absorb much moisture. Summers on the Mediterranean are usually very sunny.

In winter the Dinaric hills and mountains tend to block the advance of cold air from the east. January average temperatures on the coast tend to be relatively high for these latitudes because of the continuous release of energy stored in the sea in the summer months. Rainfall for the region comes at this season. The Azores high-pressure centre migrates southward in the winter, allowing Europe's cyclonic storms to travel a more southern trajectory. In many coastal villages one can still find giant stone aprons built to catch winter rainfall and store it in cisterns for the drought of summer. Despite summer dryness, annual totals of precipitation are notably higher than those of the Danubian plain, particularly where mountains rise abruptly above the sea. In the Gorski Kotar range above Rijeka and the Mount Lovčen area of Montenegro it can exceed 100 inches.

It is difficult to generalize about climates of the highland zone except to state 'diversity'. The region exhibits elements of the other climatic regions, but local differences in elevations, exposures to the sun and channels of air-mass movement result in great variations in annual patterns of temperature and precipitation. Generally speaking, higher elevations are cooler and western slopes exposed to prevailing winds are rainier. Precipitation notably declines from west to east, with the Morava–Vardar corridor area receiving less than 20 inches annually.

Vegetation

The wild vegetation of Yugoslavia is a response to these varying patterns of temperature and precipitation. However, it also reflects millennia of interference by man. Thus, the coastal region and Dinaric Alps at one time were covered by evergreen oak and cypress forests. A constant need for construction and household firewood eventually led to a destruction of the forests. Natural and man-set fires also contributed to their demise, as did the general practice of grazing goats, who consumed new tree growth before it could become re-established. The result was a denudation of the land. Without tree roots to hold the soil, slopes became bare rock. In pockets where soil remained, trees were replaced by a summer drought-resistant scrub known locally as *maki*. (In California such vegetation is known as 'chapparal'.) It is interesting to note the beginnings of forest regrowth since post–war Yugoslav law required the tethering of family goats.

A similar alteration of vegetation occurred in the Danubian plain. Although the past density of oak forests on the plain remains a matter of debate, it had become a vast grassland by the time the land was reconquered from the Turks in the seventeenth century. In the modern period most of this rich area has become farmland. Trees are now found on hilltops and on the soggy margins of streams.

In the highland zone the prevailing vegetation is deciduous forest. In areas of greater elevation beech trees dominate, while lower slopes are covered by varieties of oak.

The Peoples of Yugoslavia

The name 'Yugoslavia' literally means 'The Land of the South Slavs', and an overwhelming majority of the inhabitants of Yugoslavia indeed can be classed as South Slavic in language. However, the sharing of similar languages has never meant a similar sharing of ideas and values among the several South Slavic groups who coexist within the Yugoslav state. Moreover, a number of non-Slavic peoples also live within the boundaries of Yugoslavia, including Albanians, Hungarians, Italians and Gypsies. These groups seldom have found common cause with their Slavic neighbours.

To begin to understand the present diversity of ethnic groups in

Yugoslavia and their often mutual antipathy, it is necessary to grasp the principal outlines of centuries of migrations, political controls and cultural influences. The many distinctive groups now living in Yugoslavia are a product of a multitude of events that have beset the Balkan Peninsula.

Archaeologists have found remains of prehistoric peoples in several places in Yugoslavia. Settlement began in this area perhaps 10,000 years ago when climates began to warm up in Europe as the great glaciers melted away. It is evident that in addition to practising rudimentary agriculture, some early peoples knew how to smelt iron and copper from readily obtainable ores located in the mountains.

During the early period of the flourishing Aegean Sea civilizations to the south, the Balkan Peninsula appears to have been dominated by two Indo-European groups with related cultural patterns: the Thracians and Illyrians. Thracians lived mostly east of the Morava river, and dominated the present areas of Romania and Bulgaria. Illyrians lived to the west, and their ancient language and traditions are reflected in the present culture of the Albanians. In addition, in the eighth to sixth centuries BC, Greeks established trading colonies at such Adriatic coastal sites as Trogir and Korčula. Celtic groups are known also to have moved into northern Yugoslavia in the fourth century BC.

Rome made its presence felt in the region in the third century BC when it began attacking coastal pirates. By AD 9 all of present-day Yugoslavia had come under Roman control. The Romans are noted for building roads, parts of which are still in use locally. Along these routes they established strings of cities for administration and control. Many are urban sites today, including Emona (Ljubljana) and Siscia (Sisak).

Military colonies of Romans were also planted along the Adriatic coast. The rectangular forms of their system of apportioning agricultural lands (*centuriation*) can still be observed on the coastal plain outside Split and other communities. Ancient cadastral boundaries have been preserved by twenty centuries of farmers piling rocks on field edges.

The Roman impact on the landscape was largely destroyed by invasions of Huns and other barbarian tribes as the Roman Empire weakened. Cities in the Balkan Peninsula were put to ruin, and surviving Latin-speaking inhabitants fled to refuge areas on the coast or in the mountains.

At the end of the sixth and beginning of the seventh centuries AD, Slavs first appeared on the territory of contemporary Yugoslavia as allies of the Asiatic Avars. The invaders had moved southward from a common Slavic cultural hearth region in southeastern Poland at about the same time that related tribes were pushing westward to the Elbe and eastward to the Volga.

The initial advance of the South Slavs was into the great valleys of the Drava, Sava and Morava rivers on the periphery of the Hungarian plain. They also moved along the Adriatic coast. Only later did they begin to penetrate the mountains. In many highland communities their presence was never complete, and Illyrian and Latin (Vlach) speakers there have managed to retain distinctive identities up to the present. In the coastal zone Roman traditions held out in several city states, including Ragusa (Dubrovnik) and Spalato (Split).

The subsequent differentiation of the South Slavic invaders by language, religion and other aspects of culture reflects contrasting external influences to which they were subjected. Thus, the Slovenes, perhaps earliest of the Slavic groups in the region, came under continuous control of Frankish Germans in the eighth century. The Croats, who had formed a kingdom of their own in the tenth century, were dominated by Hungarians from the end of the eleventh.

Slavic tribal groups that had settled to the east and south of Slovenes and Croatians came under the influence of the Byzantine Empire. The early Serbian states of Zeta and Raška recognized the authority of Byzantium, although they were not controlled by it for any appreciable length of time. Further south, the Slavic ancestors of the present-day Macedonians were dominated more directly by the Byzantines and then, in the ninth century, by the Bulgarians.

The widening religious breach in Christianity led the Byzantine-influenced peoples along a notably different path from that of the South Slavs to the west. The Serbs, Montenegrins and Macedonians adopted the Orthodox rite of the church and employed the Cyrillic alphabet for their written languages. In contrast, the Slovenes and Croats, who followed Rome, began to use the Latin alphabet, although initially they too had utilized the Greek-influenced Glagolitic alphabet created by Saints Cyril and Methodius in the ninth century, and its tenth century successor Cyrillic.

A further force differentiating the South Slavs was the Turks, who moved northward into the Balkan Peninsula in the fourteenth century. They decisively defeated the Serbs in 1389 in Kosovo Polje (Blackbirds Field). By 1463 they had conquered Bosnia, and eighty years later, at the Battle of Mohacs in the Hungarian plain, they routed a combined Hungarian–Croatian army. As a consequence of this defeat, Croatian nobles selected Ferdinand of Austria as their king, and subsequently remained under Habsburg authority until 1918.

In the twelfth century, long before the Turkish invasion, a distinctive form of Christianity had emerged among Slavic tribes in Bosnia. Rejecting both eastern and western branches of the church, the so-called Bogomils adopted a belief system that appears to have had its origins in Bulgaria. Persecuted as heretics by both Rome and Byzantium, most Bogomils found it advantageous to adopt the Muslim religion following the Turkish conquest. Not only did Islam have many similarities to Bogomil beliefs, but its acceptance also had the practical effect of allowing landowners to retain their hereditary estates. Bosnian Muslims rose to high positions in the Ottoman Empire, and their Slavic-speaking descendants have preserved a Middle Eastern ambience in the heart of the Yugoslav lands ever since.

The Turks were also responsible for introducing new ethnic elements into the area. A modest number of Turkish-speakers settled in Macedonia and elsewhere. Of more lasting significance were the Gypsies, a proscribed Indian caste, whom the Turks brought in as leather- and metal-workers for their cavalry.

Fear of the Turks led to mass refugee migrations of Slavs northward. Many settled in the forested hill country of Zagorje, northwest of the Croatian capital of Zagreb, and, for the most part, became Roman Catholics. Their abandoned farmlands were taken over by other groups, particularly Albanians in Kosovo. After the Habsburgs in the mid-sixteenth century had succeeded in reconquering the Hungarian plain from the Turks, they resettled incoming Eastern Orthodox refugees in military-style colonies along the newly established political boundary that followed the Una and Sava rivers.

This region was organized as a 'Military Frontier', and its inhabitants had special privileges in return for lifetimes of duty as border guards. In contrast to the earlier refugees to Zagorje, the majority of the new residents retained their Orthodox religion. Their descendants identify themselves today as Serbs and constitute a significant regionally concentrated minority of more than a half million in modern Croatia.

As the Turks were effectively pushed southward, the Habsburgs also settled other groups on newly won territory, particularly in the Vojvodina region of the southern Danubian plain. There villages of Czechs, Slovaks, Croats, Slovenes, Serbs, Hungarians and Romanians appeared in a fertile territory long void of population under the Turks.

The Turkish march northward into the core of the Balkan Peninsula was matched by an expansion southward of Venice along the coastlands facing the Adriatic. Dalmatia's Italianate city states and their Slavic-speaking hinterlands had all (with the exception of Ragusa) become Venetian by 1420. The long association of Croatians of Dalmatia with cultural traditions of Italy has left an imprint that still distinguishes them from inland Croatians who were for so long bound to the Hungarians.

Between Venetians and the Turks, a small group of Eastern Orthodox Slavs maintained a precarious independence in the mountain country north of the Albanians. The Montenegrins have remained divided among a number of tribes to modern times.

Thus, by the end of the eighteenth century, the territory of present-day Yugoslavia lay divided between Habsburg and Ottoman Empires, with the coastal strip of Dalmatia under Venetian control, and Montenegro and Ragusa stubbornly resisting outside rule. The nineteenth century saw several major changes. Napoleon seized Venice and its Dalmatian holdings in 1797 and then Ragusa in 1805. Both became part of the Habsburg Empire after 1815, following Napoleon's defeat. The Serbs began a protracted revolt against Ottoman oppression in 1804, and their right to self-rule was at last formally recognized by the Sultan in 1830. Turkish domination of the peninsula was further weakened by the Austro-Hungarian seizure of Bosnia and Hercegovina in 1878.

Habsburg holdings in the Yugoslav lands were significantly affected by a 'compromise' (*Ausgleich*) of 1867 in which the Austrians gave the Hungarians self-rule and dominion over half the empire. The Vojvodina and Croatia proper, including its eastern territory of Slavonia, were assigned to the Hungarians. Dalmatia and the Croatian military frontier continued under Austrian control, although the frontier was joined to the rest of Croatia in 1881.

In the early twentieth century Serbia expanded southward and westward at the expense of a weakened Ottoman Empire. It acquired a substantial area inhabited by South Slavic Macedonians, and also the Kosovo basin with its large numbers of Albanians.

The nineteenth and twentieth centuries witnessed another political phenomenon that has had repercussions to the present. The French Revolution of 1789 is often taken as the starting point of the mass adoption of nationhoods throughout Europe. The notion of the rights of a people to control their political destinies accompanied the Continent's social upheavals associated with industrialization and urbanization. The Balkan Peninsula was not immune to these currents.

Particularly significant was the influence between 1797 and 1814 of Napoleonic occupying forces in the so-called 'Illyrian Provinces' of Dalmatia, Istria, Western Croatia, Slovenia and Carinthia. Peoples whose identity formerly had been based upon family and religion came to see themselves as 'nations', with collective values, symbols, aspirations and senses of history. Struggles to achieve political recognition of such distinctiveness shook the Habsburg and Ottoman Empires throughout the nineteenth century.

Both empires managed to lose the First World War. The peace treaties that followed were avowedly based on the principle of 'self-determination of nations' that had been advocated by the American president, Woodrow Wilson. Although one could hardly point to the emergence of a unified South Slavic 'Yugoslav' nation in 1918, intellectuals and political leaders of all groups were disposed for various reasons towards the creation of a South Slavic state and their endeavours were supported by the victorious allies. Thus was born in 1918 the 'Kingdom of Serbs, Croats and Slovenes'.

A problem for the new state from the very beginning was that each of these groups had become a nation already, and each nation had reasons to distrust the other two. Despite linguistic similarities, their different historical experiences and cultural attributes worked against effective political unity. Slovenes and Croats had developed economically along with the rest of Central Europe; Serbs and their fellow Montenegrin and Macedonian Eastern Orthodox Slavs had stagnated with the rest of the Ottoman Empire. The former Habsburg Slavic peoples had spent decades struggling against external domination and placed a high value upon autonomy; Serbs had enjoyed self-rule for a century and sought an ever-more strongly centralized state.

The fissures never healed. Moreover, they were complicated by the growing national awareness by other groups. The Slavic Muslims of Bosnia found their distinctive interests completely left out of the new state. The Macedonians and Montenegrins, although respectively viewed by the Serbians as 'South Serbs' and 'Mountain Serbs', increasingly found reasons for separate identities. Moreover, the nationalisms of Albanians and Hungarians living inside the borders of the Serb-Croat-Slovene Kingdom were intensified by irredentist feelings towards the nation states of their peoples across the recently superimposed borders.

Mounting and at times violent dissention within the young state led its king in 1929 to declare a royal dictatorship. The unitary name 'Yugoslavia' was adopted, and the component historic homelands of its nations were replaced by new provinces termed 'banovinas' that were named after river basins. Their territorial outlines departed only moderately from their predecessor units, although the larger territories of Serbia, Croatia and Bosnia–Hercegovina were broken into two or three parts. Agitation by Croatians led to regaining a unity within a single banovina on the eve of the Second World War, but this did little to assuage strong separatist feelings that had developed.

The nadir of Yugoslav unity came with occupation during the Second World War. The victorious Germans and Italians declared the establishment of an 'Independent State of Croatia' whose territory included Bosnia and Hercegovina. At the onset it enjoyed a degree of popular support, despite the fact that its leaders had conceded much historic Croatian coastal territory to Italy. Serbia, on the other hand, was treated as occupied territory, with civil affairs administered by a general from the pre-war regime. Montenegro again became a kingdom, but under Italian domination. Most of the Vojvodina was attached to Hungary, and Albanian inhabited areas were joined to the Italian puppet state of Albania. Slovenia was split between Germany and Italy, and Macedonia was annexed by Bulgaria.

Antagonistic national tensions were unleashed by the wartime partitioning. Yugoslavia lost perhaps as many as 1,700,000 people during the war, some 10 per cent of its population. Most were killed by other Yugoslavs rather than by the Axis occupation forces, as the various resistance movements (principally Serbian nationalist 'Chetniks' and communist 'Partisans') fought each other, as well as the occupying forces and their indigenous fascist allies.

The war was nevertheless the source of a rebirth of unity. The most effective resistance against the occupation had been mounted by the communist Partisans under the leadership of Josip Broz Tito. Ideologically opposed to nationalisms on principle, the Partisans fought a unified war against the occupiers with support coming from segments of all ethnic groups. They formulated a post-war solution to Yugoslavia's problems of national diversity based on the Soviet experience of creating 'republics' that were 'national in form but socialist in practice'. Accordingly, with the victory of Tito, 'Socialist Peoples Republics' were established for Serbs, Croats, Slovenes, Montenegrins, Macedonians and mixed inhabitants of Bosnia and Hercegovina. Further, Albanians and Hungarians were made part of 'Autonomous Regions' within the Serbian Republic.

As in the USSR, however, the establishment of centralized communist rule with paper national autonomy did not lead to a withering away of national feelings. Despite intensive efforts, it also did not erase the contrasts in economic development and culture that had plagued pre-war Yugoslavia. However, for more than three decades the forceful personality of Tito was a major element in maintaining unity.

Population

Of the more than 23 million Yugoslavs, three-quarters speak the Serbo-Croatian language. An additional 15 per cent use Slovenian or Macedonian, which also are South Slavic languages but quite distinctive from Serbo-Croatian. The remaining 10 per cent is linguistically non-Slavic, including 1,700,000 Albanians, 400,000 Hungarians, 150,000 Gypsies and 100,000 Turks.

In recent years this population has been growing at a rate of approximately 0.8 per cent or some 185,000 annually. However, significant differences in growth rates are observable among ethnic groups. Yugoslavia's Albanians are thus increasing at 2.5 per cent per year, while Croatians are experiencing a rate less than 0.4 per cent. In Montenegro, Macedonia and Bosnia–Hercegovina growth rates range from 1.1 to 1.4 per cent. Generally speaking, birth rates are highest in the southern and eastern regions, which are also the economically least-developed parts of the state. The average annual income in Kosovo in 1979 was US$604 per capita; in Slovenia it was US$4,000.

Yugoslavia's population is concentrated in the two-thirds of the country lying north and east of a line stretching from Ljubljana to Skopje and passing through Sarajevo. To the south and west lie the relatively empty Dinaric mountain zone and the coastal region.

People in the latter areas are found in isolated clusters in fertile poljes (Mostar) or around widely separated port cities (Rijeka, Split, Dubrovnik). In northeastern Yugoslavia the Danubian lowland is more or less evenly settled. Other areas with noteworthy concentrations of people are the zone between Zagreb and the Hungarian border, the middle Sava valley around Brod, and the Morava–Vardar corridor in Serbia and Macedonia.

It is tempting to ascribe differences in population densities to differences in economic opportunities afforded by the physical environment. However, the environment is only one factor, and a passive aspect at that. Much of the explanation for differences in settlement patterns has roots in historical and political factors. Thus, the steep slopes and poor soils of the hill regions of Zagorje north of Zagreb and Šumadija south of Belgrade support unusually high numbers of inhabitants. This is accounted for by the roles these areas played in the past as refuges for Christians fleeing Turkish conquest. Similarly, the modest populations of the coast reflect large outmigrations to America and elsewhere in the nineteenth century following the steamship's destruction of sailing as an occupation and the phylloxera plague that destroyed the region's once flourishing vineyards. More recently, Dalmatians have been more prone to seek employment in Western Europe than the population of other areas, particularly those of the south. Similarly the high density of population in the Kosovo basin is a consequence of the high birth rate of its predominantly Albanian population and their reluctance to migrate to non-Albanian parts of the country.

Nearly 50 per cent of the population is now urban. Half this number is concentrated in the sixteen largest cities and towns. The seven with the greatest populations are political capitals, reflecting tendencies for each to become 'primate cities' within their increasingly disconnected republics and autonomous regions.[1] Belgrade is the largest, with more than a million inhabitants. It is both the federal capital and the capital of Serbia. The Croatian capital Zagreb ranks second, with 600,000 population. The other large towns are industrial centres, including Osijek, Rijeka and Split in Croatia, Maribor in Slovenia, Mostar and Banja Luka in Bosnia–Hercegovina, Niš and Kragujevac in Serbia and Subotica in the Vojvodina.

Urban populations have grown rapidly in recent decades, mainly

---

1. The term 'primate city' refers to the tendency of the capitals of sovereign states generally to become the largest and most industrialized urban centres within their countries, and to have the highest quality and variety of social and cultural amenities.

by migration of young people from villages to towns and cities. More than 40 per cent of the rural communes in Yugoslavia lost population between 1971 and 1981. Too many farms had too little land. They concealed a major problem of underemployment and poverty. Urban settlements offered better living standards, a defined working day, higher status work, better medical care, schools and entertainment.

However, the creation of new jobs in the towns did not match demands for them. Among the socialist countries, Yugoslavia has suffered most from a high rate of unemployment. The problem was relieved in the 1960s by permission for individuals to seek temporary work in foreign countries. Between 1965 and 1971, for every new job found within the country, two others were secured abroad. In fact, many of the low-paid unskilled jobs that were found by rural migrants in Yugoslav cities had resulted from former job-holders seeking more remunerative opportunities outside the country. The census of 1971 recorded 672,000 Yugoslavs employed as 'guest workers' (Gastarbeiter) in West Germany, France, Sweden and other countries. (For a variety of reasons it is probable that the census seriously underestimated the size of these migratory flows. See chapter 5 by Mesić, below.) Recession in Western Europe during the 1970s dried up new employment opportunities, however, and the 1981 census indicated that only 578,000 Yugoslavs had temporary jobs abroad.

The decline of external employment opportunities meant that those seeking to leave rural villages had to find new homes and jobs within the country. For most, such migration was to towns and cities within republic or autonomous region borders. However, members of minorities tended to migrate to cities of areas that were dominated by their own groups, that is Croats in Bosnia and the Vojvodina moving to Croatia and Muslims in Montenegro leaving for Bosnia. Rural–urban migration thus has not resulted in a mixing of peoples, but rather has strengthened the ethnic exclusivity of most republics. The exception is prosperous Slovenia, which saw absolute numbers of other national groups within its borders double and triple in the inter-censal period between 1971 and 1981. More than 97 per cent of Yugoslavia's Slovenes live within that republic, but they now constitute only 90 per cent of its population.

A critical situation of potential conflict among peoples has arisen in Kosovo. There the Albanian majority has long pressured local Serbs and Montenegrins to migrate to their nominal republics. A forced exodus has become apparent in recent years. This has enraged particularly the peoples of Serbia, who view Kosovo as their national cultural hearth. They have demanded stronger control over the Albanians and vigilance in protecting the remaining Serbian minority.

Farming in Yugoslavia

The farm population of Yugoslavia stood at 4.3 million in 1981. At the time of the 1948 census it was 10.3 million. As a percentage of total population, the farm population declined during these years from 67 per cent to less than 20 per cent. The value of agriculture in total national income is now 14 per cent.

Although Yugoslavia is an avowedly socialist state, the socialist sector in agriculture accounts for only 17 per cent of total farmland. After attempts in the immediate post-war period to institute Soviet-style state and collective farms, the regime changed course and ceased pressures upon peasants to merge their lands. It did, however, limit farm sizes to 25 hectares (62 acres). In 1953 permissible size was reduced to a maximum of 10 hectares (25 acres). Socialist farms remained principally in the productive Danubian plain, where former lands of German settlers had been nationalized and resettled by a quarter of a million migrants from land-poor areas of Bosnia and Montenegro.

Some 3,400 cooperative farms now operate with a workforce of a quarter of a million employees. Despite their relatively small amount of land and labour, these farms produce a quarter of the gross output and nearly half of the country's marketable surplus.

In contrast, there are approximately 2,600,000 private farms. A high proportion have to be classed at the subsistence level. More than a third have less than 5 acres of cropland, often in several widely separated plots. Equipment in the smallest units consists of simple wooden ploughs pulled by oxen. Families survive by having one or more members work at other occupations in nearby towns. It is these farms particularly that have provided migrants to the cities. As the young men and women leave for better opportunities, cultivated land is decreasing and villages are being abandoned.

Still, the private farming sector has seen improvement in recent years. The number of privately owned tractors grew from 8,600 in 1963 to nearly 700,000 in 1983. Many of these are owned by workers returning from temporary employment abroad. They often hire themselves out to cultivate and harvest adjacent farmlands owned by an increasingly ageing population. Crop yields per acre have more than doubled over pre-war production. An early, distinctive feature of socialist farms in Yugoslavia was the assistance given to private farmers in seeds, fertilizers, machinery and marketing. This has led to a thriving, commercialized private sector, particularly in the Danubian plain.

It is useful to consider farming in terms of five contrasting regions: the Danubian plain, the foothills marginal to the plain, the mountain belt, the coast and the Vardar valley in Macedonia. The Danubian plain is the most productive area. Its soils are fertile, its growing season warm and long, and its summer rainfall usually adequate. It contains one-fifth of Yugoslavia's farmland, but produces more than half the country's commercial grain, a quarter of its dairy products, and two-thirds of its industrial crops, including sugar beets, sunflowers (for oil and cattle feed), soy beans and hemp. At any one time 60 per cent to 70 per cent of its area is in crops. Two-thirds of this cropland is given over to grain, with maize outnumbering wheat by a ratio of 2 to 1. The maize is fed to animals, particularly to some 2½ million pigs.

The plain was settled essentially in the eighteenth century after the occupying Turks had been pushed south of the Sava River. Large villages became the rule, a legacy of clustering for protection against the possibility of more depredations from the south. Even now settlements average 2,000 to 3,000 inhabitants, and a number have populations of 10,000 to 20,000 or more. As the Turkish threat declined, many families established farmsteads away from villages to avoid long trips to their lands. These isolated *tanjaci* or *salaši* result in a rural landscape reminding one of southern Australia or the American Midwest.

The foothill belt extends along the fringe of the Danubian plain from Ljubljana and Zagreb in the northwest to the Serbian city of Niš in the southeast. Many parts of it have population densities as great as those of the plain itself. About half the cultivated acreage is sown to maize, which is principally used as a feed for beef cattle. On the smaller, more subsistence holdings one often finds beans and squash grown simultaneously on the same plots as the maize. This is also a zone of truck crops for the adjacent large urban markets and of wine production on south-facing slopes up to 2,000 feet elevation.

The mountain belt principally focuses on animal husbandry.

Most of Yugoslavia's 8 million sheep are raised here, and large numbers of beef cattle are also produced. In contrast to intensive stall-feeding in the Danubian plain and foothills zone, animals in this region are generally raised in extensive fashion on grassland pastures. Some of Europe's last vestiges of transhumance still occur in parts of the southern mountains. From upland villages men and boys drive their animals in the autumn to winter pastures on the Sava river plain or in the coastal zone, often not returning to family homes for six months or more. Generally less than 10 per cent of the land is cultivated, and in Montenegro it is only 5 per cent. In the karst zone, cultivation most often is in the poljes or where pockets of soil have accumulated in small depressions formed by collapsed caves in the limestone rock. The region is particularly noted for its production of Turkish tobacco. It also has a large share of Yugoslavia's 74,000,000 plum trees, which yield the basic raw material for home production of *šlivovica* (plum brandy).

The mild winters of the Adriatic coast permit the growing of olive and citrus trees, particularly in the south. Vineyards are also significant, including the famous *dingač* wine produced on the Pelješac peninsula. However, agriculture has declined in many coastal areas as the population has emigrated and the growing tourism industry has offered less onerous alternative employment. Thus, in the Ravni Kotari area near the port city of Zadar one encounters huge olive plantations which are no longer managed nor harvested.

The Vardar valley region of Macedonia has a distinctively hot and dry summer climate. In contrast to the other republics, it produces twice as much wheat as maize. Its farmers raise all of Yugoslavia's million tons of cotton each year and nearly half of its tobacco. It is also important for vegetables, yielding a quarter or more of the country's commercial rice, tomatoes and paprikas. More than half of Yugoslavia's irrigation equipment is located in Macedonia, supplementing the marginal rainfall.

Industrial Development

Over the past seven decades Yugoslavia has transformed itself from a land of agricultural subsistence to one of respectable industrial production. Manufacturing output is now valued at roughly twice that of agriculture. Among able-bodied people, one person in every six works in a factory. In addition to primary production of a range of metals and fuels, Yugoslavia manufactures a wide variety of consumer and industrial goods. A significant share is exported abroad, including the 'Yugo' automobile produced by the Crvena Zastava plant in the Serbian city of Kragujevac.

In contrast to the pronounced regional concentrations of industry found in most states, Yugoslavia's production tends to be dispersed fairly evenly throughout the country. This in part is a result of a conscious effort to redress inherited economic inequalities between north and south. A rather even dispersion of industrial facilities does not, however, translate into an equality of well-being. Sharp contrasts exist between northern and southern republics, reflecting inherited differences in development and productivity.

Yugoslavia began industrializing rather late on the European scene. Its lands had been peripheral to the Habsburg and Ottoman Empires, and generally had been neglected economically. However, the territory had a number of favourable factors for industrial development, including a variety of mineral, fuel and other resources and a large potential labour force and market.

Before independence, development beyond subsistence farming occurred almost entirely in the north. Early in the nineteenth century the Habsburg Empire built all-weather roads in Dalmatia and elsewhere. Later in the century Austrians and Hungarians constructed railroad lines from their capitals into Slovenia and Croatia, and, after 1878, into Bosnia and Hercegovina. The primary motivations for building railroads were to gain access to Adriatic ports and to tap agricultural surpluses of the South Slavic lands for domestic and foreign markets. However, the rail lines did constitute an infrastructure that permitted the beginnings of mining and industrial production.

In southern areas there was little development. The stagnation of more than four centuries of Turkish feudal domination weighed heavily on the population. Too often they had suffered from the rapacity of local officials who operated even beyond the control of the central government. Entrepreneurship did not find encouragement. Official corruption, political instability, and low purchasing power of the inhabitants discouraged investment from the outside. Moreover, most communities lacked transportation connections within the Ottoman Empire and with the outside world. The Turks, unlike the Austrians, were not noted for building roads. They did collaborate with foreign investors to construct a railroad from Thessalonika through Macedonia to Kosovo at the end of the nineteenth century, but it did not link up with the Habsburg lines.

Serbia on the eve of the First World War – a century after breaking away from Turkish domination – was still characterized by rural isolation, economic subsistence, and a sense of fatalism in its population. Montenegro was similarly backward, though it had never been under effective Ottoman control. Of industrial enterprises in the Kingdom of Serbs, Croats and Slovenes in 1918, 83 per cent were in the former Habsburg lands, while only 14 per cent were in Serbia and less than 3 per cent in Montenegro and Macedonia.

As in other Habsburg successor states, newly independent Yugoslavia had a tendency to seek to produce as many goods and services as possible that had previously come from the imperial capitals. However, only 16 per cent of the population of the young country lived in cities. The country itself lacked the capital necessary to build plants and provide machinery. Foreign capital was borrowed, accounting for half of total investments on the eve of the Second World War. Virtually all mining of ores and their processing into metals was in the hands of foreigners, as was 60 per cent of textile production and half of wood-processing. The number of industrial plants did double in the inter-war period. However, per capita production and income remained extremely low, only Portugal having a lower level within Europe. In 1939 three-quarters of the population was still engaged in agriculture.

The war destroyed much of the hard-won industrial development. The transportation network suffered heavy damage, and 40 per cent of the factories were put out of action. A new regime came to power that saw the experience of the Soviet Union as a model for modernization. This model included nationalization of existing plants and a bias towards new investment in heavy industry. Communist ideology also called for a territorial evenness in development.

Tito's regime immediately began restoration of facilities, with output reaching pre-war levels by 1946. It also set about improving the transportation infrastructure. A new highway between Belgrade and Zagreb was constructed by volunteer youth labour, and work began for improvement of the railway network, including double-tracking, widening of several narrow-gauge lines, and filling in gaps between the inherited Austrian, Hungarian and Turkish systems.

Several major industrial facilities were constructed in the southern regions. Almost immediately such installations were dubbed 'political factories', since many were sited in locations that virtually guaranteed that costs of transportation and raw materials, to say nothing of untried labour, would exceed the value of finished product. A steel mill in the remote Montenegrin town of Nikšić was particularly singled out in this regard. Moreover, there was more than a suspicion that specific communities were selected for investment on the basis of influence exerted by former residents who had risen to high positions in the new regime, rather than as a result of careful economic analysis.

Whatever the merit of these generally held perceptions, investments in the southern areas as a whole have been far less profitable than similar developments in the north. Despite massive transfers of funds from northern republics, the south continues to lag behind in development. This is reflected in a variety of statistics. In the Albanian region of Kosovo, output per capita is less than one-third of the all-Yugoslav average; in Bosnia–Hercegovina, Macedonia and Montenegro it hovers around 60 per cent. In contrast, per capita output in Croatia is 130 per cent of the average, and in Slovenia it is more than double.

Leaving aside the question of the individual productivity of a southern labour force steeped in an Ottoman-based culture, the north had inherent advantages in agglomerative economies. Advantages of an early start in the industrialization process are evident everywhere. The outputs and even waste products of existing factories can constitute components or raw materials having minimum transportation costs for plants constructed nearby. A skilled labour force perpetuates itself and can be tapped by new enterprises. Utilities, communication facilities, and transportation routes are in place and can be utilized after minor investment. This contrasts with the necessity to construct an infrastructure from scratch in an undeveloped region.

In recent years there has been a tendency towards economic autarchy of constituent republics and autonomous regions. Each political unit appears to be investing in the production of as wide a range of goods as possible in order to promote local development and to avoid dependence upon other republics with which there are tensions. As a result, market areas of plants tend to be limited to the borders of their administrative units, which precludes scale efficiencies associated with mass production.

The pattern of industry in Yugoslavia consists of four primary clusters that focus on the capitals of republics: Belgrade, Zagreb, Ljubljana and Sarajevo. The first three are linked by excellent rail and highway connections along the plain of the Sava River. Each of the three produces approximately one-sixth of the country's total industrial production, while the Bosnian cluster yields somewhat more than 10 per cent. Outside the clusters are a host of minor regional developments.

1. The Belgrade region is the largest industrial area of the country. It is noted for its production of transportation equipment and agricultural machinery. A wide range of consumer goods are produced, including clothing, television sets and food products.

2. The Zagreb area ranks next, and is particularly important for its electrical-engineering equipment, petrochemicals and machine tools. Its array of consumer-goods production includes textiles, paper products and furniture.

3. The industrial area of Slovenia around Ljubljana and Maribor produces a host of products from aluminium, high-quality steels and trucks to electrical appliances, cotton fabrics and shoes.

4. The central Bosnian area focused on Sarajevo is the most recently developed, and stands out for its heavy industry, particularly iron and steel.

Outside of the major clusters, some industrial activity is to be found in each city and town.

To support this industry requires a substantial production of electricity. Currently Yugoslavia generates roughly one-quarter of the electricity produced in the United Kingdom and about one-sixth of that produced in West Germany. Despite the development of a variety of energy resources, Yugoslavia suffers from chronic shortfalls of power production. This is particularly due to high demands from industry, which now consumes two-thirds of the country's electricity. The problem has been exacerbated by recent expansion of industrial enterprises that are high-power consumers, including aluminium and copper smelting, steel production in electric furnaces, and plants producing industrial chemicals.

In contrast to most other countries of Europe, Yugoslavia generates up to 50 per cent of its power by hydroelectric dams – an unusually high share. About one-third of the country's water-power potential has thus far been developed. The largest single hydroelectric installation in Europe is the Djerdap plant, built jointly with Romania and opened in 1972 in the famous Iron Gates gorge of the Danube, east of Belgrade. It has a capacity of more than 2,000,000 kilowatts, ranking close to Grand Coulee Dam on the Columbia River in the United States. A second power plant, with a capacity of 400,000 kilowatts, has recently been constructed further downstream on the Danube. Numerous smaller power stations have been built in the Alpine mountains on the upper Drava and Sava rivers and in the central mountain belt on the Neretva, Drina, Vrbas, Vardar and other river systems.

Yugoslavia's first atomic power plant has been opened at Krško, which lies northwest of Zagreb, just inside the Slovenian border. It has a capacity of 632,000 kilowatts. Additional atomic installations were planned, but growing protests based on radiation fears have delayed and in all probability prevented their construction.

The remaining share of electricity production is produced by burning coal. Giant generating plants have been built in the vicinity of major beds, particularly in Serbia, Kosovo and Bosnia. Although Yugoslavia has extensive coal reserves, most beds are relatively small and low in quality. Lignite accounts for 90 per cent, whose potential is generally limited to electricity generation.

Coal is, of course, a vital raw material in the production of iron and steel, chemicals and other industrial goods. For producing iron in blast furnaces a baked bituminous coal termed 'coke' is required. Relatively small amounts of coking coal are mined in Bosnia. Some coke is also produced using an East German process that transforms lignite. However, the largest share of coking coal is imported, principally from the Soviet Union. It is processed in coke ovens in Bakar, just outside the northern port city of Rijeka.

In addition to coking coal, Yugoslavia also imports substantial quantities of petroleum. Some oil is produced in the Sava River valley and the Vojvodina region, but not enough to satisfy demand. In fact, up to 40 per cent of total energy needs must be satisfied by imports. Oil comes from the USSR via barges up the Danube and from the Middle East by tankers that unload in ports in the vicinity of Rijeka. Several refineries have been constructed in the Danube and Sava river valleys, and they are now being supplied with imported crude oil by a 350-mile-long pipeline from the island of Krk near Rijeka to the industrial town of Pančevo lying north of Belgrade.

Yugoslavia produces about 4 million tons of steel per year, which is roughly a third of that produced in the United Kingdom and tenth of that produced in West Germany. It meets most domestic needs, although some rolled steel is imported. Steel is produced in mills in each republic, but nearly half comes from Bosnia and Hercegovina, which benefits from its rich beds of iron ore and an early start during the period of Habsburg control. The country's largest integrated steel works is located in Zenica, just west of Sarajevo. Because of the paucity of coking coal, a significant portion of the country's iron and steel is smelted in electric furnaces using hydroelectric power. Particularly noteworthy is a new electric steel complex in Skopje using western Macedonian ore.

In addition to iron and steel, Yugoslavia produces a variety of other metals, including ferroalloys, copper, lead, zinc, nickel and aluminium. It stands in Europe second only to Poland in copper production, based on mines in Bor and Majdanpek east of Belgrade. It also mines more bauxite ore than any other European country and produces significant amounts of aluminium, much of it for export. The Trepča mines in Kosovo are noted for their lead and zinc ore and metal production. Most smelting of non-iron metals occurs in Serbia and Macedonia, though some production is found in each republic.

While primary metal production is concentrated in southern regions, some 90 per cent of machinery manufacturing is located in the three northern industrial complexes around Belgrade, Zagreb and Ljubljana. Skilled labour and transport connections account for this disparity. Northern factories also produce most of the country's textiles, chemicals and forest products. Most types of modern manufactured goods are produced in Yugoslavia, with perhaps three-fourths of its domestic needs being met by home production. A significant proportion of industrial output is exported, but an equal amount is imported from other countries. Yugoslavia has been noted particularly for its export of ships of all types.

In discussing industrial development a word must be said about the environmental consequences of modernization. The air, water and forests of Yugoslavia have deteriorated, as volumes of wastes from chimneys and outfalls continue to multiply. Smog lingers in mountain basins and quality fish have disappeared from streams. The mining and metallurgical areas of central Bosnia and eastern Serbia have been particularly hard hit, but all regions have felt the consequences of environmental pollution.

In the early post-war stages of development, emphasis was upon meeting production quotas at whatever cost. Subsequently, as environmental problems became evident, legislation was passed to

minimize pollution. However, in the decentralized political organization of Yugoslavia, enforcement was patchy and weak.

Public concern about the quality of life has noticeably increased
in the past decade. In Slovenia a 'Green Party' dedicated to protection of the environment has emerged with a significant degree of
support. It mirrors similar groups that have formed throughout
Europe, both East and West.

The Tourism Industry

Yugoslavia's third-ranking industrial branch after agriculture and
industry is tourism. It employs 4.4 per cent of the work-force and
earns at least 3 per cent of the gross national product.

Despite the fact that transactions and activities take place inside a
country's borders, those segments of tourism that cater to foreign
visitors properly are viewed as an export industry. More than half of
Yugoslavia's provision of services and accommodation is for the
estimated 9 million foreigners who bring at least US$1.3 billion in
hard currency to the country each year.[2] This amounts to at least 8
per cent of the country's total hard currency earnings, and covers
some 65 per cent of its negative trade balance. Catering to foreign
tourists yields 300 per cent to 1,000 per cent higher price-returns
than more conventional exports.

The benefits of the tourism industry to Yugoslavia are not just its
hard currency earnings. In addition to the multiplier effect of
imported money upon regional economics, growth of the tourist
industry has tended to stabilize local populations and to promote
better housing and public health in formerly backward areas. By
providing alternative employment opportunities it has arrested out-
migration to foreign countries or to other regions within Yugoslavia.

Foreigners are drawn primarily to the country's coastal region.
Although many also visited interior attractions, foreign tourists in
Yugoslavia in 1987 spent more than 88 per cent of their nights in
coastal accommodation. Tourism on the Adriatic coast is part of the
massive tourist attraction of the Mediterranean region, which draws
a third or more of total world tourist flows.

Although the airline distance of the coast from the Italian border

2 Officially reported tourism income is grossly underestimated due to evasion of
foreign currency controls by individuals offering rooms and meals. Yugoslav experts
on the tourism industry place current annual earnings at US$3.2 billion.

to Albania is less than 400 miles, Yugoslavia's shoreline actually adds up to more than 3,700 miles, including stretches around inlets on the mainland and along the margins of its 725 islands, 47 of which are inhabited. Most of this coastal zone is rocky, with only a few sandy beaches . However, in contrast to many parts of the Mediterranean, the Yugoslav coast is relatively unpolluted.

Beyond azure water and sun, the attractiveness of the coast includes numerous artefacts of ancient and medieval civilizations – a Roman emperor's palace and aquaduct in Split, a well-preserved arena in the Istrian Peninsula town of Pula, cities surrounded by walls at Dubrovnik and Kotor, and numerous old churches and monasteries. Although tourism has transformed much of the economy of the coast, tourists are also able to catch glimpses of a vanishing subsistence way of life, as fishermen repair their nets and their wives still patiently ride donkeys into the highlands to harvest vegetables or hay for their animals.

Legacies of the past also draw tourists to the interior. Sarajevo, Mostar and other southern cities reflect much of their Islamic heritage, including mosques, Turkish baths and colourful bazaars. Ancient Christian monasteries with spectacular frescoes are scattered throughout the country. Castles dot the landscapes of Slovenia and Croatia. Zagreb has maintained its medieval old town, and Ljubljana has preserved much of its striking baroque core.

The natural beauty of much of Yugoslavia affords a sharp contrast with heavily industrialized regions of Western Europe. The government has set aside twenty-two areas as national parks. Plitvice in the Croatian karst regions, with its spectacular waterfalls and travertine-dammed lakes, is perhaps best known. Among other preserved areas are the environs of Mt. Triglav in the Slovenian Alps and the mountainous zone along the Djerdap gorge of the Danube.

Tourists also come to Yugoslavia for ski facilities in the Slovenian Alps and the 1984 Olympic games complex around Sarajevo. Summer hiking and sight-seeing vacations in the mountains are significant. Upland game, deer and wild boar draw significant numbers of hunters from abroad.

The largest proportion of foreign tourists comes from Central Europe. More than 30 per cent arrive from West Germany and nearly 10 per cent from Austria. Italians make up 13 per cent, and Britons 8 per cent. No other groups exceed 5 per cent. Collectively, about 9 per cent are from socialist states of Eastern Europe, and just under 3 per cent are from the USSR.

Some 232,000 Americans visited Yugoslavia in 1987, constituting 2.6 per cent of the total. This was slightly less than the 247,000 Soviet citizens who visited Yugoslavia that year. Americans more than other groups appear to be fascinated by Dubrovnik's medieval charm. Nearly half the arrivals from the USA manage to visit that south coast city. In addition to Yugoslavia's natural and historical attractions, many Americans are drawn by family ties, particularly to relatives in Croatia left behind by turn-of-the-century émigrés.

Tourism development began in the middle of the nineteenth century with the Austrian construction of a railway from Vienna to Trieste and its establishment of a steamship line calling at a number of communities along the Dalmatian coast. Opatija, west of Rijeka, became the empire's principal winter resort when rails were extended there in 1873. During the inter-war period of independent Yugoslavia, tourism development continued, particularly along the coast. It suffered major setbacks with the destruction of facilities during the Second World War, but the new regime had rebuilt domestic and foreign tourism to pre-war totals by 1946.

American assistance after Yugoslavia's post-war break with the Cominform countries permitted the opening of a modern highway along the coast in 1964. That improvement in infrastructure plus heavy investment in new facilities led to a rapid increase in foreign tourists, whose numbers grew at an annual pace exceeding 15 per cent during the decade of the 1960s. After ups and downs reflecting changing world economic fortunes, current growth in visitors is about 6 per cent per annum. Two-thirds arrive by private automobile, 20 per cent by air, and 10 per cent by bus. Although only 1 per cent come by boat, numbers using this mode have more than doubled since 1983.

Yugoslavia now has accommodation for at least 1,350,000 tourists at any one time. A quarter of these are in hotel rooms, and a third are in private homes and guest-houses. An additional quarter are at public campgrounds, with the remainder principally vacation facilities for children or groups of workers.

The tourism industry suffers from a number of problems. Seasonality is a principal one. Most tourism workers are idle for half the year, adding to Yugoslavia's chronic unemployment problem. Conflicts exist with other economic activities. Coastal processing of imported raw materials degrades many developed and potential tourist sites. A cement plant outside Split and a carbide plant near Omiš are particularly noteworthy in this regard. The use of the coastal highway and other roads for long-distance hauling of goods exacerbates an already bad traffic congestion generated by increasing tourist flows.

The ubiquitous building of weekend houses (*vikendice*) is also lessening the attractiveness of many areas. Nearly a quarter of a million such second dwellings have been built, a third of them along the coast. They have proliferated for a variety of reasons, including easy credit, lack of planning control, and especially the fact that the regime until now has severely limited other avenues of investment of private funds. Some significant channelling of such surplus funds into hotels and restaurants is likely, if a recently passed Croatian law permitting unlimited investments in tourism facilities is approved by the federal government.

The rapid growth of domestic tourists also has affected foreign tourism. In 1987 more than 13 million Yugoslavs were recorded as tourists within the country, constituting 60 per cent of the total. In 1939 only 4 per cent of Yugoslavia's population was able to take vacations; in 1987 a full 57 per cent took such holidays. Only 30 per cent of domestic tourists now spend their time along the coast, however, a much lower proportion than of foreign tourists. This probably reflects higher costs of coastal facilities that have been bid up by more affluent foreigners.

Among current complaints about the state of the tourism industry is the uncertain and often contradictory role of the government in development, regulation and promotion. As in many other countries, it is not seen as a 'real' industry entitled to the same share of infrastructural and other investment and other incentives as manufacturing and processing establishments. Facilities are short in training and increasing the qualifications of employees. Marketing abroad is not sophisticated. There is still a pronounced bias against many forms of private initiative.

Summary

Yugoslavia is a diverse country situated at the intersections of numerous contrasting European physical, cultural, political and economic phenomena. To many it would seem a political–geographic impossibility, held together by royal dictatorship before the Second World War, and by communist dictatorship after it. Yet it has survived so far the passing of Tito as it survived the assassination

of King Alexander and the bitter wartime fragmentation and divi-
siveness. It has modernized and urbanized, providing a viable way
of life for its citizens. Its fund of natural resources and its increasingly skilled and sophisticated population give promise for continued progress in the future.

Bibliography

Bodrich, V. V. and L. A. Avdeichev (1970), *Yugoslavia: Ekonomiko-
Geograficheskaya Kharakteristika* (Yugoslavia: Economic–Geographical
Characteristics), Moscow, Mysl

Carter, F. (1968), *A Bibliography on the Geography of Yugoslavia*, King's
College, Cambridge, Department of Geography, Occasional Papers A 1

Carter, F. W. (1972), *Dubrovnik (Ragusa). A Classic City-state*, New York,
Seminar Press

Debardeleben, J.(ed.) (1989), *Environmental Problems and Policies in Eastern Europe*, Washington D.C., The Wilson Center

East, W. G. (1966), *An Historical Geography of Europe*, 5th edn, New
York, E. P. Dutton

Fisher, Jack C. (1966), *Yugoslavia – a Multinational State: Regional Difference and Administrative Response*, San Francisco, Chandler

Geografski Atlas Jugoslavije (Geographical Atlas of Yugoslavia) (1961), ed.
Petar Mardesić and Zvonimir Dugački, Zagreb, Znanje

Hamilton, F. E. L. (1968), *Yugoslavia – Patterns of Economic Activity*,
London, Bell

Hoffman, G. W. (1977), The Evolution of the Ethnographic Map of
Yugoslavia. A Historical Geographic Interpretation, in F. W. Carter
(ed.) *Historical Geography of the Balkans*, London, Seminar Press, pp.
437–91

—— (1986), 'The Transformation of the Urban Landscape in Southeastern
Europe', in M. P. Conzens (ed.), *World Pattern of Modern Urban
Change*, Chicago, University of Chicago, Department of Geography,
Research Paper No. 217–18, pp. 129–50

—— (ed.) (1989), *Europe in the 1990's: A Geographic Analysis*, New York,
Wiley

Lukaš, Filip (1922), *Geografija Kraljevine Srba, Hrvata i Slovenaca* (A
Geography of the Kingdom of the Serbs, Croats and Slovenes), Zagreb,
Nadbiskuske Tiskare

Mellor, Roy E. H. (1975), *Eastern Europe: A Geography of the Comecon
Countries*, New York, Columbia University Press

Milošević, Miodrag (1966), *Geografija Jugoslavije* (A Geography of Yugoslavia), Belgrade, Naucna Kniga

Osnove Ekonomske Geografije Jugoslavije (Foundations of the Economic Geography of Yugoslavia) (1974), ed. Hrvoje Turk, Zagreb, Grafokon

Pavić, Radova and Nikol Stražičić (1970), *Ekonomska Geografija Jugoslavije: Udžbenik za IV razred ekonomskih škola* (The Economic Geography of Yugoslavia: A Textbook for the IV grade of Schools of Economics), 3rd edn, Zagreb, Skolska Kniga.

Pounds, Norman J. G. (1964), *Eastern Europe*, London: Longman

Rogić, Veljko and Stanko Zuljić (1964), *Geografija Jugoslavije: Udžbenik za IV razred gimnazije* (The Geography of Yugoslavia: A Textbook for the IV grade of High School), Zagreb, Skolska Kniga

Rugg, D. S. (1985), *Eastern Europe*, The World's Landscapes Series, London and New York, Longman

Singleton, Fred (1970), *Yugoslavia: The Country and Its People*, London, Queen Anne Press

—— (1976), *Twentieth Century Yugoslavia*, New York, Columbia University Press

Veliki Geografski Atlas Jugoslavije (The Great Geographical Atlas of Yugoslavia) (1987), ed. Ivan Bertić, Zagreb, Sveučilišta Naklada Liber

2

The Economy of Yugoslavia: Structure, Growth Record and Institutional Framework

Ljubomir Madžar

Introduction

Among a rather heterogeneous collection of socialist nations Yugoslavia stands out as a unique case. In formulating her policies and shaping her institutions Yugoslavia did what no other socialist country had been able to undertake: she completed a thorough and far-reaching social reform at a time when in other socialist countries even far smaller changes appeared to be unthinkable. Moreover, the reforms undertaken some fifteen years later in other socialist countries turned out to be much less radical and less effective in shaking their bureaucratic foundations. The socialist world is still waiting for a reform which will represent as radical a departure from the existing, firmly established ideas and institutions as was the case with Yugoslavia's introduction of self-management. In China and elsewhere there may be bold attempts to provide a vast array of opportunities for mobilization of foreign and even domestic capital; but they are still far from affecting the entire economy, and their scope is therefore significantly narrower.

Nation-wide experiments are almost non-existent; and Yugoslav institutional turnaround is a unique act of social engineering of world-wide significance. Firstly, it gives a valuable indication of the potential of social engineering. Has Man acquired sufficient knowledge and political stamina to interfere with the institutional basis of society and to initiate massive changes in all spheres of social life without grave dangers to overall stability and efficiency? Secondly, the experiment is an excellent opportunity to learn the effects of a particular type of institutional transformation. As the number of strategic alternatives open to socialist countries for further institutional improvement is not particularly great, knowing what a specific avenue of social change brings obviously carries considerable practical significance.

Almost all other socialist countries have by now undertaken their own reforms. All of these have represented attempts to create more efficient organizational frameworks for economic and other social activity. As such they are living proofs of the unsatisfactoriness of existing institutional arrangements. By retaining so-called 'social property' in the means of production, Yugoslavia remains a member of a wider class of socialist economies. Her radical experiment is valuable as yet another attempt to construct an efficient economic mechanism on the common base of social ownership of the means of production. It thus greatly contributes to our understanding of the economic implications of social ownership. Can it be made compatible with the efficient allocation of economic resources? Should the Yugoslav way of institutionalizing social ownership turn out to be inefficient, that would be another valuable piece of empirical knowledge. Evidently, the probability of finding an economically efficient system based on social ownership declines as the number of unsuccessful alternatives which have been tried increases.

The Economic Potential of Yugoslavia

Economic potential is considered here under two headings. The first relates to Yugoslavia's natural resources, and the second to her economic strength in the narrow sense of the word: income, economic structure and a few physical production indicators.

Natural Resources

With an area of 255.8 thousand square kilometres, Yugoslavia is a relatively small country on a world scale, but at the same time, is one of the larger European countries. Among the 164 countries of the world Yugoslavia occupies 102nd place; whereas she ranks 10th among the 33 European countries. Except for Italy, Yugoslavia has a larger area than any of her neighbours. She has a slightly larger area than Romania and surpasses the remaining five neighbours by between two and five times.

The geographic position of Yugoslavia is generally considered to be favourable. She is located at the crossroads between the highly developed Western and Northern Europe on the one hand, and serves as a bridge to the oil-rich and strategically important Middle East, on the other. International routes connecting Northern Europe to the Mediterranean and to most of Africa also cross Yugoslavia. With a long and extremely convenient Adriatic coast she has worthwhile access to the Mediterranean and further to the world seas. Her access to the Danube, of which she has the largest part, provides a valuable connection with Eastern and Central Europe and the link with the Rhine provides a cheap and efficient navigation route to the most industrialized parts of the Continent.

The population of Yugoslavia in 1986 was 23.3 million, which gives her somewhat higher ranks both in the world and in Europe than was the case with geographic area: 32nd place in the world, and a relatively high 7th place in Europe. The population of working age is 15.1 million (65 per cent), and the economically active population is 11.3 million (44 per cent). The share of the agricultural population is 19.9 per cent. Total employment in 1986 amounted to 6.7 million, of which 2.6 million were women. Social (non-private) sector employment accounted for 97.8 per cent of total non-agricultural officially recorded employment and for 59.2 per cent of the economically active population. The rest is by and large absorbed by privately owned and operated agriculture. An impressive 3.1 per cent of the population has had a university education (1986); but the illiteracy rate is also impressive, and amounts to 9.5 per cent. The rate of population growth is rather low (0.63 per cent in 1986), being the result of quite low natality and mortality rates (1.54 per cent and 0.91 per cent respectively). Infant mortality is in line with what could have been expected on the basis of other demographic indicators (2.8 per cent), and compares favourably with most other countries.[1] The World Bank puts Yugoslavia in the group of so-called 'upper middle-income developing countries', in relation to which her demographic indicators stand out as favourable. Her crude birth and death rates in 1985 (16 and 9 per thousand) compare favourably with the rates (36 and 28) of this group, and to especially even higher rates (42 and 30 per thousand)

1. Original data on area and population are taken from various issues of *Statistički Godišnjak Jugoslavije (SGJ)* (Statistical Yearbook of Yugoslavia) mostly from *SGJ, 1987*, pp. 79–131. The information on the rank of Yugoslavia with respect to area and population is from D. Marsenić (1981, pp. 120–1).

for the entire collection of the developing economies. Similarly, her infant mortality rate in the same year was 27 per thousand, slightly below the average 52 of her group, and 71 of the larger set of the developing countries.[2]

With 14.4 million hectares of agricultural land and 9.9 million hectares of arable land, Yugoslavia cannot be considered as either richly endowed or visibly poor in her natural resource-base for agricultural development. At 58 per cent the area of agricultural land as a proportion of total area is significantly below the world average but her per capita arable land exceeds by 22 per cent the average for the world. In comparison with European averages, however, she comes out quite favourably: in the two categories mentioned the Yugoslav average exceeds the corresponding averages for Europe by 35 per cent and 50 per cent. The area covered with forests is approximately 9 million hectares, which puts Yugoslavia significantly above the European average, but leaves her far below the world average. The wooded area is large and still growing, but its structure and quality are not quite satisfactory.

Mineral resources are versatile, but unequally available. Reserves of oil suitable for exploitation are estimated at 140 million tons, which at the present rate of production is sufficient for twenty-odd years. Much richer are the exploitable reserves of coal, estimated at 13 billion tons, which is sufficient to sustain the present intensity of extraction for about three centuries. The unfavourable feature of these reserves is the predominance of low-quality lignite. The situation is much more favourable with hydroelectric potential, which amounts to 110 billion kilowatt hours, with potential yearly profitable production of 55 billion kilowatt hours.[3] In this respect Yugoslavia is one of the richest countries of Europe and of the world.

The known reserves of iron ore – the quality of which is quite modest – are sufficient to sustain the present rate of production for another one-and-a-half centuries. The country has been reputed for her riches in ores of non-ferrous metals but, generally, these are being diminished somewhat more rapidly than other mineral resources, and the profitability of their exploitation is being systematically reduced due to the reduction of the ore's metallic content. Yugoslavia is well-endowed with non-metallic minerals (marl, magnesite, asbestos, a variety of clays) and it is believed that these provide a good foundation for a number of flourishing industries.

2. World Bank (1987), Table 29, p. 259.
3. More detailed information can be found in D. Marsenić (1987, pp. 70–4).

Ljubomir Madžar

Income and Production Capacity

The briefest way of portraying the size and strength of the Yugoslav economy is to indicate her share in area, population and gross national product (GNP) in appropriately selected larger geographical areas (see Table 2.1). The areas to be considered are (a) the group of upper-middle-income economies; (b) the more comprehensive group of middle-income economies; (c) the entire group of developing countries (according to the World Bank classification); and (d) the world as a whole. Yugoslav per capita GNP will also be expressed as a ratio to the average GNP in each of these four areas. This indicator will be calculated as a ratio of the Yugoslav share of GNP to her share of population of the respective areas.

GNP is expressed in 1975 US dollars. The fourth line is calculated as a ratio of the numbers in the second and the third lines.[4] In the group of upper-middle-income countries Yugoslavia is evidently above the average. Her level of development markedly exceeds that of the middle-income countries in general, which are a wider subset of the set of developing countries. With respect to the level of development of this latter set, Yugoslavia has a towering advantage, exceeding it by no less than 3.5 times. Nevertheless, Yugoslavia remains below the world's average, falling short of it by more than one-fifth.

Structural features of the Yugoslav economy indicate a rather advanced stage in the process of industrialization, a stage which is visibly above her general level of development. No doubt this is the result of a highly biased development policy, which was firmly committed to restructuring the economy along the lines of technological modernization and creating entirely new sectors.

The share of agriculture is characteristically low,[5] and still displays a persistent declining trend; it dropped from 23 per cent of

4. Calculated on the basis of World Bank (1987), Table 1. The table does not contain information on per capita GNP for non-reporting, non-member economies. The lacuna is filled by estimating the percentage GNP for this group of countries: the ratio of their GNP per capita to that of the world is taken from Ivo Vinski (1978) and with adjustment for the differences in the rates of growth, applied to the estimate of the GNP per capita for the world *without* non-reporting countries. This estimate made it possible to calculate the share of the Yugoslav GNP in the world's GNP. Due to the well-known upward bias in the officially reported rates of growth of the centrally-planned economies, the world's total income is overestimated and, consequently, the Yugoslav share in global GNP and her relative position are underestimated.
5. Unless otherwise conveyed, quantitative indicators to be discussed until the end of this section are calculated on the basis of World Bank (1987).

Table 2.1 Relative Size of the Yugoslav Economy (percentage shares and ratios)

	Upper-middle-income countries	Middle-income countries	Developing economies	World
Area	1.2	0.7	0.4	0.19
Income (GNP)	4.6	3.0	2.1	0.37
Population	4.1	1.9	0.6	0.48
Relative income	112.2	157.9	350.0	77.1

Source: World Bank (1987), Table 1.

GNP in 1965 to only 12 per cent in 1985. It thus approximated fairly closely the corresponding figure for the group of upper-middle-income countries (the more advanced category of the larger set of developing nations). The relevant figures for this advanced group show a decline from 15 per cent to 10 per cent; and for the bundle of developing countries as a whole from 29 per cent to 20 per cent. In contrast to agriculture, the shares of industry and of services are both high and increasing. In the years 1965 and 1985 these shares were 42 per cent and 46 per cent of GNP for industry, and 35 per cent and 42 per cent for services. (The upper-middle-income countries had 34–35 per cent for the first, and 54 per cent for the second sector, whereas the analogous figures for the entire cluster of developing countries were 29 per cent and 34 per cent vs. 42 per cent and 47 per cent). The structure of employment diverges from that found in both of the groups of countries of which Yugoslavia is a member. Thus the share of the agricultural labour force in 1965 and 1980 was 57 per cent and 32 per cent (upper-middle-income countries 45 per cent and 29 per cent; developing countries 70 per cent and 62 per cent). The share of the labour force in industry vs. services in Yugoslavia in these two years was 26 per cent and 33 per cent vs. 17 per cent and 34 per cent. This can be compared to 23 per cent and 31 per cent vs. 32 per cent and 40 per cent for the upper-middle-income countries and to 12 per cent and 16 per cent vs. 18 per cent and 22 per cent for the larger assemblage of developing countries.

Equally indicative for ascertaining the type and the level of the country's development is the structure of her foreign trade. The requisite information is assembled in Table 2.2.

Table 2.2 The Structure of Foreign Trade for Yugoslavia and Reference Groups of Countries in 1985 (%)

	Exports					Imports				
	1	2	3	4	5	1′	2′	3′	4′	5′
Yugoslavia	8	12	33	46	9	5	27	14	25	30
Upper-middle-income countries	37	16	18	30	9	10	17	7	32	33
Middle-income countries	40	19	14	27	9	11	18	7	31	33
Developing countries	39	21	13	28	10	11	17	7	30	34

Key: 1 = fuels, minerals and metals, 2 = other primary commodities, 3 = machinery and transport equipment, 4 = other manufactures, 5 = textiles and clothing; 1′ = food, 2′ = fuels, 3′ = other primary commodities, 4′ = machinery and transport equipment, 5′ = other manufactures.

Source: The World Bank (1987), Tables 11 and 12.

On the export side one is struck by a very low share of primary commodities which make up only one-fifth of the total; conversely there is an extremely high share of manufactures in which the important category of machinery and transport equipment constitutes more than 40 per cent. Typically all of our reference groups of economies display strikingly different structural features; so that Yugoslavia stands out as having an advanced and diversified structure of exports. The structure of imports shows broadly analogous traits, with a relatively high share of primary commodities. The form of both aggregates is a result as well as an indicator of the process of modernization that has been going on for almost half a century.

A frequently used development indicator is energy consumption per capita. Here again Yugoslavia is above the average of the respective groups of countries into which it is classified: with 1,926 kilograms of oil equivalent in 1985, it compares favourably with upper-middle-income countries (1,510), middle-income economies (886) and the entire set of developing economies (502). Similar conclusions can be drawn out on the basis of fertilizer consumption (measured in hundreds of grammes of plant nutrient per hectare of arable land): with 1,178 grammes, Yugoslavia exceeds significantly the average of her subdivision of upper-middle-income economies (684), not to mention the broader classes of countries which, on average, fall well behind Yugoslavia.

Another illuminating gauge of development is daily calorie supply per head. Here Yugoslavia seems to be occupying a particularly favourable place: with 3,602 calories she is far above the average for the upper-middle-income states (2,987), not to mention the developing economies (2,470). Significantly enough, in this respect she surpasses even the group of highly developed market economies (3,417).

One of the rare indicators with respect to which Yugoslavia is below variously defined averages is the degree of urbanization. In 1985 Yugoslavia had 45 per cent of her total population in urban settlements, which falls short not only of the corresponding percentage for her subdivision of the (more advanced) developing countries (65 per cent), but even of the degree of urbanization of the entire collection of middle-income societies (48 per cent). Of course, the set of developing countries as a whole has a lower degree of urbanization (31 per cent).

Considered on an international scale, Yugoslavia is indubitably a relatively egalitarian society. In his exhaustive and well-grounded comparative analysis Milanović (1987, pp. 311–19) found Yugoslavia to be among countries with the highest degree of equality of income distribution. Rough indicators presented by the World Bank are in full accord with this finding.[6] In 1978 the lowest 20 per cent of the population received 6.6 per cent of income, whereas the highest 10 per cent received 22.9 per cent of income. Both results compare quite favourably with most other countries.

An extremely unfavourable structural characteristic of Yugoslav society, however, can be identified in the regional dimension of its development. The country is bedevilled with unusually large differences in per capita income (and other indicators) between the various parts of her territory and population. As these differences coincide with ethnic boundaries, the problem acquires particularly adverse political and social overtones. The firmly established, and by now almost traditional classification, subdivides eight federal units (six republics, and two autonomous provinces which are, together with Serbia proper, parts of the Socialist Republic of Serbia) into the group of the developed (Slovenia, Croatia, Serbia proper and Vojvodina) and the group of the underdeveloped units (Bosnia and Hercegovina, Montenegro, Macedonia and Kosovo). Taken as a whole, the developed areas are in terms of per capita

6. World Bank (1987), Table 26.

gross material product (GMP) about twice as developed as the underdeveloped areas: in 1986 the ratio of corresponding per capita magnitudes was 2.02 to 1. The distance between the most developed (Slovenia) and the least developed (Kosovo) is much more striking, and reaches the astounding ratio of 7.4 to 1. The alarming fact is that these differences display a clearly visible rising trend, because of which the entire complex of regional development remains one of the central issues in development policy.[7]

Foreshadowing subsequent discussion, it is of some interest to cast a brief glance at the country's rate of growth, and to compare this with the growth record of her environment. Taking two periods, 1965–80 and 1980–85, one immediately observes that Yugoslavia experiences a drastic deceleration of growth: the rate of growth of her gross domestic product (GDP) drops from an impressive 6.1 per cent in the first to only 0.8 per cent in the second period. This, in a sense, follows the general pattern of growth of the world economy; but the decline of the speed of development is more pronounced. The rates of growth for the same periods were 6.6 per cent and 1.7 per cent for upper-middle-income countries; 6.5 per cent and 1.7 per cent for middle-income economies; and 6.0 per cent and 3.3 per cent for the entire collection of the developing countries. Obviously, some far-reaching changes took place in the Yugoslav economy's growth process, to which we now turn.

A Summary Analysis of Yugoslav Economic Development

The Growth Experience of Pre-War Yugoslavia

Yugoslavia was created on 1 December 1918. The constituent parts came from societies of widely differing economic and political backgrounds. The north-western areas were parts of the large, developed and well-organized Austro-Hungarian Empire. Serbia and Montenegro were independent kingdoms, with a significantly lower level of economic and general social development. The rest of the country came from the backward and obsolete Turkish Empire, carrying with them all of the latter's unfavourable social attributes. As Bićanić (1972, pp. 4–10) points out, one part of the country had the experience of a wide, largely competitive national market, and of

---

7. The differences calculated on the basis of the *SGJ, 1987*, pp. 446, 473.

modern ways of pursuing business; the other part had very little or none of these. One part was market-oriented and ready to fight for policies based on liberal economic philosophy; the other part had a strong inclination towards state interference in economic activity, autarchic policies, and a high level of protection of its relatively undeveloped industry. These differences in outlook were to survive for a long time, and left a deep imprint on attitudes towards policy issues and directions of institutional development in the entire post-war period. The level of development was low and uneven. The national income per capita was, in the (formerly) Austrian part of the country, 5,200 dinars, in the Hungarian part, 4,400 dinars, and in the country as a whole only 3,000 dinars. The value of fixed assets fell between 1909–12 and 1919 by 8 per cent – whereby most of the losses occurred in Serbia and Macedonia – and regained its pre-war level only in 1925 (Bićanić, 1972, p. 3). A remarkably high degree of tariff protection produced spectacular changes in relative prices, opened a price scissors (the widening gap between the prices of manufactured good and agricultural products) by unprecedentedly depressing agricultural prices, and unleashed a process of massive income redistribution with far-reaching long-run consequences. The speed of development varied enormously across various parts of the country – Slovenia, for example, increased its per capita industrial investment 2.5 times faster than Serbia, 6 times faster than Bosnia and Hercegovina and 25 times faster than Montenegro (Mišić, 1957, p. 271). Economic power was extremely unequal: no less than 50 per cent of the country's bank capital was located in Croatia (Bićanić 1972, p. 4). Southern parts of the country were practically without any industrial capacity (Čobeljić, 1972, p. 21).

The unenviable economic structure of the new state is perhaps best illustrated by the composition of its population: the share of the agricultural population was in 1921 no less than 78.7 per cent, and it declined very slowly to 76.2 per cent in 1931 and to 74.8 per cent in 1938 (Čobeljić, 1972, p. 22). The growth of industrial employment was only sufficient to absorb about one-twelfth of the increase of the economically active population. Agriculture and forestry accounted for 58.1 per cent of the national income in 1923–25; this share was to be reduced only slowly to 52.9 per cent in 1936–39. At the same time the share of industry, mining and handicrafts increased from 20.5 per cent to 28.7 per cent over the same period (Čobeljić, 1972, p. 23; Bjelogrlić, 1973, p. 8).

The rate of growth of pre-war Yugoslavia was modest, albeit not at all low by the then prevailing international standards. In the period 1926–39 national income grew at an average rate of 2.14 per cent which barely exceeded the average rate of growth of population of 1.44 per cent, implying a rate of growth of income per head of only 0.7 per cent (Stajić, 1947, p. 8, cited in Čobeljić, 1972, p. 22). Marsenić (1981, p. 23) also found that per capita national income in 1938 reached a level of only US$60 measured by the purchasing power of that year. International comparisons show how small this income was; in the same year the US per capita income was $521, that of Germany $337 and of France $236. The process of industrialization was to a significant degree propelled and financed by foreign capital. In highly cartelized sectors, such as cement, chemicals, textiles and food industries, foreign firms owned and operated between 51 per cent and 97 per cent of capacities (Bjelogrlić, 1973, p. 8). In the production of metals these accounted for about four-fifths of capacities (Marsenić, 1981, p. 78).

Income distribution in pre-war Yugoslavia is believed to have been rather unequal. Bjelogrlić (1973, pp. 7–8) found that in 1938 the top 3 per cent of the agricultural population appropriated 20.9 per cent of national income in agriculture, and that the top 10 per cent of the non-agricultural population received 35 per cent of the income of the non-agricultural sector. On the other hand, 34 per cent of the non-agricultural poor were able to get only 12 per cent of the corresponding income.

Thus, pre-war Yugoslavia was poor and nearly stagnant. Her development was heavily dominated by foreign capital, and income distribution was overly asymmetrical and unequal.

Post-War Reconstruction and the Socialist Transformation of the Economy

Few countries came out of the Second World War as badly damaged as Yugoslavia. According to some estimates, perhaps as many as 1.7 million people (almost 11 per cent of the pre-war population) succumbed tragically during the war.[8] Among them about 90,000

---

8. This figure has recently been seriously challenged. From a number of quarters the arguments have been advanced that the number of war victims could have reached the limit of 1.2 million at the most. Whatever figure turns out to be right, it is too much. We therefore stick to the standard figure with the caveat that it might be revised some time in the future. See also chapter 4 by Pleština, below.

skilled industrial workers and 40,000 highly trained specialists lost their lives. The loss of national wealth was estimated at $9.1 billion (purchasing power of 1938). The heavy toll of war destruction included, among other things, 36 per cent of industrial capacity, 52 per cent of standard gauge railways and 33 per cent of narrow gauge railways. All thirteen large railway bridges were destroyed. Yugoslav war losses made up 17 per cent of the total losses of the eighteen Western allied countries. While these countries lost 0.7% of their population, the Yugoslav population was decimated, in a way which produced a number of far-reaching, adverse long-run consequences (Bjelogrlić, 1973, pp. 10–11).

The period of reconstruction was at the same time a period of decisive and irreversible institutional transformation. In a number of consecutive moves the bulk of available productive potential was transferred to the state sector. The first step was taken as early as 1944, when the property of quislings and war criminals was confiscated. Then came two agrarian reforms, in 1945 and 1953; the first affected a land area of 1.6 million hectares, half of which was distributed to poor and landless peasants, and the other half went to the state. The second reform reduced the maximum size of private holdings to only 10 hectares, a constraint which has survived up to the present day.[9]

There have been three waves of nationalization; and the sequence of these is highly indicative. In the first move (December 1946) banks, insurance companies and other financial institutions, mining, basic and highly concentrated manufacturing industries were nationalized. These require the smallest number of decisions for their running. Other sectors which are highly intensive with respect to decision-making capacity came in for nationalization only in 1948. Small businesses were generally transferred to the social sector; the only exceptions consisting of small craftsmen relying predominantly on their own labour force. The object of the third nationalization campaign (1959) was residential housing, when the owners were allowed to retain only two large or three small apartments (Bićanić, 1972, pp. 22–8, Horvat, 1976, p. 7). Agriculture was not covered by nationalization until 1949, when a massive campaign of forced collectivization was launched. This experiment was short-lived, however, and by 1953 most cooperatives were dissolved. (A

---

9. The most recent constitutional changes provided for an increase of the maximum to no less than 30 hectares.

part of the socially owned property was formed by nationalizing concerns owned by foreigners other than those who had collaborated with occupying enemy forces. This, however, entailed more or less fair compensation).

Two additional sources greatly contributed to the formation of the social (at that time state) property. The first is the substantial amount of war reparations and other forms of foreign aid. As these were administered on an inter-governmental basis they went automatically into the state (social) sector. The other is state property from the pre-war period: large expanses of forests, railways and roads, defence and some other manufacturing industries, a dozen coal mines and five large banks, including the National Bank of Yugoslavia, which had been owned and operated by the government (Bićanić, 1972, p. 25).

Because of the revolutionary enthusiasm of the people, the application of force by the strong, monolithic government, the inflow of foreign resources and drastically depressed personal consumption, the process of reconstruction unfolded quickly. The level of industrial production in 1946 was 20 per cent below that of 1939; but by 1947 this pre-war level was surpassed by 19.6 per cent. Agricultural production did not reach the 1930–39 ten-year average until 1957 (Bjelogrlić, 1973, pp. 18–19).

The first five-year plan was formulated for the period 1947–51. Its over-ambitious targets can best be illustrated by the fact that it envisaged an approximate doubling of GMP, increasing industrial production by about five times, and increasing the production of heavy industries by seven to ten times (depending on the sector). It foundered on account of the economic blockade brought about by the rupture of political ties with the bloc of Eastern socialist countries. Loans were cancelled and practically all financial and commercial ties were severed. Of course, it is highly questionable whether the plan could have been implemented under the best of circumstances. The mutilated economy, saddled with a heavy burden of defence spending and several unheard-of-droughts, achieved a rate of growth which fell far short of the target: while the planned growth rate of GMP was 16 per cent (Sekulić, 1985, p. 129), the actual rate reached 1.9 per cent (Marsenić, 1986, p. 80).

This period was characterized by a heavy investment effort, investment reaching almost a third of GMP. The policy of maximizing savings was pursued in a ruthless way, relative prices were drastically distorted and the notorious price scissors opened widely at the expense of agriculture. A political and an economic aim were simultaneously served in this. Income was taken from private agriculture, as a remnant of the capitalist economic set-up, and accumulation was siphoned off to fuel the process of industrialization. No wonder, at such low prices, that the sale of agricultural products had to be made compulsory.

The Rate and Efficiency of Economic Growth Since the Introduction of Self-management

The introduction of labour management entailed a major institutional metamorphosis of the Yugoslav economy. Following its introduction a thorough-going adjustment was needed, which was aggravated by a couple of extremely unfavourable agricultural years in the early 1950s. It is generally considered that a period of normal growth started in 1953; moreover 1952 is usually taken as a base year of analysis. One caveat is, however, in order here. Due to the disastrously slow growth in the 1949–52 period, much of the subsequent growth record is accountable in terms of the recovery from the preceding stagnation. High growth rates during the 1953–60 period are thus partly a consequence of the low rates experienced prior to it. One way of ameliorating the bias resulting from this abrupt change of development trends is to take 1953, rather than 1952, as the base year of the analysis. This does not eliminate all the difficulties, and the periodization of Yugoslav economic growth remains a controversial issue both among Yugoslav and foreign scholars. With this caveat in mind, the rates of growth of the principal macroeconomic aggregates are presented in Table 2.3. To minimize the bias resulting from periodization, a variety of suitably chosen time periods is presented.

The table clearly reveals that the choice of base year does matter: the shift of the base from 1952 to 1953 lowers significantly most rates, with the most pronounced change in the rate of growth of GMP in the private sector, caused by the especially low agricultural production in 1952. This incidentally illustrates the extraordinary fluctuations of agricultural production, and its striking vulnerability to the weather conditions – a well-known attribute of underdevelopment.

The long-run tendency of a decline of the rate of growth is readily apparent. Two years – 1960 and 1964 – could be alternatively taken as the dividing lines. With 1960 as the separating year, the rate of

Table 2.3 Rates of Growth of the Yugoslav Economy (%)

Period	Total GMP	GMP Social sector	GMP Private sector	Population	GMP per capita
1952–60	8.91	9.55	7.37	1.14	7.67
1953–60	7.95	10.05	3.57	1.10	6.78
1960–64	8.11	10.41	1.13	1.10	6.93
1964–70	5.11	5.63	2.99	0.97	4.10
1970–80	5.74	6.34	2.64	0.91	4.79
1980–86	1.15	1.12	1.33	0.71	0.44
1953–64	8.01	10.18	2.67	1.10	6.83
1964–80	5.50	6.08	2.77	0.93	4.53
1953–80	6.52	7.73	2.73	1.00	5.47
1964–86	4.30	4.70	2.38	0.74	3.53
1953–86	5.52	6.50	2.47	0.95	4.53
1950–60	6.46	6.79	5.63	1.19	5.21
1960–70	6.30	7.52	2.24	1.02	5.23
1970–80	5.74	6.34	2.64	0.91	4.79

Source: *Statistički Godišnjak Jugoslavije (SGJ) 1987*, (Statistical Yearbook of Yugoslavia) p. 92, *SGJ, 1979*, p. 79, *SGJ, 1977*, pp. 81, 102.

growth of social-sector GMP is reduced by almost a third (31.0 per cent). When the present period of stagnation (1980–86) is excluded from the analysis, the rate of growth of the total GMP is reduced somewhat less drastically (24.3 per cent). The corresponding declines with 1964 as the separating year are 40.3 per cent for social-sector and 31.3 per cent for total GMP. The phenomenon of deceleration shows much less clearly in the mechanical periodization presented by the last three rows of the table; one cannot even speak unequivocally about a slowing down of the growth of the private sector. This applies to the 'normal' period of development ending with 1980; in the subsequent years the economy plunged into the present phase of protracted stagnation, the end of which cannot even be guessed for the time being. This is a qualitatively different and evidently inferior part of the growth process, for which a separate explanation will be given.

The chosen periodization follows institutional changes in the economy, and should reflect roughly the efficiency of the underlying solutions. Institutional criteria for defining periodization are among the most frequently used in the empirical analyses of Yugoslav economic development, but the number of deep changes and the inescapable lags in their effects are among the factors which make the separation of various sub-periods far from simple (Madžar, 1974). Another reason why extreme caution in interpreting these results is necessary is the fact that (as will be shown below) the growth process has continuously been subject to the influence of many powerful forces which had no connection whatsoever with the existing institutional framework, and because for a long time some of these developments effectively suppressed and concealed serious deficiencies in economic mechanisms and policies. Even so, it could be said that up to 1960 the business autonomy of firms was restricted to matters of routine daily management; in particular, investment policies and income distribution were not under the decision-making authority of firms, and were regulated by the state. In fact, the regulation giving the firms the authority to distribute their available income as personal income and retained earnings (the economic accumulation) was enacted in 1958, although it started actually to be applied only around 1960. Another far-reaching institutional change was the abolition of state investment funds in 1963, when enterprises started to take over the important function of planning their own long-run growth, and to undertake independently the corresponding investments. This coincided with the beginning of the gradual diminution of the so-called use-price of social capital. This was a sort of capital tax whose function was to serve as an instrument of social accumulation, to ensure appropriate pricing of scarce capital and to equalize the economic conditions under which working collectives were operating. This last function was performed by slicing off from enterprise income the contribution of capital and making it impossible to distribute this in the form of personal income. The use-price of capital was reduced gradually – the marked inter-sectoral and even inter-enterprise differentiation having been its salient characteristic – and it was finally abolished in 1971. It has become customary to locate the effects of this deep change in the institutional mechanism regulating savings potential and investment activity at the end of 1964. The economic reforms of 1965 inaugurated an entirely new set of policies and underlying decision-making rules which marked the beginning of a new philosophy of economic management. This was a decisive break with the traditional socialist way of steering economic development by turning to decentralized mechanisms, which, due to serious institutional weaknesses at the microeconomic level of the system, could not possibly give satisfactory results. Thus 1965, the year of the beginning of the new system of regulating investment and shaping growth policies, seems to be a convenient benchmark separating two institutional set-ups and two regimes of functioning of this most important segment of the economy. This way of periodizing post-war Yugoslav economic growth is also subject to raging controversies (Sapir, 1980, 1986; Bajt, 1986), so that whatever conclusions happen to be drawn must be interpreted with some caution. Yet, this change seems to be sufficiently significant that it probably remains as relevant as any other for defining the periodization.

The institutional determinants of Yugoslav economic development will be the subject-matter of the next section. However, a tentative conclusion can be drawn now: the changes in the institutional setting of the Yugoslav economy have in all likelihood exerted an unfavourable influence on its growth performance. With more caution one could say that they certainly have not improved the growth record of the economy.

To complement the analysis of growth rates, it is desirable to glance at some indicators of macroeconomic efficiency. The proverbial incremental capital-output ratio (ICOR) will be relied upon in the attempt to highlight changes in efficiency. The analytical limitations of the ICOR are well known; but it still gives worthwhile information on the efficiency of use of investible resources. The ICOR is probably more appropriate in a labour-rich country such as Yugoslavia, a country which has for decades been saddled with serious problems of unemployment, than in more typical economic environments in which both basic production factors could be considered scarce. To give a complete picture of the development effort and of the resulting performance, the rates of investment, defined as shares of investment in fixed assets in GMP, are separately presented. Furthermore, the rates of investment are presented in two versions, as (a) the share of total and (b) the share of 'economic investment', in GMP. 'Economic investment' comprises allocation to those sectors which are, according to the Yugoslav version of Marxist national accounting theory, productive in terms of generating economic value. Such sectors as housing, education, health, social insurance and government are excluded. Thus, taking a more narrowly defined investment rate, based on 'economic' investment, is probably more consistent with the definition of GMP, and therefore analytically more relevant. (See Table 2.4 for the results).

Table 2.4 Rates of Investment and the ICORs (%)

Period	The rate of investment	The rate of 'economic' investment	The ICOR	The 'economic' ICOR
1953–60	27.80	21.10	3.12	2.37
1961–64	34.47	22.50	4.25	2.77
1965–70	30.43	21.18	5.96	4.15
1971–80	32.26	22.72	5.62	3.96
1981–86	23.47	16.87	20.41	14.67
1953–64	30.73	21.72	3.55	2.51
1965–80	31.76	22.30	5.78	4.06
1965–86	25.71	20.34	5.98	4.73
1953–86	26.53	20.57	4.57	3.54

Source: Table 2.3 for the rates of growth and *SGJ, 1987*, pp. 92 and 162; *SGJ, 1982*, p. 152; *SGJ, 1979*, p. 85; *SGJ, 1978*, p. 144; *SGJ, 1974*, p. 136; *SGJ, 1973*, p. 114; *SGJ, 1972*; p. 116. Economic investments estimated by applying their share in total investments *in current prices* to the series of total investments in constant (1972) prices.

Parallel to that which could have been deduced from Table 2.3, two strikingly different periods can be distinguished, the first one ending in 1980, and the second one following it and comprising the present stage of economic stagnation. The exorbitantly high ICORs in both versions are the result of the coincidence of slow growth, (approximating stagnation) and a still relatively high level of investment. However, in the 'normal' segment of the process under examination one easily identifies some striking elements of deterioration: from about 3 the ICOR jumps by more than one-third in the next sub-period and then to about 6 in the period following it. Thus, in a time-interval of fifteen or so years the ICOR practically doubled, a result which provoked serious concern among both Yugoslav scholars and policy-makers. Subsequent decline of the ICOR is only slight, so that Yugoslavia remains with respect to the efficiency of investment vastly inferior to comparable countries with similar levels of development. The changes in the 'economic' ICOR are noticeably less pronounced, reflecting the changes in the share of 'non-economic' investment; but the tendencies are the same, and deterioration of this performance indicator is just as spectacular as the soaring of the conventionally defined ICOR.

Global Factor Productivity as an Indicator of Efficiency

More sophisticated analyses of macroeconomic efficiency, based on production functions and corresponding indices of global factor productivity, give results which are in broad agreement with the conclusions derived from the changes in the ICORs. By fitting a non-homogenous Cobb–Douglas production function, with both factors – capital and labour – corrected for the degree of their utilization, and with two specifications – one containing the exponential technical progress term and the other one not containing it (Bajt, 1985, pp. 7–9) – one finds that the contribution of technical progress to the rate of growth is rather low: 33.6 per cent for industry and 25.6 per cent for the economy as a whole. An alternative methodological route was taken by Bazler-Madžar (1984), who did not make corrections for the degree of utilization of the factors of production, and treated this simply as a component of a generalized variety of overall productivity. Moreover, she separated the period under examination into two sub-periods, 1952–64 and 1965–79. By experimenting with alternative specifications of the Cobb–Douglas and the Constant Elasticity of Substitution (CES) production function – contrary to Bajt (1985) – she found that elasticity of the GMP of the non-agricultural segment of the economy with respect to labour is much higher than that with respect to capital. At the same time she found a positive contribution (27 per cent of the then high rate of growth) of the increase of global factor productivity in the first sub-period, and that it was negative in the second sub-period. As this latter result was not statistically significant, the application of an alternative non-parametric way of measuring global productivity gave in this latter time-interval a very meagre contribution of technical progress – only 10 per cent (Bazler-Madžar, 1984, p. 200). In another work Bazler-Madžar (1985, p. 17) established a pronounced declining trend in all macroeconomic performance indicators, and demonstrated that the rate of technical progress was 2.6 per cent in the first, and only 1.14 per cent in the second sub-period. Subsequent analyses of Yugoslav growth not only confirm but strongly emphasize and reiterate its faltering efficiency.

Unlike Bajt and Bazler-Madžar, who concentrated on the usual decomposition of the rate of growth, Sapir (1980) turned to the capital-intensity bias which is a corollary of the maximization of income per worker, and which is clearly implied by the theory of labour-managed economies (Ward, 1958; Vanek, 1970; Meade, 1972). To simplify in a somewhat extreme way: the route towards a high income per worker (an objective of the labour-managed collective) certainly does not lead through the expansion of employment but through abundantly equipping the employees with complementary factors, the chief among which must certainly be capital. Sapir finds that, due to a low elasticity of substitution (1980, p. 299), the excessive substitution of capital for labour results in spectacular decreases in elasticity of output with respect to capital; this then reduces (p. 301) the contribution of both capital and labour expansion to the rate of growth. The contribution of technical progress remains unchanged in both periods under examination (1955–65 and 1966–74). Bajt (1966), among others, questions Sapir's periodization, criticizes the proposition that 1965 was the year of a major institutional turnaround, and points to other factors which could have caused the same observed movements. In his recent reaction (1987) to Sapir's reply (1986) Bajt reiterates some of his criticisms. In his recently published book (1987, pp. 48–52) Labus reinterprets Sapir's arguments, finds them convincing, and adds a number of observations of his own, confirming the idea of a capital intensity bias as the cause of the serious misallocation of resources. Among many analyses and underlying disagreements – which incidentally confirm the old belief that economics is still as much an art as it is a science – one can discern a clear common message. For one set of reasons or another, the efficiency of the Yugoslav economy is unsatisfactory and, moreover, it exhibits a clearly visible declining trend.

In this long-lasting and by now truly voluminous discussion, one crucial factor seems to have escaped the attention of the analysts. It refers to the role of foreign resources in Yugoslav economic development. Abundant inflow of supplementary resources from abroad started as early as 1950 (and probably earlier) and lasted up to and including 1980. For most of the time these were unilateral transfers, such as foreign aid, war reparations and workers' remittances. During the 1970s these gifts grew gradually into loans, at first on concessionary and then on commercial terms. On the basis of the extensive study by D. Gnjatović (1985, pp. 46–70), one can infer that, expressed as a share of GMP, the inflow of foreign resources reached really impressive levels: in 1952–60, 9.0 per cent; in 1961–64, 5.9 per cent; in 1965–70, 5.5 per cent; in 1971–75, 8.5 per cent; and in 1976–81, 7.6 per cent. Expressed as a share of net investment, this inflow reached, in the same periods, the following percentages: 42.6 per cent, 23.8 per cent, 25.9 per cent, 40.7 per cent and 32.9 per cent. Despite such a massive utilization of supplementary foreign resources, Yugoslav international indebtedness did not start to grow rapidly until the second half of the 1970s. In 1971, for instance, the net international debt amounted only to US$2.7 billion, and in 1975 to a still modest US$5.8 billion (Gnjatović, 1987, p. 301). It was only in the second half of the 1970s, when loans had to be used in place of unilateral transfers, that foreign indebtedness experienced its spectacular expansion. Its present amount of about US$18.8 billion[10] proved too much of a burden for repayment according to previously agreed to schedules, and the country had to resort to repeated reprogramming. It is the firm conviction of the present author (Madžar, 1987) (a conviction not infrequently disputed by many economists) that the development of the Yugoslav economy cannot be understood without seriously taking into account the contribution of foreign resources. As these figures concerning the relative level of foreign resource inflow clearly indicate, the changes in the economy's rate of growth are not unrelated to the volatile intensity of this resource transfer. The contribution of these resources to growth is certainly underestimated. A number of factors account for this: (a) the dinar was persistently overvalued, thus leading to underestimation of these resources, (b) they helped activating past investments made under the regime of the Soviet-type central planning, (c) this was a perfectly mobile component of resources, which was readily directible to the most important priority sectors where it could give the largest effects, and (d) it provided a perfect way of compensating for the numerous allocational defects of the prevailing institutional mechanism – by removing bottlenecks it simply made other investments more effective than they would otherwise be. The most suggestive indication of the importance of foreign resources is the fact that the dramatic precipitation of the growth path of the Yugoslav economy takes place at the beginning of 1980s when the inflow of foreign resources was replaced by their intensive outflow.

Retardation of growth is not the only trouble bedevilling the Yugoslav economy. Space permits only a mention of such problems as galloping inflation, heavy and still-growing unemployment, dif-

---

10. The latest available official figure refers to June 1987; see Narodna Banka Jugoslavije, *Bilten Narodne Banke Jugoslavije*, Vol. 16, Nos. 7–9, 1987, p. 3.

ficulties with a balance of payments and growing discrepancies in the level of development among the country's already highly differentiated regions.

The Institutional Roots of Yugoslavia's Economic Hardships

The institutional determinants of untoward developments in the Yugoslav economy have been foreshadowed in the preceding analysis. They cannot be dealt with in detail here. Yugoslavia is in this respect such a peculiar country that works devoted to her institutional system constitute a new branch of economics, a new discipline in the strict sense of the word. Without pretending to an exhaustive analysis, only a few points will be indicated here.

The Implications of Social Ownership

In the first place, the Yugoslav institutional system is based on social property and thus shares all (dis)advantages of the class of systems relying on this type of ownership. Rational husbanding and expansion of any type of property, including social, can be secured either through decentralized arrangements based on the motivation of economic agents or, it is to be hoped, through the intervention of the government and forceful and administrative means of augmenting productive potential. Indicative planning and indirect economic policies are a theoretically possible combination of the two. For a number of reasons, including the absence of any political mechanism for arriving at a social consensus (see Milenkovitch, 1971, pp. 295–6), government-based mechanisms for steering economic development and preserving and expanding the social means of production were discarded, while the necessary institutional preconditions for securing a proper motivation of the economic agents were not being created. The well-known 'property rights problem' (Furubotn and Pejovich, 1970; Milanović, 1983) makes it simply unattractive for workers to accumulate and invest in the firms in which they are employed. Empirical trends seem to have verified this, one might say, obvious proposition. The final outcome of the institutional disorder in the field of property rights is the notoriously dangerous and economically irrational divergence of rewards and efforts, and of authority and responsibility (Madžar, 1988) which, just as in the case of communal grazing in Africa, stimulates the agents to use the available resources to the utmost without motivating them to expand the resources and to economize on them. Yet, here too, controversies have developed and disagreements persist (Horvat, 1986a; Madžar, 1986; Horvat, 1986b).

The lack of motivation on the part of working collectives to accumulate and expand the assets of their enterprises, combined with the absence of a governmental mechanism for the direct or indirect regulation of social savings, has produced a number of undesirable consequences. For one thing, as is frequently emphasized, and as has been shown in various ways many times (e.g. Korošić, 1979; Kovač and Madžar, 1986, pp. 41–3; Sojić, 1986), the savings potential of the social sector of the economy has been drastically reduced. In fact, when adjustment is made for a fictitious component generated by inventory revaluation under inflationary conditions (Madžar, 1985; for a concise and yet exhaustive analysis of theory and method see Lydall, 1987), it turns out that since 1979 the social-sector business savings have been either around zero or negative.

Distortions in Factor and Product Pricing

The corollary to the disinclination to save has been, on the average, a fast growth of personal incomes which have frequently outstripped the increase in labour productivity and caused lasting distortions in the functional distribution of income (Popov, 1987). Thus the abundant factor (labour) became artificially expensive, while capital (a notoriously scarce factor) was and is still being priced at an inadmissibly low level. Due to the abolition of the use-price of capital, it acquired the characteristics of a free good; and due to nominal interest rates persisting below the rate of inflation, its most valuable financial component became and remained negatively priced. Another disadvantage is the fact that factor shares had been lumped together, which made it possible to distribute in the form of personal incomes the contribution of the complementary production factors. As labour is – due to technology and other objective reasons – in different sectors combined with vastly varying quantities of production factors, it is clear that possibilities for raising personal incomes above labour's true contribution varied widely across sectors and between firms. Some of the determinants of total income, differentiating the ability of firms to remunerate workers, are even unmeasurable; such are, among others, internal technologies, which are private to the firm (Lydall, 1984, pp. 32–3). This is the reason why the socialist principle of remuneration according to work done was drastically violated and, as Popov (1983, pp. 156–70) has shown, on the level of industrial branches (the economy is divided into some forty branches) the discrepancies in remuneration of the same type of work go up to 1:2. Of course, the discrepancies on the next (lower) level of aggregation are much larger, and reach a surprising 1:3.7 (Popov, 1983, p. 161). International comparisons demonstrate that such differences are far out of line with what is customary in other economies (Popov, 1980). Wide variation in the pricing of labour and, more generally, the fundamental divergence of factor pricing and factor endowment, could not fail to produce troubling disparities in product prices (Kovač and Madžar, 1986, pp. 38–41). This greatly reduced the allocative efficiency of the market: it generated wrong signals and, what is more, produced inappropriate motivation regarding the alternatives to which resources were to be allocated. In short, with systematically distorted factor and product prices the market(s) could not function properly.

Another consequence of institutional disorder in the field of income distribution and the resulting factor pricing is the permanent tension of the cost-push inflationary processes. This is one of the best understood problems in Yugoslav economic thought, and one to which numerous research-efforts have been devoted (Bajt, 1971, 1983; Jovanović, 1981; Popov, 1976; Mencinger, 1971, 1987). Inter-sectoral differences in capital intensity – as well as a large number of other exogenous factors, particularly including objectively determined variations in the rate of technical progress – produce substantial differences in income per worker. These in turn lead to the above-mentioned differentiation of the remuneration of labour. Due to the demonstration effect, and to some mobility of labourers, the lagging sectors, in trying to catch up, exert a powerful pressure on prices. The effects of sectoral price increases get quickly transmitted throughout the economic system with a steady tendency to increase of the general price level as the unavoidable final result. Moreover, the uncontrolled and in the present institutional setting almost uncontrollable (save for extrasystemic direct state interventions) increase in personal incomes also had its important demand-pull aspects. Once won, they tended to be spent quickly, the more so in view of the absence of capital markets, readily obtainable alternatives for productive investment or some other ways of rationally deploying the financial surplus. Inflation has, in turn, in many ways further twisted factor and product prices, contributing, among other things, to a progressive decline of the real interest rate.

The Macroeconomic Policy Framework

The weak microeconomic foundations of the economy – the absence of the impulse to accumulate capital in the enterprises, low mobility of investible and other resources, extremely inadequate factor pricing, distortions of product prices, the lack of a rational stance towards risky ventures (Gams, 1987, pp. 130–2; Popović, 1984, pp. 116–23), overly complex and cumbersome arrangements for decision-making and the resulting sluggishness in reactions and low adaptability – certainly call for energetic and efficient macroeconomic regulation of the economy. This was, however, rather inefficient. Macroeconomic planning does not function in a satisfactory way (only one out of seven medium-term plans – the plan 1957–61 – was implemented). The reasons are legion (see Madžar, 1982, 1987; Čobeljić, 1987), but they can be grouped in two broad classes: (a) those having to do with the deficiencies of the political mechanisms for interest mediation and grinding out strategic decisions which are acceptable to all relevant power factions, and (b) those reducible to the incompleteness and malfunctioning of the mechanisms for plan implementation. In particular, the process of controlling the economy and steering its development is decentralized, so that the federal states have a decisive role in it with all the concomitant problems of co-ordination. Many instruments of economic policy are lacking and their distribution among the institutional carriers of economic policy is dysfunctional; and the process of strategic decision-making is not separated from current policy issues, so that many matters of minor importance become politicized, and decisions are taken in a sluggish and inefficient way. Many domestic and foreign observers (e.g. Schrenk *et al.*, 1979, pp. 111–35) have noticed the flagrant segmentation of the fiscal system – both regional (with a preponderant role of the federal states) and functional (with some 17,000 autonomous parafiscal entities which collect revenues and, without much co-ordination, decide on how to spend them). This makes it impossible to pursue the policies of functional finance or, for that matter, any kind of well-conceived and effective stabilization policies.

Organization of the Economy

Self-management has long been pursued as a social goal of its own, as an end in itself, without much regard to its underlying efficiency implications. As workers cannot fully exert their influence in large concerns, which because of their complexity are dominated by the technostructure, there has been a country-wide, massive process of splitting up large organizations and creating substantially smaller ones, called Basic Organizations of Associated Labour (BOALs), in which workers' management can more fully come to the fore. The process was initiated by constitutional amendments and completed by the new Constitution of 1974 and the Law on Associated Labour of 1976. Actual processes of reorganization dragged on for another quinquennium. Many consequences sprang from this colossal overhaul of the entire society, but only some of them can be cited here. First, there has been significant duplication of administrative apparatus in the economy. The number of directors, secretaries, accountants and clerical staff increased beyond expectation, and so did the corresponding material base – office space, office equipment, information infrastructure and other components of the decision-support systems. Second, an enormous increase took place in the complexity of decision-making. What used to be daily routine decisions became the object of exceedingly complex arrangements, not infrequently sanctioned by formalizing agreements to which a number of now independent parties had to give their consent. Third, some natural entities were broken up and technological ties severed. This in some cases led to technological disunity of the systems, whose efficiency crucially depends on that unity itself. A special, semi-colloquial term was coined to describe the process of disintegrating organizations inspired by the desire to make self-management more practicable; the nearest English translation of that term would be *boalization* (creating BOALs). Now that the impact of boalization is well understood, an opposite process is (and has been for about three years) in full swing. This too gave birth to a new word – *deboalization*. Much of the loss of micro-economic efficiency is ascribed to such spectacular organizational changes which reduce the strength and adaptability of the entire economy in many ways, but in particular by: (a) adopting an institutional framework which is meant to serve other ends than enhancing the power of the economy, and (b) seriously undermining organizational stability which is an essential prerequisite for

89

a satisfactory economic performance. Present constitutional amendments (IX–XXXVII, especially X and XI) go a long way towards rectifying the above-mentioned organizational weaknesses. Some interesting theory has developed in anticipating, guiding and justifying constitutional changes in this field (e.g. Babić, 1988; Ranković, 1988).

A Peculiarity of the Financial System

A final reflection of these institutional deficiencies and resulting structural discrepancies is a substantial financial deficit, a sort of accumulated *negative* capital of the social sector as a whole. The high propensity of this sector to distribute large personal incomes – a penchant which the state very frequently had to check with crude administrative means (see Sekulić, 1985, pp. 139–47), as well as an insufficient impulse to economize, which seems to be a common characteristic of all social-property-based systems, has steadily driven the social-sector firms towards financial deficits. The lack of financial discipline, caused by the fact that sanctions for any failure to pay fall not on private but on common property, has greatly exacerbated this problem. From the point of view of the firms – but not of the economy as a whole – the difficulties were alleviated by hidden but nevertheless substantial subsidies contained in bulky credits extended under negative real interest rates, a natural resultant of the inflationary conditions. If the social sector of the economy was the winner, the losers were other institutional sectors – households, the state and to some extent the private sector of the economy. With negative prices, the demand for credits was and remains practically infinite, which is one of the determinants of high foreign indebtedness. But a very interesting by-product of the extensive utilization of foreign loans developed in the late 1970s and early 1980s. These are the so-called negative foreign exchange differences (the appropriate terminology exists in the Yugoslav languages alone). This phenomenon has been exhaustively and, one is inclined to say definitively, discussed by Mates (1987).

'Foreign exchange differences' are simply a debt of the banking system towards households and the foreign sector, that is towards all those agents who have deposited foreign exchange with it. The essential point is that these liabilities are not matched by any claims of the banking system on the non-banking sectors. To understand this phenomenon one has to take into account the fact that the recipients of bank credits (by and large the enterprises of the social sector) have become permanently adjusted to negative real interest rates, and to the implicit subsidies conditioned by them and contained in practically all credits. In fact, this has practically become a necessary prerequisite of their financial viability. Giving credits on the basis of the dinar deposits does not create any imbalances in the banking sector because inflationary depreciation erodes both the assets and the liabilities side of its balance sheets. The banking system, however, has been receiving substantial amounts of foreign exchange denominated deposits, and on the basis of these has extended dinar credits. The dinar-denominated value of the foreign exchange liabilities has been rapidly increasing on account of the inflation-induced and accelerating devaluation of the dinar. The corresponding assets have not been fully revalued because they were partly converted into dinars, and advanced to the social sector in the form of extremely soft loans (i.e. at a nominal rate which significantly fell short of the rate of inflation). The banking system simply did not charge its customers the true costs of the financial resources on the basis of which credits had been advanced to the social sector. The excess of costs over revenues produced an imbalance, and eventually accumulated into a large amount of debt to which no claims towards anybody can be juxtaposed. The largest part of these uncovered debts is accumulated in the National Bank of Yugoslavia. This is an effect of the special legal arrangements without which the business banks would not be interested in accepting foreign exchange under such unfavourable conditions. Be that as it may, a paradox has developed: due to the inflationary redistribution of wealth, induced by negative real interest rates, the economy has a favourable financial position as seen through its equity-assets ratio, the budgets of all levels of the state are balanced, the household sector has substantial financial assets, and yet new deficits are yearly piled up without any of the sectors being financially burdened by an equivalent amount. This is yet one more institutional peculiarity of the unique regulating mechanism of the Yugoslav economy. Some economists are inclined to interpret this amassed deficit as just an internal reflection of the foreign exchange indebtedness of the social sector of the economy – either to the rest of the world or to the household sector, which has financed the economy by forming foreign exchange deposits with the banking sector.

One last question concerns why banks behaved so irrationally as to willingly incur losses by borrowing dearly and lending cheaply.

Ljubomir Madžar

The answer throws light on another important institutional trait of Yugoslav society. The banks are founded by their clients; they are managed by these clients on the principle: one founding member–one vote. The capital subscribed is not significant and does not determine their voting power. The banks are, therefore, run by their debtors, whose 'interest' is to lend at interest rates as low as possible. This is the reason why a law had to be passed prohibiting the banks from granting too unprofitable and insecure loans. This fact alone tells much of the story of the evolution and harmful effects of the existing institutional arrangements of the Yugoslav economy.

Conclusion

By its growth record and by the very atypical configuration of its underlying development trends, the Yugoslav economy has been and probably will remain an attraction for economic and other researchers. Especially attractive has been her unusual and in many aspects unique institutional system. Yugoslavia has in a sense been the biggest laboratory in the world. As such, she is a fascinating country both to observe and to live in, even though it may not be always pleasant to reap the fruits of the experiments. In an unrelenting course of institutional transformation Yugoslavia has tried out a vast number of widely varying solutions. A lot of experience has been acquired and many things have been learned the hard way. Certainly, some of them did not yield much tangible benefit; but they have added to the world's repository of knowledge in the important field of the merits and demerits of alternative courses of institutional development, and thus acquired significance which widely surpasses the boundaries of Yugoslavia. Right now Yugoslavia is embarking on a new bold and far-reaching change of her institutional system. It is hoped that she will not only take the lead once again among reforming socialist countries, but also reach solutions which will enhance the efficiency of her economy and society at large. This will perhaps contribute to the pool of the world's knowledge of the potential value of various policies and institutions as well as to the ability of other countries to shape more successfully their own economic and social systems.

Bibliography

Babić, Manojlo (1988), 'I dalje sa neadekvatnim i kontradiktornim rešenjima', *Ekonomika udruženog rada*, Vol. 36, Nos. 1–2, pp. 27–30

Bajt, Aleksander (1971), *Inflacija osebnih dohodkov*, Ljubljana, EIPF

—— (1983), 'Mehanizmi inflacije u Jugoslaviji', in B. Šoškić (ed.), *Savremeni problemi ekonomski stabilizacije*, Titograd, Savet Akademija Nauka i Umetnosti SFRJ–CANU

—— (1985), 'Trideset godina privrednog rasta (Problemi efikasnosti i društvenih odnosa)', *Ekonomist*, Vol. 38, No. 1, pp. 1–20

—— (1986), 'Economic Growth and Factor Substitution: What Happened to the Yugoslav Miracle?: Some Comments', *The Economic Journal*, Vol. 96, December, pp. 1084–8

—— (1987), 'Economic Growth and Factor Substitution: What Happened to the Yugoslav Miracle? A Post Festum Comment', *Ekonomska analiza*, Vol. 21, No. 4, pp. 469–71

Bazler-Madžar, Marta (1984), *Tehnički progres i privredni rast*, Belgrade, Institut Ekonomskih Nauka

——, Marta (1985), *Efficiency of Resource Use in the Yugoslav Economy*, Fourth International Conference on the Economics of Self-management, Liège, 15–17 July

Bićanić, Rudolf (1972), *Economic Policy of Socialist Yugoslavia*, Cambridge, Cambridge University Press

Bjelogrlić, Dušan (1973), *Dvadeset pet godina ekonomskog razvoja Jugoslavije*, Belgrade, Izdavački Centar 'Komunist'

Čobeljić, Nikola (1972), *Privreda Jugoslavije*, Bk 1, Belgrade, Savremena Administracija

—— (1987), *Plan i tržište – otvoreni problemi i pokušaj sinteze*, Scientific Conference on Plan and Market in Yugoslav Economic System, Kragujevac, 17–18 December

Furubotn, Erik and Svetozar Pejovich (1970), 'Property Rights and the Behaviour of the Firm in a Socialist State: the Example of Yugoslavia', *Zeitschrift fur nationalökonomie*, December, pp. 431–54

Gams, Andrija (1987), *Svojina*, Belgrade, Institut Društvenih Nauka – Centar za Filozofiju i Društvenu Teoriju

Gnjatović, Dragana (1985), *Uloga inostranih sredstava u privrednom razvoju Jugoslavije*, Belgrade, Ekonomski Institut

—— (1986), 'Platni bilans i zaduženost Jugoslavije u inostranstvu 1971–1986', *Jugoslovenski pregled*, Vol. 31, No. 6, pp. 297–304

Horvat, Branko (1969), *Privredni ciklusi u Jugoslaviji*, Belgrade, Institut Ekonomskih Nauka

—— (1976), *The Yugoslav Economic System*, White Plains, N.Y., M. E. Sharpe

—— (1986a), 'Farewell to the Illyrian Firm', *Ekonomska analiza*, Vol. 20, No. 1, pp. 23–9

—— (1986b), 'The Illyrian Firm: An Alternative View: A Rejoinder', *Ekonomska analiza*, Vol. 20, No. 4, pp. 411–16

Jovanović, Slobodan (1981), 'O globalnom odnosu realnih zarada i produktivnosti rada', *Ekonomska politika*, 15 June, pp. 29–31

Korošić, Marijan (1979), 'Akumulativnost organizacija udruženog rada', *Jugoslovenski pregled*, Vol. 23, No. 5, pp. 201–6

Kovač, Oskar and Ljubomir Madžar (1986), *Employment Policies in the Programme of Structural Adjustment of the Yugoslav Economy*, World Employment Programme Research Working Papers, Geneva: ILO

Labus, Miroljub (1987), *Društvena ili grupna svojina*, Belgrade, Naučna Knjiga

Lydall, Harold (1984), *Yugoslav Socialism: Theory and Practice*, Oxford, Clarendon Press

—— (1987), 'Efekti inflacije na procenu realnog proizvoda', *Ekonomska politika*, No. 1815, 12 January, pp. 27–8

Madžar, Ljubomir (1974), 'Problemi i perspektive razvoja Jugoslovenske privrede', *Ekonomska misao*, Vol. 7, No. 1, pp. 9–36

—— (1982), 'Privrednosistemske dimenzije društvenog dogovaranja o osnovama plana', in B. Šoškić (ed.), *Problemi samoupravnog privrednog sistema*, Vol. 2, Titograd, Crnogorsk Akademija Nauka i Umjetnosti–Odjeljenje Društvenih Nauka, pp. 189–205

—— (1984), 'Privrednosistemska izgradnja kao komponenta dugoročne razvojne strategije', *Zbornik matice srpske za društvene nauke*, No. 76, pp. 35–61

—— (1985), 'Revalorizacija zaliha, fiktivna akumulacija i iluzija rasta', *Ekonomist*, Vol. 38, No. 3–4, pp. 327–49

—— (1986), 'The Firm in Illyria: An Alternative View', *Ekonomska analiza*, Vol. 20, No. 4, pp. 401–10

—— (1987), 'Zbilja i iluzija u predstavama o relativnoj uspešnosti Jugoslovenskog privrednog razvoja', *Ekonomika*, Vol. 23, No. 5, May, pp. 3–8

—— (1988), *Iluzija i stvarnost u institucionalnom oblikovanju društvene svojine*, Scientific Conference on Social Property and Other Forms of Ownership, Herceg Novi, 11–13 May

Marsenić, Dragutin (1981), *Ekonomska struktura i privredni rast Jugoslavije*, Belgrade, Savremena Administracija

—— (1986), *Ekonomska SFR Jugoslavije*, Belgrade, Vojnoizdavački i Novinski Centar

Mates, Neven (1987), 'Some Specific Features of Inflation in a Heavily-Indebted Socialist Country', *Ekonomska analiza*, Vol. 21, No. 4, pp. 419–31

Meade, James E. (1972), 'The Theory of Labour-Managed Firms and of Profit Sharing', *The Economic Journal*, Vol. 82, No. 325s, March, pp. 402–28

Mencinger, Jože (1971), 'Inflacija potražnje ili inflacija troškova', *Eko-*

nomska analiza, Vol. 5, No. 1–2, pp. 1–22

—— (1987), 'Acceleration of Inflation into Hyperinflation–The Yugoslav Experience in the 1980's', *Ekonomska analiza*, Vol. 21, No. 4, pp. 399–418

Milanović, Branko (1983), 'The Investment Behaviour of the Labour-Managed Firm: A Property Rights Approach', *Ekonomska analiza*, Vol. 17, No. 4, pp. 327–40

—— (1987), *Nejednakost u raspodeli dohodaka u Jugoslaviji*, Belgrade, Ekonomski Fakultet, Ph.D. Dissertation

Milenkovitch, Deborah D. (1971), *Plan and Market in Yugoslav Economic Thought*, New Haven, Conn., Yale University Press

Mišić, Dimitrije (1957), *Ekonomica industrije FNRJ*, Belgrade, Naucna Knjiga

Popov, Sofija (1976), *Uloga ličnih dohodaka u formiranju i kretanju cena*, Belgrade, Ekonomski fakultet, Ph.D. Dissertation

—— (1980), 'Medjunarodna uporedna analiza veličine raspona ličnih dohodaka', *Ekonomski anali 29*, Vol. 25, No. 68–9, July–December, pp. 377–415

—— (1983), *Lični dohoci i inflacija troškova u Jugoslaviji*, Belgrade, Ekonomika

—— (1987), 'Uskladjenost tempa rasta ličnih dohodaka i produktivnosi rada i privredna kriza u Jugoslaviji', *Ekonomska misao*, Vol. 20, No. 4, pp. 28–48

Popović, Strasimir (1984), *Ogled o privrednom sistemu Jugoslavije*, Belgrade, NIO Poslovna Politika, Marksistički Centar Organizacije SK u Beogradu

Ranković, Jovan (1988), 'SOUR – Ni udruženje ni složeno preduzeće', *Ekonomika udruženog rada*, Vol. 36, No. 1–2, pp. 9–14

Sapir, Andre (1980), 'Economic Growth and Factor Substitution: What Happened to the Yugoslav Miracle?', *The Economic Journal*, Vol. 90, June, pp. 294–313

—— (1986), 'Economic Growth and Factor Substitution: What Happened to the Yugoslav Miracle?: Further Comments', *The Economic Journal*, Vol. 96, December, pp. 1089–90

Schrenk, Martin, Cyrus Ardalan and Narwal A. Tatawy (1979), *Yugoslavia – Self-Management Socialism, Challenges of Development*, Baltimore, Md, Johns Hopkins University Press

Sekulić, Duško (1985), *Tržište, planiranje i samoupravljanje*, Zagreb, Globus

Stajić, Stevan (1947), 'Realni nacionalni dohodak Jugoslavije u periodu 1926–1939 i 1947–1956', *Ekonomski problemi*, Belgrade Ekonomski Institut FNRJ

Šojić, Milan (1986), 'Akumulativna i reproduktivna sposobnost društvenog sektora', *Jugoslovenski pregled*, Vol. 23, No. 5, May, pp. 201–6

Vanek, Jaroslav (1970), *The General Theory of Labour-Managed Market Economies*, Ithaca, NY, Cornell University Press

Vinski, Ivo (1978), *Kretanje društvenog proizvoda svijeta od 1910. do 1975. godine*, Zagreb, Ekonomski Institut

Ward, Benjamin (1958), 'The Firm in Illyria: Market Syndicalism', *American Economic Review*, Vol. 47, No. 4, September, pp. 566–89

World Bank (1987), *The World Development Report 1987*, New York, Oxford University Press

3

Contemporary Yugoslav Society: A Brief Outline of its Genesis and Characteristics

Zagorka Golubović

Introduction

The analysis of contemporary Yugoslav society must take into account two facts: firstly, that post-war Yugoslav society was modelled after the Soviet pattern, and secondly, that it staged a new, specifically 'Yugoslav road to socialism' after the break with Stalin in 1948, which was named 'self-governing socialism'. Within this context analysis must suggest answers to the following questions: (1) Does Yugoslav society still belong to so-called 'real socialism'? (2) How does it differ from East European societies, and are these differences of degree or of kind? (3) Has the 'Yugoslav road to socialism' offered a genuine alternative to Soviet-type society? (4) How can one explain the genesis of the crisis of present-day Yugoslav society?

The emergence of a new concept of socialism in Yugoslavia, in contrast to the Soviet model, represented only a first step, necessary but insufficient in itself, in the transformation of post-war Yugoslavia. The break with Stalin was easier and less painful to make than a more profound break with Stalinism as a way of thinking and acting, whose impact we are still witnessing in various features of the post-war development of Yugoslav society.

The new approach to socialism, which the concept of 'self-government' implied, called for changes in the entirety of those social relationships inherited from both the pre-war tradition and the post-war imitation of a Soviet-type regime. The most urgent changes assumed by the concept of the 'Yugoslav road to socialism' can be summarized as follows: (a) a reorganization of the centralized (command) type of management of the economy and society and a reconstruction of the authoritarian type of work organizations, with their established hierarchies implying the domination of the managerial staff and the workers' subordination in the decision-making process, (b) a reconstruction of the existing distribution of power, and power monopoly in the political structure, with a domination of politics over all other sub-structures, and (c) a change in the position of the workers (and the other population) as citizens, clearly defining citizens' rights and liberties and creating democratic institutions to guarantee their use.

One cannot describe the level and nature of development of contemporary Yugoslav society without first analysing, at least very briefly, its genesis. In analysing the current crisis, we shall see that Yugoslavia underwent a crisis in the 1970s and 1980s because the social changes initiated in 1948 were neither theoretically conceptualized, nor given coherent shape as a political programme. That is to say these changes were conceptualized and implemented half-heartedly, constantly shifting back and forth under the influence of an ideological legacy which the Yugoslav leadership has never fully abandoned. For this reason one may speak of an identity crisis in contemporary Yugoslav society.[1]

Hence new elements of a market economy, and new institutions of workers' councils, were merely built onto (a) the already established structure of social and production relations, based on the nationalization of the means of production in industry, which gave birth to the monopoly of state ownership, and (b) the political structure, based on the monopoly power of the state/party apparatus.

Consequently, self-government as a symbol of the 'Yugoslav road to socialism', inevitably bears the mark of controversies which Yugoslav society has not been able to resolve so far. Due to its ideological burden, the concept of self-government takes on a variety of interpretations and satisfies a diversity of social interests. An apparently uniform façade conceals a multitude of tendencies and interests, which different social groups pursue in both the economic and political spheres, without real possibilities for adjusting them with the existing institutional framework.

1. My book *The Identity Crisis of the Contemporary Yugoslav Society* (in Serbo-Croat) has been recently published in Belgrade by Filip Višnjić, 1988, of which this presentation is a summary.

The phases of post-war development

It was in 1950 that the law was brought in inaugurating the establishment of workers' councils in the factories, under the slogan 'Factories to the workers'. The foundation of a clear conceptualization of the process of change, and social changes themselves, were laid in 1952–53. This period saw the adoption of laws which opened up possibilities for structural changes in economic relations, and challenged the hitherto inviolable form of a centralized economy. A major step was taken with the law on 'planned management of the national economy', according to which the Social Plan related only to macroeconomic planning, while enterprises were given the autonomy to decide on their own production plans, with an eye to the demands of the market. Further liberalization in the management of the economy was manifested in the greater portion of the producer's income which was left at the disposal of the enterprises.[2] In economic policy, there was a shift away from the absolute priority of heavy industry and towards consumer goods production.

Another trend of importance for the further course of development was a reduction of the state administrative apparatus (by means of the reorganization of federal ministries, stemming from the reconceptualization of social planning). Accordingly, processes of decentralization began to take place, transferring a measure of power, primarily in economic management, from the state apparatus to the enterprises and communes.

The character of this period (from 1950 to 1960) was signalled by the concept of 'workers' democracy', built after the pattern of the Paris Commune, and relying on Marx's key concept of 'free associations of producers'. This implied that the workers should take control over the management of production, and there should be a corresponding decentralization and liberalization of management.

2. Fred Singleton (in *A Short History of the Yugoslav Peoples* (Cambridge, Cambridge University Press, 1985), see chapter 11) saw these changes as 'more symbolic than real', because it was still up to directors and managers to make the vital decisions (p. 228). A Yugoslav author also warns that the changes were made only in the distribution of the social product between the state and the enterprises, while everything else remained the same. The state continued to set prices and retain in its hands the foreign currency system and foreign trade, there were no changes in either the monetary system, or the system of accumulation and expanded reproduction, or the planning system (D. Bilandžić, *Ideja i praksa društvenog razvoja Jugoslavije 1945–1973* (The Ideas and Practice of Yugoslavia's Social Development 1945–1973), (Belgrade, Komunist 1973), pp. 203–7).

Emphasis was placed on workers' participation in the workers' councils following the principle of the workers' majority, making them the real subjects of the decision-making process in economic matters within the factory walls. (This fact should be kept in mind, because it indicates the fundamental limitations of a concept of self-government whose implementation was confined to the shop-floor level, and to economic matters alone.)

A second phase began in the 1960s, gaining full ideological and political legitimacy in the Eighth Party Congress (1962). It indicated a profound shift from a 'workers' democracy' defined in terms of the democratization of *production management*, to a 'market democracy' primarily focusing on the democratization of *trade* through the mediation of the market, and turning from the changes in the process of production to the field of distribution. What mattered were no longer producers but the enterprises, as 'self-managing producers of commodities'.[3] This is why this period came to be described as 'self-managing market socialism' (or as a foreign analyst called it, 'laissez-faire socialism').[4]

Having seen during the 1950s the transmission of managerial rights from the governmental bureaucracies to the producers' units and the producers themselves, decentralization primarily focused in the 1960s on the enlarged independence of the enterprises *vis-à-vis* the state and political power. In this phase the question of workers' participation was left aside, as current policy was no longer principally interested in changing the structure of power within the factories. (From that period on, all sociological analyses confirmed the fact that an oligarchic structure of power re-emerged in the enterprises, with rapidly falling percentages of workers' participation.)

At the Tenth Party Congress, and continuing in the 1970s, the grounds were laid for a third phase whose slogans announced a suppression of commodity production and a break with the 'liberalization of the economy'. Hence, a specifically Yugoslav pattern of economy was born, based neither on centralized control over economic processes, nor on economic laws, but on 'agreement' and

---

3. See E. Comisso, *Workers' Control Under Plan and Market, Implications of Yugoslav Self-Management* (New Haven, Conn., Yale University Press, 1979), pp. 119ff.

4. Dennison Rusinow uses this term to explain the character of this phase of Yugoslav economy's development. See *The Yugoslav Experiment 1948–1978* (London, C. Herst, 1977).

consensus among the national, republic state powers. This 'new course' represented a regression from the point of view of those who demanded the reinforcement of the state's role in the economic processes, and the control of the party over all the spheres of social activity. When this peculiar type of economy was inaugurated both self-government and the market were suppressed in favour of the new political aspirations of national–republic states. The meaning of 'decentralization' was changed once again, primarily focusing now on the transfer of power from the federal state to the regional state powers. The 'new course' saw another 'original' invention, which was called 'integral self-government'. This aspired to cover all society's sub-structures and provide an overall pattern of social organization based, so it was proclaimed, on self-government principles. The network which was then established under the name of 'self-governing communities of interests' has turned into a mere façade, because the latter were, in fact, semi-state services acting on behalf of the bureaucracies.

Given the fact that this policy was based on agreement between representatives of national states, the role of the state was reinforced at the cost of both the self-government bodies and market mechanisms, reaffirming thus once again the domination of politics over economic (and other) affairs. The newly created self-government bodies were, in fact, semi-state services acting on behalf of bureaucratic interests, which completely demotivated people to take part in the decision-making processes, the latter being once again manipulated thanks to the multiplication of centres of state and semi-state powers. To this phase a foundation was laid in the 1974 Constitution, which can be said to have generated the main causes of the current crisis in Yugoslav society.

The major changes and results of the post-war development of Yugoslav society

Although peasants constituted the majority of the Yugoslav population before the Second World War, Yugoslav society followed in its post-war development a course of accelerated industrialization, which gave priority to heavy industry, neglecting in particular agricultural production. A rapid change of the structure of the village population produced by a great exodus to the industrial centres, however, and the continued economic progress throughout the 1940s and 1950s, resulted in a marked growth of industrial products until 1976.[5] In its present level of development Yugoslavia is a medium industrially developed country, thanks to a rapid sixfold rise in the volume of industrial output. But the legacy of major regional differences was not eroded by Yugoslavia's impressive economic growth. Although special funds were set up to provide economic aid to underdeveloped regions, these were used nonrationally and even often abused.[6]

Prolonged steady industrial development inspired Fred Singleton to conclude that: 'The sustained growth in industrial output during the 1950s was faster than that achieved during the same period by any other country in the world, whether in socialist Eastern Europe, capitalist Western Europe or the Third World.'[7] This kind of industrial growth was due more to factors connected with the building of new factories and to large interest-free foreign loans (aid), than to an improved organization of production, the more rational use of the resources, or raising the productivity of labour. (Although this did grow, it was constantly below the employment rate and the growth of personal incomes. This latter was 24 per cent above the level of the social product, and 44 per cent above the growth rate of productivity.)

Given the circumstances of this basic inconsistency in the development of the Yugoslav economy, its course showed an up-and-down curve, which may be described as follows. A policy of accelerated industrialization, with gross investment consisting of 32 per cent of national income, and an enforced collectivization of land during the period 1949–52, were replaced during the mid-1950s by a more balanced economic development. After the heavy impact of the Soviet economic blockade, a new economic expansion was manifest between 1952 and 1968, when the economic product increased 3.5 times, industrial output 5 times, agricultural produce 2.5 times and employment 3 times.[8] (These growth rates decreased

---

5. Albert Meister compares the annual growth rate in Yugoslavia, which was 7.6 per cent from 1952 to 1962, with that of Japan, which was in first place at that period. See A. Meister, *Où va l'autogestion Yougoslave?* (Paris, Editions Anthropos, 1970), p. 270.

6. The figures indicate the increase of differences between regions – from 1:3 to 1:6; and the most underdeveloped part, Kosovo, is much behind the average growth. The highest unemployment rate is also found there: 27.3 per cent as against 15.8 per cent in Serbia proper and 1.5 per cent in Slovenia.

7. Singleton, *A Short History*, p. 232.

8. According to the information presented by B. Horvat in *Privredni sistem i ekonomska politika Jugoslavije* (The Economic System and Economic Policy in

after 1959, however, and this is the reason why Branko Horvat speaks about the myth of high growth rates in the Yugoslav economy.) Throughout the 1960s growth rates constantly declined; and when they are compared with those of other countries of a corresponding stage of development, the figures show that Yugoslavia lags behind.[9]

One of the continuing problems of the post-war development of the Yugoslav economy was the inadequacy of agricultural policy because of the dogmatic concept inherited from the Bolshevik tradition. According to this, the village was viewed as a 'bastion of a counter-revolution'. The lack of a coherent policy of agricultural development can be confirmed by the course of the enforced collectivization of land in 1949 in response to Stalin's accusation that the Yugoslav Communist Party had abandoned 'a socialist road' in the villages.[10] The compulsory purchase of agricultural products provoked a sharp conflict with the peasants; and this, taken with under-attention to the sustaining of agricultural production in the development plans, resulted in a low rate of production. It also led to a proportional reduction of the contribution of the agriculture product in national income. The social effect of such a policy was reflected in an exodus from the village, producing a significant change of the structure of the village households, which were reduced to their elderly population. Even though the collectivization of land was abandoned in the early 1950s, a long-term policy of agricultural development did not follow, which might have made a more rational use of the natural resources available in Yugoslavia, and for a more efficient agriculture. For these reasons Yugoslavia still has difficulty in feeding its population, and is compelled to import agricultural goods.

In the mid-1960s a policy of economic reforms was launched in order to escape from the recession which showed its face at the end of the 1950s. The main aims of the economic reforms were a

Yugoslavia) (Belgrade Economske studije 3, Institut Ekonomskih Nauka, Belgrade, 1970), p. 31.

9. B. Horvat provides data confirming the above statement: Romania had a growth rate of 9.4 per cent (1964–75) and Albania 7.8 per cent as against 5.4 per cent in Yugoslavia at the same period. See B. Horvat, *Privreda 1965–1983, Prognoze i kritike* (Economy 1965–1983, Prognoses and Critiques) (Zagreb, Cankarjeva založba, 1984), p. 220.

10. While the policy towards collectivization of the land was mild from 1945 to 1948, the rise in the numbers of the collective farms was rapid in 1949, increasing from 6,625 to 340,000. Documents confirm that peasants were forced to join the collective farms.

redistribution of the social product on behalf of the enterprises, a greater share of the latter in accumulation, and a limitation of the state's role in investment policy. The intention of these measures was to put a stop to galloping inflation, and to achieve a more balanced relation between personal income and investments. Because the economic reforms remained isolated from the wider reformation of the political and social system, however, they left intact the main obstacle to more efficient production, that is the domination of politics over the economy. Since the economic reforms were not framed within a long-term policy they soon began to reveal their negative side: a rise in the prices of basic articles and the cost of living, which in turn pushed up personal incomes, but without being accompanied by a corresponding growth in productivity and in the social product. Introduction of the principle of enterprise profitability caused a reduction of the labour force and a strong rise in unemployment (from 1962 to 1970 the unemployment rate climbed from 8 per cent to 14 per cent in 1982, the highest in Europe). This, along with economic emigration to Western Europe, entailing the loss of a large number of the skilled labour force, posed new unresolvable problems.

Orientation towards the market-economy without contemplating the mechanisms needed to adjust the random working of the market to the necessarily planned development of a 'self-governing' society, created a broad set of problems. It increased social inequalities; there was a growth of the structural disproportions in the economy, instead of a more balanced relation of the basic and the consumer-good industries, which was reflected in decreasing accumulation. The latter, especially with the disintegrating economic effects due to the creation of closed republican state economies, jeopardized normal social reproduction, on the one hand, and led to the multiplication of capacities and 'lame investments', on the other. A hybrid semi-planned and semi-market economy, with quasi-self-management and semi-wage labour relations, has generated basic contradictions and problems which it has proved incapable of solving. The persistent rise in the prices of elementary goods, and the ever-stronger pressure of inflation broadening the gap between the developed and underdeveloped regions, the rise in uncontrolled indebtedness to foreign banks, the decline of the capacity for accumulation (the rate of accumulation dropped in the mid-1970s to 12 per cent from 27 per cent in 1962) all prevented the Yugoslav economy from taking the necessary steps towards income redistribution on behalf of accumulation, and the necessary restriction of excessive consumption. They also prevented the elimination of fragmentation and the multiplication of investments, and the monopolistic conduct of certain firms in the market. In other words, according to one economist: 'The microeconomy became dominant, producing an entropy of the macrosystem.'

These developments led to the atomization of work organizations as commodity producers, which found themselves torn between the market, as the only factor that connected them, and state interventions, when the random working of the market went too far. State intervention became a necessity, but resulted in a continued restriction of the enterprise share in investments, the imposition of numerous taxes (accounting for the twenty-seven kinds of taxes a work organization has to pay), and last but not least, a reinforced dependency of the enterprises on governmental mechanisms, and correspondingly the declining influence of self-management.

The end point of these accumulated contradictions was the disintegration of the Yugoslav economy into a series of closed national economies. The division of the Yugoslav market prevented the normal circulation of capital, goods and labour within the country. Politically, the process led to a re-feudalization of the former power monopoly, while economically it produced an impending economic crisis and a complete malfunctioning of the economic system. The end result was the creation of an inconsistent economic system based, on the one hand, on the restricted influence of economic laws due to administrative interventions in their effects, and on the other, to an inconsistently implemented planning function, incapable of adjusting to economic laws. Having relied upon heterogeneous premises, economic development became thus 'institutionally and functionally unmatched', and characterized (according to the Yugoslav economist Kosta Milhailović) by the opposition between plan and market, centralized and decentralized decisions, and social and individual criteria, as well as between short-term and long-term ends.[11]

As to the political structure, there have been no impressive changes. This is one reason why an immanent incongruence between economic and political factors has remained one of the basic

11. See K. Mihailović, *O privrednom sistemu* (On the Economic System) (Belgrade, Ekonomski institut, 1977), pp. 231–2.

characteristics of the present-day Yugoslav system. Since 1952 (at the Sixth Party Congress) when the reform of the Communist Party was planned but very soon abandoned, progress towards a liberalization of the political system has fallen behind. By 1953 warnings could already be heard from the top party echelons that the liberal interpretation of the future of one-party rule had gone too far. (In particular, the idea of a 'withering away of the party' as a precondition of society's democratization was put forth by Milovan Djilas, in 1954; but he was accused of opposing the party line, dismissed from the leadership and expelled from the party.)

The early reconciliation with the Soviet leadership (in 1956) was one of the decisive reasons for reported shifts back and forth, and a hard-line policy regarding change of the political structure.[12] The radically critical attitude towards the USSR after 1948 (which affected the Yugoslav leadership's critical re-examination of its own past as well) was changed in the mid-1950s, with the consequences of both ideological retreat and a more conservative policy.

Although since the 1950s the Yugoslav political system can no longer be interpreted as a 'dictatorship' (or simply as a 'system of commands') it does not automatically follow that it has made the necessary democratic transformation implied by the concept of self-government. Instead of opening doors to democratic processes within the political system and society at large, the Yugoslav leadership undertook frequent reorganizations of the existing institutional system but without really changing it. New democratic institutions were not created; but the old ones were merely altered either by being one-sidely decentralized, or merely reinterpreted giving them a more democratic appearance. (For example, the federal state transmitted some of its functions to the republics, restricting, at the same time, the functions of self-government instead of enlarging them. The National Front changed its name to the Socialist Alliance, suggesting a more democratic coalition of political opinion groups while still remaining in practice a transmission belt of the party.) What remained intact was the very backbone of the political system, namely, the 'leading role of the Party', which remained a

---

12. This was the almost unanimous conclusion of the old-guard party leaders whom this author interviewed during 1983–84. They found that the reconciliation with the Soviet Union, which happened to be not only a renewal of normal state relations, but was also a restoration of ideological dependency, had become the main obstacle to the announced process of liberalization. (The interviews form a part of *Identity Crisis of Contemporary Yugoslav Society*, see note 1.)

state party constitutionally grounded in the 1974 Constitution.

The brief episode of a parliamentary multi-party system in Yugoslavia from 1946 to 1947 could not have influenced post-war political developments, although if it had lasted longer one might have expected more favourable conditions for democratic processes after the break with the Soviet leadership. Instead, other parties were prohibited, and one-party rule was sustained as the only acceptable framework from which policy was derived, irrespective of the fact that an adjustment of the political system to 'self-governing socialism' was desperately needed. This had its effects on the very conceptualization of self-government, not only through its constant restriction, but extending to the inversion of its basic principles. Self-government has come to be treated as an appendix to the state-party apparatus, serving as a means of ideological legitimation of the powers that be, instead of preparing the ground for a transformation of the bureaucratic and oligarchic structure of power.

Consequently, constant organizational change (with frequent changes of the Constitution) has not led to change in the basic features of the system, but rather has produced a very complicated and incoherent social organization which has become dysfunctional. What is assumed at the shop-floor level is self-management of the organization of production; while at the macro-level there exists an oligarchic structure of political power submerging the self-management institutions. Furthermore, the organization of the state is assumed to be based on a federal constitution; but the latter is negated by the Constitution itself, which bestows almost full autonomy on the republics *vis-à-vis* the federal state. Behind this constitutionally defined institutional system, however, real political power lies in the hands of the party leadership, or rather, belongs to non-institutional policy lobbies which in fact make all the vital political and economic decisions. Because of this identification of party and state in a 'party state', it is incapable of providing an efficient administrative apparatus which can coordinate and regulate the network of institutional bodies. There is a saying that: 'The state is there where it is not needed (i.e. in its political function), but it is not there when it is needed (i.e. in its administrative function).'

Due to this extensive and one-way decentralization the current political system may be characterized as a 'polycentric statism', which has led astray self-government, even at the shop-floor level at which it used to have certain functions in the 1950s. The widely proclaimed 'withering away of the state' turned in practice into an enormously diffused bureaucratic apparatus, which prescribed numerous taxes and excessively enlarged the budget, becoming more and more expensive at the cost of economic efficiency. This affected the standard of living, which has declined significantly over the last decade. It has also resulted in an excessive 'normativism', directly related to the expansion of the state apparatus.

The stability of the regime, whose legitimacy was provided in the 1950s by the introduction of self-government as a model opposing the Soviet-type system, was shaken at the end of the 1960s and in the early 1970s. Two events in that period challenged the party's monopoly of power: (a) growing nationalism, tending towards disintegration, and (b) the left-wing students' movement, which arose spontaneously in 1968. Although mutually opposed, these events challenged the established monolithic political organization and party ideology. They warned the party leadership of the steps which they had to take in order to regain control over the social processes which had been getting out of hand. They signalled not only the reinforcement of repression, but also the reintroduction of old mechanisms and measures ensuring the party's penetration of decision-making at all levels, in order to prevent an irreversible process of liberalization.

Having put down both left-wing and nationalist movements, the party leadership asserted once again its control contending that 'liberalization' had had such negative effects that the party had to respond in order to defend the 'achievements of the revolution'. The real reasons for returning to a 'firm-hand' policy were, on the one hand, a growing threat to the party's ability to control current processes, and on the other, the fact that the expansion of freedom was threatening to ruin the entire 'construction of socialism' which was still based on a single-party rule and the preservation of its monopoly of power.

The change of the electoral system in 1974, which transformed the direct election of representatives at all levels into a delegate system as a 'filter election' (F. Singleton), made it possible for the *nomenklatura* system to be reintroduced, allowing the party committees to play a decisive role in the recruitment of 'cadres' to important social positions. It certainly did not contribute favourably either to the system's legitimation through democratic mechanisms, or to the improvement of the state of law. On the contrary, by stubbornly opposing the demands of a critical public opinion concerning the necessary liberalization of politics and the improvement of citizens' rights and liberties, official policy itself provoked a legitimation crisis. The manifestations of this have been the mass demonstrations and populist waves in the 1980s which have denied credit to the powerholders and underlined their incapacity to deal with the problems generated by social crisis. The so-called integral (or extended) system of self-government, which was brought in during the 1970s under the slogan of the 'plurality of self-governing interests', could not have solved the basic incongruences of the system. What it did was merely to rename certain of the semi-state bodies in self-governing terms, creating at the same time a huge bureaucratic apparatus.

Even so, the political structure of contemporary Yugoslav society cannot be fully identified with a Soviet-type system. Self-management is institutionalized, regardless of the fact that it is more often formal than real. If the law is strictly followed one may find a wider scope for the implementation of self-governing rights than is the case in practice, wherein the 'customary rights' prescribed by the party still prevail.

Several features characterize the 1980s where the political system of Yugoslavia is concerned. Nationalism has been growing in all regions. In particular, the strong separatist trend in the province of Kosovo (where there has been open conflict between the Albanian majority and Serbian and Montenegrin minorities) has already jeopardized the existence of the non-Albanian population in that part of Serbia. By regarding the full autonomy of the national states as a guarantee of their own privileged position, the national bureaucracies in the other regions have supported the trend towards the disintegration of the Yugoslav state. On the other hand, the awareness of the fact that decentralization has gone too far, even threatening to destroy the Yugoslav state, has been growing, and demands for changes to the 1974 Constitution have been put forth, in order to restore integration. The emergence of a critical public opinion has become noticeable in the last decade, with more open and free use of the mass media to express critical attitudes towards the existing order, with priority given to changes in the political system. New alternative social movements have emerged, seeking to establish a 'civil society', and challenging the existing monopoly of power. There have been more open calls for political pluralism, and the abolition of the article in the penal code which defines 'verbal delicts' as political crimes. These demands have been met by a strong resistance on the part of those who have real power. Open questioning of the party's position in society, and its 'vanguard' role, is quite a new phenomenon. In the media people now question whom it is that the party represents, since workers' participation is constantly declining. Whose interests does it defend? How is it that a minority of 10 per cent of the population may monopolize social power (let alone the fact that a monopoly of political power is located within the closed circle of the top party leadership)? The feeling has become widespread that the party leadership is becoming the centre of the conservative forces upholding the status quo and arresting necessary social changes, in particular those relating to the political system.

Strong opposition on the part of the ruling political elite to social change has not been able to prevent the emergence of a new political culture which does not simply reflect the existing (static) political system. This nascent political culture only partially reflects the claims of official ideology (above all in the question of the reintroduction of Marxism as obligatory to all levels of education). It is open to the free expression of opinions, most particularly in the press, in public forums and alternative movements, while in mass culture the trends of a 'consumer society' prevail.

The emergence of a new, more diffused, although still quasi-pluralistic political culture is the result of a long process of cultural liberalization *vis-à-vis* the official ideology, beginning in the early 1960s. The 1960s have often been regarded as a 'golden age' of free creativity. This new spirit of expanded cultural freedom was announced when the new programme of the League of Communists (in 1958) committed itself to the dedogmatization of mental life in the statement: 'Nothing that has been created is so sacred that it cannot be replaced by the still more progressive, the still freer and still more humane.'[13]

The liberation of culture from ideological hegemony began in the mid-1950s, firstly in the field of *belles lettres* with a demand for the autonomy of all forms of expression, as a reaction to the previously prescribed 'socialist realism'. At the end of the 1950s and continuing through the 1960s there was a freer development of philosophy and social theory which, even while accepting Marxism as a frame of reference, adopted a new critical stance to both Marxist ideology and social reality. Both trends traced the line of a process of

13. Concluding words of the Programme of the League of Young Communists of Yugoslavia (London, International Society for Socialist Studies, 1959), p. 198.

destalinisation, which was initiated in Yugoslavia earlier than in the other East European countries.

Two phases can be followed in the development of cultural autonomy since 1948. There has been a general trend towards the dedogmatization of thought and the reinterpretation of the very concept of socialism in terms of its democratic potential. This was a relatively peaceful phase, in which both party intellectuals and relatively independent cultural producers marched together in order to get rid of the Stalinist legacy which was regarded as the main obstacle to the further socialist development of Yugoslav society. The second phase was marked by open conflict between the party ideologues and those cultural representatives who advocated a more profound alteration of the general cultural role of official ideology to the point of demanding cultural liberation. It was in the mid-1960s that the claim for cultural pluralism was voiced, demanding full autonomy for creativity in all the fields of culture. This was naturally unacceptable from both the point of view of a monolithic official ideology, and the practical aspirations of the political elite to sustain political control over the other sub-systems. Open conflicts between party officials and the humanistic intelligentsia character-ized this period, which ended with the accusation that a number of the latter were 'the inspirers of the students' movements' in 1968, and their dismissal from their university posts. The prohibition of the most liberal of the philosophical journals, *Praxis*, took place at this time, together with the suspension of the Korčula Summer School, where free debate between Marxists and non-Marxists from all over the world had been going on for a decade.

A 'critical Marxism' was born from this trend, calling for a necessary reassessment of both the theoretical foundations and the actual practices of any 'socialist development' which did not adopt a critical stance towards the Stalinist legacy. These criticisms on the part of the humanistic intelligentsia threatened to ruin both the dominant party mentality, and the actual privileged social position of the officials, by the very fact that the monopoly of control of overall social activities (a basic premise of their existence) was called into question. For these reasons the political elite resorted to 'administrative measures' against the advocates of 'liberalism', in both culture and the economy, in order to defend its own social position and prevent further uncontrollable developments. Several liberal politicians were also purged (in particular in Serbia), an-nouncing a new political freeze.

111

The liberal course in culture was thus abruptly cut off in the 1970s, and critical thought forced into silence. This may be illustrated by the fate of mainstream sociology at that time. Having shown great enthusiasm in the 1960s, when social research raised several very relevant topics for investigation, sociology suddenly abandoned its aspirations to be a critical science and became a marginal discipline interested merely in politically detached, small-scale problems. This state of affairs lasted up to the beginning of the 1980s, when once again sociologists were among the first to open doors to the emergence of a critical public opinion.

These characteristic oscillations between hot and cold in the realm of culture have continued in the last decade. The well-known 'White Book' on culture, prepared by the Ideological Commission of the Central Committee of the Croatian Party in the mid-1980s, represented a last echo of the dogmatically minded mentality of the party leadership, pretending to model culture from above.[14] But the cultural and political climate at the time did not allow the last vestiges of Stalinism to inhibit the liberation process which by that time had spread throughout Yugoslav society. A new critical spirit flooded all fields of culture from literature, through film and theatre, social sciences and the mass media – more resolutely removing the veils that had covered many taboo topics concerning both the revolutionary past and present developments.[15]

The Current Crisis: Conflicts, Dilemmas and Possibilities of Reform

Given the growing complexity of the Yugoslav social structure, social conflict springs from diverse sources, class differentiation by no means being the sole source of the conflict of interests. Class

14. This book, which was (paradoxical as it may seem) banned when published, was a peculiar remnant of the old-party mentality in that it represented a frontal assault on almost the whole production of culture at the time, from novels to films and satires. At the same time, it was a good collection of the best of cultural production (even those which had been prohibited) which was made public thanks to this ideological accusation.

15. In belletristic literature all 'revolutionary' myths have been challenged during last two decades. The 'heroic resistance' to Stalin in 1948 has been exposed as a typically Stalinist reaction in the light of the building of Goli Otok (the island for political prisoners). The accelerated collectivization of land and enforced purchase of agricultural goods has been represented as the use of Stalinist methods of repression. Thus the flourishing of political fiction characterizes Yugoslav literature in the 1980s.

confrontation in Yugoslav society may be assessed from two types of evidence. On the one hand, there is the evidence of the workers' strikes, which do not have a simple economic foundation, but also appear as a means of articulating political demands, that is they represent a confrontation of the working class with the bureaucratic apparatus, whether at a local or a global level. On the other hand, there is the evidence of the ruling political elite's resistance to social change, in which they are joined by their trusted political ally, the middle classes, in defending together their common interests, namely to keep their established privileged position intact.

The politicization of strikes (the combination of classical strikes with a political resistance) is caused by the fact that no other means of organization for making political demands are available to the Yugoslav workers. The trade unions and the party simply do not represent their interests – according to the workers' own statements.

According to sociological investigations, strikes in Yugoslavia have a broader meaning than appears at first glance in that the workers seem to confront merely the technocratic stratum in the factory, and not the state and the ruling class in general. Studies show, however, that beside material conditions and low wages, workers' dissatisfaction concerns also their inferior position in self-management, which undermines their influence on social change. They raise the question of their *social*, not merely their economic position, and demand the alteration of the working class's situation in society at large, and not only an improvement of the material conditions of living.[16] The fact that strikes become politicized speaks against the existence of an effective self-management, which workers do not find reliable as a means of fighting for the defence of their rights and interests.

Another expression of the workers' dissatisfaction with the existing institutional system, in particular with production relations and the distribution of income, is the so-called 'white strike'. This consists of passive resistance in the form of slowing down the rhythm of work and producing low-quality goods, so as to save energy for moonlighting jobs (from which sources it has been

---

16. Concerning strikes in Yugoslavia and their character see the following: N. Jovanov, *Radnički štrajkovi u SFRJ od 1958 do 1969* (*Workers' Strikes in Yugoslavia from 1958 to 1969*) (Belgrade, Zapis, 1979); N. Jovanov, *Dijagnoza samoupravljanja 1974–1981* (*A Diagnosis of Self-management* 1974–1981) (Zagreb, Sveučilišna naklada Liber, 1983); N. Popov, 'Studentski pokreti u Jugoslaviji' ('Students' Movements in Yugoslavia), *Sociološki pregled*, No. 1–2, 1985.

estimated that on average more than 40 per cent of their monthly income is obtained).

Next to strikes as an expression of open conflicts, come clashes based on national and regional divisions, which threaten to destroy the unity of the Yugoslav state. These have become the focus of social conflict in the 1980s, very often hiding class divisions behind a national homogenization which redirects conflict outwards, against the other nations.

After having kept up an illusion for forty years, that the national question was solved in the Yugoslav liberation war, Yugoslavia faces nowadays a very serious problem of how to reconcile the diverse national aspirations, although the Constitution guarantees autonomy not only to republics but also to the various national minorities. A mass nationalist movement which began in Croatia in 1971 (soon crushed by Tito's authority) has spread all over the country in the 1980s, being particularly pronounced in the growing antagonism between Slovenes and Serbs, on the one hand, and between Serbs–Montenegrins and Albanians in Kosovo, on the other.

The situation raises the question of the causes of such an eruption of nationalism, which certainly were not generated during the post-war period alone, but have deep roots in the history of the creation of the Yugoslav state. Besides the diversity of historical and cultural backgrounds of the Yugoslav nations, four reasons can be found in the literature analysing this problem. Certain nations have not been fully recognized constitutionally, and have not experienced their national being in terms of their own states and political institutions. The growing social and political insecurity of Yugoslav citizens, who are neither economically (due to the increasing unemployment) nor politically protected in their rights and liberties, has caused them to orient themselves towards a super-individual entity such as the nation in order to ensure their identities. As a result of the deep contradictions of the system, social crisis leads to a loss of perspectives, in particular with regard to the possibilities for a real improvement of 'self-governing socialism' in opposition to statism. In such a setting some individuals see no other solution but the constitution of a confederation as a new framework of social organization, as against the current federal state, which they identify with a centralistic government. This latter engenders separatist aspirations, which subsequently grow into animosities towards the other nations. In addition, dissatisfaction with general economic policy, thanks to which all the nations get a feeling of being exploited by the others, 'national economies' are viewed as the only way possible of defending 'jeopardized' national interests.

Having obtained in the 1974 Constitution the grounds on which to support a tendency to strengthen the national states, these separatist trends were able to become institutionalized. Thereby, the rise of national bureaucracies as an important social force goes hand-in-hand with growing nationalist conflicts. In other words, nationalism has its political foundation in the existing Yugoslav political system.

Another expression of social conflict, which has become characteristic of all the existing socialist countries, deserves to be mentioned, that is the conflict between the individual as citizen and the state. This is manifest in a flagrant violation of citizens' rights and liberties, on the one hand, and in the citizens' more articulated resistance to these violations on the other. Such violations have produced organized revolts from which have been constituted new movements and committees for the defence of citizens' rights and liberties. What should be added to classical notions of citizens' rights in Yugoslavia, however, is the right to self-management. There are certain moves which have proved that awareness of this right is growing among workers in particular. (They give as one of the reasons for striking their disappointment with self-management.) As mentioned above, the laws guaranteeing workers' participation in self-management are larger in scope than they are realized in practice. Thus one may anticipate that a form of resistance to the existing power structure will come to rely upon reinforcement of the legal system concerning rights to self-management.

The existence of diffuse social conflict in itself does not provide a basis for social crisis, unless it becomes impossible to institutionalize the conflict and find democratic forms for its resolution. In present-day Yugoslav society it is precisely the latter which characterizes the social scene. It has become no longer possible to shut one's eyes to the manifestations of what has shown its face as a broad *social*, not only a serious *economic* crisis.

There has been an uncontrollable rise in prices, including those of basic articles, together with a continued rise in foreign debts, which are also out of public control. This has made for a constant and conspicuous decline in the living standard of the population, whose dissatisfaction increases, particularly because Yugoslavia was previously ahead in these terms in comparison with Eastern Europe.

The increasing divisions on a national scale have produced such disintegrative effects as to call into question the very existence of Yugoslavia as a state. This same trend has affected the party itself, which turned from being one of the most integrative factors into a disintegrative force, with eight parties primarily interested in the well-being of their own nations. The result of this has been not only cultural, but also economic and political disintegration, the latter manifested in the different political programmes which are offered, according to what the national parties find desirable. (For example, a programme advocating confederation is promoted in Slovenia; and another relying upon the unity of the Yugoslav state is supported in Serbia, Montenegro and Macedonia.)

A far-reaching economic effect of the crisis has been the noticeable division between the north (Slovenia) and the south (Macedonia, Montenegro, Kosovo), not only in terms of levels of social product and the standard of living, but also as quite different ways of life, value-orientations, visions and perspectives for the future of the socialist development of Yugoslav society.

This brief outline cannot end merely with a description of the existing institutional system and its accompanying social processes. A real picture of life in Yugoslavia can only be grasped if a description of everyday life is included. It is certainly everyday life and conduct that make Yugoslav society so different in comparison with Eastern Europe, even though the crisis has changed many of its features.

Up to the mid-1970s a foreigner could have got an impression of the Yugoslav people living relatively well, and suffering less from the tensions caused by an imposed politicization, than is the case in East European countries. Politics had not penetrated so deeply into the private lives of Yugoslavs, leaving them a much broader scope. The average individual seemed to be preoccupied with his or her own well-being, not with politics, and moderately participating in self-management. A traditional style of life prevailed among the village population, and a great part of the urban one too, as a result of the enormous urban influx of the peasants.

Following tradition, the family remains the centre of everyday life, although many activities no longer take place in the home, in particular because of the employment of both parents, which has caused a restructuring of family functions. It is also in keeping with a traditional lifestyle that the café remains a centre of public gatherings, where Yugoslavs talk about politics and social matters. (Although at the end of the 1980s it was the street, with its mass demonstrations, that became the new place of expression for populist movements.)

Another visible aspect of everyday life concerns consumption, which plays a great role in the preoccupation of Yugoslavs. For this reason one may speak of a 'consumer society' orientation, irrespective of the fact that Yugoslav society has not yet objectively reached that level. A high level of aspiration for consumption, and rather low average salaries, are the characteristic contradictory conditions of the majority, who typically earn less than they spend, continuing to live on loans to somehow balance their monthly budget. Family solidarity plays a great role in aiding their members to survive, even though more than a million individuals have had no employment (and not a small number of them for several years). Unlike Western societies, parents in Yugoslavia feel much more obliged to support their offspring, not only until they finish school but very often after marriage. Strong kinship ties are one of the most important resources for the improvement of material conditions of low-skilled workers, who manage to survive thanks to their having relatives, or a smallholding in the village.

Among the other characteristics of contemporary Yugoslavs is their preoccupation with the well-being of their children, and their professional promotion, which suggest a change of the patriarchal value orientation. All parents want their children, both male and female, to get as good an education as possible, which they see as the most effective means of social mobility. (Neither workers nor peasants want their children to remain in the same stratum.)

Up to the mid-1970s these aspirations seemed to be satisfactorily met, and individual and social interests harmonized. Ever-increasing social differentiation with ever more marked social inequalities, however, rapidly altered this illusory picture of social harmony. It has already been said that the growing number of strikes during the last decade, together with frequent demonstrations of factory workers and people from the most underdeveloped regions have confirmed that a relatively peaceful period characterized by tacit agreement between people and the authorities, has already passed. What will emerge as the end result? Will events follow the historical tradition of Serbs and Montenegrins in the form of uprisings? Or will there be the creation of new social movements with a more democratic orientation, capable of bringing about long-term solutions? Both possibilities are at hand. The former fits better the prevailing mentality; while the latter assumes much deeper psychological and structural changes, as well as the need to overcome the powerholders' resistance to such independent movements.

The scope for freedom of individuals in their everyday life is still noticeably greater than in several other East European countries, with their more pronounced totalitarian pretensions. Yugoslavs do not experience much repression even in their work; they do not work very hard, and do not make much effort to earn more through their employment. (They do become hard workers, however, when the second job is concerned! There is a saying: 'They can't cut my pay as much as I can cut my work'.)

With respect to political obligations, Yugoslavs are not obliged to take even a ritual part in political activities, or constantly to affirm their ideological affiliation. They are almost totally free to belong to different churches and practise religious ceremonies, and to live according to their beliefs. An average Yugoslav citizen is more or less left to himself in his private life without being under the surveillance of the state and political police. If a citizen 'minds his own business' leaving aside social, or more importantly political matters, he may live rather freely and peacefully. Unlike the enforced political participation in the Soviet-bloc, the Yugoslav leadership does not much encourage Yugoslavs to be active in politics, assuming the latter to be a field reserved for the professional politicians. (Even the party members are not much constrained by party duties.)

Furthermore, Yugoslavs are free to travel all over the country without restrictions, and abroad; they can also freely choose their place of residence; they nominally have the right to any job, although implementation of that right becomes very difficult owing to high unemployment, on the one hand, and to protection based on illicit connections, on the other.

For these reasons one may say that people are not much interested in political liberties, but are satisfied with not being greatly disturbed by the authorities in everyday life. It is believed that complaints concerning the violations of citizens' rights and liberties come more from intellectuals, while not particularly touching the average person. Yet there is a growing dissatisfaction with the continually worsening conditions of life and re-emergence of poverty in the 1980s, which mostly affects the workers, provokes politicization and raises interest in freedom of speech and gatherings

gatherings where they can express their political demands. For they where they can express their political demands. For they too have become aware of the political foundations of the current crisis.

Torn between a traditional lifestyle and rapid modernization, the way of life of Yugoslav citizens has been half-heartedly altered: the villages still remain very different from the cities, offering very little where the facilities of social and cultural life are concerned. The overcrowded cities have become incapable of solving their housing problem, which is the reason why the suburban areas look more like villages, being built by the peasant-immigrants themselves in their own styles and according to their modest means. The flood of half-peasant, half-industrial workers has lowered the standard of living, with dirty streets and ruined flats in modern apartment buildings.

The most pronounced change has occured in family life with female employment, which in Yugoslavia is rather high in comparison with more developed European countries (one-third of the employed population; in Slovenia even higher). This has mostly affected family size and its educational function in not only urban but also village families. Typically, families produce one or two children at the most (except in Kosovo, where the birth rate is the highest in Europe, and resembles that found in the Third World). The small number of children does not result simply from female employment, or from women being overworked owing to the persistence of patriarchal views on housework. It is affected also by changing values and aspirations. Parents want their children to enjoy the best conditions for education; hence, they have to reduce the number of children. The typical patriarchal extended family with many children (the latter being a criterion of family prestige) which was primarily characteristic of the southern regions, is now disappearing. (This phenomenon can be followed in villages as well.) Families have become less integrated in both the cities and villages, in terms of their members spending less time together, and relying upon other social institutions for the satisfaction of their needs. The still strong kinship ties and family solidarity, however, make for a co-existence of the patriarchal tradition with modern trends.

The values held in the conduct of everyday life continue along traditional lines, but mixed with patterns adopted from the West. Ideology has not penetrated the sphere of interpersonal relationships in Yugoslav society, which are more conducted according to a mixture of values, with a pragmatic strand prevailing. A tendency to reject utopian and global visions is gaining popularity among the younger population, who are likely to pay more attention to what is happening today, and how to deal with those 'small things' which provide immediate opportunities for a more satisfactory life.

A vague definition of values and moral norms also results in a general state of anomie, and in apathetic attitudes. Since young people suffer the most from unemployment and the resulting loss of perspectives, they are more affected by this anomie.

In general in Yugoslavia a strongly dogmatic way of thinking has not taken deep root, even among the party members, save the old-guard cadres who have been educated in Moscow. This may help to explain the more relaxed conduct of everyday life, and the lower tension in interpersonal relationships, which makes Yugoslav society closer to that in Western Europe, and different from a typical East European 'political society'.

Turning to the current crisis, one of the first things to come to mind is the inter-republican and national tensions generated by an escalation of nationalistic sentiments. These have led to a situation described abroad as 'dramatic', as if Yugoslav society is at the edge of civil war. Although this may seem an exaggeration, the situation is indeed dramatic because present-day Yugoslav society stands at a crossroads; and which path it will take in its future developments is still unpredictable. Contemporary Yugoslavia faces certain dilemmas which will prove decisive in the future. Can society be reintegrated by resolving national tensions; or will it disappear as a state? Can a market economy be installed within the current economic system across the whole territory of Yugoslavia, as a means of circulation of goods, capital and labour; or will the economy completely disintegrate into 'national economies', causing unavoidable state intervention? Will social peace continue; or will an eruption of social unrest replace it, primarily due to a permanent fall in living standards and a growing impoverishment? Last but not least: will officialdom resort to a revival of the 'firm-hand' policy as the only solution possible in a chaotic economic, political and social situation?

Such predictions are very difficult to make, because the current social, economic and political conditions support diverse but co-existing trends. Judging from current events, however, one may point to the following tendencies which speak in favour of reform.

The myth of a 'non-conflictual society' in Yugoslavia was de-mystified a long time ago, the existence of social conflicts was recognized, and an attempt made (however unsuccessfully) to establish the means for their regulation. The very fact that the myth of a 'monolithic society' was dismantled has opened doors to new actions (such as strikes, which have been tolerated although not legalized until recently), and to the emergence of new phenomena (like mixed ownership, or the growing trend towards 'small business' within the market economy). The creation of an unofficial culture, which has made a significant impact upon the development of a critical public opinion, has also begun to make room for a pluralistic society. This manifests itself in the political sphere in the 'parallel' or 'alternative' forms of communication, appearing primarily in Slovenia, but in the other regions as well.

The dedogmatization of ideology has been one of the first steps towards the affirmation of a plurality of opinions, in spite of sustained resistance to so-called 'dissident' ideas, and a political opposition has begun to find its feet even within the party itself. The destruction of both the ideological and organizational monolith, however, indicates a deeper change than one implied by merely changing ways of thinking. There has been an erosion of the very foundation upon which such a social type relies, opening doors to phenomena incompatible with a monolithic pattern.

Social organization has become more diffused, and is no longer controllable from within a single ideology and political apparatus. A 'civil society' (a more independent organization of social and cultural life) is becoming a feature of current developments in Yugoslavia. Nevertheless, even though critical opinions are increasing, the average person is more disillusioned than prepared to take a critical stance *vis-à-vis* existing conditions, and act to promote their change. It is unlikely that a mass social movement like the one in Poland will appear in Yugoslavia. First and foremost, society is disintegrated along national lines. Secondly, the Yugoslav population does not confront the state–party apparatus as sharply as is the case with Poland. There are certain safety valves (such as self-management) which play an important role in pacifying the majority with regard to their taking more radical steps. Even so, at the end of the 1980s a significant change is noticeable in terms of a growing politicization of the masses.

The institutions of self-government, whatever limitations these may have, represent a still unused potential for democratization. They serve a twofold function. Besides the possibility of popular mobilization for self-organization and self-activity, they may be

121

used (and it is the case more often than not) as a means of hindering real democratic processes when a 'semi-management' is exchanged for the genuine article. Moreover, the symbols of self-government are brought into play especially when a developing social movement is to be stopped. The powerholders claim that there is no need for such movements when self-government exists, regardless of the fact that it did not come into being through the workers' movement itself, but was imposed from above, and therefore cannot be a substitute for that movement. Yet the very existence of self-governing institutions does affect the aspirations of Yugoslav workers and intellectuals with regard to participation in management; and they express more and more often their dissatisfaction that the concept is being used as merely a façade. One must recognize the fact, however, that many use the term 'self-government' as a trademark behind which to hide quite different ideas and programmes for society's development. Nobody is openly against self-government; but the term has acquired such diverse meanings that an analysis of what it does mean for different social groups is needed, in order to understand what they are really advocating.

Regardless of these contradictions, and the irreconcilable elements of Yugoslav society, it is becoming a more modern and pluralistic society. (Some authors qualify it as 'quasi-pluralism'.) Running parallel with this process, there continues a kind of anachronism which has been termed 'refeudalization', by which the autarchic national states strive to strengthen absolute rule over their 'possessions'.

Paradoxical as it may seem, although having gone too far and produced more disintegration than democratization at the level of the redistribution of power, decentralization provided a new impetus to the appearance of a more open society and the development of diverse forms of communication. This remains true though it blocked, at the same time, inter-republic circulation. Republican differences make it possible for certain events to happen in one part of Yugoslavia which are arrested in another. What is to be approved or proscribed varies from one region to another, allowing new elements to grow at one place while they are treated as undesirable elsewhere.

One of the factors speaking most urgently in favour of social change is the crisis itself. The incapacity of the authorities to solve the basic problems of galloping inflation, ever-increasing unemployment, and a continued decline in the standard of living, makes for the constant pressure of demands for necessary reforms. When one adds to these features the specifically political aspects of the crisis (such as loss of credibility of the political leadership's avant-gardism, the growth of corruption and large-scale criminality in the use of social property for private interests) it becomes evident that reforms are a necessity. By these means, the deepening of the crisis has opened the eyes of the population, making it more capable of assessing reality of the situation. It has resulted in mass demonstrations protesting against the incapacity of the leadership to deal successfully with the crisis owing to its being popularly perceived as primarily interested in remaining in the saddle of power.

Under the political impact of the crisis, the political elite itself has become differentiated. There has been a growing pressure towards reform from inside the stratum of officeholders (although that part seems to be less strong than one which wants to keep the political structure intact). A reform of present-day Yugoslav society is not very likely, it is generally agreed, unless change is inaugurated in the political system, because without this neither the economic system nor other parts of society can be reformed. Whether the prevailing conservatism of the political elite will hinder these much-needed reforms is hard to say; but the dramatic situation in which present-day Yugoslav society finds itself will certainly wake them up, if only to save themselves by preventing disaster.

The conservatism of the ruling elite is backed, however, by rather well-situated middle classes, which have benefited the most from Yugoslav society as it is, and are therefore interested in maintaining it. Consequently, there is broader support for resistance to change, which strengthens the political functionaries' conservative stance, irrespective of the growing objective needs and demands for reforms.

Which policy is likely to be supported by the Yugoslav working class is still unknown. No investigations lend support to the thesis that the working class is conservative. The recent mass demonstrations (which can hardly be described *in toto* simply as 'nationalism'), do not confirm such a view, because as far as the workers are concerned, they were also protesting against the bureaucratic structure of power, social inequalities and powerlessness, and demanding that their self-management rights be respected. The fact that they addressed those demands to the party committees instead of inspiring a new and independent movement may possibly indicate an authoritarian viewpoint.

The question of who is likely to become the main carrier of social reforms is not easy to answer, because of the conditions already described. It is certainly the younger generation who are mostly reform-oriented nowadays, and who have most resolutely expressed the demand for radical changes of both the structure of power and those political personnel who have lost people's respect but nevertheless still remain in power. The drama of a situation which calls for reforms because they are essential, like air, can be expressed by a saying: 'Those having power to launch social changes do not want them; but those who demand reforms have no power to make them'.

Whether the existing configuration of social forces will change soon to the benefit of those demanding reforms will depend very much on whether the trend towards pressure from below will continue. If the leadership becomes incapable of controlling and stopping spontaneous movements, it will inevitably come to the conclusion that certain reforms are necessary. As East European experiences have confirmed, a *coup d'état* could not solve the problem. The mental block by which a large portion of the Yugoslav population is affected, however, makes for a significant obstacle. Having become convinced that reform of the existing system is impossible, people rationalize their own passivity and unreadiness to become committed.

There is also a dilemma as to how social change could be implemented – on a large- or small-scale basis (a utopian versus a more pragmatic level). Given the circumstances of their disappointment with a previous utopian perspective, many are likely to abstain from an engagement with actions for radical social change.

Nevertheless, all the dilemmas and problems must be soon resolved, for the crisis knocks louder and louder at the door. Yugoslav society can no longer postpone dealing with the problems, because its very survival is at stake. It is from this fact that hope may be generated regarding the possibility (and necessity) of a rational way out, even though it would be an illusion to believe that the crisis will bring by itself a solution without irresistible pressure from the people, the working class, and the intellectuals, in particular.

4

From 'Democratic Centralism' to Decentralized Democracy? Trials and Tribulations of Yugoslavia's Development

Dijana Pleština

Introduction

The first to break out of the Soviet mould and the first to set up an alternative model, pioneer of self-management and a founder and leader of the non-aligned movement, the first to legitimate a national road to communism and to base it on an increasingly open society and a 'market-socialist' economy, for thirty years Yugoslavia stood unchallenged as the great innovator and experimenter of the communist world. Then as the decade of the 1980s unfolded, Yugoslavia was caught in a downward spiral which by late-1989 seemed to have brought the country to the verge of economic insolvency and political disintegration.

There is no doubt that the current crisis is the most serious one to confront the Yugoslav regime since the 1948 expulsion from the Cominform left the country isolated and wedged between a still-guarded and suspicious West and an actively hostile Soviet Union. Indeed, the current situation is far more dangerous to Yugoslavia's survival. For while the external threat posed by Stalin and the Soviet Union in 1948 rallied the population around Tito and the Communist Party in defence of Yugoslavia's independence, the magnitude of the social, political and economic problems which have emerged in the 1980s and escalated since June 1988 are tearing the country apart. The only thing that the Yugoslavs seemed to agree on as the 1980s came to a close, was that the current situation had become intolerable both economically and politically and that unless 'something' was done, and done quickly, 'things will blow up'.

How did it happen that the precocious *enfant terrible* of the communist world had by late 1989 become the only one in East Europe not rushing to abandon communism and embrace democracy?[1] Did that resistance reflect its overall post-war development? Where does it leave Yugoslavia today, and what might it bode for its future?

This paper will attempt to answer these questions by examining first the development of the Yugoslav political system in relation to the two main goals set by the regime at its inception: economic development, and the solving of the nationality question. It will then focus on the 1980s, when the failure to solve either of these problems led to their escalation, bringing the country to the verge of economic insolvency and political disintegration. It will end with a brief speculative glance at the prospects for the 1990s and beyond.

The First Steps: From Euphoria to Optimism in the 1950s

When the Yugoslav Communist Party came to power in 1945, its avowed purpose was to create a unified, egalitarian nation-state, one in which class, ethnicity and nationality would no longer constrain a person's 'natural' rights to happiness. To create this society, the regime first had to reconcile the more than a dozen ethnic groups whose most recent experience had been the exploitation of the inter-war period, followed by the cruelties of fratricidal civil war. It also had to create a society of plenty, which according to Marxist ideology was a prerequisite for socialism.

These tasks were far from simple. The 'politics of ethnicity' which had played such havoc in inter-war Yugoslavia had also divided the Communist Party of Yugoslavia (CPY) for most of the period.[2] The position of the CPY at its formation in 1919 was that of its leader, Sima Marković, who saw federalism as opening the possibility of demagogic appeals to competing national groups. Instead, he advocated a constitutional guarantee of the 'broad

1. The usual exception here is Albania. Even in Bulgaria, events of November–December 1989 made one believe in the possibility of change.
2. For a comprehensive and excellent discussion of the inter-war period, see Joseph Rotschild, *East Central Europe Between the Two World Wars* (Seattle, Wash., University of Washington Press, 1974), chapter 5; and Fred Singleton, *A Short History of the Yugoslav Peoples*, (Cambridge, Cambridge University Press, 1985), chapters 7 and 8.

autonomy' of the Yugoslav peoples, in a state which would be 'altogether the same whether the Serbs, Croats and Slovenes are three tribes of one nation, or three nations'.[3]

For many in the party, that was not acceptable. For them, the answer to the national question was to be found in a federalism based on workers' and peasants' governments set up in every national region. The combination of federalism and self-determination would, by ensuring a just solution to the problems of national discrimination and economic exploitation, attract mass support for the CPY. Although debates over the nationality question raged within the party throughout the inter-war period, by April 1941 when Yugoslavia entered the Second World War, the CPY was cautiously forming an independent policy based on unity against the foreign aggressor and defence of national rights and social justice.

If the politics of ethnicity occupied centre stage during the inter-war period, social-economic problems were close by, exacerbating national divisions. On the eve of the Second World War Yugoslavia was still an underdeveloped country. With the peasantry constituting 76.5 per cent of the population, it had small enclaves of wealth and culture scattered in a few cities, mostly in the north.[4] The high birth-rate and slow industrialization process resulted in an actual deterioration of peasant-land ratios, with negative consequences for both the per capita national income, which in the inter-war period grew at 0.7 per cent per annum, and for the amount of surplus food for marketing and export.[5] The pattern (of industrialization) was one of extractive industry in the south, processing industry in the north, almost half of both foreign-owned.[6] The rest was largely financed by foreign capital using cheap local labour and the abundance of relatively cheap raw materials. The per capita national income for 1938 has been estimated at between US

3. Paul Shoup, *Communism and the National Question*, (New York, Columbia University Press, 1968), p. 25.

4. Todorović *et al.*, *Ekonomska politika FNRJ* (Economic Policy of SFRJ) (Belgrade, Rad, 1985), p. 188.

5. Branko Colanović, *Razvoj nerazvijenih pokrajina Jugoslavije*, (Development of the Underdeveloped Areas of Yugoslavia), (Belgrade, Medjunarodna Politika, 1966), no. 9.

6. Approximately 46 per cent of all industrial production was owned by foreign companies, mostly British, 46 per cent and French, 41 per cent. G. Hoffman and F. W. Neal, *Yugoslavia and the New Communism* (New York, Twentieth Century Fund, 1962), p. 87.

$60 and $70.[7] The illiteracy rate stood at 44.6 per cent,[8] while a mere 1.3 per cent of the population had secondary education,[9] and a miniscule 0.15 per cent had completed university.[10]

To this overall level of underdevelopment was added the devastation caused by the war, the German and Italian occupations and the civil war. The cumulative impact of these was staggering as Ljubomir Madžar has indicated.[11] Perhaps as many as 1.7 million people, 11 per cent of the total pre-war population, lost their lives;[12] and the fact that they were disproportionately the young (average age 22),[13] and the better educated, meant that the post-war reconstruction and development processes would long feel the loss. Another 22 per cent of the population was left homeless.[14] The destruction of productive facilities was even greater. The transport system was in shambles. The merchant marine was reduced to a little more than one-eighth of the pre-war registered tonnage, and the destruction in agriculture was equally awesome.[15] Finally, the financial system was in chaos, with seven kinds of currency in use in various parts of the country.[16]

Thus, two interrelated and mutually dependent tasks presented themselves to the new regime: the solving of the nationality question, and overall development of the underdeveloped, differentially developed and now also war-devastated country.

Towards the nationality question, the regime took a 'liberal' approach by creating a federation of six, quasi-sovereign republics, including a semi-autonomous region and a province within Serbia. Centuries-old yearning for national recognition and equality were thus to be satisfied. At the same time, the CPY continued to emphasize 'brotherhood and unity' between the nations and

---

7. Dennison Rusinow, *The Yugoslav Experiment 1948–1974* (Berkeley, Calif., University of California Press, 1978), p. xviii.
8. Ibid.
9. Martin Schrenk, Cyrus Ardalan and Narwal A. Tatawy, *Yugoslavia: Self-Management Socialism and the Challenges of Development*, A World Bank Country Economic Report (Baltimore, Johns Hopkins University Press, 1979), p. 13.
10. Ibid.
11. See above, pp. 74–5.
12. Ibid. New scholarship is revising this figure to approximately 1.0 or 1.1 million. See Vladimir Zerjavić, *Gubici stanovništva Jugoslavije u drugom svjetskom ratu* (Losses of Yugoslav Population in the Second World War) (Zagreb, Jugoslavensko Viktimološko Drustvo, 1989).
13. Hoffman and Neal, *Yugoslavia*, p. 86.
14. Branko Horvat, *The Yugoslav Economic System* (White Plains, New York, International Arts and Sciences Press, 1976), p. 6.
15. Hoffman and Neal, *Yugoslavia*, p. 87.
16. Horvat, *Yugoslav Economic System*, p. 6.

nationalities in the expectation that in time they would abandon the narrow confines of ethnocentrism in favour of a common Yugoslav identity. In the words of Slobodan Milić: 'After the war, the idea especially in Serbia and Montenegro was that Yugoslavia would be one country . . . that republics would be just a temporary thing.'[17]

The CPY expected that a 'romanticized' ethnic nationalism would give way to a Yugoslav national consciousness or *Jugoslovenstvo*, and sought to promote the latter by emphasizing unifying elements in the history, culture and languages of the Yugoslav nations and nationalities. Accordingly, cultural exchanges between republics were encouraged, and the Novi Sad declaration of 1954 affirmed that Serbian, Croatian and Montenegrin were one language (Serbo-Croatian or Croato-Serbian), and a Marxist, Yugoslav history was promoted.

By the mid-1950s, the first political relaxation which characterized Yugoslavia also brought the first evidence that the 'nationality question' had not been solved. Although manifestations of narrow nationalistic interests among the population at large were still relatively uncommon, among the regional party members they were frequent and serious enough to warrant public rebukes from the centre.[18] The idea that decentralization in the economy would bring greater harmony backfired as the devolution of power to republic administrations and to enterprises made each more aware of its own interests.

In the field of culture, matters came to a head in an exchange between the Serbian writer Dobrica Ćosić and the Slovenian Dušan Pirjevac, in which the latter attacked Ćosić for insinuating that the existence of republics precluded a solution to the problem of inter-republic cooperation, providing support for centralists and unitarianists.[19] This exchange brought into the open the continuing fear of a return to Serbian hegemonism, which was to play a recurrent role in Yugoslav politics. A few months later, a speech that Tito gave in Split expressed concern over the spread of national chauvinism among the youth.[20]

The height of *Jugoslovenstvo* came in 1958 at the Seventh

17. Slobodan Milić, Director of the Institute of Agricultural Economics, Belgrade, Serbia, interview 8 September 1983.
18. *Komunist*, July 1953; *Komunist*, 28 February 1958; *Komunist*, supplement, 10 May 1962.
19. *Borba*, 6 December and 14, 15, 16 December 1961.
20. *Komunist*, supplement, 10 May 1962.

Congress of the League of Communists (LCY) with the attempt to create a Yugoslav language.[21] While this was dropped only in 1967 (with the repudiation of the Novi Sad agreement), by the early 1960s the visible lack of party unity on the issue had resulted in its virtual abandonment.

In terms of nationalism, the 1950s were Yugoslavia's only relatively 'quiet' decade. For the central and regional party elites, the issue was to be taken care of by itself in the course of the development of the new Yugoslav socialist society. For the party rank and file and for the population at large, the traditionally deep-seated suspicion of foreign rule had been partly assuaged by the federal solution, which recognized the major ethnic groups as nations, granting them their own republics.

In terms of economic development, the model was the Soviet Union, and the goal 'industrialization so that the developed states continue to develop, but the less developed are enabled to catch up in "revolutionary jumps"'.[22] The method entailed highly ambitious Five-Year Plans stressing capital intensive heavy industries, which required high investments, almost one-third of the Gross Marginal Product (GMP), financed by the exploitation of agriculture and the remnants of the small private economy.

With the 1948 break with the Cominform, all treaties with the Soviet Union were abrogated, Soviet experts were withdrawn, and Yugoslavia lost its ideological compass, finding itself isolated between two hostile camps. After some ideological and political groping, including a brief attempt at collectivization, the Yugoslavs rejected Soviet-style 'State Capitalism'. To save their revolution, the Yugoslavs concluded, the state must wither away and be replaced by 'direct social self-management', by a 'free association of producers' in all affairs.

Although the 'Basic Law on the Management of State Economic Enterprises and Higher Economic Associations by the Workers' Collectives (law on worker management), was passed on 27 June 1950, its effects were hardly to be felt until the early 1960s. Nevertheless, the ideological rationale and the basic institutional frame-

21. At the Sixth Party Congress in 1952, the CPY changed its name to the League of Communists of Yugoslavia. However, in keeping with Yugoslav common usage, the term 'party' will be used here unless a specific reference warrants the use of the formal name.

22. Boris Kidrić, *Privredni problemi FNRJ* (Economic Problems of SFRY) (Belgrade, Kultura, 1948).

work for the devolution of political and economic power and for the creation of a more responsive 'market socialism' had been created.

Despite their formal rejection of the Soviet model, Yugoslav development policies continued to be heavily influenced by the views and prejudices of their old mentor. Thus, although the Soviet-dependent First Five-Year Plan was abandoned in favour of yearly plans (until 1957, when the Second Five-Year Plan was promulgated), the emphasis on industrialization of the Soviet type was continued. For in addition to their continuing belief that socialism was only possible on the basis of an industrial working class, the Yugoslavs now claimed to have compelling geo-political reasons of national security to channel their investments into heavy-industry producer-goods and other strategic investments.[23] Although this geo-political reasoning may have been valid until Stalin's death in 1953, no reorientation in industrial investment occurred until 1957, when agriculture, transportation and consumer goods were given a little more scope; and it was not until the mid-1960s that a decided break with the 'Russian-school mentality' of development was made.[24]

During this period, according to Ljubislav Marković, *Chef de Cabinet* in the government of Milentje Popović (1957–62), it was believed that mistakes in investments would not be made because 'We had nothing; therefore, everything we built was good . . . cost was never really considered; if we needed it, we built it.'[25] This view was corroborated by Svetozar Vukmanović-Tempo who had been in charge of investments from 1953 to 1957. When asked if, given the differentially developed character of Yugoslavia, the less-developed republics and regions (LDRs) were given special consideration in the disbursement of money for investment projects, Vukmanović-Tempo stated emphatically that although they did get investment projects if these coincided with what was best for Yugoslavia as a whole, no special policy of development existed until after 1957.[26]

23. Andrej Briski, Faculty of Economics, Lujbljana, Slovenia, interview 8 November 1983.
24. Ljubislav Marković, Economics Faculty, Belgrade, interview 15 December 1982.
25. Ibid.
26. Svetozar Vukmanović-Tempo, Belgrade, interview 22 January 1990. According to Tempo he was *de facto* in charge of investments from 1950.

The effects on economic development of these attitudes and policies were threefold. First, Yugoslavia achieved a very high growth rate in the 1950s, which resulted in a veritable economic boom. This growth rate (of 13.6 per cent for 1952–57 and 11.6 per cent for 1957–61) had been largely achieved by the very high rate of investment expenditures.[27] These in turn were considerably higher than the output of the economy and were largely based on borrowed resources, both domestic and foreign. Indeed, the foreign component (aid and loan) amounted to approximately US$100 million a year throughout the 1950s which according to Nikola Čobeljić, then director of the Federal Planning Bureau, was equivalent to one-third of productive investments.[28] Because the larger part of investment was geared to projects whose contribution to the economy would not be felt for some years, and because they were based on borrowing, they helped to generate inflation. In turn, inflation was reinforced by first permitting, and then encouraging a rise in personal consumption in the belief that increased consumption would stimulate production and thus act as a boost to the economy. The problem with that policy, as noted by Ljubomir Madžar, was that while it was easy to encourage consumption, it proved much more difficult to discourage it later when it became necessary to do so.[29]

Second, the growing balance-of-trade deficit was still covered by soft Western, mostly American, assistance, which was being given increasingly in the form of credit, displacing the earlier grants. Furthermore, old loans were coming to term at the same time as two years of bad weather (1960 and 1961) and bad harvests, which necessitated food imports, placed an additional strain on the balance of payments.

Finally, the processing industries were operating largely on the basis of imported raw materials previously made cheap by the availability of foreign credits, low import duties and artificially low exchange rates. With the increased balance-of-payment difficulties outside sources of raw materials were becoming less available, while

27. John H. Moore, 'Industrial Production in Yugoslavia, 1952–72', *Joint Committee Print*, East European Economics, Post Helsinki, 25 August 1977. Moore shows that the actual growth rate was about 1 per cent per year less than the official Yugoslav index.
28. Nikola Čobeljić, *Politika i metode privrednog razvoja Jugoslavije 1947–1956* (Politics and Methods of Economic Development of Yugoslavia, 1947–1956) (Belgrade, Nolit, 1959).
29. For more on this position as well as on the general debate regarding problems of the Yugoslav economy, see *Ekonomska Misao*, No. 3, September 1983.

prices for raw materials produced in Yugoslavia were so low that producers had little incentive to expand production so that the processing industries were beginning to run out of raw materials. Thus by the early 1960s investment and consumption outdistanced production and fuelled both domestic inflation and external balance-of-trade deficits, while pricing and fiscal policies further discouraged the production of necessary goods, thus hampering any spontaneous recovery. These three sets of problems together re-sulted in the 1962 recession, which spurred the first genuine open and public debate over both the actual and the desirable handling of the economy.

Before we turn to the debate of the 1960s, it is important to draw attention to the psychology of decision-makers which is revealed here, which was to affect both the further economic development and inter-ethnic–national relations. The attitude that 'since we had nothing, everything we built was good', and that cost was not a factor, created a psychology of easy spending which assumed that as long as a project was started, money would be found somehow for its completion. In the 1950s, when Yugoslavia received more than US$1,157.6 million of economic aid and US$724 million of military aid from the United States,[30] in addition to low-interest loans from other Western countries, it could get away with such financial carelessness. In later periods, this cavalier attitude towards invest-ment was to cost the Yugoslav economy dearly.

An effect of this policy was that although discrimination against the agricultural sector and extractive industries hurt all the agricul-tural and raw material producing areas within Yugoslavia and not only those of the LDRs, the options available to the LDRs were far more limited. The capital-intensive heavy-industry bias led to even greater unemployment in the LDRs than in the developed republics and regions (DRs), and created a skewed economic base which continued to create problems within the LDRs even after the decentralization of 1965 enabled them to 'choose' their develop-ment strategies. Underdeveloped and already relegated to a position of dependency, their chances for budging the economic disparity was further undermined. As a result, the difference in GMP per capita between Slovenia and Kosovo, which had been 1:3 in 1950,

30. In all, between 1950 and mid-1959, in addition to this economic and military aid, Yugoslavia also received the equivalent of US$219 million in long-term credits and grants from other Western governments. Hoffman and Neal, *Yugoslavia*, tables on pp. 348ff.

had by 1960 increased to 1:5.[31] Thus, fifteen years after coming to power, one of the regime's goals, the bridging of economic inequality, was faltering; within a few years, it was also to take on a nationalist character.

The Attempt at Reform: Shocks and Adjustments to Reality in the 1960s

The period 1961–70 was a tumultuous one for Yugoslavia's development. The Second Five-Year Plan had been completed more than a year ahead of schedule, and with its completion Yugoslavia had attained the level of a medium developed country. Urbanization had increased from 30 to 45 per cent since the war, resulting in a more differentiated society whose members had a greater span of wants and needs, which in the politically more 'open' Yugoslavia of the early 1960s, they were increasingly making known. Of these, the most potentially volatile and politically embarrassing was the public articulation of nationalist sentiments. Although these were mild compared to what they were to become in the 1970s and 1980s, they shocked the regime for they showed that nationalism was clearly more than 'a product of false consciousness of the bourgeois–capitalist stage of development'.

Along with the rise of nationalism in the early 1960s, and acting as fuel to it, came major disruptions in the Yugoslav economy via the first recognized economic cycles in a socialist country. The appearance of economic cycles led in turn to sharp and well-publicized debates over the direction of economic policy. Despite the measures taken as early as 1961 to reform the economic system, the cycle of recession-reform-recovery-recession continued throughout the 1960s.

The sharp downturn and the shock of the emergence of economic cycles after years of uninterrupted growth both exposed and exacerbated regional differences. In the prevailing atmosphere of a more open discussion over the direction of the economy and its implications for the various republics and regions, ethnic nationalism and regional economic interests become inextricably interwined. In-

---

31. Savezni Zavod za Statistika i Savezni Zavod za Društveno Planiranje (SZZS i SZDP), *Razvoj Jugoslavije, 1947–1981* (Development of Yugoslavia, 1947–1981) (Belgrade, SZZS i SZDP, 1982), p. 220.

creasingly their indivisibility also shaped the debate over the direction of the economy.

The debate which began among economists in December 1962, regarding the phenomenon of economic cycles, which soon turned into a more open and public debate over the direction of the economy, was the still mild externalization of a political struggle between those advocating liberalization and those opposing it.[32] In 1962 for the sake of party unity comprehensive economic reform was to give way to half-way measures, which not only failed to solve the economic problems but also increased social tensions along nationality lines. By late 1964 it was clear that a decisive turn toward either economic liberalization or recentralization had to be taken. It was equally clear that this choice could not be taken until the now open conflict between the 'liberals' and the 'conservatives' could be resolved.[33]

The conflict arose over the search for new directions, and it became concretized over the optimal balance between plan and market in a socialist society. For the developed republics and regions, the search led to the market system. More specifically, they argued that an increased role for the market would lead to both an increase in freedom of initiative as well as responsibility of an enterprise, over its investment as well as its production, and a general decrease of political intervention in the economy.

A second interpretation of decentralization implied a broadening of self-management from the economic to the socio-political sphere (to encompass non-productive sectors like education and medical care). As the economically stronger members of the federation, they stood to gain by the changes that both decentralization and the market might bring about.

Most of the LDRs (Bosnia–Hercegovina (BiH), Macedonia and Kosovo), though fearful of the market, were convinced by the liberals to vote for the reform by the promise that decentralization and consensual decision-making would ensure their political equality. Guaranteed economic aid through a newly created development fund was to be a sufficient compensatory measure to overcome their disadvantage in a market-based economy. Additionally, political and academic analysts from the DRs argued that under the previous

32. See Shoup, *Communism*, chapters 5 and 6.
33. See the transcripts for the Zagreb conference of 17–19 January 1963, sponsored by the Yugoslav Association of Economists and the Federal Planning Bureau and presented in full in *Economist*, Vol. 16, no. 1, Belgrade, 1963.

system of the General Investment Fund the LDRs as a group had received less in per capita grants-in-aid than the Yugoslav average; while among the LDRs, only Montenegro consistently had received more than its per capita share of investment. Thus, the LDRs had no economic interest in maintaining the status quo; support of the DRs and of the market was seen as safer than support of Serbia and its presumed goal of political dominance. Furthermore, 'the LDRs got sovereignty over the use of the money'.[34] For the DRs, who stood to gain by the market, a development fund which clearly defined the criteria and levels of development, and therefore implicitly set limits and an end to that aid, was preferable to the current 'bottomless pit' of aid.

For a number of reasons, including President Tito's support as well as Croatia's and Slovenia's deft portrayal of Serbian opposition to decentralization as masking hegemonic aspirations, the liberals won the day. With the passage of the reform of 1965, the interventions which hampered the free operation of the market as an allocator of investment and determinant of prices were to be removed.

Among the first steps undertaken in March 1965, was a price reform which began with a reduction of subsidies and an increase in the price of some raw materials to encourage their production. When as a result of the reduction of subsidies, prices skyrocketed, however, the Federal Executive Council had to resort to a 'temporary' freeze on all prices. A general reduction of investment and a virtual freeze on consumer credits accompanied the price freeze. Prices were stabilized momentarily, inflation was checked, and the deficit dropped; but unemployment increased, and the annual rate of growth for the social product in 1965 fell to 1.4 per cent from 12 per cent in 1963 and 1964.[35]

The aim of the measures had been to increase productivity by linking it directly with wages; at the same time, price reforms were to bring about structural realignment of the economy. Neither worked. For the market to operate, prices had to be free to perform their functions of allocation, distribution and so on. But because of the structural disproportions, price controls were deemed necessary in the short run; yet these in turn created further structural disproportions in the economy. Given free rein, enterprises consistently

---

34. Branko Horvat, Faculty of Law, University of Zagreb, Zagreb, interview 6 October 1989.
35. Rusinow, *Yugoslav Experiment*, p. 202.

increased wages above the cost-of-living index. As the workers' concept of justice was closely tied to the idea of parity of wages for similar work, inefficient enterprises continued to keep up in income disbursement by dipping into their reserve capital, foregoing accumulation; or they increased their borrowing to maintain high incomes, knowing that they would eventually be 'bailed out' of their insolvency. As a result, during the period 1965–70, personal incomes rose about 3 per cent per year faster than either productivity or the general price rise; income disparities between groups as well as between republics and regions were also increasing.[36] One indication of the latter is that the disparities between Slovenia and Kosovo had increased by 1970 to 1:6.[37]

The reform was faltering and the repercussions as always went beyond the economic. The first major manifestation of discontent in the post-Reform period occurred in December 1966 when BiH, dissatisfied with the development fund's allocation for 1965–70 and having in vain sought to change it, appealed to the Federal Assembly for redress. Although BiH's allocated amount of 30 per cent was not increased, it did receive some special credits as compensatory measures. More importantly, it marked the first time that a republic openly fought for and won the right to protect its economic interest. A new era of economic nationalism was to begin.

More serious were the violent demonstrations of Albanians which broke out in Kosovo and in neighbouring northwest Macedonia in November 1968.[38] The sudden increase in individual freedom and institutional reforms after twenty years of repression under the Serbian-dominated secret police and its chief Aleksandar Ranković (removed in 1966), in combination with Kosovo's continuing economic underdevelopment, had politicized a significant percentage of Albanians, who demanded the elevation of Kosovo's status to that of a socialist republic within the Yugoslav federation.

What Kosovo along with Vojvodina was granted instead, was a constitution separate from that of Serbia, though both remained constituent units of the Serbian republic. 'National minorities' were granted the same rights as the 'nations' of Yugoslavia, including the

---

36. Ljubo Sirc, *The Yugoslav Economy under Self-Management* (New York, St Martins Press, 1979), p. 129.
37. SZZS i SZDP, *Razvoj Jugoslavije*, p. 220.
38. For a comprehensive treatment of the Albanian question, see Pedro Ramet, *Nationalism and Federalism in Yugoslavia, 1963–1983* (Bloomington, Ind., Indiana University Press, 1984).

use of their native language in public institutions; the independent University of Priština was created in 1969, and steps were taken to promote more Albanians to positions of authority. The economic position of Kosovo relative to other republics and regions had been deteriorating throughout the post-war period, and the riots of 1968 were a sharp reminder that nationalism remained an unsolved question in Yugoslavia, especially prone to surface wherever the region's economy faltered.

There were other reminders of the dangerous link between perceived misdevelopment and nationalism. Half a year after the Kosovo situation had quieted down, the Slovenian road crisis threatened to bring down the federal government. The issue centred on the distribution of scarce resources to republics and regions, this time by the federal government. The planned distribution of a World Bank loan for highway construction in Yugoslavia (which had been approved partly because of the obvious need for road modernization in Slovenia) was set aside and the funds allocated to less urgent Serbian and Croatian projects.[39] Although the final outcome still favoured Slovenia, which received over half the loan, the road crisis further expanded the realm of legitimate political action by republics and regions begun by BiH.

It was in this volatile atmosphere that the reform leadership which had emerged was prompted to take decisive, if premature, action. Fearing a re-emergence of the conservative, pro-centralist, ex-Cominformist supporters and Ranković old-guard elements which had been defeated but not decidedly swept aside in 1965–66, the reformers anxiously hastened the federalization of Yugoslavia as the only way to ensure that this centralist orientation was forever discredited. This, they reasoned, would ensure the success of the reform, by removing any possibility of blockage from within. It would also definitely solve the nationality question by removing the major source of conflict, the federal government's disbursement of funds, and by creating a more open democratic, socialist system. Decentralization, de-etatization, depoliticization, and democratization were to guide Yugoslavia's development.

The further opening up of the Yugoslav socio-political system as a result of the reform, brought with it a new set of problems whose

39. For more on the Slovenian road crisis, see Rusinow, *Yugoslav Experiment*, and Steven Burg, *Conflict and Cohesion in Socialist Yugoslavia* (Princeton, NJ, Princeton University Press, 1983).

consequences were far-reaching. Beginning with the Fourth Plenum in July 1966, there occurred a devolution to republic levels of appointment of middle-level political functionaries, and thereby, a reorientation of these functionaries from the federation to the republics. There was further devolution of power as elections for leadership in the republics and the LCY proceeded from work organizations and consumers upward. The principle of rotation (which was applied at all levels) claimed to increase responsiveness of the party leadership to the constituencies they represented. At the same time, an influx of young party members, and the retirement and expulsion of older more conservative ones, as well as the general democratization of the party elections and introduction of multi-candidate lists, resulted in free and more open discussion. A separation of party and state functions was also carried out by the withdrawal of the party from direct involvement in state operations, and by forbidding the simultaneous holding of positions in party and state administrations.

The decentralization/federalization also encompassed the LCY, as the federal leadership agreed in November 1967 that henceforth the all-Yugoslav party congress would be convened *after* the republic party congresses met. This reversal in timing of party congress meetings signalled that the function of the LCY congresses had shifted from creating the guidelines which the republic parties were supposed to follow, to synthesizing the various results of republic congresses into a coherent line.

Other changes in the central decision-making bodies continued the process of federalization. In 1969 the Chamber of Nationalities, first upgraded in 1967 as a result of the Bosnia–Hercegovina initiative questioning the allocation of resources in the development fund for the period 1966–70, was elevated to a fully independent body. Furthermore, a change to equal rather than proportional representation in the Presidium of the Executive Committee of the LCY, as well as election of its members by their own republic congresses, meant a shift of their primary allegiance away from the centre toward their home republics or provincial organizations. The effect on the decision-making process within the central party leadership was dramatic. The LCY could no longer be counted on to be the guarantor of all-Yugoslav interests.

By devolving power from the federal centre to the republics and regions, the Yugoslavs sought to remove the major source of conflict; in the process they also removed the only agent of cooperation and compromise. By 1969, nine distinct units had been created whose consensus was required for most policy decisions.[40] The problem was that with the existing differences in social, political and economic development of the republics and regions both the problems facing them and the general outlook regarding solutions to these problems were likely to differ. Furthermore, the correspondence between levels of development and national territorial boundaries meant that the solutions to regional problems could and often did take on a nationalist garb. Yet, the system which had institutionalized the vocalization of these differences had not prepared a solution for reconciling them.

'Nešta Izmedju' (Something In Between): Tinkering with the System in the 1970s

The most dramatic example of the above was the Croatian crisis which culminated in the December 1971 purge of the 'left' faction of the Croatian leadership. At the root of the problem were economic grievances stemming from what the Croatians saw as their continuing exploitation by Belgrade. These were based on the incompleteness of the reform of the banking system and the general economic reform of 1965 which had left Belgrade banks still controlling more than half of all the credits and more than three quarters of foreign credits. The result was unfair distribution of economic resources and advantages among the republics and regions. Thus, although Croatia brought in about half of all foreign capital, as of 1969, according to a Croatian economist, it was allocated only about 15 per cent of the total credits, an amount insufficient for its level of development, as well as being unjust in terms of its contribution.[41] In addition, while Croatia produced 27 per cent of the Yugoslav social product, 30 per cent of its industrial production and 36 per cent of its foreign currency earnings, Serbian banks controlled 63 per cent of the total bank assets of Yugoslavia.[42] Four of the ten largest foreign trade enterprises (which accounted for 70 per cent of total Yugoslav foreign trade) were also located in Belgrade, while only one was to be found in Zagreb.[43]

40. The nine units consisted of the six republics, two autonomous regions and a representative of the army.
41. Cited in Ramet, *Nationalism and Federalism in Yugoslavia*, p. 104.
42. Rusinow, *Yugoslav Experiment*, p. 323.
43. Ibid. According to Sime Djodan, Belgrade banks controlled 81.5 per cent of

Although the initial grievances were economic, the correspond-ence of ethnic–national groups with republic boundaries facilitated interpretation as ethnic–national discrimination. This was rein-forced as the Croatian leadership, seeking to increase its positive power in relation to Belgrade,[44] first allowed then encouraged the economic issues to take on both a public, and increasingly a nationalist expression. The escalating nationalist demands voiced in the press, and the split within the Croatian leadership which evolved in the course of 1971, further polarized the positions within both the party and society. Eventually, the liberal faction's attempt to solidify their position by using nationalist appeals to mobilize broad popular support as an implicit threat to Belgrade backfired.

As Croatian demands escalated, Croatia found itself increasingly isolated within the federation, while the leadership split within the republic left the Liberal faction increasingly dependent on the student movement which they could no longer control. The student strike in late November 1971 was the last straw. Troops were called in, and amid arrests of leaders of both the nationalist and the student movements, and resignations and purges among the party elite, order was restored. With the subsequent forced resignation of the liberals in the Serbian leaderships in Vojvodina and Kosovo and in Macedonia and Montenegro, the central authority of the party was restored as well.

Justifiable economic grievances had been transformed into the most volatile political issue possible in Yugoslavia, that of ethnic-–national domination. The Croatian crisis convinced Tito that party discipline and authority had been eroded to the point where there was no longer a unified League of Communists. 'Democratization' had gone too far; it was time to reassert elements of 'centralism'.

The re-establishment of the LCY in its leading role did not mean, however, a complete turning back to the pre-reform days. Despite the 1972–74 recentralization of authority within the party and reaffirmation of 'democratic-centralism', 'dictatorship of the prolet-ariat', 'party unity,' 'purges of rotten liberals and technocrats' and

---

foreign credits while Croatia, which brought in about 50 per cent of all foreign capital, controlled only about 15 per cent of total credits. Cited in Ramet, *National-ism and Federalism in Yugoslavia*, p. 104.

44. Positive power to act, as compared to negative power stemming from its ability to merely veto decisions of the federal government; for more on this see Gregor Tomc, 'Social Stratification and National Formation in Post-War Yugosla-via', paper presented at the Wilson Center, Smithsonian Institution, Washington, DC, 4–6 September 1986.

other centralizing slogans and measures, the decentralization of the federation through the Constitutional Amendments of 1967, 1969 and 1971 proceeded on-course. Thus, self-management, interpreted as decision-making at the most basic social, political and economic levels (republic, commune, and from the mid-1970s, OOUR and SIZ), remained untouched.[45] As a result, the June 1971 amendments to the Constitution specified that the federal government should retain power only over the six areas specifically allocated to it; all residual power was vested with the republics and regions.[46]

Not only did the federation continue to have jurisdiction *only* over those matters specifically allocated to it, but in many important instances (social plans, monetary policy, foreign exchange, trade and aid to the LDRs) agreement by republics and regions was needed before the federation could act.[47] The creation of a nine-member Collective Presidency in 1969 (one member from each republic and region and the president of the Central Committee Presidium as an *ex officio* member), the creation of two federal chambers and increased grass-roots participation through the system of delegates, as well as the *de facto* obligatory parity through the 'ethnic key' (*ključ*) in most important federal organs and institutions, all show the degree of decentralization which had occurred by the early 1970s. Finally, the principle of consensus decision-making based on inter-regional consultation and harmonization of interest was reaffirmed, with President Tito as the ultimate arbiter in political conflict.

A parallel decentralization took place in the economy. The milestone in this process was the Constitutional Amendment XXI passed in June 1971, which created self-managed, semi-autonomous economic units, *Osnovne Organizacije Udruženog Rada* (OOURs).[48]

45. OOUR, *Osnovne Organizacije Udruženog Rada*, or BOAL, Basic Organizations of Associated Labour constituted in the mid-1970s – legally and financially independent units forming parts of the enterprise; SIZ, *Samoupravne Interesne Zajednice*, for social services in which 'consumers' of social services (delegates from enterprises) bargain with the 'producers' (the social-service agencies) over all aspects of social services like price, quality. The result was to be a system of checks and balances between economic units, government bodies and mass organizations. See Steven Sacks, 'Divisionalization in Large Yugoslav Enteprises', and Ellen T. Comisso, 'Yugoslav in the 1970s: Self-Management and Bargaining', *Journal of Comparative Economics*, Vol. 4, June 1980, pp. 209–25 and 192–208.

46. These federal powers are defence, foreign affairs, ethnic equality and individual liberty, a single Yugoslav market, common monetary and trade policies and upholding the 'principles of the political system'.

47. Sirc, *The Yugoslav Economy*, p. 22.

48. For more on BOALs see Laura D'Andrea Tyston, *The Yugoslav Economic System and its Performance in the 1970s*, (Institute of International Studies, Berkeley, Calif., University of California, 1980), chapter 2.

Together, Amendment XXI of 1971, the new Constitution of 1974 and the Law of Associated Labour of 1976 decentralized economic decision-making, creating a complex set of checks and balances.

One *consequence* of the above has been a high degree of 'negative power' of all republics and regions, because of their *de facto* right to veto legislation that they see as harmful to their particular interests. This 'negative power' which ensures one kind of equality of republics and regions within the federation, paradoxically also raises two dilemmas for the regime. The first, the question of fairness in representation, arises from the equal vote of republics irrespective of their size. This is most often brought up in relation to Montenegro and Serbia (proper) where the population ratio is almost 1:10. The second, is the problem of decision-making by consensus, when for objective reasons (different levels of development and therefore different interest) consensus is so difficult to arrive at. The results can range from compromises which so dilute the original proposal that its potential effectiveness is lost, to so much delay that decisions are overtaken by a changing situation, to stalemate. All three have occurred with obvious negative consequences for both economic development and ethnic–national relations.

The socio-political democratization and the devolution of power which began in earnest with the 1965 reform and continued through the late 1960s, was meant to satisfy both the ambitions of the republic elites, and the longings of their constituents, by granting them more civil freedoms and national autonomy. In the process, it was expected to bring political stability by solving the nationality problem, 'once and for all'. Similarly, the marketization of the economy was to solve the related problems of incompetent investment and disharmony between supply and demand, enhancing economic rationality and, therefore, profits. Partial democratization and liberalization which allowed for greater articulation of interests and mobilization for their protection, however, took on a nationalist garb and led to Yugoslavia's first major domestic crisis, the Croatian crisis of 1970–71. Likewise, the partial marketization and decentralization of the economy led to unintended consequences for the economy, especially in the LDRs.

There were two main negative effects of the devolution and fragmentation of economic units. First, there was a vast duplication and expansion of the bureaucracy which further burdened an already slowing economy; second, the decision-making process became far more cumbersome, time-consuming and complex, adding disincentive to any potential entrepreneurship. The goal of increased economic efficiency thus became still more elusive, as decision-making by consensus meant that more people had to reach more agreements for which there were fewer measures of enforcement and virtually no sanctions in case of non-compliance.

Despite the creation of the development fund which guaranteed the LDRs an agreed percentage of GMP for building productive facilities (for 1965–70, that represented 1.85 per cent of the GMP; for 1970–75 it was increased to 1.94 per cent), as well as budgetary grants to help them build up their social services (for 1965–70 the LDRs received 0.78 per cent of the GMP; for 1970–75, they received 0.83 per cent), their development continued to lag. The decentralization of investments resulted in capital flight to the DRs and a further weakening of the economies of the LDRs. The development fund was unable to bridge this investment gap, as the unforeseeable structural and pricing policies for the LDRs remained, while the fund's role as a source of expertise and research and development never materialized. In addition, despite low interest rates of 4 per cent, a repayment period of fifteen years (and for Kosovo, 3 per cent and nineteen years) and the slightly higher growth rate of the LDRs than of the DRs for the period 1971–75, their share of investment per capita continued to lag.[49] With 36 per cent of Yugoslavia's population the LDRs received only 28.8 per cent of investments in fixed assets.[50]

Furthermore, the distribution of investments among the LDRs did not enable the best possible development of each. Thus, both BiH and Macedonia continued to receive less than their share of investment, with Macedonia's share decreasing throughout the 1965–80 period, even though its utilization of investments was the most efficient, as shown by its growth rate of 14.9 per cent above the national average for the 1971–75 period. Finally, Montenegro continued to receive well above its per capita investment share despite evidence of underutilization of capital as shown by its growth rate in the 1971–75 period, which measured 11.2 per cent below the national average.[51]

49. *Službeni list SFRJ*, no. 33, pp. 642–5 and Marija Ivanović, *Finansiranje razvoja nerazvijenih područja Jugoslavije* (Financing the Development of the Underdeveloped Areas of Yugoslavia) (Titograd, Institut za Društveno-Ekonomska Istraživanja, 1978).

50. Ivanović, *Finansiranje*, p. 105.

51. Mihailo Mladenović, 'Neki rezultati razvoja privredno nedovoljno razvijenih republika i pokrajine Kosovo 1971–74' (Some Results of the Development of the

Some regions clearly did much better than others. Elsewhere I have sought to explain these discrepancies.[52] It is sufficient to note here that though individual republics and regions could block or at least delay legislation they could not necessarily ensure the passing of legislation which would benefit them. At most, they were able to achieve a compromise through which they would receive something more than they would have had otherwise. Thus, although the LDRs were placated by a combination of supplementary measures and promises of more investment in the future, the effect on the narrowing of regional disparity was marginal.

The danger of the continuing and even increasing regional inequality was acknowledged indirectly by the regime in its Sixth Five-Year Plan (1976–80), when the reasons given for its goals of 'faster development of the economically underdeveloped republics with the socialist province of Kosovo exceeding most of the country's development' were given as first, 'for inter-nationality relations' and second, for the 'common economic interest'.[53] It was deemed politic to supplement the ideological appeal of regional development with concrete appeals to self-interest.

The Sixth Five-Year Plan also stipulated that criteria for determining the level of development of republics and regions be formulated by no later than the end of 1978, in order to decide which republics and regions would be considered underdeveloped after 1980. Three such studies were produced: Slovenia and Croatia collaborated on one; Serbia proper produced its own; the LDRs together produced a third; Vojvodina chose not to participate. Each presented the problem of regional development from its own perspective and arrived at criteria of development which would accord best with its own interest, while claiming to be the one 'objective study'. Thus while all agreed that Kosovo was to receive preferential treatment 'for a long time', agreement on specific criteria and measures of development was not reached. Faced with an impasse and the prospect of another delayed Five-Year Plan, the Federal Executive Council (FEC) submitted its own proposals. It, too, failed to secure agreement and was withdrawn.

Economically Insufficiently Developed Republics and the Region of Kosovo, 1971–74), *Jugoslavenski Pregled*, No. 19, 1975–6, p. 224.

52. Dijana Pleština, *Politics and Inequality: A Study of Regional Disparities in Yugoslavia*, (Boulder, Colo., Westview Press, forthcoming, 1992).

53. *Društveni plan razvoja Jugoslavije za razdoblje od 1976 do 1980* (Social Plan for the Development of Yugoslavia for the period 1976 to 1980), Part 1, Section 5.1 (Belgrade, Savezni Zarod za Društvano Planivanje).

The problem highlights two key aspects of Yugoslav development which became salient in the 1980s. First, the failure of the FEC, the strongest decision-making body in post-Tito Yugoslavia, to get its measure passed even when, so shortly after Tito's death, republics and regions were particularly sensitive to the importance of presenting a united 'business-as-usual' image, shows that the influence of the central party apparatus (which had been re-established in the 1970s) was either not strong enough to override inter-regional disagreements, or itself reflected this regional conflict.[54] The second aspect which is highlighted by the failure to pass the draft agreement is that once again conflict between the republics and regions converged on the issue of regional development – a predictable point of conflict made worse by the state of Yugoslavia's economy at the close of the 1970s.

By 1978, the economic boom which had characterized most of the 1970s was showing signs of abating. In addition to the domestic factors of misdevelopment, the world-wide recession of 1974–75 reduced the demand for Yugoslav exports, while the sharp increase in the price of oil in 1973–75 and again in 1978–79 increased Yugoslavia's import bill by an equivalent of 7 per cent of GNP for 1974–76, and 8 per cent for 1978–81.[55] Foreign debt had increased to US$18 billion and inflation to 35 per cent in 1979–80.[56] Over-investment resulted in the exhaustion of Yugoslav bank liquidity and inability to meet credit commitments without further borrowing. The return of some 40,000 Gastarbeiter per year by the end of 1980 had swelled the number of unemployed in Yugoslavia to 785,000.[57] A Gross National Product (GNP) increase of only 2.5 per cent in 1980 compared to 8 per cent during the preceding years led by 1980 to a fall in real personal income to the 1975 level, the first decline in more than two-and-a-half decades.

These events were once again felt most strongly in the LDRs. In terms of overall investment for the 1975–80 period, the LDRs received considerably less than had been planned: 26.6 per cent instead of 34 per cent of total investment, and considerably less

---

54. See Burg, *Conflict and Cohesion*.
55. Balassa and Tyson, 1981, quoted in Christopher Martin and Laura D'Andrea Tyson, 'Can Titoism Survive Tito: Economic Problems and Policy Choices Confronting Tito's Successors', in Pedro Ramet (ed.), *Yugoslavia in the 1980s* (Boulder, Colo., Westview Press, 1985).
56. Martin and Tyson, 'Can Titoism Survive Tito', p. 27.
57. Kosta Mihailović, *Ekonomska stvarnost Jugoslavije*, (The Economic Reality of Yugoslavia) (Belgrade, Prosveta, 1982), p. 46.

per capita than the DRs. Nor was distribution among them optional. In BiH, Macedonia and even Kosovo, investment was cut by a third, although in Montenegro it was slightly increased. While their aid from the development fund was increased slightly from 1.94 per cent of GMP to 1.97 per cent, this only served to balance out the decrease in their supplementary resources, which were first set at 0.93 per cent of GMP and were subsequently reduced to 0.80 per cent.[58] Thus, adequate material resources for bridging regional disparity were not present.

Nor were other measures for stimulating the faster development of the LDRs successful. One such potentially significant innovation was the possibility of fulfilling up to 20 per cent of one's financial obligation to the development fund through the pooling of labour and resources of work organizations of the DRs and LDRs. The only criterion was that investments be in line with the social plans of the LDRs. The purpose of the innovation was to enhance self-management integration in the economy between the DRs and the LDRs.[59] During this period, however, a negligible thirteen ventures (or 2.3 per cent of the possible financial cooperation between enterprises of the DRs and those of the LDRs) were achieved.[60]

Further evidence of the lack of inter-regional cooperation is the development fund's failure to become a facilitator and coordinator in the exchange of experts and expertise across regional boundaries. Additional evidence is provided by the chronic malintegration of Yugoslav markets as illustrated by inter-regional price dispersion, economic specialization, personal income dispersion, location of BOALs[61] and finally, by inter-regional trade, which as Caslav Očić has shown, fell from 27 per cent in 1970 to 21.7 per cent in 1980.[62]

58. *Društveni plan razvoja Jugoslavije za razdoblje od 1976 do 1980*, Part 2, Sections 10.1.1, 10.1.2 and 10.1.3.
59. Fond Federacije (Federal Fund), *O Priticanju i usmerivanju sredstava fonda u periodu od 1976 do 1980 godine*, (On the Flow and Direction of Means of the Fund in the Period from 1976 to 1980) (Belgrade, May 1981), p. 41.
60. Mihailo Mladenović, 'Razoj privredno nedovoljno razvijenih republika i pokrajine Kosovo' (Development of the Economically Insufficiently Developed Republics and the Region of Kosovo), *Jugoslavenski Predgled*, Vol. 9, 1981, p. 64.
61. John Burkett and Borislav Skegro, 'Are Economic Fractures Widening?', in Dennison Rusinow (ed.), *Yugoslavia: A Fractured Federalism*, (Washington, DC, Wilson Center Press, 1988).
62. *NIN*, 5 June 1983, pp. 10–11.

The Post-Tito Decade: Social, Political and Economic Crisis in the 1980s

Speculated on for more than a decade before it occurred, and feared for its impact on Yugoslavia's stability, the death of the man who had led the CPY to power and had become the symbol of the post-war, socialist, self-managed, non-aligned Yugoslavia had few immediate consequences.

No *führerist putsch*, no regional supremacy, no army coup occurred; rather, within hours of Tito's death, the new president and vice-president were duly elected from among the eight representatives of the republics and regions. Ten days later the first rotation in the presidency occurred on schedule (yearly, on 14 May), and later that month the order of rotation among the republics and regions was formally established. Similarly, the Presidium of the LCY, and the FEC, the centre of political power in post-Tito Yugoslavia, functioned smoothly in terms of their rotation of power. Yet, lurking in the shadows were a growing array of problems whose successive appearance and cumulative effect by the end of the 1980s brought the country to the verge of political and economic disintegration.

The first of these problems, and the most enduring one, has been that of Kosovo. Inhabited by some 1,600,000 Albanians, 210,000 Serbs and 20,000 Montenegrins (as well as some 25,000 Gypsies and another 20,000 people of various other national minority groups), Kosovo is the only region in Yugoslavia with a majority ethnic–national group to be denied republic status.[63] Colonized by the Albanians after the Serb inhabitants fled Turkish rule in the seventeenth century, it is considered by the Albanians living there to be their birthright and their home; however, for the Serbs, Kosovo remains the cradle of Serbian civilization, and as such carries an emotional value which transcends calculation.

The more recent history of Kosovo has been marred first by the inter-war domination of Serbs, then by the frequently brutal attempts both of the Partisans to mobilize the Albanian population, and of the Albanians to even the score whenever the opportunity presented itself. The subsequent post-war repression of Kosovo by

---

63. Calculated on the basis of the 1981 census. SZZS, *Statistički godišnjak Jugoslavije 1989* (Statistical Yearbook of Yugoslavia, 1989) (Belgrade, SZZS 1989), pp. 421 and 453.

Serbia until the 1966 ousting of its secret police chief, Aleksandar Ranković, further alienated the Albanians. Finally, the region's overall economic underdevelopment and the increase in its relative backwardness in the post-war era added fuel to the fire.[64]

The steady deterioration in Serb–Albanian relations along with the new climate of openness of the late 1960s, led to the 1968 outbreak of violence, the first major instance of violence in post-war Yugoslavia. Measures to appease the Kosovo Albanians were taken, culminating in the 1974 Constitutional guarantee of regional autonomy for Kosovo. Nevertheless, inter-ethnic tensions remained high. Underground separatist organizations, student demonstrations, group and individual acts of violence resulted in trials and convictions of Albanians for subversive activity throughout the 1970s. Despite the 1974 campaign launched by the League of Communists of Kosovo (LCK) against 'particularistic–separatist Albanian nationalism', by the end of the decade more than 600 Kosovars had been arrested for Albanian separatism.[65]

According to many, the root cause of nationalist grievances was economic. The nationalist movement found most of it leaders and certainly its most vocal supporters among the educated young, many of whom were unemployed.[66] In one of Tito's last appearances, on 16 October 1979, at a joint session of the Central Committee of the LCK and the presidency of the autonomous region, he insisted that 'Kosovo truly must be the concern of all our peoples, of the entire Yugoslav union'. In relation to economic development, he reiterated that 'More equal development is in the interest not only of Kosovo, but of all of Yugoslavia.'[67]

The importance of Kosovo's economic backwardness and the relative increase of that backwardness in socialist Yugoslavia, was also recognized by the President of the Kosovo Provincial Committee in the autumn of 1980 when he linked the fulfilment of Kosovo's economic demands with the continuation of Yugoslavia's stable development.[68] Within four months of his speech, student riots in Priština had broadened into grievances over Kosovo's

---

64. For more on this see Shoup, *Communism*; and Ramet, *Nationalism and Federalism in Yugoslavia*.
65. Ramet, *Nationalism and Federalism in Yugoslavia*, p. 162.
66. *NIN*, 28 February 1982, p. 15.
67. Josep Broz Tito, *Borba za novi Svet* (The Struggle for a New World) (Belgrade, Preskliping, 1982), p. 334.
68. Radio Free Europe (RFE), *Situation Reports* (*SR*), Vol. 5, No. 58, November 1980, pp. 21–4.

general underdevelopment and high unemployment, mainly among the young.[69]

By 1980, Kosovo's situation relative to that of other republics and regions had further deteriorated, while the overall development of the LDRs had once again faltered. Instead of the growth rate of the LDRs exceeding that of Yugoslavia as a whole by 20 to 25 per cent as stipulated in the Sixth Five-Year Plan, it exceeded it by only 7 per cent.[70] As a result, the disparity between the DRs and the LDRs was not narrowed, while that between Slovenia and Kosovo increased to a little over 1:7.[71]

Thus, ten years after the Croatian crisis, economic grievances once again took on a violent ethnic–nationalist manifestation. In the decentralized Yugoslavia of the early 1980s, where pursuit of economic interest had acquired *de facto* legitimacy, where decision-making proceeded by consensus, and where no Tito-like figure had the authority to impose order, accumulated grievances proved much more difficult to contain, and by the end of the decade, impossible to subdue.

The Kosovo riots which broke out at the University of Priština in March 1981, less than a year after Tito's death, spread by May to miners and other workers throughout Kosovo; by July they had spread to Montenegro and other areas outside Kosovo that had a sizeable Albanian minority. Within Kosovo, incidents of arson, sabotage and terrorism became commonplace. The school year ended a month early so that the students could be dispersed and a state of emergency was declared. Kosovo was sealed off to the outside world for two months in the summer of 1981. A purge of the Kosovo party followed with some 1,000 members expelled by July 1982, and Mahmut Bakali, head of the League of Communists of Kosovo, resigned and subsequently was expelled from the party. Between 1981 and 1987 some 1,500 Albanians were convicted of political offences, 6,650 of misdemeanours and 1,430 of military offences. During the same period more than 40,000 Serbs and more than 9,000 Albanians emigrated, many on both sides for economic as well as political reasons.[72]

69. For more on the Kosovo crisis, see Mark Baskin, 'Crisis in Kosovo', *Problems of Communism*, March–April 1983; Ramet, *Nationalism and Federalism in Yugoslavia*, chapter 8; and Jozef Darski, 'Reformism and Nationalism: Two Responses to the Crisis of Communist Power in Yugoslavia', *Uncaptive Minds*, Vol. 11, No. 2, March–April, 1989.
70. Fond Federacije (Federal Fund), *O Priticanju*, October 1981, p. 11.
71. SZZS i SZDP, *Razvoj Jugoslavije*, p. 220.
72. Ramet, *Nationalism and Federalism in Yugoslavia*, and Darski, 'Reformism and Nationalism'.

The second major problem which began to emerge simultaneously with the Kosovo crisis, was the sharp downswing in the economy. Yugoslavia's much heralded prosperity, based on and fuelled by cheap foreign loans, began to contract suddenly and sharply in the late 1970s. The second increase in oil prices (1978–79) led to a deterioration of Yugoslavia's terms of trade, the world recession of 1980–83 reduced demands for Yugoslav exports, while the increase in interest rates drained its foreign exchange reserves.[73] By 1982, growth of the GMP was at an all-time low of 0.3 per cent, with GMP per capita experiencing a negative growth of 0.5 per cent; growth in employment also fell to a low of 2.2 per cent, while inflation was steadily rising.[74] There was an increase in foreign debt to some US$24 billion. Living standards fell to the level of the early 1970s.

In this situation of overall economic decline the awaited report of the Krajger Commission for the Economic Stabilization of Yugoslavia was completed in the summer of 1983. Its recommendations called for the liberalization of the economy with full implementation of market principles. Production was to be based on criteria of profitability linking responsibility for economic outcomes with the decision-makers involved. It was also to operate in foreign trade where the goal was to set Yugoslav prices in line with world prices, with a view to achieving convertibility of the dinar.[75]

Despite the necessity of economic reform, however, and the awareness that for its implementation political reform was a prerequisite, agreement on the latter could not be reached. The modest recovery under Milka Planinc in the first half of 1985 was undermined by the conservatives in the government led by Branko Mikulić, who succeeded her as Prime Minister.[76] Mikulić's vision of 'programmed inflation' and his series of *ad hoc* measures worsened the economic situation. By late spring 1988 when his government

73. For an overall analysis of the Yugoslav economy in the first half of the 1980s, see Martin and Tyson, 'Can Titoism Survive Tito?'.

74. Kosta Mihailović, 'Privredna Kriza Jugoslavije: urzroci i mogući izlazi' (The Yugoslav Economic Crisis: Causes and Possible Solutions) *Ekonomska Misao*, No. 16, Belgrade, June 1983.

75. For an evaluation of the Krajger Commission Report, see John P. Burkett, 'Stabilization Measures in Yugoslavia: An Assessment of the Proposal of Yugoslavia's Commission for Problems of Economic Stabilization, Joint Economic Committee, U.S. Congress', *East European Economies, Slow Growth in the 1980s*, Vol. 3 (Washington, DC, 1986), pp. 561–74.

76. For more on the economy under Planinc see *OECD Economic Surveys: Yugoslavia* (Paris, OECD), 1987.

finally took some necessary steps towards economic recovery (real interest rates, free rise of prices, devaluation of the dinar), a new factor, more difficult to control, had entered the political equation.

That factor was the growing worker unrest whose turning point came in early July 1988 with the arrival in Belgrade of the striking Borovo workers. One of Yugoslavia's rare showcases of competitiveness and prosperity, with a good track record of successful placement of its leather goods, clothing and rubber products on the foreign market, Borovo had run into serious economic problems. The fall in the world price of crude oil, which increased the Soviet trade deficit with Yugoslavia, led to a loss of the Soviet market for Borovo goods. Unable to compete in the West or to reorient its production rapidly enough, Borovo suddenly found itself with a large surplus of goods, a deficit of foreign exchange, a redundant labour force, and the need to cut back its operations. The workers, whose purchasing power had fallen to the level of 1960 as their average monthly salaries plummeted to US$150 or less, felt that they were not responsible, and naturally turned to the state demanding a 100 per cent pay increase to compensate for the previous salary freeze and high inflation, as well as a guarantee for their jobs.[77]

Yet, given the state of the economy, the government was in no position to meet the workers' demands. Yugoslavia was saddled with a foreign debt of $23 billion and a recently discovered internal debt of almost twice that amount.[78] Official unemployment stood at 17 per cent nation-wide with another 20 per cent of the population underemployed, while in Kosovo unemployment registered 54 per cent. More than one-third of industry was working under capacity, some by as much as 40 to 50 per cent.[79] The recession which in the previous two years had led to negative growth in Yugoslavia as a whole, had for the first time, in 1988, also encompassed Slovenia, the most developed and prosperous republic. In Yugoslavia GMP per capita had declined from US$3,000 in 1985 to US$2,400 in 1988.[80]

By guaranteeing all workers their jobs and agreeing to an across-the-board 70 per cent pay increase, the Mikulić government made of Borovo a model for settling economic disputes. Throughout the

77. RFE, *SR*, No. 6, 6 July 1988, p. 8.
78. For more on the origin and explanation of the 'internal debt', see the chapter by Ljubomir Madžar, above.
79. *Vjesnik*, 11 September 1989.
80. RFE, *SR*, No. 10, 11 November, 1988.

summer of 1988, busloads of workers carrying Tito's picture, making their way to the trade union headquarters and to the Federal Parliament, insisting on meeting with a variety of responsible officials, and refusing to disperse until their demands had been heard and virtually all the economic ones had been met, became a new norm.

This new 'empowerment' of the workers undermined the government's attempt at a restrictive monetary policy imposed by the International Monetary Fund (IMF) as part of the May 1988 package of reprogramming of loans, thus compromising Yugoslavia's future standing with the IMF. More dangerously, it led to the development of a crude type of populist 'quasi-democracy' which threatened any possibility of economic reform. All that was needed was a leader capable of presenting himself as champion of the 'oppressed masses', in whose interest he could then claim to pursue his vision of a new order and of his place in it. Just such a leader was emerging in Serbia.

Slobodan Milošević was the relatively young dynamic leader who, barely one year after capturing power in the fall of 1987, purged all potential opposition in the Serbian party, government, bureaucracy and media. He did this partly by promising to the liberal–nationalist wave of Serb intellectuals political democratization and economic efficiency in the market, as solutions to the various political (read Kosovo) and economic problems confronting Serbia. He appealed to the masses by presenting himself as their champion in the 'moral' struggle against the 'armchair politicians'. With the 'crusade' to free the 'oppressed and shackled' Serbia, and restore it to its position of 'equality', or rather, to its 'rightful place' within the Yugoslav federation, Milošević expanded his constituency among both intellectuals and the masses. Like many effective demagogues, Milošević cast himself as strong, resolute and effective. The lack of coherence of his programme enabled him to reach out to widely disparate constituencies. His championing of the 'small', 'impoverished', 'downtrodden' Serbian peasant–worker carried the psychological appeal that authoritarian movements often have for dislocated, frightened masses.

The hook was Kosovo, and the inability of the Yugoslav government to quell the disturbances which began in 1981. Milošević used the Kosovo situation to argue for increasing Serbia's power over its autonomous provinces to enable it to restore law and order.[81] The

---

81. For more on the abrogation of Serbian sovereignty and its repeated attempts to reclaim these, see RFE, *SR*, No. 12, 23 December, 1988, pp. 23–4.

informal campaign waged through the summer and autumn of 1988, and culminated in the *Bratsvo i Jedinstvo* (Brotherhood and Unity) rally on 19 November, the largest in Yugoslav post-war history, at which an estimated million to a million and a quarter people amassed in Belgrade in support of Milošević.[82] The campaign worked; Milošević was able to convince his federal colleagues that to restore order and to 'solve' the Kosovo question, Serbia had to be given full powers over the two autonomous provinces. Ten days later, amendments to the Federal Constitution increasing Serbia's powers over Kosovo and Vojvodina were passed.

Milošević's earlier success in amending the Serbian republican Constitution at the September meeting of the Serbian party leadership was followed in October by the forced resignation of the Vojvodina leadership, marking the defeat of his major 'in-house' opposition.[83] By November, he had engineered the fall of a part of the Kosovo and Montenegro leaderships.[84] By January 1989, those who had survived this first 'cleansing' of the party, now had their turn.[85]

The general thrust of the Constitutional Amendments passed in November 1988 was to increase the efficiency of the economy by taking a decidedly pro-market direction. Thus, among the thirty-nine amendments passed, was the lifting of all limitations to private ownership (except that of land, where the limit was set at 60 acres), allowing the formation of joint-stock companies in which decision-making power would be commensurate with the partners' investment, and ending government bail-outs of failing enterprises.[86] Although a number of amendments dealing with the polity were also passed, notably one specifying a secret vote for all government offices at all levels, and another, mandating multi-candidate lists for all public offices, the more thorny issues of the role of the party, its monopoly of power, and the question of representation were set aside for a later date.[87]

Yet passing economic reforms without the necessary political ones to implement them, meant of necessity, the inability to carry them out. When Oskar Kovač, a market-oriented economist and

---

82. RFE, *SR*, No. 11, Vol. 13, No. 48, p. 7.
83. *Vjesnik*, 8 and 9 October 1988.
84. RFE, *SR*, Vol. 13, No. 42, 30 December 1988.
85. RFE, *SR*, No. 1, 17 January 1989, pp. 9–10.
86. RFE, *SR*, No. 11, 2 December 1988, pp. 3–6 and RFE, *SR*, No. 12, 23 December 1988, pp. 3–7.
87. RFE, *SR*, No. 12, 23 December 1988, pp. 9–13.

member of the FEC, tendered his resignation over the government's unwillingness to implement market principles by increasing the interest rates (thus forcing into bankruptcy those firms with the heaviest losses) he crystallized discontent within the Mikulić government. On 30 December, having lost the support of parliament, Prime Minister Mikulić and the entire Federal Executive Council tendered their resignations, the first in the history of a communist regime.[88]

Yugoslavia at the Crossroads: 1989, The Year in Crisis

The passage of economic reforms in November, the resignation of an ineffective government in December, and the selection of a new market-oriented Prime Minister in January were all signs of hope for the future of Yugoslavia. Yet what seemed to the hopeful like a new beginning was but a very brief lull before the proverbial storm.

The crisis which led to the imposition of martial law in Kosovo in February 1989, began in January, with Milošević's ousting of Azem Vlasi, Kaćuša Jašari and Sinan Hasani, replacing them with the unpopular Husamedin Azemi as Priština's head of the party, Rahman Morina, the head of the Kosovo secret police, as head of the LCK, and Ali Šukrija as Kosovo's representative in the Central Committee of the LCY. The organizers of the November demonstrations and strikes against Serbia's proposed constitutional amendments were charged with 'counter revolutionary endangerment of the society'.[89] As strikes have been tacitly accepted since 1956, and were formally legalized by a constitutional amendment in November 1988, this obvious attempt at 'breaking' Kosovo predictably elicited mass opposition.

An informal general strike culminated in the hunger strike of 1,300 Stari Trg miners who vowed to stay underground (and if need be blow themselves up) unless the Serbian government met their demands. These consisted of the dismissal of the Serbian-installed Morina, Azemi and the Šukrija leadership and reinstatement of their dismissed leaders; the abandonment of the prosecution of those involved in organizing the strikes; and the abandonment of the

88. RFE, *SR*, No. 1, 17 January 1990, p. 3.
89. *Vjesnik*, 29 August 1989. In direct violation of the law, Vlasi and the other fourteen accused were imprisoned for more than five months before they were formally charged.

constitutional amendments which increased Serbia's power over Kosovo.[90]

The response from the presidency of the Socialist Federal Republic of Yugoslavia (SFRJ) was to declare a state of emergency, and impose 'special measures' for the preservation of peace in Kosovo, by banning all meetings and strikes, and by moving in the army. The next day, in Cankariev Hall in Ljubljana, the city's Socialist Alliance sponsored a rally at which more than 2,000 people, among them leading figures of Slovenia, including Stefan Korošec and Milan Kučan, the heads of the party and of the government, spoke vociferously against the special measures, and offered moral support to the miners. Additionally, 450,000 Slovenes signed the petition against the emergency measures, and in both Slovenia and Croatia bank accounts were opened to receive donations for the families of the miners.[91]

The counter-reaction to the Kosovo miners' strike and the sympathy it elicited was equally swift. In Kosovo, Serbian and Montenegrin miners launched a counter-strike, and Serbian and Montenegrin professors, teachers and students vowed to resign and/or leave their posts if the government 'capitulated'. In Belgrade the reaction to the Kosovo events, to the Ljubljana meeting and to the publication of a text by the president of the Slovenian Youth Alliance (in which he equated the positions of Albanians in Yugoslavia to that of Jews in the past), led to a mass protest of more than a million people, at which the mass hysteria led first to a call to arms to solve the Kosovo problem, then for the arrest of Azem Vlasi (allegedly one of the 'instigators' of the February strikes) and finally even for his death. It was answered by Milošević's 'guarantee' of Vlasi's arrest, which indeed followed a few days later.[92] Although the Serbian government took the hard line of refusing to be 'blackmailed', by the Kosovo miners' demands, Morina, Azemi and Šukrija resigned, and the miners gave up their strike. In an abrupt about-face the resigned leaders were thereupon reinstated and the Kosovo situation returned to a tense waiting period.[93]

In Croatia and Slovenia, January and February were months in which the first 'groups' or 'movements' dedicated to democratization, which had begun to form in October and November 1988,

90. RFE, *SR*, No. 1, Vol. 14, No. 10, 8 March 1989, p. 3.
91. Ibid., pp. 13–15.
92. Ibid.
93. Ibid., pp. 9–10.

took on a more public profile.[94] Although these eschewed the label 'political parties' and claimed to have no pretensions to political power, the presidency of the SFRJ formally criticized both Stipe Šuvar, the head of the Croatian party, and Milan Kučan, the head of the Slovenian party, for tolerating the formation of political parties within their republics. The presidency considered the formation of parties to be in conflict with the Constitution, and demanded that the responsible organs take the necessary measures against them.

Perhaps more astounding than the formation of opposition groups and the 'warning' by the presidency, was the response of Šuvar and Kučan. While both remained unwilling to legalize opposition groups, they defiantly refused to act against them. (Incongruously, Stipe Šuvar had risen to power in the aftermath of the 1971 crackdown on the Croatian liberals.) It was not clear whether Slovenia's and Croatia's defiance signalled their support for democracy, or whether it was only an assertion of republican sovereignty; but conflict at the very top over vastly different conceptions of Yugoslav federalism had been made public.

By late spring 1989, Kosovo had become the focus of Yugoslavia's problems. For the Albanians in Yugoslavia, national survival was seen as dependent on self-determination, which in turn necessitated full equality within the federation (i.e. republican status), and for some, complete separation. For the Serbs and Montenegrins, Kosovo had become a threat to their safety and their republic's equality within the federation; centralization and a strengthening of the party were the answers. For the Slovenes and the Croats, Kosovo had become a human-rights issue; and, for a growing minority within these two republics, Kosovo was becoming the proof that only the rule of law, political pluralism and free and open elections, could ever solve Yugoslavia's problems. Macedonia and Bosnia–Hercegovina were keeping a lower profile, though the former leaned toward Serbia and the latter toward Croatia.

Following a second miner's strike in March 1989 when twenty-four Albanians were killed, a relative calm lasting some five months spread over the country. Kosovo remained under martial law, Azem Vlasi and fourteen other 'organizers' of the November strikes remained in prison, and the Kosovo problem continued to defy any solution based on repression. Even in that relative calm however,

---

94. *Borba*, 24 August 1989, p. 3; *Vjesnik*, 23, 26 and 29 August 1989; and *Danas*, 5 September 1989.

incidents of nationalism continued to proliferate. The 600th anniversary of the Serbian defeat by the Turks at Kosovo Polje (on the outskirts of Priština) drew hundreds of thousands of Serbs to Kosovo and to Knin in Croatia for celebrations. The accompanying Serbian nationalist songs, chauvinist slogans and pictures of Milošević left no doubt about the link in these 'pilgrims'' minds between the glories of their nation's past and the embodiment of their hope for its revival.

Instances of individual harassment or even of physical attack because of one's ethnic identification abounded. There were daily reports of brawls between youths at dances or in taverns, tyre-slashing, rock-throwing, and name-calling, most frequently in areas of mixed populations and especially in resort towns, typically involving Serbs or Montenegrins with Croatians or Slovenians.[95]

More frightening than the nationalistically motivated random acts of violence and harassment, were their results on the pysche of the average citizen. A feeling of incomprehension and fear of the 'other' was creeping into daily life which was to increase during the autumn and winter of 1989–90. Evidence of this was the fact and the frequency with which discussion of inter-nationality relations became the topic of conversation. Even one's travel plans became subject to questioning by family and friends who sometimes 'softened' the questioning by joking over what could happen to one in the 'foreign lands' outside of one's republic.

The second topic which continued to preoccupy the public was the state of the economy. Throughout the spring and summer of 1989 the government of Ante Marković was occupied with keeping the ethnic–national fires from spreading. There was neither the time nor the energy, and least of all was there a consensus, for the reforms necessary to marketize the economy. Not surprisingly, the economy continued its downward spiral adding more fuel to nationalist suspicions.

The long-expected 'hot autumn' (*vruća jesen*) of 1989 arrived with Slovenia's amendments to its constitution, granting the local parliament ultimate sovereignty over its territory, including the

95. An extreme example of the above and one which became another minor near-crisis in a year of crises, was the beating by a Belgrade policeman of Boris Muževič, one of Slovenia's representatives to the Presidency of the CC of the LCY for jumping a red light. See among others, *Vjesnik* and *Borba* from 27 September 1989 to mid-October 1989.

right to secession. Amendment LXII embodied the essence of the six controversial amendments:[96]

> If the federal organs adopt a decision contrary to their constitutionally specified authority and thus encroach on the constitutional position and rights of the Socialist Republic (SR) of Slovenia, the Parliament of the SR of Slovenia is duty bound to pass measures to ensure the protection of the constitutionally defined position and right of the SR of Slovenia.

The amendments gave rise to a virulent debate throughout Yugoslavia, especially in Serbia where they were seen as another instance of Slovenia's selfishness, and proof of its covert plan to separate from the rest of Yugoslavia.[97] That the Slovenian Constitutional amendments created such an uproar is understandable in view of the fact that they raised the question of the nature of the Yugoslav federation. The question was an old one, which predated the formation of the first Yugoslavia in 1918 and remained on the agenda throughout the inter-war period.

To the dilemma of creating a nation-state composed of disparate ethnic–national groups, carrying historical animosities compounded by differentially developed economies, the 'north' (Croatia and Slovenia, and in the post-war period Vojvodina) and the 'south' tended to favour different solutions. The most explosive post-war examples of the different concepts of the nature of the Yugoslav federation were the Croatian 'spring' of 1971 and the Kosovo uprising which began in March 1981 and has continued into the 1990s. In both of these cases, national aspirations were joined to the self-interest of a large segment of the party *aparat* leading to an attempt to increase republican or regional autonomy.

In the case of Slovenia where the Constitutional amendments of September 1989 raised this issue, defence of the republic's autonomy was a result of a genuine grass-roots push for democracy which first began in spring 1988.[98] The arrest of Janša, Tasić, Borštner and Zavrl on charges of military espionage provoked widespread protests in Slovenia. A Committee for the Defence of Human Rights was formed, petitions were signed and demonstrations

---

96. *Amandmani dele Jugoslaviju* (Amendments are Dividing Yugoslavia), special edition of *Borba* (Documents), Belgrade, October 1987, p. 2 (author's translation).

97. Actually, strengthening republic sovereignty was only one of the three key areas of change in the Slovenian constitution; the other two dealt with regulating human rights and reforming the economic system. *Vjesnik*, 28 September 1989.

98. *Nedeljna Borba*, 4–5 November 1989, p. 11.

on their behalf took place. The military trial (conducted in Serbo-Croatian) and the resulting conviction of the four, outraged the Slovenians and led to a critical re-examination of the political system. The staged trial and conviction, which had been meant as a warning to the liberal elements in Slovenia, and especially to the irreverent magazine *Mladina*, had the opposite effect. Issues previously articulated only by those on the margin of society took centre-stage in Slovenian public discourse, while those previously unmentionable suddenly found a new voice.

Through the summer and autumn of 1988, Slovenians debated and agonized over the possible democratization of their republic. By early November, in a series of open letters to Kučan and the Slovenian LC, liberal elements questioned the right of the party to rule and called for the abolition of the one-party system and the establishment of democracy. The Slovenian leadership's agreement to the Serbian proposed amendments of the Yugoslav Constitution, which reasserted Serbian control over Kosovo and Vojvodina, were met in Slovenia with demonstrations.

When Milošević's quest for power led to the 'political differentiation' of the party leaderships in Vojvodina, Kosovo and Montenegro, Slovenia protested. During the Kosovo miners' strike in February 1989 the Slovenian party *aparat*, intellectuals and populace united in support of the striking miners and their families. Thus, Slovenia's constitutional amendments of September 1989 were a natural extension of the process of democratization and liberalization which had been taking place in the republic, a process during which the Slovenian party had been forced to catch up with society, or risk obsolescence.

In Serbia, the Slovenian amendments provided Milošević with a needed source of evil around which to mobilize the masses, for, by November 1989, the first signs of opposition to the leadership of Milošević began to appear, when the hitherto obedient Serbian Socialist Youth Alliance declared itself in favour of a democracy based on a multi-party system. It was soon joined by Ljuba Tadić's Committee for the Defence of Freedom of Thought and Expression[99] and other groups whose membership was drawn largely from disaffected intellectuals. By the autumn of 1989 many were abandoning Milošević's camp in the face of continuing and increasing evidence of his centralist and anti-democratic stance.

99. *Delo* (Ljubljana), 13 November 1989 and *Borba*, 16 November 1989.

Milošević's vilification of Slovenia was also meant to distract from Kosovo, where an international commission which visited the province in September reported gross violation of human rights, further evidenced at the trial of Azem Vlasi and his fourteen 'co-conspirators' which began on 31 October. In the spotlight Milošević went on the offensive. The Committee of the Association for the Return of Serbs and Montenegrins to Kosovo, Milošević's front organization which had organized and led 'people's *mitings'* in Vojvodina, Kosovo and Montenegro and toppled their leaderships, now sent a letter to the Central Committee of the LC of Slovenia and alternative movements informing them of their intention of holding a 'peaceful protest *miting'* in Ljubljana on 1 December.[100]

By mid-November, there were daily polemics in the media between the Kosovo committee and individuals and organizations throughout Slovenia who were consistently saying that there was no need for a *miting*.[101] The fear of violence unleashed by an unruly mob (whose numbers according to the organizer were first to be close to a million, then were revised to 100,000 or 150,000, and by 17 November were further revised to 10,000 to 12,000) increasingly frightened the Slovenes. The prospect of a 'mission' to 'bring the truth', even if, as one of the organizers stated in a television interview, it meant 'cracking a few heads',[102] led Slovenia to declare a state of emergency, thus making all public meetings illegal. On the day of the announced meeting, Ljubljana was deserted except for some three dozen media people and a dozen protesters. Having met with total failure in his Ljubljana venture, Milošević launched an economic boycott of Slovenia. Between 1 December 1989, and 9 January 1990, it was alleged that 483 business ties were severed, although the extent to which this form of action was sustained is unclear.

While Serb–Slovenian relations had created a climate which, according to the media, was bringing the country to the brink of a civil

---

100. *Borba*, 14 November 1989.
101. *Delo*, 13 November 1989 and *Borba*, 16 November 1989.
102. Such fear may seem exaggerated when looked at from a distance. But in Yugoslavia in November 1989, it was real. After all, before the announced Ljubljana meeting, there had been the attempted destabilization of Macedonian and BiH leaderships (*Večernji List*, 11 August 1989; *Vjesnik*, 18 and 30 October 1989); also, while the Slovenian parliament was still discussing its proposed constitutional amendments, Momir Bulatović, party head of Montenegro, had stated (in front of television cameras) at a *miting* organized by the Montenegrin LC, that the Slovenians, 'shouldn't reproach us, if we (Montenegrins and Serbs) ask for arms'. *Vjesnik*, 29 September 1989.

war, preparations for republican party congresses were under way. These were to be held in December, in time for the republican parties to clarify and solidify their positions before the Fourteenth Extraordinary Party Congress, which after much debate and delay, had finally been scheduled for 20–22 January 1990. On 12 December, the Croatian LC surprised everyone by repudiating the leading role of the party, declaring itself to be in favour of multi-party elections, and choosing the liberal Ivica Račan for its party head.[103] The Slovenian LC which had broken with the 'Stalinists' two months earlier was by then generally considered a little extreme.[104] It was thus the Croatian LC, which had managed to keep out of the recent major nationalist debacles, whose repudiation of party monopoly set a new tone.

Over the following few weeks, it became clear that the challenge of democracy sweeping across East Europe had been taken up in Yugoslavia. Only Serbia remained for the time being decidedly recalcitrant. 'The most democratic elections held in Serbia thus far',[105] according to Milošević, renewed Milošević's mandate as president of the republic with 86 per cent of the popular vote – in an election which it was subsequently discovered brought a record 107 per cent of the electorate to the poll booths.

In the midst of these republican and regional party conferences, the government of Prime Minister Marković announced its long-prepared economic programme. As part of that preparation, both President Drnovšek and Prime Minister Marković had travelled to the United States to explain Yugoslavia's position to the Bush administration, to business representatives and to the IMF.[106] Closer to home, meetings were held with European Free Trade Area (EFTA) representatives and with the General Secretary of the OECD.[107] In all cases they received support. Foreign experts were also brought in, including Jeffrey Sachs, of whom *Borba* wrote: 'Famous Harvard "economic wonderkid" – doesn't consider Yugoslav economic situation tragic.'[108]

At home, consultation with working groups for economic reform as well as with business people and other interest groups continued.

103. *Vjesnik*, 12–13 December 1989.
104. *Vjesnik*, 26 October 1989.
105. *Borba*, 3 November 1989, p. 3.
106. See transcript of interview given to the US public broadcasting station PBS and reported in *Borba*, 18 October 1990.
107. *Borba*, 17 October 1990; *Borba*, 15 October 1989.
108. *Borba*, 16 November 1989.

In addition, Marković made a special effort to engage the general populace through frequent television and newspaper interviews in which he sought to explain the government position. This effort to reach out and include the population in the government economic reform programme and to make the government's actions intelligible won him a solid base of support in spite of the fact that the economic situation was creating chaos in everyday life.

With daily inflation of 1.5 per cent and price-changes occurring every two to three weeks, an incredible amount of energy was expended in shopping for articles with (two-week) 'old' prices, or standing for hours in bank queues to change dinars into foreign currency as a hedge against inflation, only to change it back to dinars in a few days and another long queue later to pay overdue bills. For those not lucky enough to have foreign-currency accounts, credit cards or bank cheques, all of which provided a few weeks of 'time' before payment, effectively cutting the merchandise cost by 50 per cent or more, the situation was much worse.[109] The psychological insecurity caused by galloping inflation and the talk of needed economic restructuring which would lead to job losses for many, were all-pervasive.

The general economic crisis was felt most strongly in the LDRs, where all the economic indicators began their downward spiral earlier and faster, all that is, except for unemployment which was increasing rapidly, and in Kosovo had reached 60 per cent by the end of the decade.

The development fund was unable to make any progress in bridging the economic disparity between the DRs and LDRs. Furthermore, its criteria for membership and basis of operation became a point of virulent controversy. Feeling the pinch of their own near zero and (later) negative growth, the DRs protested the handing over of so much of their money to the LDRs, whose development, despite the effort and financial commitment, was progressing at snail's pace. The LDRs, all but BiH, facing total bankruptcy, refused ('for the moment') to change the fund's basic parameters. In post-1974 Yugoslavia, where decision-making proceeded by consensus, they could not be forced to do so.

A compromise of sorts was reached by an agreement to decrease

---

109. Buying on credit had been made illegal earlier in the autumn. School books and other school supplies were exempted since otherwise many children would have been unable to attend school, as some workers' *monthly* salaries were barely large enough to pay for the school supplies for even one child.

the obligatory 'loan' of the DRs to the fund from 1.97 per cent of the GMP of all firms (1975–80), to 1.86 per cent for 1981–85 which was further decreased to 1.56 per cent for the period 1986–90.[110] In addition, the previously specified 20 per cent of the fund's assets for joint ventures between the DRs and LDRs was increased to 50 per cent, thus giving the DRs more say over how their money was spent, and more interest in helping the LDRs to spend it wisely.[111] The supplementary resources for infrastructure were also decreased from 0.80 per cent to 0.50 per cent of the GMP. Finally, as the (by far) least developed, Kosovo received 48.1 per cent of all funds given to the development fund for the development of the LDRs.[112]

The disbursement of scarce resources in a contracting economy will almost by definition lead to a conflict. The likelihood of conflict is increased if the participant units are composed of ethnic-national groups, coterminous with political boundaries. If vast differences in political culture and economic development also exist, creating differences in both world-view and interest, even a minimum degree of intelligibility may be jeopardized. In Yugoslavia, all of these conditions were present. As a result, both the political and economic situations were at an all-time low as the government prepared to present its economic programme to the nation.

On 18 December, at 3.00 pm, a calm and smiling Ante Marković stunned parliament and the country by announcing the linchpin of his economic reform: the convertability of the dinar, pegged to the Deutschmark, and fixed for a six-month period at US$1 to 12 (new) dinars. Other measures of the reform were a tight fiscal policy including the fixing of wages for a six-month period; liberalization of foreign investments and of private property; freeing of 85 per cent of prices, devaluation of the dinar and the refusal to bail-out failing industries.[113] After more than thirty years of tinkering with 'market socialism', Yugoslavia had taken a decisively market orien-

110. *Nedelnja Borba*, 8–9 July 1989.
111. The stipulation that 50 per cent of prescribed percentage be given to the LDRs in cash and 50 per cent (equivalent) in joint-venture investment, was increased to 60 per cent in favour of joint ventures for the 1986–90 period.
112. SZDP, *Izvještaj o trošenju sredstava fonda u SAP Kosovo u tekućem planskom periodu* (Report on the Spending of the Means of the Fund in the Autonomous Province of Kosovo in the Current Planning Period), Belgrade, July 1989, 07 br. 271/2.
113. Additionally, US$150 million was set aside for special retraining programmes in the LDRs, and another US$100 million for social security and unemployment benefits in the poorest areas; Serbia's debt of US$1 billion was also taken over by the federal government.

tation. Amid heated debate (and despite Milošević's call for a general strike) the economic programme was voted in with an impressive two-thirds majority. Marković's bold move had passed the first test; he now had six months for the second.

Search and Struggle for a New Identity; Yugoslavia in the 1990s

For Yugoslavia, the decade of the 1990s began in December 1989 when the Croatian and Slovenian League of Communists formally repudiated their party's monopoly of power and Prime Minister Marković announced his economic programme. The post-war period of communist rule ended a month later, the night of 22–23 January, when the Slovenian delegation walked out of the Fourteenth Extraordinary Party Congress.

Milošević's attempt to isolate Slovenia by forming a new quorum failed. The insistence of the Croatian LC (backed by the Macedonian) on adjournment of the Congress under threat of their own walk-out convinced the majority. While the Congress was interrupted for 'a twenty minute consultation recess', a bitter struggle took place behind the closed doors. When the Congress reconvened four hours later (around 4.00 am), the liberal elements had won. The Fourteenth Extraordinary Party Congress was adjourned for an indefinite length of time. The next day *Borba's* headlines proclaimed in bold letters: *SKJ više ne postoji* (The LCY No Longer Exists).[114]

A few hours later the morning café talk in Belgrade was rife with speculation over the meaning and consequences of the events of the past few hours. Yet it was the Prime Minister's statement, as the Congress folded, that captured the popular imagination. When asked what he thought of the Slovenian walk-out and its possible repercussions on Yugoslavia, the unflappable, smiling Marković replied: 'The government can function without the party.' Sometime during the month-and-a-half between the Croatian Party Congress of 12–14 December and the adjournment of the LCY Party Congress of 20–23 January, an era had to come to an end. A new one is still in the formative stage. Yet, so far, Marković's words have proven true. The government has continued to function without

114. *Borba*, 23 January 1990.

the party, no small feat after forty-five years of direct and indirect party rule.

On the economic front, the signs have been encouraging. The inflation rate, which for the month of December had climbed to 56 per cent, had by the end of January fallen to 17.3 per cent; by February it was down to 8.4 per cent, by March to 2.4 per cent and for April it registered only 0.2 per cent. Foreign-currency reserves which at US$5.4 billion in December were strong enough to permit the convertability of the dinar, had increased by January to US$6.5 billion and by May to US$8.5 billion. Industrial productivity has also increased and foreign loans have been secured to aid the restructuring of the economy. These good signs in no way guarantee the success of the economic programme. For the major adjustments, the restructuring of the economy by closing failing factories, and the consequent massive lay-offs, at the time of writing are still to come. Nevertheless, Marković has managed to galvanize a degree of support and energy after a decade characterized by cynicism and apathy.

He will need support as he leads a Yugoslavia much changed from when he assumed power. The dissolution of the LCY in January 1990 may have been little more than a symbol of dissolution which had been taking place for some twenty years, and had occurred *de facto* sometime during the decade of the 1980s. Nevertheless, the formal break-up further accelerated the changes, whose sometimes contradictory directions can barely be discerned.

One trend which is discernible, is that in fits and in starts, at different paces in different republics, political democratization is occurring. The leading role of the LCY has been abandoned as has its monopoly of power. Movements and groups have been legalized into opposition parties. The party spectrum ranges from old-style communist parties to right-wing nationalist ones, with most falling in the liberal to social democratic range. Since the beginning of March 1990, a group of alternative parties has met in Mostar to discuss the Kosovo situation in an attempt to find a peaceful solution. In Kosovo, martial law has been lifted, and Vlasi and his fourteen co-defendants have been freed.

April was also the month in which the first post-war free multi-party elections were held in two of Yugoslavia's eight federal units. The result in both Slovenia and Croatia was an impressive 55 per cent popular vote for the Slovenian Democratic Opposition of Slovenia (DEMOS) coalition, and an astounding 70 per cent for Franjo Tudjman's Croatian Democratic Union. This vote shows the degree of frustration felt by the Slovenes and Croats. The object of that frustration was, first of all the LCY, which was judged responsible for bringing the country to the brink of economic disaster. Second, there was fear of Serbian expansionism reawakened by Slobodan Milošević. Third, this was an anti-centralization vote.

In the continuing constitutional dispute over the reapportionment of power between the federal and republic governments, Slovenia and Croatia have shown themselves determined to keep or enhance their republic's power. For, in addition to the fear of Serbian expansionism and consequent Serbianization by the country's most numerous group, political sovereignty has specific economic repercussions.

The 27 per cent of the Yugoslav population residing in Slovenia and Croatia (who contribute more than 60 per cent of the national GMP) tend to perceive the federal government as unsympathetic and often hostile to their problems, and investments in the LDCs as motivated by local politicians' desires for aggrandisement at the cost of efficiency, solvency and development. As a result, they chose to give the electoral mandate to political parties whose platforms rest on the defence of their nation's economic interest, integrity and sovereignty. In the process, they declared themselves to be first and foremost nationalists, and if need be separatists.

Today, much like in 1948, Yugoslavia is facing a crisis of identity; and today, much like in 1948, it is at a crossroads. Having opted for a multi-party system, the question now arises of the direction that the popular mandate will take, its effect on Yugoslav stability, and even on its survival. In Yugoslavia as throughout Eastern Europe, the discrediting of communism is leading to a search for roots. A return to tradition and one's past is not an illogical first step. Nor need it surprise us that a variety of outcomes including nationalist ones are likely to follow (especially at first), as they have in Slovenia and Croatia.

There is of course the danger that nationalism could be substituted for democracy. The likelihood of this substitution occurring is increased when fear of economic exploitation is intertwined with aspirations of distinct ethnic–national groups inhabiting their own geographically and politically defined regions. It happened in Croatia in 1971, in Kosovo from 1981, in Serbia under Milošević; and it may happen in some of the republics during the initial period of multi-party democratization.

There is however one important difference between the previous cases and today. In the Yugoslav one-party system of old, increased devolution of power in the absence of legitimate competing groups quite naturally led at the republic level to an increase in power of regional and communal elites. In today's multi-party Yugoslavia, where the electorate can hold its officials responsible for any abuse of power, this is much less likely. As a result, under the old system, given the choice between 'imported' authoritarians or the 'home-grown' variety, the people may well have chosen the 'home-grown' in the hope that room for manœuverability would then be more easily increased. Today, however, when the choice is between a variety of competing programmes and leaders, authoritarian leaders who do not represent and promote the interests of their constituents, even if they do come to power, are less likely to remain.

Thus, although the April 1990 election results in Slovenia and Croatia may raise the spectre of national chauvinism which but a generation ago led to a devastating civil war, they also have a more hopeful side. After all, in both Slovenia and Croatia, multi-party elections with free and equal media access to all have been held; the communist parties of both republics have stepped down; in both, new governments have been constituted. The elections held in Slovenia and Croatia in April 1990 have been the most democratic and peaceful elections since Yugoslavia's first unification in 1918.

In terms of a political arrangement conducive to ethnic–national sovereignty, economic development and all-Yugoslav unity, a federation granting even more power to the constituent political units is not only the most likely outcome, but is also the only one that can save Yugoslavia from disintegration. To those who argue that federalism only exacerbated nationalist tensions and led to political and economic chaos in Tito's Yugoslavia, one may point out that *that* was federalism within a one-party system. Consensus-based decision-making among a non-accountable (and often irresponsible) oligarchic elite in the multi-national, differentially developed country, did not work. In a freely chosen, pluralist state, however, a dialogue between the genuine representatives of the people could well lead to a still regionally differentiated, but more democratic federal union.

PART II

Choices and Constraints

5

External Migration in the Context of the Post-War Development of Yugoslavia

Milan Mesić

Introduction

External migration from a given country is always determined in the context of its entire social, economic and political development, as well as that of the destination country. (Here I don't mean individual and occasional migration, but rather migration as major social phenomenon.) In migration studies (as for social studies in general) post-war Yugoslavia is an extremely interesting case, since it is the only socialist country which has been drawn into and become a constituent part of European labour-migration flows.

External migration flows from Yugoslavia cannot be understood unless we keep in view the integral development of the self-management system, which was at first gradual, but after the 1965 reform amounted to a radical transformation of the socialist model of industrialization. To some extent the reverse could also be said: one cannot fully understand Yugoslav post-war social development unless the manifold effects of external migration are included in the analysis.

In this chapter, I shall distinguish three different migration situations corresponding to the three phases of the post-war social development of Yugoslavia. Looked at from another point of view, these are analogous to changes in the migration strategies of the industrially developed receiving countries. This second, *key* determinant of Yugoslav external migration – European and other world capital accumulation centres and their requirements for a 'reserve (migrant) labour army' – will be treated only in passing. First, I shall concentrate on some basic directions of the internal development of Yugoslav society in connection with external migration.

171

Milan Mesić

Phase I: Migration as an Escape from a Closed Society: Exit (from Socialism) Forbidden; Entry (into Capitalism) Freely Encouraged

It is essential to keep in mind that Yugoslav communists began the revolution with a negative political attitude towards external migration, and this was one of the constitutive moments of the strategy of post-war social development.[1] This attitude had its own implicit class-ideological dimension – in a worker's country working people have the right to work and have no need to migrate. At this very point the Yugoslav social model approached the Soviet system, even after the break with the Cominform. At the same time, it had its national aspect – emigration is harmful, even shameful for the country and nation – and only an anti-national regime can stimulate and tolerate it. In precisely this lies a paradoxical similarity with some right-wing ideologies and practices in relation to external migration.

One of the direct consequences of the national-liberation war and socialist revolution in Yugoslavia during the Second World War was political emigration. It has been estimated that about 300,000 people fled from the country at the end of the war.[2] For the most part they were members of defeated armed and political forces linked with the fascist occupiers and the puppet pro-fascist regimes which had been set up in some parts of the country. They were joined by pro-West-oriented groups which did not accept fascism, but could not reconcile themselves to the new communist order. These people (among whom were also war criminals) spread all over the world from refugee camps, and many of them have become active adversaries of socialist Yugoslavia. This was the first migration experience of the country, and it has remained a negatively loaded political issue.

1. Yugoslav communists of that time reduced all the problems of social development to the problems of capitalism in itself, believing that the developmental problems of society could be solved (simply) (according to the Soviet pattern) by the mere removal of the capitalists. The semi-colonial position of pre-war Yugoslavia was defined by the following characteristics: the impact of foreign capital; a poor peasantry; a working class deprived of rights; national inequality and, finally, external migration – all these were consequences of the capitalist socio-economic system. Outflows from the Yugoslav countries before the establishment of a unified state could be explained in part by foreign rule and indifference towards the Yugoslav nations. There was, certainly, some truth in this, but the problem was not exhausted by this explanation, as the external-migration experience of socialist Yugoslavia has proved.
2. Dušan Bilandžić, *Historija SFRJ, Glavni procesi* (A History of the SFRY) (Zagreb, Školska knjiga, 1978), p. 99.

Post-war repatriation of the numerous German national minority (*Volksdeutsche*) from Vojvodina and Slovenia can also be considered as political emigration, although of a different character. There are no data published about it; yet it is widely known that about a half a million Germans lived in Yugoslavia before the war, while later censuses indicated the Germans only as an insignificant minority. Consequently, one can easily imagine the proportions of this exodus, which could hardly have passed without conflicts and human dramas.[3]

The so-called 'optants' also fall under the heading of political migration. Namely, a large part of the population (about 300,000) from territory formerly under Italian government, having been returned to their mother country on the basis of free choice, opted for departure to Italy. Somewhat later (1956–60) another national minority would emigrate on a massive scale to its native country. They were the Turks from Kosovo.

Additionally, all those who left the country illegally, for various reasons (since legal emigration was exceptional) until the beginning of the 1960s, are included in the category of political migrants. Because of the difficulties of making a livelihood it is quite possible that a large number of these migrants were motivated by economic reasons in the first place, although the West (at least at the beginning) was opening its doors partly for reasons of political propaganda. Nevertheless, they were all regarded as deserters in a negative political sense.

If one speaks about *purely* economic emigration, there was practically no external migration from Yugoslavia until the mid-1960s; or rather, it was negligible. Yet in the period between 1953 and 1960 the total number of emigrants ranged annually from 13,000 to 57,000. The emigration wave was extremely strong between 1955 and 1958, when annual emigration flows ranged from 40,000 to 57,000. In the next two years there were about 20,000 emigrants; while after 1960 stabilization at a relatively lower level of about 1,000 took place for a certain period of time. At the same time, on average about 1,000 per annum were *returning* to the country. According to official statistical data, the country's total external net-migration during the decade amounted to 277,675 persons.

3. In 1948, 55,000 people declared themselves as Germans. See Fred Singleton, *Twentieth Century Yugoslavia*, (New York, Columbia University Press, 1976), pp. 218–19.

However, the estimated figure for the inter-census period was over 500,000 people. This number may be somewhat exaggerated, and at the same time, the statistical data are probably neither very accurate nor reliable.[4]

A few words are in order about the socio-economic basis on which Yugoslavia's 'closed society', rested in this first phase. Even before the end of the war the initial prerequisites for a socio-economic system modelled after the Soviet pattern were created in Yugoslavia. On the one hand, they included the new structure of political power which had grown with the national-liberation struggle and socialist revolution; on the other hand, they included the material basis for such a revolution. In the liberated territories the partisan authorities carried out revolutionary economic measures such as confiscation, dispossession of war profits, sequestration and the like, which affected a large number of entrepreneurs and rentiers accused of collaboration with the occupiers. In such a manner the new state acquired possession of more than 80 per cent of the industry (primarily heavy industry) and of almost all the banks, traffic, foreign trade and wholesale trade. Capitalist ownership of the means of production was essentially limited in agriculture by the law on agricultural reform by which the landowners were deprived of land in excess of 30 hectares, while the second reform reduced this limit even more, to merely 10 hectares. By the end of 1946 this nationalization was given formal and legal support by the first Constitution, and thus the state's economic monopoly was definitely established.

All this was intended to achieve a faster industrialization. The party–state leaders wanted the country to leave behind its semi-colonial position as a backward exporter of agrarian products and raw material. Filled with enthusiasm by military and political victory in the war, and deeply convinced of their being on the right track of modern historical development as affirmed by the teachings of Marxism–Leninism–Stalinism and the Soviet experience of 'building socialism', they believed that Yugoslavia could catch up with the industrial countries by means of several five-year plans. But both nationalization and industrialization had a 'higher goal' – the establishment of a socialist society. Their objective was to create a

4. Vladimir Grečic, *Savremene Migracije Radne Snage u Evropi* (Contemporary Migration of the Labour Force in Europe) (Belgrade, Institut za Medjunarodnu Politiku i Privredu, 1975), p. 196.

prosperous economy and a modern industrial working class as the dominant category of social structure.

In accord with the Soviet model the First Five-Year Plan (issued in 1947) was primarily directed towards the building of 'heavy' basic industry, the 'production of means of production' (Marx) as the basis for the total development of the economy. The plan was incredibly ambitious: it predicted a fivefold increase in gross industrial output, a fourfold increase in electric power, etc. Leaving aside the question of the fundamental rationality of the plan,[5] which was redefined because of the economic blockade by the East European countries after Yugoslavia's conflict with the Cominform, it should be emphasized that it relied on drawing the peasant masses into industry. Efforts were made to replace the lack of capital, equipment and skill by the mobilization of an abundant stock of labour from the villages. Thus the peasant question was to have been *definitely solved* by the socialist transformation of society.

Even such a powerful state, however, having in its hands almost complete control, not only of nationalized industry but also of private agricultural production (by means of obligatory sales at fixed prices), had great difficulty at the beginning in moving the peasants from the private to the social sector, and from the village to the town. Because of overall poverty, the village offered a better living standard for a certain period of time. Furthermore, the peasants did not accept the socialist project of nationalization and collectivization, but only the agrarian reform and the distribution of land. Nevertheless, the traditional peasant communities and the traditional peasant way of life were shaken by the national liberation war and the revolution, which was soon to shape the initial internal migration flows in two aspects. First, by means of the spatial transfer of peasants from the poor highlands to rich lowlands (especially to the land of the displaced German national minority in Vojvodina). Second, by means of the village–town migration (which was, later on, to assume a character of inter-regional movement from the poorer south towards the richer north).

In order to stimulate a sufficient influx from the village (as well as to satisfy the regime's doctrinal–ideological suspicion of small

---

5. There are various opinions concerning this matter. Compare: D. Rusinow, *The Yugoslav Experiment 1948–1974*, (Berkeley, Calif. University of California Press, 1978), p. 20; L. Sirc, *The Yugoslav Economy under Self-Management* (New York, St Martin's Press, 1979), pp. 2–4; I. F. Hamilton, *Yugoslavia: Patterns of Economic Activity* (London, 1968).

private producers who 'bring forth capitalist tendencies everyday, every moment') the state gave various privileges to those employed in the state-owned sector and their families. This was the reason why state employment very soon came to hold out the ideal of an easier way of life for peasants, and proved very attractive, especially for peasant youth. Having built up a certain momentum, this social and cultural aspect of the exodus from the village (the other side of the industrialization process) became a self-supporting process which began to put pressure on further extensive employment. Those who had taken an active part in the national-liberation war moved first and most easily; while under their influence (even pressure) their relatives, friends and others did the same.

The numerous army and state apparatus for control over the economy and society was recruited from their ranks. A good deal of the enormous increase in employment in the early post-war years could be ascribed to the establishment of this extensive state apparatus for control over the economy and society. In 1945 there were 461,000 employed workers; in 1946, 721,000; 1947, 1,167,000; 1948, 1,517,000 and in 1949, 1,990,000. From 1945 to 1961, then, about 160,000 people per annum, on average, moved from the sector of private agricultural production and handicraft to the 'socialized sector' (as the nationalized economy was defined after introduction of self-management), including industry, administration, service trades and others. If we want to make comparisons, it might be noted that the increase in the number of people employed annually at that time was almost the same as in the whole inter-war period 1919–39. In this way the entire population increase plus 30,000 of the rural surplus was absorbed annually. This meant that the channels for social advancement were wide open, particularly for the rural population masses, although jumps to the highest hierarchic positions ceased to be possible any more, as they had been immediately after the war. Unemployment was marginal, and regarded as only a temporary occurrence and not a structural one.

In the light of these facts, a significantly strong economic motive for external migration could hardly have existed. To this should be added the dominant ideology that external migration was not acceptable in a socialist (self-managing) system. Furthermore, the still-living memories of the horrors of war meant that going away to work, especially to Germany, was treated as a national treachery. Nevertheless, the development of self-management, followed by the liberalization of commodity production (the introduction of elements of a market), de-etatization and the democratization of public life together with changes in the international position of Yugoslavia, were gradually rendering anachronistic the model of a 'closed society'. The point is, that these previous changes in the social structure and in the value system should be taken into account in order to understand how socialist Yugoslavia came to be included in mass European migration flows 'all of a sudden'.

Phase II: Migration as a Two-Way Road: Exit (from the homeland) Free; Entry (into a host country) Welcomed

During the early 1960s the strategy of extensive industrialization exhausted its development potential, and after a decade of remarkable growth the economy experienced a slowdown. Economic reform was the order of the day.

Other Southern European countries, with different socio-political systems, found themselves faced with similar problems at the same time: 'Because of the lower productivity development implicit in policies of extensive industrialization, internal and external, economic *disequilibria* arose which could be cured only by the adoption of a new strategy of intensive industrialization.'[6]

The necessary inclusion of the Yugoslav economy in the international division of labour required a competitive economy with high labour productivity; and this could not be achieved without an intensification of production, without a more rational use of economic factors in order to ease the path to accelerated internal economic growth: 'but at the same time the rapid growth of productivity opened a pronounced gap between production in industry and the absorption of the work force in this sector'.[7]

The simultaneous development of self-management, which was initially introduced as early as 1950 on the micro-level of the enterprise, came into increasing conflict with the prevailing state-run system. In the ongoing controversies about the further development of self-management the opinion which took hold with the leadership was that the self-managed enterprises should act autonomously (from the state) in the market. The market was now seen as

6. Heiko Korner, 'The Experience in the Main Geographical OECD Areas, European Sending Countries', in *The Future of Migration* (Paris, OECD, 1987), p. 71.
7. Ibid.

a prerequisite, as a necessary though controversial environment, for self-management to expand.

The new system of development was articulated in legal terms by the great economic and social reforms of 1965, defined by Western scholars as 'market socialism'. As the state no longer guaranteed the entire salary fund to work collectives, they became interested in creating as large an income as possible from as little labour as possible, in order to be able to pay larger salaries. The enterprises, given the right to dispose freely of the income earned in the market (after paying certain taxes), became interested in economizing on labour and investing in new technology. Thus intensive industrialization of the economy and the economic liberalization of the global socio-economic system resulted in a decrease of the employment rate, and even reduced the level of employment in the public sector in the first and most radical years of the reform. (This suggested underemployment under the previous, labour intensive model of development.) Tens of thousands of workers lost their jobs, and thus 'a floating industrial reserve army' appeared. This happened just when the first post-war 'baby-boom' generation finished its schooling and began looking for work, and while the villages still retained a 'relative industrial reserve army'.

Under the pressure of increasing unemployment (and other forms of social differentiation) the attitude began to prevail in the Yugoslav political leadership that the departure for temporary work abroad is a democratic right of citizens, as well as a social necessity in the years of restructuring the economy. It is, however, hard to speak about a pronounced Yugoslav emigration 'policy' at the end of the 1960s. Because of ideological considerations which represented socialism as a society of universal equality and full employment, political structures were neither willing to initiate public discussion about the problem of external migration, nor to take an open political attitude towards it. Nevertheless, the negative rigid posture towards external migration started to evolve into a tacit acceptance and tolerance of migrants looking for jobs abroad at the beginning of the 1960s. In 1962, along with political refugees, there was a legal amnesty even on those who went abroad illegally seeking employment.

During the following years the legislation relating to working migrants was expanded. First, an 'Instruction on the Procedure for Employment Abroad' was issued in 1963 by the Federal Secretariat for Labour. This introduced a term which became a constant blueprint for Yugoslav migration policy: 'worker temporarily employed abroad'. This means that a migrant is a Yugoslav citizen, and as such is still subject to its rules and regulations. In addition, the instruction initiated closer links between the Yugoslav diplomatic representatives abroad and migrants, broadening the traditional tasks of the workload of diplomats. It placed some restrictions on those who could leave to seek employment abroad (although in practice these restrictions did not prove effective). Those temporarily unemployed were given priority in going abroad; while employed workers had to be given permission by their work organizations. Skilled workers were particularly discouraged from migrating.

A few years later, when external migration reached a more massive scale and became harder to control, restrictions on the departure of skilled workers were cancelled, in spite of trade-union opposition; but new procedures designed to subject migration flows to social control were introduced. Instead of an unorganized search for employment by workers on their own, the government services on three levels (federal, republican and local) now began to arrange for the employment of migrants by placing them in contact with foreign firms and employment bureaus. (Even so, potential migrants were not bound to accept these official offers, and quite a few in fact did not.) In short, by 1966 employment abroad became legally a 'normal' form of employment, and was even encouraged.

The increased social contradictions of 'market socialism' in the second half of the 1960s, manifest most obviously in the form of intensified social inequalities, still evoked strongly egalitarian values among the general public. Discontents and social tensions rose to a crescendo in the students' demonstrations of 1968 in the large university centres: Belgrade, Zagreb and Ljubljana. In a letter addressed to President Tito, on 4 June 1968, the students of the Red University of Karl Marx (as Belgrade University was called) pointed out:

We do not fight for our own material interests. We are embittered by great social and economic differences in our society. We are against the fact that only the working class should bear the burden of economic reform. We support social self-management from the bottom to the top, but it can't be realized unless self-managing and representative bodies consist of representatives of the direct, self-managing workers. We are against those individuals who are getting more and more rich on the account of working class. We are for social property, and against the attempt to establish capitalist joint-stock companies. *We are badly hurt by the thousands of workers who are obliged to go away in order to serve and work for world capital.*[8]

The students, however, didn't manage to move the workers to mass political action (as, for example, in France or Italy), although a large number of workers undoubtedly shared the students' dissatisfaction with their social position, as well as their negative sentiments towards market 'injustices'.

At least a partial explanation for this inaction can be looked for in external migration itself. After a standstill, caused by the short recession of 1967, the strongest wave of external labour migration from Yugoslavia started in 1968, reaching its highest point in the period 1970–71. According to official statistical records (which probably have not registered a segment of the migrant stock), in that year, 57,238 Yugoslavs left the country for 'temporary work' abroad, and the number of those leaving in the course of the next three years is as follows: in 1969, 123,639; 1970, 239,779; 1971, 116,724. By 1971, over a million Yugoslav migrants, for the most part economically active young men (in fact the most agile part of the working class) found themselves on the West European labour markets and many others were ready to follow in their footsteps. For those who had already left, and for those who were about to leave, migration offered a solution to their existential problems by resort to an *individual*, directly *private* action outside of the existing self-management system and independent of the class (collective activity) to which they objectively belonged. Thus, freedom to leave the country, along with the possibility of entering foreign labour markets at that historical moment acted as a neutralizer of the pressure of unemployment, as well as of broader social tensions.

The indisputable fact is that the Reform sharpened the problem of unemployment; and it is obvious that unemployment would have been considerably more severe if there had been no massive external labour migration. In fact unemployment seems to have been the main motive for migration. Several questionnaire-based studies (sometimes, admittedly, of a dubious representativeness) have shown that in the interval from 1967 to 1971 every fourth or even

8. The same sentiments were repeated at several student meetings, e.g. by the students of the Faculty of Law on 5 June 1968. *Praxis*, June 1968, Documents, pp. 161–2.

every third migrant gave unemployment as the reason for departure to work abroad. By comparison, in a research project undertaken in 1971 respondents were asked if they were employed before going away, to which 77 per cent of them answered affirmatively. The highest percentage of migrants examined in these questionnaires (somewhat less than two-thirds of the responses) pointed to 'higher wages' as the key motive for their decision to migrate.[9] This contributes to the thesis that many of the migrants saw in migration not only the possibility of solving their existential problems, but a chance for escape from the working class as well. Consequently, they did not adopt a strategy of political activity, but rather the path of obedient service to capitalist employers, self-denial and above all, *saving*. Higher earnings, along with saving, gave an opportunity for a better standard of living, for a solution of essential existential problems, such as housing, but also raised expectations that people might take charge of their own economic destiny. (The more so because many migrants owned a bit of land.) Other reasons for migration have also been mentioned, such as agricultural over-population, housing problems and others; but they exclude the previous ones.

As has been mentioned in the introduction, Yugoslav external migration is a special case because of the country's socialist character, although, naturally, it cannot be understood exclusively from the perspective of the internal post-war development of Yugoslav society and its system. It is a segment of broader migration processes, especially on a European scale. As Yugoslavia came to be included in international migration flows, with the opening up of Yugoslavia's borders (as well as those of the receiving countries) the impression was created that individual potential migrants autonomously evaluate the possible positive and negative sides of 'temporary work' in some more developed country, and that they make *their own private* decisions. They had the right to leave their homeland in search of work; while the countries which offered relatively better-paid jobs kept their doors wide open. With regard to the migrant masses the only question was, who would migrate and on what conditions, since freedom to remain in the country of origin, in more or less favourable circumstances, was open to everyone. At this level, the migration phenomenon was strikingly expressed by the *push–pull* theory which became popular in Yugoslavia at that

9. Grečić, *Savremene Migracije*, pp. 207–11; 213–16.

time.[10] Inventories were created of *push* factors – the reasons, from economic to cultural, forcing potential migrants to (temporarily) leave their country, and of *pull* factors – the siren calls of the richer labour-importing societies.

What actually enables and moves migrant masses from one side of continents to the other (and between continents) at a given historical moment, however, surpasses the scheme of push–pull factors. As soon as the West European borders were practically closed 'overnight' to new migrants, this theory was of little further assistance. The theory developed by Castles serves us better. He found that contemporary European migration, in spite of the particularities in some countries, and different initial forms (e.g. Great Britain and West Germany), was primarily labour migration induced by a certain level of development of the world capitalist system. There are two key theoretical concepts which explain this. These are Marx's notion of the 'industrial reserve army' within the framework of the accumulation theory, and the thesis of Samir Amin of the unequal development within capitalism of two separated but mutually conditioned types of socio-economic formation: 'capitalism of the centre' and 'capitalism of the periphery'. The *underdevelopment* of *peripheral* countries, according to this theory, is not only a remnant of the past, but is also the consequence of a subordinate role played by suppliers of labour, and of certain kinds of both goods and markets, for the industrial production of the *centre*. The work of migrants is a form of this 'hidden transfer of value from the periphery to the centre, since the periphery has borne the cost of education and training this labour power'.[11]

The import of the migrant labour force for the industrially developed countries in market conditions had (particularly in the short term) several advantages. 'Finished' workers arrived on the labour market, whose price of social reproduction had been borne by their countries of origin. Due to the noticeably higher wages than they were able to get in their home countries, migrants were ready to do the most difficult and the most dangerous jobs, under more unfavourable conditions than indigenous workers. And last, but not least, it was expected that in the case of recession or crisis, these guest workers, mobile and inadequately protected with tem-

10. Silva Mežnarić, 'Sociology of Migration in Yugoslavia', in *Migration in Europe*, part 1, *Current Sociology*, Vol. 32, No. 2, 1984, p. 50.
11. Stephen Castles, *Here for Good* (London, Pluto Press, 1984), pp. 2–3.

porary working and residence permits, were the first to be dismissed and sent back to their countries of origin, thus transferring to them the social costs of unemployment. Yugoslav migrants, in addition, being comparatively more educated and more qualified than the Portuguese, Spanish, Greek and Turkish ones, fitted perfectly into the Gastarbeiter migration strategy.[12] At the same time, Yugoslav migration policy received an ideological (socialist) justification on the basis of two assumptions: that it was a question of temporary work and residence abroad, and that migrants formed an integral component of the Yugoslav working class. Their position in the countries of work as well as their return was not merely their own private affair, but the concern of the whole socialist community – and precisely in this, it was believed, lay the specific (socialist) character of Yugoslav external migration.

Social concern about migrants showed itself in various forms. First, employment bureaus at federal, republic and local levels were given the right and the duty to organize the departure of Yugoslav migrants, to make contact with foreign employers, to make bilateral agreements and collective contracts, and to organize vocational training programmes.[13] Employment contracts were signed with France (1965), Austria and Sweden (1966), West Germany (1969), Belgium, the Netherlands, Luxembourg and Australia (1970). Social security conventions which had already previously been concluded with France, Belgium and Luxembourg (1954) and Switzerland (1964) received a new significance, while new ones were signed with West Germany (1969) and Norway (1974).

Second, Diplomatic–Consular representatives, besides undertaking standard consular functions, were also given new tasks: to concern themselves with the protection of Yugoslav migrants' interests and especially the application of inter-state agreements; to inform migrants of their rights and obligations, and to help them to organize clubs and associations. In a word, they were expected to serve as a permanent bridge between migrants and their native country. Due to these obligations, the consular network abroad was enlarged (between 1969 and 1975, seventeen new consulates were opened). Diplomats were joined by social workers dealing with growing social problems, as well as by teachers in Yugoslav supplementary

12. Ibid., p. 134.
13. The amendment of the law on the Organization and Financing of Employment, *Službeni List*, No. 47, 1966. 'Right and duty' is one of the peculiarities of the Yugoslav legal system.

schools and departments. These contributed to the preservation of national and cultural identity, and prevented assimilation by teaching migrant children their mother tongue and culture.[14]

Third, in accordance with the self-management system, migrants were encouraged towards 'social-organization' through clubs and associations.[15] This self-organization, as in Yugoslavia itself, took place mainly under the patronage of state–political structures (in this case consulates).

Fourth, a network of institutions for the social care of migrants was built up at all levels. Besides employment bureaus, other government agencies and/or services were included in this network, particularly those in communes, in self-managed communities of interest for employment, and in self-managing institutions and 'socio-political organizations' (as the League of Communists, the trade unions, the Socialist Alliance of Working People are called in Yugoslav terminology). Trade unions had priority in political activity since they had been the first to deal with migration problems by criticizing the government's migration policy.[16] A highly developed institutional network was expanded by the Socialist Alliance, which in the Yugoslav political system is conceived of as a 'front-line political organization', whose collective members are other political organizations, including the League of Communists. Hence 'coordinating committees for activities towards Yugoslav citizens on temporary work and residence abroad' were created under the wing

14. Educational and personal development activities in the mother tongue for Yugoslav children and youth abroad has been undertaken in an organized manner since 1970. It applies to all ages, although with unequal coverage of population and diverse degrees of success. There are limited facilities for pre-school children in the labour-importing countries, while curriculums for elementary school pupils are based on the regulations of those countries; thus the inclusion of this group was considerably greater. Some receiving countries offer organizational, professional and material help, naturally serving (also) their own interests in this. Out of about 1,100 permanent and part-time teachers in Yugoslav supplementary schools, one half are in a contractual relation with the Yugoslav authorities, and the other half with the authorities of the receiving country.

15. Since the beginning of the 1970s, more than 1,000 clubs, associations, communities, coordination committees, unions and other forms of 'self-organization' of Yugoslav citizens abroad have been founded. A significant role in the organization of spare time and the preservation of the cultural identity of Yugoslav migration communities has been attributed to them. The inadequacy of these institutions and their programmes, however, especially for the so-called second generation, women and intellectuals, is being criticized more often nowadays, both in the countries concerned as well as in Yugoslavia, and their modernization is being demanded.

16. In 1986, a Commission of the Central Council of the Trade Unions on Questions of Employment Abroad was established. The Sixth Congress of Yugoslav Trade Unions, held in 1968, was the first federal political body to discuss publicly external migration as a *problem. Sindikati*, Vol. 9, No. 2, 1968, p. 181.

of the federal and republic conferences of the Socialist Alliance. Their task was to coordinate the manifold social and political activities concerning migrants (a task which is hard to achieve in conditions of radical decentralization and of the unequal level of organization and effectiveness of 'political infra-structure' in some republics and provinces). Finally, there was revision of the legal regulations relating to migration.

Yugoslavia is a multi-national community with immense inherited differences in the level of development of some parts of the country. The historical boundary between the former Austro-Hungarian countries and the Turkish Empire has remained a line of division between the relatively developed Yugoslav north and the backward south. Therefore, the opening of borders and inclusion in the international division of labour, and consequently in the international labour market, have *unequally* (particularly in the beginning) impinged upon certain republics and provinces, and various sub-regions within them. Contemporary migration was also influenced by migration traditions dating back to the turn of the century and the inter-war period.

As may have been expected, the north-western parts of the country were the first to be grasped by mass external labour migration, as much because of their proximity to the main migration destinations as their historical connections and their earlier inclusion in the international division of labour. Disproportionately high shares of the migration stock in the 1960s were drawn from Croatia, both as a republic and as a nation, so that migration at that time can be said to have been primarily a Croatian phenomenon.

Data about outflows by years (see Table 5.1) show that the contribution of Croatia to total Yugoslav migrant stocks in the 1960s ranged from 56 per cent (1960, 1962) to 36 per cent (1965), after which it increased till 1968. Moreover, one must bear in mind that among the migrants from Bosnia and Hercegovina, Croats were over-represented. Citizens on 'temporary work' were included for the first time in the 1971 census, when 671,908 workers (or 763,000 Yugoslav workers and their family members) were registered.[17] Croatia was practically affected by massive labour migration far more since it had proportionately the oldest population (after Slovenia) and a low birth-rate (after 1971 the lowest in

17. Most of the researchers consider that the census results must be corrected by a certain increase. A statistical expert, Ivo Vinski, has estimated that there was an under-recording in the census of 5 per cent. *Vjesnik*, 23 November, 1972.

Table 5.1 Percentage of Yugoslav Workers Abroad, 1960–70 (by Republic)

Republic	1960	1961	1962	1963	1964	1965	1966	1967	1968	1969	1970
Numbers of Yugoslav Workers Abroad	15,342	4,288	8,131	8,682	10,204	20,373	25,855	26,920	57,238	123,639	239,779
Bosnia–Hercegovina	8.6	15.2	14.7	16.2	17.5	14.6	13.3	14.9	16.7	19.1	21.6
Croatia	56.0	51.2	56.0	50.6	39.2	36.3	39.9	40.2	42.4	37.8	28.7
Macedonia	7.8	5.9	4.8	4.6	6.4	7.2	6.8	8.2	6.9	7.3	9.1
Montenegro	0.8	0.4	0.6	0.6	0.5	0.7	0.7	1.0	1.5	1.5	1.3
Slovenia	16.2	15.6	11.7	9.6	12.2	13.2	12.7	10.0	9.4	7.2	5.1
SR Serbia											
Serbia proper	7.1	8.5	8.4	13.3	17.6	19.3	17.4	16.8	12.7	13.5	19.5
Kosovo	0.4	0.3	0.3	0.3	0.3	0.6	0.5	0.6	1.5	2.9	4.7
Vojvodina	3.1	2.9	3.5	4.8	6.3	8.1	8.7	8.2	8.9	10.7	10.0

Source: Savezni zavod za statistiku, 'Lica Na Privremenon Radu u Inostrantvu', *Statistički Bilten*, No. 679, 1971, p. 9.

Yugoslavia). Therefore it is not surprising that external migration became one of the key questions on which Croatian nationalism rested.

The large emigration of Croatian workers to Western Europe, which had formerly been construed as an economic opportunity was suddenly viewed as a Serbian plot to move able-bodied Croats out of their homeland. An official source recorded that 9.6% of the Croatian labour force was employed abroad in 1971 – the highest proportion of all the federal units, and significantly higher than the Yugoslav average of 6.6%. Bosnia was a close second with 9.2% of its labour force employed as Gastarbeiter; but Serbia and Slovenia were far behind with rates of 3.7% and 5.4% respectively.[18]

At the beginning of the 1970s, however, the regional pattern of external migration began to change, pulling in more and more strongly the south-eastern parts of the country and decreasing the proportion from the north-west. This trend would 'naturally' have been continued if there had been no closing of the West European borders.[19] The 1981 census data reflect this shift, for the most part occurring after 1974. The number of Croatian migrants decreased by 73,000. At the same time, despite the decline of the total Yugoslav migration population by 46,000, there were about 50,000 more persons from Serbia proper abroad in 1981 than there had been in 1971 (see Table 5.2).

It has been said that the concept of open borders for migrants emerged as a by-product of the reform strategy of intensive industrialization and market socialism. External migration is regarded as a temporary safety-valve for the unemployed. This implied a simple-minded view of the Yugoslav 'labour-market'. (The self-management system did not acknowledge a labour market, because work collectives in enterprises were constitutionally defined as collective contractors.) Emigration was assumed to regulate emigration of the unemployed, in the first place, and then of the underemployed and those underactive at the village level. In fact, however, the considerably higher wages available in Western Europe moved first the

18. Pedro Ramet, *Nationalism and Federalism in Yugoslavia 1963–1983* (Bloomington, Ind., Indiana University Press, 1984), p. 110.
19. The most recent illegal emigration flows exemplify this. Among some 20,000 asylum seekers from Yugoslavia in West Germany in 1988, according to German sources (for the most part clandestine labour migrants), Romanians from southern Serbia and Albanians from Kosovo constituted the greater part. In the same way, the majority of unrecorded migrants in Italy came from the south-eastern parts of the country.

Table 5.2 Percentage of Yugoslav Workers Abroad, 1971–81 (by Republic)

Republic	1971		1981	
	% of Total Yugoslav Population	% of Workers Abroad	% of Total Yugoslav Population	% of Workers Abroad
Bosnia–Hercegovina	18.3	20.4	18.4	21.4
Croatia	21.6	33.4	20.5	24.3
Macedonia	8.0	8.1	8.5	9.3
Montenegro	2.6	1.2	2.6	1.6
Slovenia	8.4	7.2	8.4	6.7
SR Serbia				
Serbia proper	25.6	17.1	25.4	24.5
Kosovo	6.1	3.6	7.1	4.6
Vojvodina	9.5	9.0	9.1	7.7

Source: William Zimmerman, *Open Borders, Nonalignment, and the Political Evolution of Yugoslavia* (Princeton, NJ, Princeton University Press, 1987) pp. 84–5.

most agile parts of the labour force, including a remarkable share of those already employed, and a very large proportion of skilled and highly skilled workers, thus causing great changes in the national economy.[20]

Migration started to be considered as a special problem, and was highlighted by President Tito at the end of 1971 with his image of state security affected by the 'three big armies' situated abroad.[21] Eventually, on 5 February 1973, migration was placed on the agenda of the highest government and political bodies of the country, the presidency of the SFRJ and the presidency of the League of Communists. It was claimed that economic migration to Western Europe raised problems of national security and posed obstacles to social development. It was concluded that a comprehensive migration policy should be formulated at all levels of social organization, and that corresponding organs for the coordination and implementation of migration policy should be set up. In the discussions which followed, migration problems were reinterpreted and extended to include not only the question of the reasons for departure, but also those concerning the conditions of residence in the destination countries, problems of living, language and culture, problems of the family and children, and finally the return of migrants. From then on, return became a focal point of migration policy, not something that is taken for granted and left to the migrants themselves.

Almost at the same time, while Yugoslavia was reconceptualizing its migration policy, the first oil crisis broke, contributing to the closing of the borders of the Western European receiving countries, the reversal of their migration strategies, and accounting for the break-up of the Gastarbeiter migration model. Thus began the third migration phase.

Phase III Crisis: Exit Free; Entry Closed

The 1965 reform began with expectations that the restructuring of the economy and its inclusion into the international division of

---

20. Direct social damage can be reckoned on the basis of the price of the social reproduction and training of skilled workers. Since technicians were also leaving, observers began to speak of the 'brain drain' which has continued till the present, becoming one of the key developmental problems of the country gripped as it is by deep crisis. Analysing the 1971 census results, M. Nikolić found that employment in the country and abroad were not mutually conditioned in such a way that the decrease of migration abroad was significantly affected by greater employment in the country.

21. *Borba*, 9 December 1972.

labour would bring about – in the short term – certain social costs, such as greater social inequalities, unemployment and external migration. The forces of reform obtained their ideological justification, however, from the thesis that the further development of self-management could not be achieved without commodity production and enterprise autonomy. Workers in 'work organizations' (the definition of firms according to the 1963 Constitution) were expected to manage 'socially owned capital' as collective contractors in the place of the formally dispossessed state. This proved to be illusory. Under the conditions of a market economy, social power, instead of going to the self-managers, passed into the hands of a new social stratum – managers or the technocracy.

Since then, indeed during the whole period of institutional development of the self-management system, there has been no 'grass-roots' self-management movement among the working class; and as the tendency to 'technocratism' strengthened, the League of Communists itself (self-management being its creature after all) delivered a blow to technocracy. 'Technocratic counter-revolution' was said to account for stagnation in regard to economic and social development, the increase of social tensions and the undermining of the social position of the working class. (In this context, the question of the return of Yugoslav migrants and their position as an integral part of the Yugoslav working class was raised.) Reconceptualization of the self-management system was started in the hope that it might be possible to prevail over the worst excesses of the market, while avoiding a return to *etatism*.[22] Regardless of the theoretical, or even the doctrinal, justifiability of the critique of technocratism and of capital relations as 'non-self-managing' relations (or indeed of the claim that self-management may be considered to be an integral new system of production and social relations) the true social victor of the political reversal at the beginning of the 1970s was the political bureaucracy. The new self-management model, in spite of its normative intentions, in practice began to glide towards a barely concealed *etatism* whose 'bearer' (in Marxian terms) is the political bureaucracy. In conflict with the neo-liberal revival of market powers at the international level, *etatism* everywhere showed itself to be inferior, and thus pulled the country into deep crisis.

22. Milan Mesić, 'Evropska Migracijska Situacija i Perspektiva' (The Current Situation of Migration in Europe), *Migracijske Teme*, Vol. 4, No. 4, 1988, pp. 371–94.

A new system of 'associated labour', with a 'delegate system' as its 'political superstructure', was included in the Constitution of 1974 and the Associated Labour Law of 1976. By these measures, the self-managed rights of the workers were further extended, and self-management procedures complicated to the utmost (although scientific researches in the 1960s showed that even then workers did not realize their rights, nor were they capable of securing them).[23]

Since the Yugoslav market was still protected, it was possible to build the costs of the uneconomic business operations of 'organizations of associated labour' into the 'price' of products and services, through 'self-management contracts' and 'self-management agreements'.[24] The new constitutional definition of a firm stressed *labour* and *associated labour* expressly, which implied *labourers* regulating economic flows *consciously*, and *stipulated* the resort to markets only as an auxiliary means. Labour and its self-management (plus the means of production) were considered to be the main factors of production. This means the more work (and hence, the more workers) the greater the social wealth. But in practice 'agreements' have led to self-management monopolies; while the total protection of the employed (alongside a million-strong army of the unemployed) has resulted in the non-economic utilization of labour. The ruling ideology of 'associated labour' and the dominant egalitarian system of public values created pressure towards excessive employment. It was expected that 'associated labour', depending on large investments financed mostly by foreign loans, would restore the former high growth rates of the economy. By these means, new work-places would be opened for the unemployed, for new generations of young educated people as well as for returnee migrants.[25]

23. Josip Obradović and W. N. Dunn, *Workers Self-Management and Organizational Power in Yugoslavia* (Pittsburgh, Pa., University of Pittsburgh, 1978), pp. 175–278; H. Lydall, *Yugoslav Socialism, Theory and Practice* (Oxford, Clarendon Press, 1984), pp. 109–152.
24. The 'self-management agreement' as well as the 'social compact' were conceived as self-management acts, based on free negotiation among the various interested parties. In this way traditional state intervention in various social activities was replaced. Self-management agreements regulate relationships among the relevant self-management bodies specifically in the pooling of labour, planning, the distribution of income, the setting of prices, the regulation of the mutual rights, obligations and liabilities of workers in associated labour, as well as in other domains. The social compact is an agreement concluded by self-management organizations and communities. It can be concluded in different spheres of social life such as planning, social development, price control, incomes policy, and employment.
25. Yugoslavia had very high rates for the growth of new employment from the beginning of this second phase, as it has been analytically defined here. Between 1974 and 1980 these ranged from 4 per cent to 5 per cent. Even later, from 1974 to 1984,

Many investments turned out to be unsuccessful however, and the public was shocked to discover, in 1980, that the country was US$20 billion in debt. A deep economic crisis set in, leading even to political crisis, and the chances of overcoming it in the near future are uncertain.

Returning to migration problems; the enormous body of legal regulation of the new self-management model[26] is institutionalized and partly extended to cover migrants as well. The Law Concerning Basic Conditions for Temporary Employment of Yugoslav Citizens Abroad and their Return from Employment Abroad was enacted in 1973. By this law Yugoslav legislation undertook to protect Yugoslav workers' rights abroad. Migrants' protection comprised: health disability and pension insurance; health care; children's allowances and other social taxes; safety at work, accommodation and nutrition; work and residence permits in the country of employment; protection in legal proceedings in the country of employment; regulations concerning the transfer of savings; information dissemination; regulations on the basis of work in the country of unemployment; conditions for pre-school education of children and of youth in their mother tongue; and temporary unemployment insurance.

This was followed in 1974 by the 'social compact', concluded between the republics and provinces on Temporary Employment of Yugoslav Citizens Abroad and their Return from Work Abroad. Besides these commitments referring to employment and protection while working abroad, obligations were laid upon all 'subjects' (in Yugoslav parlance this means the competent political bodies) to form conditions for the gradual return and active incorporation of returnees into the economic and social life of the country, by this 'compact'. The Federal Executive Council (Cabinet), being one of

---

the annual employment rate remained at the relatively high level of 2.5 per cent (especially if the crisis is taken into account). *Jugoslovenski Pregled*, Vol. 29, No. 2–3, 1985, pp. 45. In the years 1974–77 about 850,000 people were added to the employed labour force.

26. The 1974 Constitution, being one of the longest in the world due to the number of its articles was surpassed in length by the Associated Labour Law. Even so, the Constitution and the Associated Labour Law had to be worked out in detail by numerous so called 'systemic laws', at the federal and republication levels. All this – together with the self-management by-laws – 'self-management agreements' in 'organizations of associated labour' etc., was reproduced in hundreds of thousands of editions. In order to be legalized, all aspects of the organization of working people and of inter-personal relations had to be fixed in self-management enactments. M. Mesić, 'Alcune controversie inerenti al modello jugoslavo d'autogestione', *Affari Sociali Internazionali*, Vol. 16, No. 1, 1988, pp. 131 and 28.

the 'subjects', produced in 1976 the Programme of Measures and Actions for the Gradual Return of Yugoslav Workers from Temporary Work Abroad and their Working Engagement in the Country. In the programme the basis of a series of relevant rules was created, and special 'programmes of measures and actions' on the part of republics and autonomous provinces, of communes and organizations of associated labour were initiated.

By prolonging the stay abroad, and by uniting the families of migrants in the labour-importing countries, the emphasis of concern with migration problems shifted from employment (by then only sporadic) to the question of the protection of migrants and their families. Thus the Law on the Protection of Yugoslav Citizens on Temporary Work Abroad (1980) was primarily oriented towards *protection*, relying on international conventions and bilateral treaties with the receiving countries of Yugoslav migrants.

Among the socialist dogmas persisting longest and striking the deepest roots, is the problem of private ownership over the means of production, or private small enterprises. (Until recently the number of workers that the private owner was able to hire was limited to five.) The Yugoslav self-management system addressed this question very ambivalently. On the one hand, periodic political campaigns were led urging the greater engagement of private resources in small-scale business (instead of consuming them or depositing them in bank vaults). On the other hand, fear of the renewal of capitalism and 'enrichment' was warmed up once again. The all-powerful high handedness of communal administration in determining taxes, the general public atmosphere and legal uncertainty made it impossible to develop this sector of the economy.[27] Since a number of the migrants abroad and returnees have significant savings in foreign currency at their disposal,[28] discussion lasted for several years on the possibilities and need for their useful engagement. Under the circumstances of economic crisis, unemployment and the lack of investment means, the question became

---

27. Marginalization of the private sector outside agriculture is shown by its share of less than 1 per cent in GNP.

28. There are various conjectures concerning resources held by Yugoslav migrants in foreign banks. The figure of US$20 thousand million is often mentioned. In his interview for *Vjesnik*, a German banker and Vice-Chairman of the German–Yugoslav Friendship Association set out more moderate estimates. Yugoslav workers in Germany earn annually about DM 7 thousand million, spend a half of that sum, one fourth is sent to Yugoslavia while the other fourth is deposited in German banks or invested in business.

even more urgent. Returning migrants have taken an interest not only in opening their own workshops, but also in investing in the public sector, under certain conditions and granted the possibility of their own employment, employment of their children or elder members of their families. During the public debate on the Draft Bill on Acquiring Means from Citizens for the Enlargement of the Material Base of Organizations of Associated Labour opinions differed a great deal. (Thus in the youth organization, it was pejoratively called the 'law on buying workplaces'.) Even so, after several modifications, the law was enacted in 1986.[29]

It has been indicated that return was the core issue of migration policy in the third phase of social and migration development. Return-flows started even during the period of the mass departure of Yugoslav migrants; but the migration balance was clearly negative. The turning-point was the year 1974. Since then, return has been prevailing over departure, the latter being considerably reduced in relation to previous levels, keeping to around 15,000 per annum during recent years. The strongest wave of returnees occurred at the time of crisis for the Western European economies, during which the annual return-flow settled for a while at about 30,000 per annum, subsequently diminishing once more.[30]

There are remarkable differences between the estimated figures for returnee fluctuations, and the official census results. According to the 1981 census no more than 183,000 migrants returned (for good). Other estimates for just the two first years (1974–5) of mass return, however, range from 155,000 to 200,000; while 30,000 to 60,000 left at the same time. For 1977 alone an estimated figure of 62,000 has been given.[31] In the period between 1964 and 1975 as many as 2.3 million Yugoslav citizens, including dependent family members, might have been living and working for some time as

---

29. It is estimated that about 40,000 people got a job as a result of savings investments. The law itself, however, has not so far lived up to expectations. On the contrary, employment on this basis has not been noticeable. The possibility of establishing so-called 'contractual organizations of associated labour' on the basis of private capital investments and cooperation with the public sector existed before the law was enacted. Over 200 such organizations were founded, but this means of employment likewise did not achieve any great effects. The Fund for Increasing Employment in Insufficiently Developed and Explicit Emigration Regions has been in force for a decade, providing work for 10,000 people in areas with high emigration rates by its programme. Initially, there were returnees, but also other job seekers from such regions – in fact, potential migrants.

30. *YU-Novosti*, Vol. 24, No. 504, 1989.

31. Ivica Nejasmić, 'Statističko Pračenje i Neka Kvantitativna Obilježja Jugoslavenske Vanjske Migracije', *Migracijske Teme*, Vol. 3, No. 3–4, 1987, pp. 289–301.

migrants in Western Europe, out of which 960,000 might have returned.[32] The Yugoslav national report for the OECD National Experts' Conference on the 'Future of Migration' (13–15 May 1986) offers a figure of 220,000 returnees in the years 1980–84. At the same time, most researchers agree that there are still a million or more Yugoslav migrants living and working in the European labour-importing countries.

Taking the census data to be more trustworthy (although recognizing the possibility of some intervening factor, and thus the need to correct these by a factor of 20 per cent) Schierup explains the difference between estimates and statistics by the 'migrancy' phenomenon. This suggests that a certain number of migrants are 'commuting between the labour-importing country and country of origin – perhaps for years – perhaps throughout their lives':

> Yugoslav writers on migration seem to take for granted that the bulk of the returnees every single year have returned for good and reintegrated themselves in some way or the other upon return ... Our subsequent analysis of conditions for reactivation of returnees in the Yugoslav economy indicates that this presumption is highly dubious. Hence, *the factor of re-emigration is almost totally neglected.*[33]

We accept Schierup's explanation, anticipating in addition that in the case of Yugoslavs, as distinguished from perhaps Greeks or the Portuguese, the tendency towards 'migrancy' will be inhibited more and more by their position in the European Economic Community (EEC) and the other European immigration countries as well.

The legal status of Yugoslav workers in the EEC is becoming increasingly uncertain, as the (announced) decision to introduce visas for Yugoslavs in West Germany proves. Further, I suppose that these re-emigration flows (at least partly) are directed towards overseas destinations as well and partly through clandestine channels.[34]

32. Živan Tanić, 'Povratak Radnika iz Inozemstva i Zapošljavanje' (The Return of Workers from Abroad and their Employment), *Ekonomski Pregled*, Nos. 11–12, 1976.

33. C. U. Schierup, *Migration, Socialism, International Division of Labour, One Century of Yugoslav Labour Migration* (Zagreb, Institut za Migracije i Narodnosti, forthcoming), chapter 7, pp. 14, 13.

34. About 50,000 Yugoslavs working clandestinely are supposed to have gone to Switzerland as early as 1982. *YU-Novosti*, No. 387, 1982, p. 7. On the German clandestine labour market, Yugoslavs provide the largest contingent after Turks. The presence of unregistered Yugoslav workers in the Italian clandestine economy is getting even greater. Emil Hersak, 'Immigration in Mediterranean Europe', *Razvoj/ Development – International*, Vol. 2, No. 1, 1987.

The greater part of the (registered) returnees are being employed in the public sector of the economy – about 70 per cent. As opposed to the cliché of returnees as capitalists, the 1981 census found out that hardly 7.4 per cent of the total number of active returnees were persons who were either independently or in association performing business activities with private means of production. Moreover, the Yugoslav return-flow confirms that the global pattern of the selectivity of return-flows is unfavourable for the sending countries: 'Experience shows that the majority of the returnees is older, less skilled, in worse health and more affected by personal or family problems than the average of the emigrants. Migrants who have acquired a good occupational qualification and have managed to overcome many problems of living in the societies of the industrial countries do not tend to return.'[35]

Conclusion

In conclusion, it can be said that the actual effects of external migration on Yugoslav social development are certainly less significant than expected; nor are they unambiguously negative. In the long run the crucial problem of unemployment was not solved, nor did migration improve the expertise of the workforce, particularly not of that part which returned.[36] Migrant income flowing into the country provided an incentive for consumption, especially of imported products, or products dependent on raw material from abroad. This, on the one hand, brought about pressure to increase imports while, on the other, the inflexible domestic economy responded to the increased demand by upping prices (instead of with greater and more efficient production), and this led into an inflationary spiral. At the very moment when the influx of migrant remittances began to decrease it became clear that the country had become dependent on it, so that instead of decreasing its independence, it had become even more dependent on the developed countries. Since, however, those countries which kept their borders

35. Korner, 'The Experience in the Main Geographical OECD Areas', in *The Future of Migration*, p. 78.
36. One of the subsequent rationalizations for the mass exodus of Yugoslav migrants expected them to acquire industrial experience and new qualifications in the more developed economies. Not only did migrants have little upward social mobility, however (Castles, *Here for Good*, p. 138), but they also tended to find work in jobs at a lower level than their qualifications.

closed (although they did not entirely manage to prevent migration) also went through crises and increased their dependency on the developed capitalist countries, it is obvious that Yugoslavia cannot attribute the guilt for this situation entirely to its migration policy of open borders. Even from today's pessimistic standpoint, based on a concrete historical analysis, the opening of the borders to free migration should be considered a reasonable developmental move. The question remains of the later mis-moves in both migration policy and in developmental strategy in general.

Not until the prolonged and deepened crisis had set in, were the political structures of the country forced into new economic (and political) reforms oriented towards a (renewed) market economy. In this respect the first series of constitutional amendments has already been brought in, radical legal changes have been executed, while new ones are being prepared. Among these changes, the maximum agricultural holding has been increased to 30 hectares, and the number of workers permitted in private small business has been raised to 100.[37] Conditions for foreign capital investments are being extended and made easier. Some of these changes are expected to stimulate the engagement of migrant capital to a high degree and to move the country's economy. On the other hand, the most recent political events involving conflicts between nationalists are hardly conducive to this.

Yugoslavia today, at least in the short-term perspective, has high migration potential at its disposal.[38] The paradox is that its borders are wide open to migration, while those of the West European destination countries are practically closed, except for the 'brain drain' which leaves behind long-term negative effects. The public has suddenly recently become aware of the real and potential danger to social development caused by the loss of the most agile young professionals. This was more worrying since reliable data on the dimensions of this on-coming catastrophe did not exist. Replying to the frequent questions of news reporters, scientists and representatives of various state institutions have given diverse, widely differing

37. The agricultural maximum is regulated in Amendment XXIII, Constitution of Socialist Federal Republic Yugoslavia, *Službeni List SFRJ*, No. 70, 1988. The maximum number of workers in private business is defined in the Enterprises Law, *Službeni List SFRJ*, No. 77, 1988. The precise scope of the activity of private enterprises has been deferred for regulation by republican law.

38. Simon Gildas places Yugoslavia (along with Portugal) in the group of countries with a still-high migration potential: 'Migration in Southern Europe: An Overview', in *The Future of Migration*, pp. 266–7.

estimates on the actual number of these migrants in annual and long-term migration flows. In various places discussions are being conducted on the reasons why professionals emigrate, and on the possibilities of curbing their departure, or of ensuring scientific cooperation with professionals of Yugoslav origin who have established themselves in various scientific fields in developed countries. The impossibility of emigration, however, makes radical economic reform more difficult, and perhaps even calls it into question. It is to be understood that in a situation of economic crisis not much can be done to accelerate and increase return-flows. Unemployment in the country is much greater then in the period of mass external migration. Therefore the Yugoslav policy of 'socialist' migration with the onset of the crisis, revealed a deepening discrepancy between the declared principles of temporary labour migration and the possibilities of the country to realise this goal. At the same time, hopes that labour-importing countries would be prepared to help the return and reintegration of Yugoslav migrants proved futile. What remained was the possibility that radical changes in the economic, and therefore necessarily in the political system, would motivate the migrants themselves, especially those with entrepreneurial ambitions, to find their own economic interest in returning, and thereby help in overcoming the crisis. In this respect the strong forces of socialist dogmatism (which have so far blocked radical reforms in the entire socialist world) would have to be overcome.

6

The Role of the Yugoslav Intelligence and Security Community

Marko Milivojević

Introduction

This chapter is based upon two related assumptions. First, Yugoslavia's post-war political system cannot be properly understood without some knowledge, however fragmentary and incomplete, of the Yugoslav intelligence and security community (henceforth YISC). Second, the YISC is worthy of study in and for itself, in that its nature is, in many respects, unique in comparison with the intelligence and security communities of the Soviet-bloc countries, and the Soviet Union in particular. The uniqueness of the YISC is, in turn, related to Yugoslavia's unique brand of communism, which developed after the Yugoslav–Soviet split of 1948.

Yugoslavia's brand of communism has, of course, attracted a great deal of attention in the West, which has led to the creation of a vast secondary literature on the country. One subject that has received comparatively little attention in that literature is the YISC.[1] This is partly due to the paucity of publicly available information on the subject, but is also, in part, due to its controversial and politically sensitive nature.

Any analysis of the YISC must, at the very outset, make it clear that the primary sources on its subject matter are virtually non-existent; that the number of operatives who have defected from that community to the West is very small; that the secondary literature

---

1. This chapter is both a summary and revision of a book by the author on the subject: Marko Milivojević, *Tito's Sword and Shield: The Story of the Yugoslav Intelligence and Security Community* (London, The South Slav Research and Study Centre, 1989).

on its subject matter is sparse, fragmentary, incomplete and scattered throughout numerous obscure publications; and, that any analysis of the YISC, and its operational–organizational structures in particular, must, perforce, rely greatly on intelligent speculation, analogy, on secondary sources, frequently undocumented and unprovable statements. However, despite these inevitable limitations, enough material exists to come to some sort of tentative conclusions about the origins, development, operational organization, politics, operations (domestic and foreign) and problems of the YISC, and the various ways in which that community is similar to, and different from, the intelligence and security communities of the Soviet-bloc countries, and the Soviet Union in particular.

Figure 6.1 shows that the YISC, like its counterparts in the Soviet-bloc countries, is made up of two major and distinct components: *political* intelligence–security and *military* intelligence–security. The service nomenclature of the former has been changed many times since its creation in 1943, which is also true of the latter, though to a lesser extent, since its creation in 1941.

As is also the case with the KGB in the Soviet Union, the existence and role of the post-war Yugoslav political intelligence–security services have always been matters of public knowledge in Yugoslavia. The existence and role of the post-war Yugoslav military intelligence–security services, as is also the case with the GRU (Glarvoje Razvedjvatelmoje Upravlenije) in the Soviet Union, have never been publicly acknowledged in Yugoslavia. This has also been true of the third distinct component of the YISC, also shown in Figure 6.1, which was President Tito's personal intelligence service. This service was, until Tito's death in 1980, located in his Personal Secretariat.

Origins and Development

National Liberation–Civil War, 1941–45

Yugoslavia's first communist intelligence–security service was the military intelligence section of the High Command of the National Liberation Army (NLA), which was created by the Communist Party of Yugoslavia (CPY), and commanded by Tito throughout the national liberation–civil war of 1941–45. From late 1941 to early 1944, when sheer military survival was Tito's number-one priority

Figure 6.1   The Yugoslav Intelligence Community, 1941–87

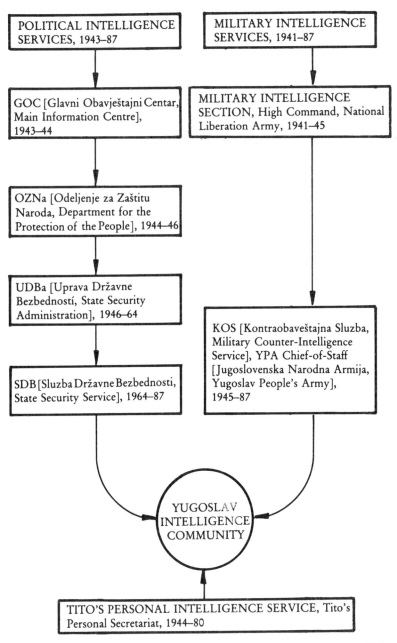

in the face of formidable Axis forces intent on destroying the CPY–NLA, the military intelligence section of the NLA's high command was of absolutely critical importance.

This was also the case as regards the CPY–NLA civil war with the Croatian Ustaše, the Serbian Četniks of Draža Mihailović and the Slovenian Domobranci. Not until early 1944, when an NLA military victory over its domestic enemies became increasingly certain, did the CPY's newly formed political intelligence–security services begin to overshadow the NLA's military intelligence section in the new YISC.

These wartime political intelligence–security services were two in number. First, and soon after Tito had proclaimed the formation of a new provisional Yugoslav government at the second session of the Anti-Fascist Council of National Liberation of Yugoslavia (AVNOJ) in late 1943, the GOC (Glavni Obavještajni Centar, Main Information Centre) was formed. The man entrusted to head the GOC in 1943 was Dalibor Jakaš. Second, on 13 May 1944, the provisional GOC was replaced by OZNa (Odeljenje za Zaštitu Naroda, Department for the Protection of the People), which was co-founded and subsequently headed by Aleksandar Ranković[2] and Svetislav Stefanović.[3]

Tito, an experienced Comintern agent before the war, knew the importance of good intelligence and counter-intelligence security in political and military warfare. The CPY, of which Tito became Secretary-General in 1937, had been illegal in Yugoslavia since 1921, and he was therefore well versed in clandestine underground activities (of which intelligence operations for the Comintern was one) long before war broke out in Yugoslavia in 1941, at which time a large agent network of secret CPY members, sympathizers and fellow travellers was in place for wartime work for the CPY and later the NLA.

2. One of the four men who dominated the CPY immediately before, during and after the war, and who co-founded and headed OZNa from 1944 to 1946. Thereafter, Ranković was Federal Secretary for Internal Affairs, which gave him political control of the Yugoslav political intelligence/services until he was purged by Tito in 1966. At the same time he was also a CPY Politburo member and an organizational secretary of its central committee. Aside from Tito, the other two dominant men were Milovan Djilas (purged in 1954) and Edvard Kardelj (died in 1979).

3. Stefanović had been trained by the Soviet NKVD during the 1930s. For his NKVD connections see Milovan Djilas, *Rise and Fall* (London, Macmillan, 1986), p. 5. As well as co-founding OZNa with Ranković in 1944, he was the second most important man in it until 1946, after which he was operational head of the Yugoslav political intelligence–security services until he was purged with his mentor, Ranković, in 1966. For Stefanović's long career see Dennison Rusinow, *The Yugoslav Experiment, 1948–1974* (London, C. Hurst, 1977), p. 185.

It is now reasonably certain that the wartime CPY, through the NLA's military intelligence section (and through GOC–OZNa later in the war), had a large and generally very effective agent network in the ranks of its domestic political enemies and among the civilian employees of the Axis military occupation administrations. It also had, from the earliest days of the war, an elaborate and very effective counter-intelligence apparatus, designed to prevent hostile penetration of the CPY–NLA by their enemies. The strategic objectives of this considerable intelligence–counter-intelligence effort were as follows:

1. To obtain, via agents and other methods, important and timely intelligence on its domestic and foreign enemies, so as to aid the achievement of strategic CPY–NLA political and military objectives during the national liberation–civil war of 1941–45.

2. To manipulate, via influential agents, the hostile organizations of its domestic political enemies (especially the Ustaše and Četniks), so as to use, discredit and weaken them, thereby aiding the achievement of strategic CPY–NLA political and military objectives during what was, for all concerned, mainly a civil war.

3. To prevent, via counter-intelligence work, hostile agent penetrations of CPY–NLA ranks at all levels, thereby ensuring that they remained internally secure.

4. To safeguard, via effective security procedures, the security of wartime CPY–NLA radio communications, both in Yugoslavia and with reference to Tito's radio contact with Moscow during the war.

Tito's wartime radio communications with Moscow, which he kept secret from even his closest colleagues, are of particular interest, as long after the war it was revealed that Tito, through a man called Josip Kopinić located in Ustaše–controlled Zagreb, had had a secure radio link to Moscow throughout the war.[4] Because of effective NKVD training in such matters before the war, CPY–NLA field radio communications in wartime Yugoslavia were also secure, which contrasted sharply with poor Četnik radio-communications

---

4. A fascinating biography of Kopinić, which covers his wartime intelligence work and much else besides in great detail, was recently published in Yugoslavia: Vjenceslav Cenčić, *Enigma Kopinić*, 2 vols. (Belgrade: Rad, 1983).

security – an oversight that the Četniks would come to regret, as the British, from SOE (Special Operations Executive), Cairo, were thus able to read all Mihailović's radio communications throughout the war.

Consolidating Power and Soviet Subversion, 1954–53

Having played an important role during the civil war, which ended with a complete CPY–NLA victory in November 1944 when a new communist regime was established in Belgrade, the YISC was then to have an even more important role in the immediate post-war period, when the new regime consolidated its power and, even before the Yugoslav–Soviet split of 1948, was faced with the reality of Soviet subversion in the country.

The first two years of the new regime saw two important developments in the YISC. First, in 1945, the NLA's military intelligence section was replaced by KOS (*Kontraobaveštajna Služba*, Military Counter-Intelligence Service), which was part of the Chief-of-Staff/ General Staff of the YPA (Jugoslovenska Narodna Armija, Yugoslav People's Army), itself formed with KOS in 1945. The founder of KOS and its first head was Svetozar Vukmanović-Tempo.[5] Second, in February–March 1946, the Federal Secretariat for Internal Affairs (FSIA) was formed, with Ranković as Federal Secretary, while OZNa was replaced by UDBa (Uprava Državne Bezbednosti, State Security Administration), which was henceforth under the political control of the FSIA.[6]

Though specifically concerned with political intelligence–security matters, OZNa had, in fact, always been organizationally a part of the armed forces, reporting directly to, and under the exclusive control of, Tito, as Commander-in-Chief of the NLA and later the YPA. This was a natural development at the time, as when OZNa was formed, for example, war was still raging in Yugoslavia. OZNa,

---

5. Vukmanović-Tempo was a very important CPY–NLA figure during the war, thereafter going on to hold many key positions at the same time as heading KOS, which he largely created. That alone makes him a key figure in the early years of the YISC. His other positions included heading the CPY's Main Political Administration in the YPA and the office of Military Prosecutor. His time at KOS, however, was relatively brief, as by 1950 it is known that YPA General Srečko Manola was head of KOS. For this early period of KOS see A. Ross Johnson, *The Role of the Military in Communist Yugoslavia: An Historical Sketch*, Rand Paper, No. 6070 (Santa Monica, Calif.: Rand Corporation, 1978), p. 4, and Djilas, *Rise and Fall*, p. 269.
6. For the 1946 YISC organizational changes see Djilas, *Rise and Fall*, p. 32.

and its successor, UDBa, were both paramilitary intelligence–security organizations. OZNa remained a paramilitary organization throughout its entire existence, from 1944 to 1946, while UDBa only became a purely civilian intelligence–security organization in 1952. All that the 1946 organizational changes did was to place UDBa under the political control of the FSIA.

It was at this time that OZNa–UDBa gained an absolute ascendancy over KOS and the YPA in general in the YISC, as KOS, as its very name suggested, was given limited and highly specific responsibilities: military counter-intelligence–security and the gathering of tactical intelligence on countries likely to be at war with Yugoslavia in the future. OZNa–UDBa, on the other hand, had far greater responsibilities, involving political counter-intelligence–internal security, control of the country's penal system, CPY leadership security, the gathering of all foreign strategic political and other intelligence, and the monitoring of the YPA for the CPY, whose political instrument it was first and foremost.

As the CPY's chosen political instrument in the consolidation of the new regime's power, OZNa–UDBa, following the Soviet NKVD in such matters, had unlimited powers during this period. OZNa's and UDBa's mission was, in the words of Tito, 'to strike *terror* into the bones of those who do not like this kind of Yugoslavia' (my emphasis):[7] a mission that gave OZNa–UDBa the power to monitor, arrest, detain, mistreat, sentence (by secret tribunals), deport or even execute at will, while being everywhere in their fearful presence throughout Yugoslav society. This situation was noted by a Captain Frank C. Waddams, a British Liaison officer to the NLA during the war and later British Consul in Ljubljana, who wrote of OZNa's role in early 1946 in the following terms:

> The most unpleasant feature of life in Yugoslavia today is the existence of the all-powerful OZNa, the secret police. This body is responsible for the permanent terror in which the vast bulk of the population lives. It possesses its agents in every block of flats, in every street, in every village and in every barrack room. OZNa has complete control over the life, liberty and property of all citizens, and if it chooses to arrest, to imprison without trial, to deport or to 'liquidate' anybody, no one may protest or ask the reason why. That is why the populace is in such a state of terror.[8]

---

7. Quoted in Wayne S. Vucinich (ed.), *Contemporary Yugoslavia* (Berkeley, Calif., University of California, 1969), p. 129.
8. In 1946, upon his return to the UK, Waddams privately and anonymously

This CPY-directed mass OZNa–UDBa terror did succeed in consolidating the power of the new regime, but at a terrible price, as one estimate has put the number of people killed by mass shootings, forced death-marches and incarceration in concentration camps at 250,000 during the period 1944–46,[9] while another estimate has put the number of people who went through OZNa–UDBa prisons and concentration camps at one million during the period 1944–48.[10]

Aside from consolidating the power of the new regime, UDBa and, in military matters, KOS, had a vast counter-intelligence security task during the 1946–53 period: countering Soviet subversion in the country, which was as extensive as it was dangerous, notwithstanding very close Yugoslav–Soviet relations during the period 1945–48, as Stalin's understanding of this so-called 'friendship' was to prove, as time went by, a direct threat to the security and very survival of Tito's regime.

Soviet subversion, via NKVD and GRU agent penetration, began immediately after the war ended, concentrating on the CPY and the YPA, where, according to Adam Ulam: 'The Soviet attempt to penetrate the army and to infiltrate the officer corps and to turn its highest leaders from their allegiance to Tito, were among the most important factors in convincing the Yugoslav regime that for its sheer *survival* it had to stand up to Soviet Russia.'[11] Developing and perfecting the counter-intelligence–internal security capabilities of UDBa and KOS, therefore, was not a matter of choice. The regime's very survival, in the face of extensive Soviet subversion, depended on these capabilities being effective, which indeed proved to be the case. At no other time, before or since, had Tito's regime depended so much on the YISC.

This Soviet subversion started at the very top of the CPY. Andrija Hebrang, Politburo member, and Sretan Žujović, central committee member, were arrested as Soviet spies in May 1948. The former was reportedly killed, while the latter was imprisoned. In the YPA high command many Soviet spies were discovered by UDBa, including

published a report on conditions in Yugoslavia entitled, 'Today in Yugoslavia, by a British Officer', *Yugoslav Information Sheet* (Bromley, Kent, 1946). The extract quoted in this paper is quoted in Nora Beloff, *Tito's Flawed Legacy – Yugoslavia & the West: 1939–1985* (London, Victor Gollancz, 1985), p. 133.

9. Borivoje M. Karapandzich, *The Bloodiest Yugoslav Spring, 1945 – Tito's Katyns and Gulags* (New York, Carlton Press, 1980), p. 20.

10. Beloff, *Tito's Flawed Legacy*, p. 135.

11. Adam Ulam, *Tito and the Cominform* (Cambridge, Mass., Harvard University Press, 1952), p. 57 (my emphasis).

YPA General Arso Jovanović, one time NLA Chief-of-Staff, who was reportedly killed, while YPA Colonel Vlado Dapčević managed to escape to the Soviet Union.

As during the period 1944–46, UDBa terror was required during the period 1948–50 to purge thoroughly the CPY and YPA of all Soviet spies and pro-Soviet elements (Cominformists), but it is very difficult to exactly estimate how many such people were arrested, imprisoned and liquidated during this still politically sensitive UDBa operation, which did not fully end until as late as 1952. At that time, Ranković claimed that 13,700 Cominformists had been arrested and imprisoned during the period 1948–52.[12] This figure is almost certainly an under-estimation of the true figure, although later Western estimates, which talk of 250,000 Cominformists being purged during the period 1948–53, are almost certainly exaggerations.[13]

A figure of around 100,000 expelled (from the CPY, including people in the YPA), arrested and imprisoned is probably about right, or around 20 per cent of the CPY's membership in 1950. Estimating the number of Cominformists liquidated by UDBa at this time is even more difficult, as these secret political killings on the Adriatic island of Goli Otok were a strictly taboo subject until after Tito's death in 1980. A recent memoir published in the West by a survivor of Goli Otok speaks of 'tens of thousands' of Cominformists being killed by UDBa on Goli Otok after 1948.[14] Whatever the true figure, UDBa's ruthless and highly successful countering of Soviet subversion enabled Tito's regime to survive the period 1948–53 intact and greatly strengthened.

Organizational Changes and Purges, 1953–66

The year 1952, when the CPY became the League of Yugoslav Communists (LYC), was a significant one for the YISC, which was extensively reorganized at the time, as part of a wider political and ideological revolution in Yugoslavia, rejecting Soviet-type

---

12. Rusinow, *The Yugoslav Experiment*, p. 39.
13. Christine von Kohl, *Neue Zurcher Zeitung* (Zurich), 7 May 1982. This Swiss journalist claims this figure came from semi-official Yugoslav sources, but it is rather improbable, as total CPY membership in 1950 was only 500,000 people.
14. Venko Markovski, *Goli Otok: The Island of Death – A Diary in Letters*, East European Monograph, No. 163 (Boulder, Colo., East European Monographs, 1984), p. viii. This is almost certainly an exaggeration. The true figure is probably in the thousands, as only a hard-core of Cominformists and dangerous Soviet spies were killed. The majority of Cominformists were imprisoned for varying periods of time.

communism as a direct result of the traumatic events of 1948–52. Such a revolution could not but affect the role of the YISC in Yugoslav politics and society.

In 1951, in the first of a number of campaigns for 'stricter legality' that continued throughout the 1950s, Ranković made a totally. unprecedented public statement admitting that during 1950 47 per cent of UDBa arrests had been 'unjustified' and that 23 per cent had been for crimes of 'minor significance', and that the entire judicial system had been guilty of 'converting ordinary crime into political criminal offences in an indiscriminate manner'.[15] Consequently, the number of officially admitted UDBa arrests was reduced from over 36,000 in 1950 to 15,500 in 1952.[16] In addition, under the new criminal code of 1951 there could be no crime or administrative punishment outside the normal legal process. Arbitrary UDBa action, which had been the norm during the 1940s, became more selective and hence exceptional during the 1950s.

A seasoned observer of Yugoslavia at this time remarked that: 'The judicial reforms of the early fifties, by placing greater emphasis on legality, and by pushing the administrative security services into a more *discreet* background, went a long way towards making the regime more secure.'[17] 'Discreet' is a good description of the more limited, selective and less overt role of UDBa in Yugoslavia during the 1950s and 1960s – a period of increasing economic prosperity, great social changes, a more legitimate political order and a stronger sense of international security, especially after the Soviet–Yugoslav *rapprochement* of 1955 and the *de facto* adoption of a non-aligned foreign policy by Tito in the same year.

In 1952 UDBa became a purely civilian intelligence–security service, stripped of all its earlier paramilitary forces, which included the National Defence Corps (became the YPA Border Guard), internal security troops (became the FSIA's Workers' State Militia, which now numbers around 150,000 men), CPY leadership security (became special YPA troops assigned to Tito's Personal Secretariat), and penal system troops (became FSIA's penal system guards). In this respect UDBa became very different from the Soviet KGB, which retains large border, internal security, penal system and

15. Quoted in George W. Hoffman and F. W. Neal, *Yugoslavia and the New Communism* (New York, Twentieth Century Fund, 1962), p. 92.
16. Ibid., p. 389.
17. Stevan K. Pavlowitch, *Yugoslavia* (New York, Praeger, 1971), p. 237 (my emphasis).

leadership security paramilitary forces to this day.

Though UDBa's role was more discreet and selective in Yugoslavia during the 1950s and 1960s, it remained, on account of Ranković's powerful position in the regime, an important actor in the convulsive, prolonged and bitter power struggles at the very highest echelons of the regime. In 1961 a struggle began for the future destiny of Yugoslavia, in which Ranković's UDBa played a key role, as did KOS and Tito's personal intelligence service, and which ended in the purging of Ranković and his UDBa associates in 1966.

The full issues, manoeuvres and personalities of this struggle over the reform process in Yugoslavia are beyond the scope of this chapter,[18] which will focus on events in the YISC during the period 1965–66, when the aforementioned power struggle came to a head, with rumours that Ranković was plotting to replace Tito. Whether this was true is hard to say, but in March 1966, Tito, in an indirect public censure of Ranković, threw him to his numerous political enemies.

The plot to get rid of Ranković seems to have begun in late 1965, when Milan Mišković, a Croat, replaced Ranković's lackey, Vojin Lukić, a Serb, as Federal Secretary for Internal Affairs.[19] With Ranković's ally, Stefanović, as head of UDBa, Mišković soon discovered that his power over it was purely nominal, which led him to use KOS, headed since 1963 by his brother, YPA Colonel-General Ivan Mišković, against the Serb-dominated UDBa HQ in Belgrade, which he, as a Croat, could not directly penetrate.[20]

A very complicated KOS–UDBa intrigue reportedly followed, seemingly also to have involved Tito's personal intelligence service, which KOS provided with incriminating evidence of extensive and illegal wiretapping of prominent LYC leaders (including Tito) by

18. For the background on the reform process and the political struggle over its implementation prior to 1966 see Rusinow, *The Yugoslav Experiment*, expecially chapter 6. Basically, Ranković, a Serb centralist conservative, was against the more liberal and politically decentralized reform process, which had strong support in Croatia and Slovenia. After the implementation of the reformist 1963 SFRY Constitution Tito fully supported the reform process, while Ranković did all in his power to block its implementation at grassroots level in Yugoslavia. Conflict was inevitable, but it was not until late 1965 that Tito decided to start a chain of events that would culminate in Ranković's removal from office in 1966.

19. Rusinow, *The Yugoslav Experiment*, p. 185.

20. Yugoslav conspiracy theorists suggested, not without reason, that Tito's appointment of Milan Mišković in 1965 as head of the FSIA was the first step in a plot to 'get' Ranković's UDBa, as Mišković's access to KOS in 1965–66 (through his brother) was no coincidence. According to this line of thought, Tito used KOS (and the YPA in general) to purge UDBa in 1966, just as he had used UDBa to purge the YPA of pro-Soviet elements in 1948–50.

Ranković's UDBa since the late 1940s. By the early summer of 1966 Tito, through Milan Mišković and his personal intelligence service, had enough evidence to get rid of Ranković once and for all.

On 9 June Tito appointed the Crvenkovski Commission fully to investigate the allegations against Ranković, Stefanović and UDBa HQ in Belgrade. The Crvenkovski Commission's report found the allegations to be true, and Ranković was dismissed from all his offices on 1 July 1966 at the famous fourth plenum of the LYC's central committee on Tito's island, Brioni.[21]

This seminal event, however, did not end the rumours, as it soon became clear that there was far more to these murky events than the official version of them would have the world believe. Stefanović, who was kicked out of UDBa and the LYC with Ranković, denied outright that UDBa had wiretapped Tito's offices and private residences, suggesting KOS was behind it, which was given credence by the dismissal of Tito's personal military *aide-de-camp*, Luka Vožović, in late June 1966. Vožović was almost certainly a KOS operative.[22]

Yet despite this probable KOS wiretapping of Tito (possibly discovered by his personal intelligence service), the Crvenkovski Commission's brief was limited to alleged UDBa wiretapping activities, as set out in the 'evidence' provided by KOS, which itself was not even mentioned. All of which strongly suggested that the deliberations of the Crvenkovski Commission were not really concerned about the morality and illegality of wiretapping *per se*, but about finding a convincing pretext in the alleged misdeeds of UDBa to get rid of Ranković and his cronies for wider political reasons.

Given all this KOS–UDBa plotting and counter-plotting it seems, in retrospect, that at the root of it all was a plot by Tito, aided by his personal intelligence service, to get rid of Ranković, end UDBa's role at the *haute politique* levels of the regime, and raise up KOS, at UDBa's expense, in the YISC, while also purging KOS of unreliable elements such as Vožović. A revealing story, later retold by Paul Lendvai, about the Ranković affair, seems to bear out that Tito's intelligence service had always been very active in the regime, none of whose leading figures was ever entirely trusted by Tito, as:

---

21. Also known as the Brioni plenum, whose published proceedings included the Crvenkovski Commission's report on the Ranković affair – see *Četvrti Plenum Centralnog Komiteta SKJ* (Belgrade, 1966). The fact that the report was made public was unprecedented, leading to a prolonged anti-UDBa campaign in the Yugoslav press which continued well into 1967.

22. Rusinow, *The Yugoslav Experiment*, p. 187.

'During a debate about the Ranković affair in the small circle of Tito's closest collaborators, Kardelj is reported to have remarked, "I had noted years ago that my telephone was tapped." "Why didn't you tell me?," snapped Tito. "I thought *you* might have ordered it . . .", Kardelj said quietly.'[23] With such a mutually suspicious crew, who is to say that Kardelj was wrong in assuming what he did?

The most important immediate consequence of the Ranković affair was that KOS gained ascendancy over UDBa in the YISC, with the head of KOS, YPA Colonel-General Ivan Mišković, becoming head of UDBa in 1966, whereupon he conducted a thorough purge of all Ranković and Stefanović loyalists, who had dominated UDBa and OZNa before it for over two decades. Mišković also, in the words of a well-informed CIA analyst, 'probably retained effective authority over his successor as KOS Chief',[24] YPA Lieutenant-General Stjepan Domankušić. This gave Mišković, in an unprecedented development, total control of the entire YISC, with the notable exception of Tito's personal intelligence service, one of whose primary functions – as the events of 1966 showed – was to monitor the YISC for Tito.

KOS–YPA Control of the YISC, 1966–87

The real changes of 1966, unlike the alleged 'changes' of 1964 (when UDBa became the SDB – Služba Državne Bezbednosti, State Security Service),[25] can be seen, in organizational–operational matters, as leading thereafter to increasing KOS–YPA control of the YISC.

The head of UDBa and the *de facto* head of KOS, Ivan Mišković, went on to serve as Special Adviser on security to the State President (one of the select few who had daily access to Tito) and Secretary of the Council for State Security Affairs of the Presidency of the Federation. He retained his position as YISC overlord until

23. Paul Lendvai, *Eagles in Cobwebs: Nationalism and Communism in the Balkans* (Garden City, N.Y., Doubleday & Co., 1969), p. 162 (emphasis in original).

24. Robert W. Dean, 'Civil – Military Relations in Yugoslavia, 1971–1975', *Armed Forces and Society*, Vol. 3, No. 1, November 1976, p. 40. This article, and its section entitled 'Lessons from the Mišković Case' (pp. 40–3), in particular, offers an excellent discussion of Mišković's pivotal role in the Ranković affair of 1966, and his subsequent role as YISC overlord, which ended with his dismissal by Tito in 1973.

25. This final change of name from UDBa to SDB did not displace the former among ordinary Yugoslavs, who use it to this day to refer to the SDB. For that reason UDBa will be used throughout the rest of this chapter.

his dismissal in 1973, for alleged UDBa failings during the Croatian disturbances of 1971–72.[26]

Before that dismissal, however, the YISC under Mišković saw further important changes in 1968–69. In 1968, when the Soviet invasion of Czechoslovakia indirectly threatened Yugoslavia's security, the interconnected systems of Total National Defence (TND) and Social Self-Protection (SSP) were created. The former, as the 1970s progressed, increasingly became the responsibility of the YPA, while the latter – a comprehensive nationwide internal security system – was the responsibility of the FSIA and a YISC dominated, in turn, by KOS and the YPA high command in general.

On 13 May 1969, the twenty-fifth anniversary of OZNa's formation was celebrated on a grand scale, as early 1969 saw the full rehabilitation of UDBa in Yugoslavia. Tito clearly felt that the post-1966 anti-UDBa campaign in the press and elsewhere had gone too far. At that time Mitja Ribičić, Slovenian OZNa/UDBa chief in the 1940s and holder of various high UDBa positions thereafter, became chairman of the Federal Executive Council (FEC), or Yugoslavia's Prime Minister,[27] an appointment that was a clear sign that a purged and reorganized UDBa was fully rehabilitated.

In the same year Tito placed the YPA, which had done well out of the events of 1966, more fully under his control, by dismissing the Federal Secretary for National Defence, YPA General Ivan Gošnjak, and the YPA Chief-of-Staff, YPA General Hamović. However, the head of UDBa, Colonel-General Ivan Mišković, was not affected by these changes in the YPA high command, which strongly suggested that the 1969 rehabilitation of UDBa and the downgrading of the YPA in the same year did not appreciably change the post-1966 KOS–YPA control and domination of the YISC.

The military domination of the YISC, which had no precedent in Yugoslavia (other than the special wartime organization of OZNa), nor in the communist world in general (where such a development was unthinkable, especially in the Soviet Union), turned out to be an important preface to the 1970s and 1980s story of increasing

---

26. Adam Roberts, *Nations in Arms: The Theory and Practice of Territorial Defence* (London, Macmillan, 1986), 2nd edn, p. 204.

27. Ribičić is still active in Yugoslav politics, where he has acquired a notorious reputation for justifying past OZNa/UDBa activities, no matter how distasteful. In 1982, for example, he said 'we must not be ashamed of Goli Otok. All that happened there was legal because it was revolutionary': quoted in Markovski, *Goli Otok*, p. ix.

YPA power and influence in Yugoslav politics and society as a whole, which became very pronounced during and after the Croatian disturbances of 1971–72.[28]

In 1974, for example, YPA Colonel-General Franko Herljević became head of the FSIA, which gave the YPA direct political control of UDBa (and the YISC as a whole through KOS), the Workers' State Militia and the ordinary criminal police. All of which represented an unprecedented concentration of intelligence and security service, paramilitary force and police power in the hands of one prominent YPA figure, who, in another unprecedented development, was head of the FSIA from 1974 to 1984.[29]

Herljević's YPA boss (and hence ultimate head of the YISC), YPA General Nikola Ljubičić, held the office of Federal Secretary for National Defence from 1971 to 1984, after which he became the State President of Serbia. Ljubičić was elected to the LYC central committee and its all-important Presidium at the Tenth (1974), Eleventh (1978) and Twelfth (1982) LYC Congresses, which made him one of the most important and powerful figures in the LYC, in addition to his high military position – second only to Tito as Commander-in-Chief prior to 1980, while being *de facto* Commander-in-Chief from 1980 to 1984.

Ljubičić's successors, YPA Admiral Branko Mamula and General Veljko Kadijević, are just as powerful in Yugoslavia. As with General Jarulzelski in Poland in 1981, Kadijević's control of the YISC would be a vital requirement if and when the YPA, under his or his successor's operational control, mounts a military *coup d'état* in a Yugoslavia afflicted with its most serious political, economic and social crisis since the end of the Second World War.

28. For a wider discussion of increasing YPA power and influence in Yugoslav politics and society in the 1970s and 1980s see Marko Milivojević, 'The Political Role of the Yugoslav People's Army in Contemporary Yugoslavia', in Marko Milivojević, John B. Allcock and Pierre Maurer (eds.), *Yugoslavia's Security Dilemmas: Armed Forces, National Defence and Foreign Policy* (Oxford, Berg; New York, St Martin's Press, 1988), pp. 15–59.

29. Slobodan Stanković, *The End of the Tito Era: Yugoslavia's Dilemmas* (Stanford, Calif., Hoover Institution Press, 1981), p. 129. In addition to being head of the FSIA, Herljević was also elected a member of the LYC central committee at the Tenth (1974), Eleventh (1978) and Twelfth (1982) Congresses.

Organization and Politics

Political Organization

The State Presidency is currently the ultimate executive authority in Yugoslavia, while the LYC (the CPY prior to 1952) has held a monopoly of political power since November 1944. Until his death in 1980, Tito was SFRY State President, Secretary-General of the LYC (and the CPY before it) and Commander-in-Chief of the armed forces. Tito exercised tight political control of the YISC throughout his long political career, both through the appointment of people whose loyalty to him personally was very strong and through the independent monitoring of that community by his personal intelligence service in his Personal Secretariat – the source of all real power in Yugoslavia until Tito's death in 1980.[30]

It is unclear whether the post-Tito State Presidency, whose chairmanship rotates on an annual basis, maintains any sort of independent secret intelligence capability to monitor the YISC. What is clear, however, is that the State Presidency is the ultimate political master of the YISC, working through its advisory Councils for State Security Affairs,[31] Protection of Constitutional Order[32] and National Defence,[33] while the Federal Secretaries for Internal Affairs and National Defence are responsible for the day-to-day political control of UDBa and KOS–YPA respectively.

30. Considering its importance, it is rather odd that Tito's Personal Secretariat has been virtually ignored in the secondary political literature on Yugoslavia. Its nearest equivalent was Stalin's Secret Chancellery, through which Stalin exercised direct control of the NKVD and GRU. For this question see Erik Niels Rosenfeldt, *Knowledge and Power; The Role of Stalin's Secret Chancellery in the Soviet System of Government* (Copenhagen, Rosenkilde & Bogger, 1978). Tito almost certainly modelled himself on Stalin in such matters as controlling and monitoring the YISC through his personal intelligence service and his Personal Secretariat. A *modus operandi* that served him well, especially in 1966 with the Ranković affair.

31. By tradition chaired by the head of UDBa – as, for example, Ivan Mišković (1966–73) – see Roberts, *Nations in Arms*, p. 204. In recent years, however, it has been chaired by the head of the FSIA.

32. By tradition chaired by an important and trusted LYC figure. For many years before Tito's death in 1980, for example, this Council was chaired by Dr Vladimir Bakarić, a very powerful figure in post-war Yugoslav politics and one of Tito's closest political associates – see Stanković, *End of the Tito Era*, p. 52.

33. Chaired by Tito as Commander-in-Chief of the armed forces. Since 1980 chaired by the chairman of the State Presidency, assisted by the Federal Secretary for National Defence. In wartime this council would become the government of the country, with full and unlimited military and political powers, subject only to a formal declaration of war (if this was needed and possible) by the SFRY Federal Assembly, which has only got this right under the 1974 SFRY Constitution.

Since the early 1970s the Federal Secretary for National Defence (always a YPA general) has been politically more important than his counterpart at the FSIA. At the present time, for example, the Federal Secretary for National Defence is an ex-officio member of the State Presidency, where policy is formed, and which he is indirectly involved in, although he has no voting rights. His FSIA counterpart, on the other hand, merely executes policy as laid down by the State Presidency and its relevant advisory councils.

By tradition, both the Internal Affairs and National Defence Federal Secretaries are members of the LYC central committee, as well as being full voting members of the FEC, whose chairman (the Yugoslav Prime Minister) is responsible for the execution of all policy decisions made by the State Presidency, including those pertaining to internal affairs and national defence. The FEC, as the executive organ of the SFRY Federal Assembly (Skupština), is also responsible for all budgetary matters, the appointment of all major officials below the rank of Federal Secretary (who are directly appointed by the State Presidency) and the monitoring of the performance of all Federal Secretariats and other state organizations.

Further down the line, at the operational level, the head of UDBa reports directly to the Federal Secretary for Internal Affairs, while the head of KOS reports directly to the YPA Chief-of-Staff, who is the first deputy of the Federal Secretary for National Defence. The heads of UDBa and KOS will, as circumstances dictate, attend meetings of the Councils for State Security Affairs, the Protection of Constitutional Order and National Defence, although here they are only secondary to their respective Federal Secretaries, who attend such meetings as a matter of course, being permanent members of these three advisory councils.[34]

Finally, the LYC, through its committees in UDBa and the YPA, operates politically at all levels of UDBa, KOS and the YPA in general. Membership of UDBa and KOS (like the YPA high command in general) is, of course, conditional on membership of the LYC, whose monitoring organs pay particular attention to the political reliability, activism and general attitudes of all UDBa and

---

34. Though the LYC has, since the death of Tito in 1980, become a very loose and highly un-Leninist coalition of *republican* political factions (as is also true of the State Presidency, which draws its members from the Presidium of the LYC's central committee). These two committees, and the LYC Committee in the YPA in particular, are nevertheless still of great political importance. Ljubičić and Mamula (past and recent Federal Secretaries for National Defence) both began their rise to power in the LYC Committee in the YPA. See Stanković, *End of the Tito Era*, pp. 132–3.

KOS operatives, no matter how insignificant. In this key respect at least the YISC is nearly identical to its Soviet counterpart, where full CPSU(b) political control of the KGB and GRU (Soviet Army) has always been a top priority for the ruling party leadership.

Operational Organization

While the political organization of the YISC is reasonably clear, little is known about the operational organization of UDBa and KOS. Only operational generalities, and not details, are available to observers of the YISC, as such matters have always been highly classified and covered by official secrecy in Yugoslavia. However, enough secondary material exists to give a general sketch of the operational organization of the YISC.

UDBa HQ in Belgrade is the operational core of the entire organization, engaged in centralized control functions, analysis, the provision of services and all foreign operations. As is also the case with the Soviet KGB, UDBa's domestic section is its most important component, employing the majority of its operatives. UDBa HQ (Belgrade) is also, and with reference to its domestic section, the republican UDBa office for Serbia (with sub-offices in Novi Sad and Priština). The other republican offices are Zagreb (Croatia), Ljubljana (Slovenia), Skopje (Macedonia), Titograd (Montenegro) and Sarajevo (Bosnia–Hercegovina). The operational functions of UDBa's domestic section are domestic politics and dissidents, the YPA, surveillance and counter-intelligence.[35]

UDBa's foreign section, which is known to be controlled by its SID (Služba za Informaciju i Dokumentaciju, Service for Information and Documentation),[36] is entirely the concern of UDBa HQ in Belgrade. Its functions are strategic intelligence, hostile émigrés, surveillance of SFRY citizens abroad and ciphers–communications security. It is known that SID has always worked very closely with the Federal Secretariat for Foreign Affairs, whose SFRY embassies and consulates provide a legal cover for the posting of UDBa operatives abroad (posing as diplomats).[37] Like the KGB's

---

35. The republican operational organisation of UDBa was confirmed in the final report of the Crvenkovski Commission in 1966, which was made public (see note 21 for further details of this report).

36. Hans Peter Rullmann, *Assassinations Commissioned by Belgrade: Documentation about the Yugoslav Murder Machine* (Hamburg, Ost-Dienst, 1981), p. 33.

37. In the opinion of one well-informed observer of UDBa's foreign operations this Federal Secretariat has always been 'the extended arm of the Belgrade secret

First Chief Directorate (responsible for foreign operations), UDBa's foreign section/SID is believed to contain the *crème de la crème* of UDBa operatives.

KOS HQ in Belgrade is known to be a part of the YPA's General Staff, though organizationally separate from them in operational terms, and providing centralized control and other functions and services for its seven counter-intelligence–tactical intelligence directorates located at the HQ's of the YPA's seven (as of 1988) military districts: Belgrade (West Serbia), Niš (East Serbia), Zagreb (Croatia), Ljubljana (Slovenia), Skopje (Macedonia), Titograd (Montenegro) and Sarajevo (Bosnia–Hercegovina). As its very name implies, KOS is mostly concerned with counter-intelligence, while tactical intelligence operations against countries likely to be at war with Yugoslavia in the future are its secondary concern. Like the Soviet GRU, it is probable that KOS is involved in some foreign strategic intelligence operations, which would involve some liaison with UDBa–SID and the Federal Secretariat for Foreign Affairs.[38] Lastly, KOS is responsible for all YPA ciphers and communications security.

Nothing whatsoever is known about how many operatives UDBa and KOS employ, nor the amounts of money allocated to them, but it would be reasonably safe to assume that manpower–money allocated – as is the case in all communist countries without exception – have always been substantial, especially as regards KOS–YPA, as the YPA accounts for around 50 per cent of the federal budget at the present time. The YPA, and hence KOS, is financed at the federal level of government, while the FSIA (of which UDBa is part) is reportedly financed by a mixture of federal, republican and communal resources.

As is also the case with the KGB, prolonged and thorough training (including intensive political indoctrination by the LYC) of UDBa operatives is reported to have always been a top priority in the organization, with training taking place at UDBa's Faculty of Security and Social Self-Protection in Belgrade, which is reportedly

---

police' – ibid., p. 8. According to this source Dalibor Jakaš, wartime head of GOC and OZNa – UDBa foreign section head in the 1940s and 1950s, went to Latin America in the 1950s as a 'diplomat' looking for the Ustaše leader, Ante Pavelić. He found him in hiding in Argentina. In 1957 Jakaš personally attempted to assassinate Pavelić, who was paralysed by his wounds, eventually dying in Spain in 1959. Jakaš indirectly confirmed the above in an interview with the Zagreb newspaper, *Vjesnik*, 13 May 1974 – the thirtieth anniversary of OZNa's foundation in 1944.

38. Rullmann, *Assassinations*, pp. 8–9.

Marko Milivojević

modelled on the KGB Academy in Moscow. It is also reported that senior UDBa operatives have attended and continue to attend the KGB Academy in Moscow – known as the 'highest school' in UDBa circles[39] – for advanced intelligence and security training. This UDBa–KGB training relationships does not seem to have been affected by past changes in Yugoslav–Soviet relations, with the notable exception of the 1948–53 period.

Although the YPA has a number of elite training institutions, such as the High Military Academy in Belgrade, it is unclear as to whether KOS has a special training facility for its operatives. It is highly likely that it does have such a facility, which is probably modelled on the GRU's Military-Diplomatic Academy in Moscow. It is also highly probable that some sort of KOS–GRU training relationship has always existed, as it is known that YPA officers have received advanced military training at a number of Soviet military academies in the past.

YISC Internal Politics

The post-war distribution of power within and between the constituent components of the YISC is what made it, after the seminal events of 1966, unique in the communist world in general, with the notable exception of post-1981 Poland, which was ruled by General Jarulzelski's military regime. Figure 6.2 is a diagramatic representation of this changing distribution of power within the YISC during the post-1948 period, which also presents the relationship of the ruling CPY–LYC (and Tito in particular) to the two constituent components of the YISC: KOS–YPA and OZNa–UDBa.

From 1944 to 1966, OZNa–UDBa were in a position of political dominance over the YPA, which was matched by the institutional dominance of OZNa–UDBa over KOS in the YISC. This situation was ordered by Tito; and following standard Soviet practices in such matters, the YPA was kept in a subordinate political position relative both to the CPY–LYC and OZNa–UDBa, with the help of the latter. At this time, the YPA was very much outside mainstream politics, while Ranković's UDBa was, as has already been seen, very politically active at the highest levels of the regime, especially during the period 1961–66, which ironically was to prove its undoing in 1966.

39. Thomas Plate and Andrea Darvi, *Secret Police: The Inside Story of a Network of Terror* (London, Robert Hale, 1982), p. 51.

Figure 6.2 The Yugoslav Political System, post-1948 period: Structure and Distribution of Power

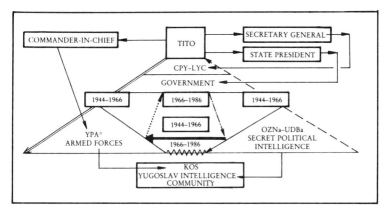

Key:

*	Includes military service, KOS. Controlled by, and reporting to, YPA Chief-of-Staff. KOS institutional rival of OZNa–UDBa in Yugoslav intelligence community.
◄—	Political dominance of OZNa–UDBa over YPA, and institutional dominance of OZNa–UDBa over KOS in the Yugoslav intelligence community.
∿►	Political dominance of YPA over SDB, and institutional dominance of KOS over SDB in the Yugoslav intelligence community.
↘	Power of SDB, under Ranković, became so great as to endanger implementation of post-1963 reform process, and possibly Tito's own political dominance. Tito, therefore, purged Ranković and SDB with assistance of YPA, and KOS in particular, in 1966.
↘	SDB placed under tighter LYC political control by Tito in 1966, through purge and reorganization of SDB. SDB rehabilitated by Tito and his new Prime Minister, Mitja Ribičić (ex-Slovenian OZNa Chief), in 1969.
⇑	YPA kept in subordinate political position by Tito, relative to CPY–LYC and OZNa–UDBa, with help of the latter. In 1966, however, YPA became more politically powerful due to purge of SDB by Tito.
↑	Increasing power and influence of the YPA, relative to the LYC and SDB, although partly reversed in 1969 when Tito purged YPA General Ivan Gošnjak. After Croatian disturbances of 1971–72, however, power and influence of YPA continued on its upward path, culminating in its dominant political position in the post-Tito Yugoslavia of the 1980s, especially after the disturbances in Kosovo in 1981.

The purging and public humiliation of Ranković's UDBa in 1966 and thereafter completely changed the distribution of power within the YISC, with the YPA gaining a position of political dominance over UDBa, which was matched by the institutional dominance of KOS over UDBa in the YISC. Again, this situation was ordered by Tito, and unique to Yugoslavia in the communist world at the time, with UDBa placed under tighter LYC political control with the assistance of the YPA and KOS, whose increasing political power and influence in Yugoslav politics and society was only slightly reversed with the full rehabilitation of UDBa in 1969 and the purging of YPA General Ivan Gošnjak in the same year.

The political advancement of the YPA and KOS was to prove, despite the slight reversal of 1969, the first major step in the YPA's full entry into mainstream regime politics thereafter, and especially during and after the Croatian disturbances of 1971–72; an entry that was, however, made at Tito's behest, both in 1966 and 1971–72.

This increasing YPA power and influence in Yugoslav politics and society, which became ever-more pronounced during the 1970s (when the YPA became the ultimate guarantor of the regime), was at its most profound in the YISC, where full YPA–KOS control has been operative from 1966 to the present day. More generally, and especially after the Kosovo disturbances of 1981 and thereafter, the increasing YPA power and influence has extended into the post-Tito era, during which the YPA remained the only real Yugoslav institution in an increasingly *de facto* con-federal political system confronted with, and unable to resolve, the country's most serious multi-faceted crisis since the end of the Second World War. A crisis that could, in time, lead to a YPA military *coup d'état*, which would certainly be expedited by full YPA–KOS control of the YISC – a key factor in any plan to mount a successful *coup d'état* in Yugoslavia.[40]

YISC External Politics

To look at the external political impact of the existence of the YISC involves, in a very real sense, post-war Yugoslavia's entire political, economic and social development, which is what makes the YISC so

40. A question discussed in more detail in Milivojević *et al.*, *Yugoslavia's Security Dilemmas*, especially Figure 1.3, which diagrammatically summarizes the historical origins, institutional forms, associated political problems and future variables of the YPA's political role in contemporary Yugoslavia.

politically important. An importance incomprehensible in Western political systems, where the role of intelligence and security communities is modest, but perfectly comprehensible in communist political systems of the Yugoslav variety, where political power is in the shape of a triangle, with the ruling party at the apex, while the army and political intelligence–security service make up the other two corners.

From 1944 to 1948, the CPY was a purely Leninist–Stalinist political party ruling Yugoslavia with an iron hand, tolerating no opposition (real and imaginary) and emulating Stalin's Soviet Union in all things, including the unlimited powers and mass terrorism of the YISC during this early period. The very ruthlessness and counter-intelligence effectiveness of the YISC enabled Tito's regime to survive the total Soviet blockade of Yugoslavia during the period 1948–53.

However, that Yugoslav rejection of the Soviet Union during the period 1948–53 was to have revolutionary political, economic and social consequences, which the new LYC in 1952 symbolized and henceforth espoused, while these changes were, in time, to lead to major changes in the YISC itself, although this process was not to be finally completed until the events of 1966 in the YISC.[41] First, during the 1950s and 1960s the role of the YISC became, as has been seen, highly selective, discreet and exceptional as regards the number of people whose lives it touched, which contrasted sharply with its more extensive role in the 1944–52 period. Second, and during the period 1961–66 in particular, the then key component of the YISC – Ranković's UDBa – tried, unsuccessfully as it turned out, to reverse the reform process in Yugoslav politics and society, which had been agreed upon in the form of the 1963 SFRY Constitution, and whose ultimate cause was the aforementioned political, economic and social revolution of the early 1950s.

Ranković's UDBa, created and developed before the events of 1948–53, clearly wanted to retain a dominant position in politics and society, the development of which during the 1950s and 1960s it found highly distasteful. By 1963, this was no longer tenable as the

---

41. How that 1948–53 rejection of the Soviet Union was ideologically justified, and with what future political and social consequences, is discussed in detail in A. Ross Johnson, *The Transformation of Communist Ideology: The Yugoslav Case, 1945–1953* (Cambridge, Mass., MIT Press, 1972). A rejection of the Soviet experience, in which the role of the NKVD – KGB was unquestioned, could not but affect the role of the YISC, which was (as regards UDBa) questioned in public in 1966.

political and social forces that favoured the reform process of the 1960s could not be stopped. Tito, though he had much sympathy for Ranković's political views, came to accept this situation, given his fine appreciation of the balance of political and social forces in the country in the 1960s.[42]

For all these reasons the power and influence of Ranković's UDBa was broken in 1966. And broken in a humiliating public manner, involving extensive purges of old operatives, reorganization, criticism in the media and the redefining of its future role, which was no longer to involve dangerous intrigues at the *haute politique* level of the regime, but was to lead to a more professional service with limited responsibilities dealing with the designated domestic and foreign political enemies of the LYC regime.[43]

The public humbling of UDBa, despite its rehabilitation under YPA–KOS control in 1969, was to have important political consequences in Yugoslavia, as the events of 1966 would, in the words of Dennison Rusinow, have 'an enormous impact on political behaviour and popular attitudes'.[44] Consequences that first manifested themselves in 1968, with serious disturbances in Kosovo, where a UDBa-directed policy of mass terror – not seen in the rest of Yugoslavia since the 1940s – had been fully operative from 1944 to Ranković's fall in 1966. This mass terror was fuelled by anti-Albanian Serbian xenophobia in UDBa HQ in Belgrade and led to disturbances which were to be repeated, though for different reasons, in 1981 and thereafter.

However, the most significant consequence of Ranković's fall was, in time, to manifest itself in the Croatian disturbances of 1971–72, which was the most serious domestic threat to Tito's regime since the end of the national liberation–civil war in 1944. Disturbances whose secessionist tendencies were to be eliminated by the YPA–KOS-dominated YISC, but whose republican–nation-

42. In this, as in so many other instances (especially before the Croatian events of 1971–72, which Tito seemed to endorse in 1970–71), Tito acted in an opportunistic manner, the trademark of all political survivors, who have no real ideas of their own or any firm convictions, which is the general view of Milovan Djilas, *Tito – The Story From Inside* (London, Weidenfeld & Nicolson, 1981).
43. Mišković's post-1966 reorganization of UDBa was based on the recommendations of the Crvenkovski Commission, whose final report (see note 21) recommended that UDBa's reorganization should be on the basis of the removal of incompetent and/or corrupt operatives, the ending of blatantly political appointments, improved professionalism and training, strengthened LYC political supervision, and that its operations should be confined to dealing with designated (by the LYC) domestic enemies and threats from abroad.
44. Rusinow, *The Yugoslav Experiment*, p. 188.

alist aims were, in part, achieved in the 1974 SFRY Constitution, by which the LYC regime operates to this day.

The post-1966 loosening-up of Yugoslav politics and society (which saw, among other things, a resurgence of the old 'national question' in the country) continued throughout the 1970s and 1980s, thereby creating numerous problems for the YPA–KOS dominated YISC, whose primary function became the containment, and if possible the elimination, of the political and social forces that had, in the last analysis, been released and strengthened by the events of 1966.

Operations and Problems

Operational Objectives and Methods

Despite extensive changes in its political–operational organization and methods, the YISC remains a key component of a political system that is an example of what John Dziak, writing about the Soviet Union, calls a counter-intelligence state, which displays:

> an overarching concern with 'enemies', both internal and external. Security and the extirpation of real or presumed threats become the premier enterprise of such systems – and are among the few state enterprises that work with a modicum of efficiency and success. The fixation with enemies and threats to the security of the state involves a very heavy internal commitment of state resources. Further, this fixation demands the creation of a state security service that penetrates and permeates all societal institutions (including the military), but not necessarily the claimant to monopoly power, usually a self-proclaimed 'revolutionary' party. This security service is the principal guardian of the party. I would label such a system the counter-intelligence state.[45]

The ruling LYC, though bitterly divided organizationally and politically, was still in agreement about one thing. It wished to retain its monopoly of political power, with the assistance of what has long been a YPA–KOS-dominated YISC, whose operational objective has always been to deal with this regime's real and presumed domestic and foreign enemies, although its operational

45. John J. Dziak, *Chekisty: A History of the KGB* (Lexington, Mass., Lexington Books, 1988), pp. 1–2.

methods have changed a great deal since 1944. Since 1966 the YISC, dominated by the YPA, has existed within a wider and extremely comprehensive national security–counter-intelligence–internal security system, which is shown in Figure 6.3.

The *domestic* (1–2) and *foreign* (3–6) operational objectives and methods of this system are as follows:

1. To protect and perpetuate, through UDBa's domestic section, the political monopoly of the LYC (and the CPY before it) regime against its designated political and other enemies, real and presumed. The methods used being surveillance (agent informers, covert monitoring of communications, covert and overt human surveillance), administrative measures, unlimited powers of arrest and pre-trial detention, political trials within a politicized judicial system, special political prisoner regimes in the country's penal system, and unlimited powers to harass and persecute ex-political prisoners upon their release from prison.

2. To protect, through UDBa–KOS counter-intelligence, the country's internal security, and the internal security of its major institutions (LYC, YPA and all state bodies) in particular, from foreign espionage, active measures, special warfare, subversion and the electronic and other interception of strategic and other communication systems in the country. The methods used being surveillance, administrative measures, unlimited powers of arrest and pre-trial detention, secret *in camera* trials (for domestic agents of foreign countries), and expulsion (for foreigners with diplomatic immunity involved in espionage).

3. To gather, through UDBa–SID and KOS, strategic intelligence abroad on the political intentions of hostile and friendly governments towards the LYC regime. The methods used being espionage, active measures (especially agents of influence, disinformation and overt propaganda, all of which also aim to influence the policies of foreign governments towards the LYC regime) and the covert interception and monitoring of strategic and other communications systems in targeted countries abroad.

4. To gather, through KOS, tactical intelligence on the military capabilities of hostile and friendly governments whose military policies are of relevance to Yugoslavia's security, and especially the military policies–capabilities of governments with which the

Figure 6.3 The Yugoslav National Security/Counter-Intelligence/
Internal Security System

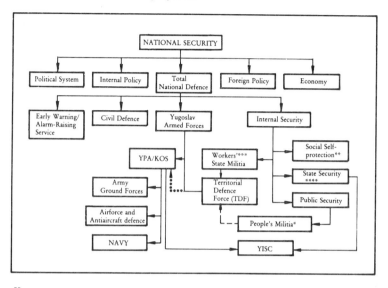

Key:

*	The country's armed police would became part of the TDF in wartime.
**	Social Self-protection is not a separate part of internal security, but is an integral part of every component of the country's national defence system.
***	Paramilitary internal security force under the control of the FSIA that would become part of the TDF in wartime.
****	Known as the SDB (State Security Service) since 1964. Previously known as UDBa (1946–64) and OZNa (1944–46).
••••••	Though the TDF remains an organizationally distinct entity within the Yugoslav Armed Forces (YAF) in *de jure* terms, it is now under the *de facto* command of the YPA Chief-of-Staff.

Source: Milan N. Vego, 'The Yugoslav Ground Forces: A Look at the Past and the Present', *Military Review*, Vol. 60, November 1980, Fig. 1, p. 17, plus additional insertion (YISC) by author of this chapter.

LYC regime and YPA may find themselves at war in the future. The methods used being espionage and the covert interception and monitoring of strategic and other communications systems in targeted countries abroad.

5. To monitor and disrupt, through UDBa–SID, the political and other activities of hostile émigrés of Yugoslav origin and their

numerous organizations, which are one of the legacies of the 1941–44 Yugoslav civil war. The methods used being espionage, active measures (especially agents of influence, disinformation, assassinations and kidnappings) and the covert interception and monitoring of emigre communications, especially with people inside Yugoslavia.

6. To monitor, through UDBa–SID, all SFRY citizens abroad, whose numbers have been extensive since the early 1960s, due to the labour export policies of a LYC regime confronted with high domestic unemployment. The methods used being espionage, active measures (especially agents of influence and disinformation), administrative measures and the covert interception and monitoring of the communications of such people, especially with people inside Yugoslavia.

Domestic Operational Targets

Looking at UDBa's domestic operational targets involves, at the very least, asking two key questions: *how* (methods) and *why* (politics) the CPY–LYC regime, through UDBa's domestic section, dealt with them in the way that it did since coming to power after the civil war ended in 1944.

The 'how' question, briefly, can be easily answered by understanding the extent of the operational changes that have taken place in UDBa's domestic section since the mass terrorism of the 1940s, which affected a substantial proportion of the country's population at the time. Since the early 1950s, as has been seen, UDBa's operational methods in the domestic political and internal security sphere have been characterized by discretion, selectivity and surgically precise targeting of politically troublesome individuals and groups. This has been a generally very effective operational strategy, which carefully utilized extensive operational capabilities (means) to changing political ends (objectives), and described in the following terms by a group of émigré observers:

> The Yugoslav regime's political terror, employed by the state through its judiciary, the police and various political bodies, is designed to make its impact with the least possible means, but for the victims of those means – and per capita, in this respect, Yugoslavia stands foremost in Europe – it is the Gulag revisited. There is no need to terrorize the entire population:

the persecution of a carefully chosen 5 per cent achieves the same effect.[46]

The 'why' question, equally briefly, can be answered by understanding changing political conditions in Yugoslavia, conflicts with foreign countries (especially the Soviet Union) and the very nature of the CPY–LYC's Marxist–Leninist ideology, which places permanent class struggle and/or conflict (and hence the search for enemies) at the centre of political and social life. All of which has made it necessary for UDBa's domestic section to deal with a long list of major and minor domestic and foreign enemies – a never-ending search for enemies that does not seem to have been affected in the least by wider political, economic and social changes in Yugoslavia since 1948, although these changes have, as has been seen, necessitated changes in how, and within what parameters, that search has been conducted.

UDBa's major domestic operational targets have included, as is shown in Figure 6.4, the CPY's civil war enemies (1940s), Cominformists (1940s and 1950s), Croatian nationalists (1970s) and ethnic-Albanian nationalists (1980s), while UDBa's minor domestic operational targets have included dissident intellectuals, religious believers and radicalized workers. These domestic operational targets have, in turn, always been treated as a counter-intelligence problem, as domestic political opponents of ruling communist regimes are, without exception, given largely imaginary foreign connections, whose purpose is to label domestic political enemies as 'traitors', 'hirelings' and 'spies', who are allegedly controlled by foreign countries, and their intelligence and security services in particular.

However, real foreign connections have existed in the past. The Cominformists, for example, have had proven and extensive connections with the Soviet Union and its Warsaw Pact allies,[47] who have always been the major foreign operational targets of UDBa

46. Committee to Aid Democratic Dissidents in Yugoslavia (CADDY, New York), 'The Yugoslav Oppositionists and the US State Department: An Exchange of Views', *Survey*, Vol. 28, No. 3 (122), Autumn 1984, p. 69.
47. Most extensive, for obvious reasons, during the period 1948–53, but still of some significance until as late as the early 1970s, when the Soviet Union played the Cominformist 'card' with a secret Cominformist Congress in Yugoslavia in 1974 by the so-called 'Communist Party of Yugoslavia', which Moscow had created and supported for many years. For this affair, which UDBa dealt with its usual ruthlessness (culminating in a number of political trials in 1975 and 1976), see Christopher

Figure 6.4 Operational Targets (Domestic and Foreign) of the YISC, 1944–87

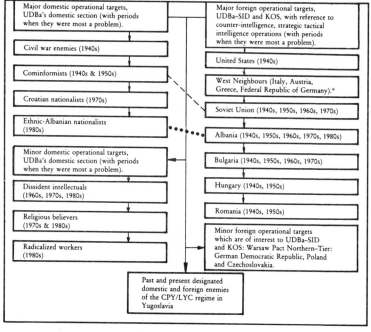

Key:

*   For most of the post–1944 period relations with these four countries have been more bad than good. As regards Italy and Greece, relations did not really become good until 1974, when the Greek military regime fell in Athens, and the Yugoslav–Italian dispute over Trieste was finally resolved. Good Yugoslav–Austrian relations go back before 1974, but the Yugoslav–Austrian dispute over Carinthia remains unresolved to this day, although Yugoslavia has long pursued a policy of not making a public issue of this dispute for wider economic and political reasons. Yugoslav relations with West Germany, though of great economic importance since the 1960s, remain politically difficult and sensitive due to past history, the presence of hostile émigrés in the FRG and the treatment of SFRY citizens working in West Germany as guestworkers since the 1960s.

– – –   Proven and extensive connections between the Yugoslav Cominformists and the Soviet Union, especially during the period 1948–53. Thereafter, the Soviet Union and its Warsaw Pact allies remained the main foreign operational target of the YISC. Of these allies, Bulgaria has been the most consistently hostile, due to the Yugoslav–Bulgarian dispute over the Yugoslav republic of Macedonia.

••••••   Proven, though limited, connections between ethnic–Albanian nationalists and Albania, which has been consistently hostile towards Yugoslavia since 1948 for ideological and political reasons.

and KOS as regards counter-intelligence and strategic–tactical intelligence operations. This was an inevitable consequence of the 1948 Yugoslav–Soviet split, as well as later Soviet willingness to attempt to subvert Yugoslavia through a manipulation of its internal political problems.[48] Of the Soviet-bloc neighbours of Yugoslavia, Bulgaria has always been the most hostile due to the issue of Macedonia, although this Bulgarian hostility was reduced during the 1980s following a major improvement in Soviet–Yugoslav relations at this time, and especially after the coming to power of Gorbachev in the Soviet Union in 1985.

Proven, though limited, connections have also existed (and probably still exist) between ethnic-Albanian nationalists in the troubled province of Kosovo and neighbouring Albania, which has been virulently and consistently hostile towards Yugoslavia since 1948. This is malignant enmity that became particularly dangerous during and after the 1981 disturbances in Kosovo.[49]

As regards the West, and Yugoslavia's three Western neighbours in particular (as well as the US, further afield), periodic Yugoslav charges that its governments (and that of the US in particular) have been involved in subversive activities in Yugoslavia – via a manipulation of its internal problems – are largely unproven. They are also highly improbable to any rational observer, as since 1948 the primary strategic objective of Western governments in Yugoslavia has been the survival of the LYC regime, and not its subversion.[50]

Foreign Operational Targets

While counter-intelligence operations against the espionage, ac-

---

Cviic, 'A Pro-Soviet Plot in Yugoslavia', *The World Today*, October 1974, and Gavriel D. 'Ra'anan, *Yugoslavia After Tito: Scenarios and Implications* (Boulder, Colo., Westview Press, 1977), pp. 51ff.

48. Apart from playing the Cominformist 'card' in 1974, the Soviet Union also, during the Croatian disturbances of 1971–72, seemed to have toyed – via covert KGB contacts with Croat émigré organizations such as the so-called 'Croatian Communist Party' – with also playing the Croatian nationalist 'card' in the early 1970s. For this affair see Slobodan Stanković, 'Belgrade Protests Against Soviet Support for Anti-Yugoslav Emigrés', Radio Free Europe, *Research Papers*, No. 1034, 11 June 1971, p. 3.

49. For the issue of ethnic-Albanian nationalist Albanian connections (especially during and after the 1981 disturbances in Kosovo) see Stevan K. Pavlowitch and Elez Biberaj, *The Albanian Problem: Two Views*, Conflict Studies Nos. 137–8 (London, Institute for the Study of Conflict, 1983); especially the Pavlowitch paper.

50. A point convincingly argued in CADDY, 'Yugoslav Oppositionists' though this source sees continued Western (especially US) support of the current LYC regime as being both morally objectionable and politically short-sighted in the extreme.

tive measures, subversive, disinformation and communication interception and monitoring activities of the YISC's major foreign operational targets (since 1948, largely the Soviet Union and its Warsaw Pact allies, as shown in Figure 6.4) have always been a top priority for UDBa's domestic section and KOS (which is, first and foremost, a counter-intelligence organization), purely foreign operations – such as strategic–tactical intelligence gathering – have also been given a great deal of attention by these two organizations, as was also probably true of Tito's personal intelligence service when it existed.[51]

KOS tactical intelligence gathering, which is concerned with the military capabilities of Yugoslavia's neighbours (especially the Soviet-bloc countries to the east), is centrally directed by KOS HQ in Belgrade, while the actual gathering (as at 1988) is almost certainly (for reasons already given) on the following basis: KOS Belgrade/West Serbia (Albania, Hungary, Romania and the Soviet Union, especially Soviet forces in Hungary),[52] KOS Niš/East Serbia (Romania and Bulgaria, especially Soviet forces in Bulgaria),[53] KOS Zagreb/Croatia/Split naval region (Hungary, plus all foreign naval forces in the Adriatic and East mediterranean seas), KOS Ljubljana/ Slovenia (Italy, Austria and Hungary), KOS Titograd/Montenegro (Albania) and KOS Skopje/Macedonia (Bulgaria, Greece and Albania).[54] Though not bordered by any foreign country, KOS Sarajevo/Bosnia–Hercegovina is also reported to be of great import-

51. From 1961, when the non-aligned movement was formally inaugurated in Belgrade, Tito's major preoccupation was foreign policy, which remained very much his personal responsibility until his death in 1980: a responsibility that would have entailed having good and timely intelligence on the numerous foreign policy issues he was concerned with over the years.

52. Budapest, at the time of writing (1989), is the HQ of the Soviet Southern Group of Forces (SSGF), which commands all Soviet forces in South-east Europe, (Hungary and Bulgaria). It is now known that in 1951, when a Soviet invasion of Yugoslavia was planned, Budapest–Hungary were the key to Soviet military strategy against Yugoslavia. For this plan see Bela K. Kiraly, 'The Aborted Soviet Military Plans Against Tito's Yugoslavia', in Wayne S. Vucinich (ed.), *At the Brink of War and Peace: The Tito–Stalin Split in a Historic Perspective*, War and Society in East Central Europe, Vol. 10 (New York, Social Science Monographs, Brooklyn College/ Columbia University Press, 1982).

53. According to Kiraly, *ibid.*, also a key country in the 1951 invasion plan, from whose territory Soviet and Soviet-controlled forces would make for Niš in Eastern Serbia and Skopje in Macedonia, while Soviet and Soviet-controlled forces from Hungary would make for Novi Sad–Belgrade and Zagreb–Ljubljana. Any future Soviet invasion of Yugoslavia would, in essential matters, be based on this 1951 plan.

54. Since leaving the Warsaw Pact in 1961, Albania's puny armed forces have not posed a direct threat to Yugoslavia's security, but Albanian intrigues in Kosovo are an indirect threat, which could conceivably lead to war between the two countries in the future.

ance for the gathering of tactical intelligence and other military activities.[55]

Strategic intelligence gathering, which is concerned with the political intentions of Yugoslavia's neighbours (plus West Germany, US and Soviet Union further afield), is jointly and centrally directed by UDBa HQ (SID) and KOS HQ in Belgrade, with the former traditionally dominating such operations, working throughout in close cooperation with the Federal Secretariat for Foreign Affairs. How efficacious such operations are is unknown, but it is doubtful whether UDBa–SID has ever made much progress in gaining strategic intelligence in the Soviet Union, which is the archetypal 'counter-intelligence state', wherein the largest Western intelligence–security services, such as the US CIA, have always found it very difficult to penetrate, especially as regards the top echelons of the Soviet government.

Nor is it at all likely that UDBa–SID have ever penetrated the highest ruling echelons of its major Western operational targets – West Germany and US – although its active measures operations (propaganda, disinformation, agents of influence – especially in the Western media)[56] have, over the years, been very successful in putting over a generally favourable view of Yugoslavia to Western governments, who have long fully supported the LYC regime,[57] as well as ensuring a key position for Yugoslavia in the non-aligned movement, where Yugoslavia has always been very well regarded.

---

55. Since 1968 the YPA high command has, as a matter of policy, located many strategically important military and logistical assets in the Bosnia-Hercegovina military district, which are thought to include important KOS–YPA cipher and communications, and electronic communications intercept and monitoring facilities. The entire military district has been turned into a natural fortress, which would play a key role in any future war with the Soviet Union and its Warsaw Pact allies. For this issue see A. Ross Johnson, *Yugoslavia: In the Twilight of Tito*, The Washington Papers Vol. 2, No. 16 (Beverly Hills & London, Sage Publications, 1974), chapter 4.

56. Active measures operations, which aim to manipulate and influence foreign political systems to the political advantage of those doing the manipulating, have long been a major operational priority of the KGB's First Chief Directorate. A subject discussed in Richard H. Shultz and Roy Godson, *Dezinformaltsia: Active Measures in Soviet Strategy* (McLean, Va., Pergamon/Brassey's International Defence Publishers, 1984). It is highly likely that UDBa–SID emulated the KGB in the area of active measures, which successfully applied can yield immense political dividends externally for a comparatively modest outlay of domestic resources.

57. This is not just due to Yugoslavia's post-1948 foreign policy stance, which Western governments have found useful to their security, but is also due to extensive and generally successful Yugoslav courting, manipulation and influencing of Western public opinion, which has had a generally positive view of Yugoslavia since 1948; a positive view that has, without a doubt, proved most beneficial to Yugoslavia over the years.

Extensive Soviet influence in the Third World has, in recent years, however, made Yugoslavia's position in a movement largely created by Tito increasingly marginal.[58] This marginalization became especially marked after Tito's death in 1980.

Finally, UDBa–SID has had two further strategic objectives: monitoring SFRY citizens abroad and monitoring and disrupting the activities of hostile émigrés and their organizations. The first objective, made necessary by the labour export policies of the LYC regime in the 1960s and 1970s, involved a massive surveillance operation, as by 1975 around 1.5 million SFRY citizens were employed abroad, with around 650,000 of the total figure resident as 'guestworkers' in West Germany in 1975. This total figure fell a little during the late 1970s and early 1980s, but it is still substantial, posing a major problem for the LYC regime, which is unique in the communist world in allowing so many of its citizens to go beyond its borders – and hence its direct control – for purely economic reasons.

Having so many SFRY citizens abroad also had its advantages, however, enabling relatively easy UDBa agent infiltration into Western countries, plus large SFRY diplomatic and other presences in certain Western countries, notably West Germany, which unwittingly became host to a large number of UDBa operatives posing as 'diplomats'. All of which greatly aided UDBa–SID strategic active measures and other operations against hostile émigrés and their organizations.

Such operations included surveillance, penetration, active measures (especially agents of influence, propaganda and disinformation) and counter-intelligence work in Yugoslavia to discover links between such hostile émigrés and people inside the country. In addition, and especially since 1964, UDBa–SID has adopted a campaign of general intimidation, assassination and kidnapping to deal with particularly troublesome émigré operational targets.

It is now reasonably certain that 1964 saw a key meeting in UDBa HQ in Belgrade, attended by its then chief, Svetislav Stefanović, the Croatian UDBa chief, Uroš Slijepčević, and the head of the Zagreb UDBa, Marijan Odak.[59] At this meeting, and upon Tito's direct

---

58. Some recent Western observers, such as Beloff, *Tito's Flawed Legacy*, chapter 2, claim that Yugoslavia has always been non-aligned against the West, while at one and the same time covertly advancing Soviet interests in the so-called non-aligned movement, which is now almost exclusively pro-Soviet in its attitudes.

59. Rullmann, *Assassinations*, pp. 10ff. From the very first this work was very

orders, a new assassination department was reportedly set up within SID, and modelled on its KGB counterpart, whose brief was to assassinate or kidnap prominent émigrés as and when ordered to do so.[60] One source has estimated that UDBa agents assassinated around seventy-two émigrés all over the world from 1945 to 1981, with all but seven of these assassinations taking place after 1964 when the new department was reportedly set up.[61] This assassination campaign continues, though on a reduced scale, to this day.[62]

Operational Problems and Challenges

Though this paper is entitled the *Yugoslav* Intelligence and Security Community, the truth of the matter is that UDBa and KOS have always been dominated by *Serbs*, while the other peoples of Yugoslavia have never, at any time since 1944–45, been represented in these two organizations in proportion to their numbers in the country as a whole. This state of affairs is at heart a political problem, but the existence of a Serb-dominated YISC has created unique operational problems in the area of domestic politics, in that this Serb domination of UDBa and KOS has, in the eyes of the

---

dangerous for all concerned in it, as those present at the reported 1964 meeting had knowledge of Tito's reported secret order to liquidate the most dangerous hostile émigrés. This followed the first Croat émigré terrorist incursion into Yugoslavia in 1963, which was followed by a larger incursion into the country in 1972. Of the three men present at the 1964 meeting, Stefanović was purged in 1966, while Odak died in a mysterious car crash in 1984 – a favourite UDBa device for disposing of operatives who had outlived their usefulness.

60. Prior to the creation of this new department, UDBa assassinations had been carried out on an *ad hoc* basis, such as Jakaš's attempt on the life of Pavelić in 1957 (see note 37). After 1964 the entire business was more organized, involving the training of assassins (usually ex-criminals), and almost certainly involving KOS in some way (for armaments and explosive devices). The new UDBa–SID assassination department was almost certainly based on the KGB's notorious Department 13 (1954–68) – later known as Department V (1968–72), and now known as Department 8, Directorate S (Illegals), First Chief Directorate, KGB (1972–present). For this issue see Dziak, *Chekisty*, Appendix B.

61. Rullmann, *Assassinations*, pp. 72–4. According to this source, of these seventy-two assassinations around fifty-six were Croat émigrés, which proved that the Croat émigrés were considered the most dangerous by the LYC regime. Some of those assassinated were leading Croat émigré terrorists, notably the leaders of the Croatian Revolutionary Brotherhood, who organized the 1963 and 1972 incursions into Yugoslavia. However, most of the victims were legitimate political leaders, editors of émigré publications and writers of material hostile to the LYC regime.

62. Since 1981 a number of UDBa assassinations have taken place (mostly in West Germany – the favourite UDBa killing ground since 1964), most notably that of Stjepan Djureković, a Croat INA official who had fled to East Germany, who was murdered by UDBa agents in Wolfratshausen on 29 July 1983. For this case see *ibid.*, p. 72.

non-Serbs, belied the allegedly supranational Yugoslav identity of these two intelligence and security organizations.

Finding statistics on this politically sensitive problem is hard, but quite a lot more is known about KOS – a part of the YPA General Staff – than about UDBa. Yugoslav sources have admitted that around 70 per cent of the YPA officer corps is Serb,[63] while Western sources have put this figure as high as 80 per cent.[64] However, at the YPA high command level (which includes the higher echelons of KOS), Serb domination is less marked, as 38 per cent of the top twenty-four commanders were Croats in 1971.[65] On the whole, therefore, the lower echelons of KOS have always been dominated by Serbs, but its higher levels have always been more balanced, with Croats – Manola (1950–?) and Mišković (1963–66) – often occupying the position of KOS chief, which has mostly been occupied by Croats in the post-war period.

In the case of OZNa and UDBa, however, Serb domination has always been more marked, although the changes of 1966 did lead to a more balanced ethnic composition at the command level in UDBa HQ in Belgrade. From 1944 to 1966, under Ranković and Stefanović, this Serb domination in OZNa and UDBa was reportedly absolute, although the evidence for this is more anecdotal than statistical, as no figures on this question have ever been published in Yugoslavia. This state of affairs, which also existed in the FSIA and the ordinary criminal police (People's Militia) at this time, caused great resentment among non-Serbs, and the Croats and ethnic-Albanians in particular, but it was nothing new, as before the 1941–45 war Croats and ethnic-Albanians regarded the absolute Serb domination of the then political and ordinary criminal police as the most brutal manifestation of a wider Serb position of dominance in Royalist Yugoslavia.[66]

---

63. Stanković, *End of the Tito Era*, p. 36, which cites Dr V. Bakarić as the source for this figure.

64. A. Ross Johnson, *Role of the Military in Communist Yugoslavia*, p. 16. Since this study was published the numerical preponderance of Serbs in the YPA officer corps has not significantly changed. For the situation in the 1980s, see Robin Alison Remington, 'Political – Military Relations in Post-Tito Yugoslavia', in Pedro Ramet (ed.), *Yugoslavia in the 1980's* (Boulder, Colo., Westview Press, 1985).

65. Bogdan Denitch, *The Legitimation of a Revolution: The Yugoslav Case* (New Haven, Conn., Yale University Press, 1976), pp. 197ff. Since 1971 no further figures have been published in Yugoslavia on the ethnic composition of the YPA high command (or on the YPA officer corps in general), but it is believed that the principle of ethnic proportionality at the YPA high command level has been maintained as a matter of high policy by the LYC regime to this day.

66. Elizabeth Wiskemann, *Undeclared War* (London, Macmillan, 1967), p. 111.

After the 1966 purges in UDBa, whereby removed Serbs were simply replaced with other Serbs, little reportedly changed at the lower (republican) levels of the organization, but as with KOS (where the process began much earlier), the ethnic composition at the command level in UDBa HQ in Belgrade became more balanced, with Croats such as Mišković (UDBa Chief, 1966–73) and Herljević (head of the FSIA, 1974–84) at the high operational and political levels in UDBa and the FSIA respectively.

For non-Serbs, however, these high-level changes in the FSIA, UDBa, KOS and the YPA high command in general did little to alter their perceptions of a Serb-dominated concentration of intelligence and security service, military, para-military and ordinary police power, which became so dominant and influential in Yugoslav politics and society during the 1970s and 1980s.

This ethnic imbalance in the YISC, which mirrors a similar imbalance in the institution that has controlled it since 1966 (the YPA), will make it even more difficult for the YISC, and UDBa in particular, to discharge its assigned domestic role in a Yugoslavia afflicted with what one recent observer calls a state of 'general chaos'[67] – a chaos characterized by *de facto* political con-federalism and the near-anarchy that goes with it at the level of the federal government, economic collapse, and rising social discord, which makes it very difficult, if not impossible, to determine what, exactly, is or should be the role of the YISC, and UDBa in particular, as regards domestic politics.[68]

Turning to external challenges to the YISC, both as regards counter-intelligence and strategic–tactical intelligence gathering (as well as active measure operations), its role is clearer, as the major

---

Also see Cynthia H. Enloe, *Ethnic Soldiers: State Security in a Divided Society* (Harmondsworth, Penguin Books, 1980), p. 88.

67. Sabrina P. Ramet, 'The Role of the Press in Yugoslavia', see below, chapter 14. The role of the YISC, like that of the press (or any other community or institution for that matter), exists and is largely determined by wider political, economic and social conditions in Yugoslavia.

68. UDBa, though dominated by a YPA given to constant calls for 'order' in politics and society, *cannot* be separate from, nor go against, the *republican* factions and centres of power that presently, in the form of a loose coalition, make up the LYC regime. What constitutes political dissent (and hence the label of 'enemy', which brings UDBa into the case) is now, for example, very different in relatively liberal Slovenia and Croatia than in the more hardline republics of Serbia and Bosnia–Hercegovina. This confusion cannot be to the liking of UDBa, and it is known not to be to the liking of the YPA high command – for this issue see Milivojević et al., *Yugoslavia's Security Dilemmas*, whose analysis examines the possibility of a future YPA *coup d'état*.

foreign operational targets of the YISC constitute, especially as regards the Soviet Union and its allies and Albania, a permanent threat which necessitates equally permanent vigilance by all organs of the Yugoslav 'counter-intelligence state' (to borrow a phrase). A threat which could, notwithstanding a recent improvement in Yugoslav–Soviet relations, take the form of increasing foreign intrigues in a country plagued by so many problems, which have thereby created a window of opportunity for any foreign country interested in exploiting this state of affairs for its own hostile purposes.

Conclusion

This chapter ends, as it began, with two explanatory assumptions about the role of the YISC, both of which are intimately related to one another, and the separation of which in this chapter has only been done for the purposes of analysis, as in reality the political and organizational–operational aspects of the YISC cannot be separated.

The political role and impact of the YISC, and UDBa in particular, was and is a *central* one in Yugoslav politics and society, although its study has, for reasons already given, remained neglected in the secondary literature on Yugoslavia. This neglect has also existed, though on a smaller scale, as regards the intelligence and security communities of the democratic West and the communist world (and the Soviet Union in particular), which one recent observer has rightly called 'the missing dimension' of twentieth-century political, diplomatic and military history.[69]

The missing dimension of post-1944 Yugoslav politics is the YISC, whose political role and impact was of central importance during the CPY's seizure and consolidation of monopoly political power (1941–46), its historic struggle for survival against the Soviet Union (1948–53), and its high-level power struggle (in the form of the LYC) over the reform process (1961–66), whose implementation continues to dominate Yugoslavia's political, economic and social development to this day. This historic reform process could only go forward in the way intended *after* the political power of Ranković's UDBa was broken in 1966, which was also to lead to a

---

69. Christopher Andrew and David Dilks, 'Introduction', in Christopher Andrew and David Dilks (eds.), *The Missing Dimension: Governments and Intelligence Communities in the Twentieth Century* (London, Macmillan, 1984), p. 1.

general loosening of Yugoslav politics and society. This often confusing situation was, in turn, to create many problems and challenges for the YISC, and UDBa in particular, during the often turbulent 1970s and 1980s.

The seminal events of 1966, which saw a transfer of power from UDBa to KOS in the YISC, represented an organizational–operational change in that community that had no precedent in post-1944 Yugoslavia and which was unique in the communist world as a whole, where *military* control of a *political* intelligence and security service was unthinkable (especially in the Soviet Union): a situation that only General Jarulzelski's military takeover in Poland in 1981 ended.

The post-1966 YPA–KOS control of the YISC was also, it is now clear, the first major step in the YPA's subsequent growing power and influence in Yugoslav politics and society, which became so marked during the 1970s and 1980s, although the YPA's entry into mainstream politics was at Tito's behest, both in 1966 and during and after the Croatian disturbances of 1971–72. Contemporary Yugoslavia, where the YPA is now seen as the ultimate guarantor of the LYC regime, is still living with the consequences of that development, whose final forms have yet to be played out in the country.

Finally, though long organizationally–operationally unique in the communist world, the YISC (and UDBa in particular), as the 'sword and shield' of the LYC regime,[70] remains similar to its foreign communist counterparts as regards its ultimate intent and purpose: to perpetuate the political monopoly of that regime against all its real and presumed domestic and foreign enemies, which is one matter upon which that regime's otherwise divided elite is in full agreement about. In that respect at least Yugoslavia, for all its reforms, remains firmly in the communist world, and which makes its YISC very different from its counterparts in the democratic West, where the defence of the state does not mean the indefinite perpetuation of the political monopoly of a particular political party.

70. Which is the apt image that appears on the logo of the Soviet KGB, and from which the title of the book upon which this chapter is derived comes (see note 1).

7

Foreign Trade and Stabilization Policy in a Self-Managed Economy: Yugoslavia in the 1980s
Will Bartlett

Introduction

The high interest rates and low growth rates which were persistent features of the advanced capitalist economies during the early 1980s, combined with the relative overvaluation of the US dollar, exacerbated the (dollar-denominated) foreign debt position of many peripheral countries, including some of those in the Mediterranean region. Countries which have been responsibly financing economic growth expenditures through external borrowing found themselves quite unexpectedly plunged into crises of debt-service capability so that there was a sharp increase in the proportion of their export revenues going to repay previous borrowings. This meant that emergency borrowing had to be undertaken from the International Monetary Fund (IMF), which was conditional upon the implementation of so-called 'stabilization' programmes which involved deflation and often currency devaluation. Whilst this uncoordinated approach to 'muddling through the debt crisis' (Dornbusch, 1984) was successful in avoiding a collapse of the international financial system it brought about dramatic reductions in economic activity in many of the countries involved. In Latin America, for example, 'the

This chapter is based on research undertaken in 1985–86 while I was a Research Fellow at the European University Institute in Florence, and later developed at the University of Bath. I am grateful to Mario Nuti, Milica Uvalić, Phil Hanson, Colin Lawson, and participants at the Congress of the European Economic Association, Vienna, August 1986, and the Conference of the Development Studies Association, University of East Anglia, September 1986, for their helpful comments and suggestions.

size of the decline is comparable with the devastation which the developing countries experienced during the great depression' (ibid., p. 151). This 'sackcloth and ashes' (Dell, 1982) approach to policy making in the new circumstances of world-wide recession was not avoided in the self-managed economy of Yugoslavia. It is the purpose of this paper to analyse the impact of such a stabilization policy in the context of a labour-managed economy and to assess the implications for Yugoslavia in the 1980s.

Yugoslavia's Economic Crisis

Following a period of adjustment to an extensive economic reform of the mid-1960s, Yugoslavia experienced a continuation of the rapid growth which had been a feature of its earlier post-war economic performance. This new phase of growth lasted from the late 1960s until the end of the 1970s. Indeed, in the second half of the 1970s Yugoslavia's economy was the fastest growing in Europe. However, from around 1980 the economy entered a period of profound crisis with a continuous slow-down in the growth of real social product which became an actual decrease in 1983. As Bajt (1984) has indicated, previous analysis of the growth slow-down of the middle-1960s undertaken by Sapir (1980) mistook what was actually a temporary adjustment phase for a secular crisis. The experience of the 1980s, on the other hand, looks much more serious. Table 7.1 shows some of the dimensions of the present Yugoslav crisis as it began to develop in the first half of the 1980s.[1]

From 1980 onwards the growth rate of real social product fell continuously until 1983, and increased only slowly and hesitatingly in the following two years. Real net personal incomes in the social (self-management) sector fell continuously, from an index of 100 in 1980 to 76 in mid-1985, although real per-capita personal consumption fell somewhat more slowly as devaluation augmented the value of foreign currency holdings, and shadow economy sources of earnings supplemented individual incomes from employment in self-managed firms.

Nevertheless, by 1985, it was estimated that some 40 per cent of social sector workers were living near the poverty line. At the same

---

1. For a more detailed discussion see Skulić (1982), Fehr and Zloch (1983), Brera (1984), and Lydall (1989).

Table 7.1 Economic Performance in the 1980s

	1980	1981	1982	1983	1984	1985
Real GSP growth (% p.a.)	2.4	1.4	0.7	−1.3	2.0	0.2
Index of retail sales volume (1980 = 100)	100	96	96	93	89	86
Real net personal income in the socialized sector (1980 = 100)	100	95	92	82	77	76
Real per-capita personal consumption (1980 = 100)	100	98	98	96	94	89
Consumer price inflation (% p.a.)	30	46	29	39	57	80
Gross foreign debt (US$bn)	17.4	19.0	18.5	19.1	18.6	18.6

Sources: OECD, 'Main Economic Indicators', 1986; *Savezni Zavod za Statistiku, Jugoslavia 1945–1985: Statistički Prikaz*, Belgrade, 1986.

time there was a rapid acceleration of inflation, approaching 80 per cent by 1985.[2] The emergence of a serious liquidity crisis forced some firms to the point of bankruptcy as interest rates were raised to unprecedentedly high levels, in an effort to create positive 'real' interest rates, that is interest rates which would be numerically above the rate of inflation.

Foreign Trade Performance

The connection between these two phases of rapid growth and subsequent slow-down can be located in the nearly continuous current account deficit on the balance of payments which was experienced throughout the 1970s dash for growth. As can be seen from Table 7.2 the current account was in deficit in seven out of the ten years of the decade.

The problem was that imports were rising very rapidly in line with the high rate of growth of domestic demand, but exports and the net earnings from services increased much more slowly. A large part of net service income was accounted for by the remittances of workers abroad, mainly in West Germany, and as the recession in Western Europe deepened throughout the 1970s, so this flow of remittances weakened, as can be seen from the falling share of

2. See Bartlett and Weinrich (1985) for a discussion of inflation processes in a theoretical model of a labour-managed economy.

Table 7.2 Foreign Trade in the 1970s (US$m)

	1970	1971	1972	1973	1974	1975	1976	1977	1978	1979
Exports	1,678	1,817	2,241	2,853	3,805	4,072	4,878	5,254	5,671	6,794
Imports	2,874	3,252	3,233	4,511	7,520	7,697	7,367	9,634	9,988	14,019
Trade balance	**1,195**	**1,435**	**992**	**1,658**	**3,715**	**3,625**	**2,489**	**4,380**	**4,317**	**7,225**
Services (net)	847	1,079	1,412	2,143	2,532	2,622	2,654	2,798	3,061	3,564
Current account balance	**348**	**357**	**419**	**485**	**1,183**	**1,003**		**165**	**1,582**	**1,256**	**3,661**
Workers' remittances services	0.56	0.61	0.61	0.51	0.54	0.50	0.53	0.51	0.57	0.48

Note: Bold figures represent negative flows.

Source: OECD, *Economic Survey of Yugoslavia*, 1980 and 1984, Table M.

Table 7.3 Current Balance as a Percentage of GDP at Market Prices (average of annual % in each year)

	1965–9	1970–4	1975–9
	−0.43	−0.88	−2.76

Source: Lydall (1983), p. 169.

remittances in total net services shown in Table 7.2. The consequence of the failure of exports and net service income to cover the rapidly rising import bill was a steady increase in the ratio of the current account deficit relative to Gross Domestic Product (GDP) (see Table 7.3).

An earlier phase of high current account deficits had been experienced before 1965, and whilst the economic reforms of the mid-1960s have been most noted for the extension of self-management rights to the workforce of the socialized sector (Estrin, 1983), they also ushered in a development strategy supposedly geared towards a process of export-led growth in place of the previous import-substitution strategy, a feature of the reforms which has been documented by Flaherty (1982).

Table 7.4   Growth Rate of Real Value of Yugoslav Exports (% p.a.)

1965–70	1970–8	1974–9	1979–83
4.8	3.2	1.9	1.0

Source: Bartlett and Uvalić (1985).

However, whilst real export growth was initially rapid, by the end of the 1970s it had slowed noticeably (see Table 7.4), despite attempts to encourage exports by means of a system of foreign exchange retention quotas, which were further extended by the Foreign Exchange Laws of 1977. These laws also established the regional 'self-managed communities for foreign trade' (CIFERs), which were responsible for reallocating above-quota foreign exchange among the regional importers, often as a premium above the official exchange rate. Despite the existence of this export promotion measure, the balance of payments current account deficit peaked in 1979 by which time Yugoslavia had accumulated a foreign debt of US$17 billion, and found itself placed among the ten most indebted nations in the world.

It should also be noted that Yugoslav trade is diverse in its destination, with large shares of trade with both Eastern and Western blocs. This gives an added element of flexibility to Yugoslav firms in their export allocation and import purchasing decisions, but it also means that debt servicing, which is undertaken in convertible currencies, is covered by a lower level of relevant export earnings than is apparent from the global figures alone.

Stabilization Policy in Yugoslavia

In 1980, Yugoslavia agreed with the IMF to a three-year programme of economic stabilization, which was typical of those policies applied under IMF guidance to developing countries with balance of payments difficulties (Killick, 1984). Such programmes are drawn from a rather standard menu which includes exchange-rate adjustment, strengthening of the market mechanism, liberalizing foreign trade, liberalizing credit markets, restrictive monetary and fiscal policy and cuts in budget deficits. Nearly all these policies have been applied in the Yugoslav case since 1980.

The course of exchange-rate depreciation is shown in Table 7.5,

Table 7.5 Official Foreign Currency Exchange Rates (per US$) (July)

1980	1981	1982	1983	1984	1985	1986	1987	1988
27.3	36.9	49.2	98.4	154.6	273.2	408.6	739.7	2,705.5

Source: Comecon Data 1988, Vienna Institute for Comparative Economic Studies, London, Macmillan.

Table 7.6 National Bank Official Discount Rate (%)

1980	1981	1982	1983	1984	1985
		(June)	(July)	(Oct.)	(May)
6	6	12	30	47	67

Source: National Bank of Yugoslavia Quarterly Bulletin.

where it can be seen that the exchange rate of the dinar for the dollar fell from 27 dinars per dollar in 1980 to 2,705 dinars per dollar in 1988, a depreciation of about 99 per cent. The government deficit, which had been as high as 1 per cent of GDP in 1980 was held at less than 0.05 per cent of GDP thereafter. The renegotiations of 1984 produced a Letter of Intent which included measures which the *Financial Times* described as 'even more Draconian' than those of the previous stabilization phase. Further depreciation of the dinar was to be accompanied by a liberalizing of credit markets which involved the attainment of real interest rates by March 1985. The impact of this measure is shown in Table 7.6.

As it turned out this target was not achieved. The effect of the credit squeeze was so great that many enterprises faced bankruptcy and the policy was relaxed by a postponement of the target date. Nevertheless, the National Bank discount rate reached 67 per cent by May 1985, and by the end of 1987 had doubled to reach 120 per cent, although the 'real' interest rate was still negative. Further devaluation was assured by a floating devaluation of the dinar, whilst the market mechanism was 'strengthened' by the termination of a six-month price freeze which had been introduced in January 1984. A restrictive monetary policy was introduced at the same time as interest rates were increased, although control over the money supply has been frustrated by the development of extensive inter-firm crediting. The rapid increase in this form of quasi-money

243

supported the accelerating growth of prices which, as shown below, was directly associated with currency depreciation. Its importance was graphically illustrated in 1987 with the debacle at the bankrupt agricultural conglomerate, Agrokomerc, one of the leading Bosnian labour-managed enterprises which had supported its expansion by issuing unbacked bills of exchange. In effect, this enterprise, like many others to a lesser extent, was issuing its own currency with the connivance of the local political and administrative elite who were keen to promote local economic development at a time of general economic contraction. From this point on, following the purge of members of the local elite involved in the affair, the economic crisis began to spill over into a more general political crisis of increasing intensity. On the side of fiscal policy, the federal government had equally imperfect policy instruments available. Fiscal policy instruments are only weakly developed in Yugoslavia, and instead of raising taxes on personal incomes to reduce the demand for imported consumables, the main fiscal measure used to control the demand side has been sharp cuts in government expenditure, involving cuts of up to 50 per cent in capital programmes. As shown by Bartlett and Uvalić (1985), a large part of the drop in imports in the 1980s has thus been due to cuts in capital imports from the West, which has only had the effect of reducing still further the prospects for a future increase in the productive efficiency of the economy.

In April 1985 Yugoslavia received a further standby credit for 1985–86 of US$300 million, which led to the conclusion of a rescheduling agreement with several hundred Western banks on 3 August 1985 to reschedule US$3.5 billion of debt principal due. These rescheduling negotiations did not proceed smoothly, as the Yugoslavs protested at the premium over standard Eurocurrency rates which they were being asked to pay. But the IMF demanded that an agreement should be reached and threatened to withdraw its standby credit. As part of the agreement, Yugoslavia submitted to regular 'enhanced' monitoring of its economic performance by the IMF. On 29 July the *Financial Times* bestowed a rare favour of a leading article on Yugoslavia entitled: 'Yugoslavia: Time For Reform'. It commented:

> The economy is bent out of shape in many ways, partly to do with its fragmentation, or more aptly, balkanization, along the lines of the country's eight republics and provinces . . . and partly to do with the

vaunted system of self-management . . . The dilemma for the Yugoslav government is that the long-term scale for the IMF-prescribed cure for inflation, which Belgrade feels it has to follow to keep creditor confidence, does not match its increasing short-term political problems . . . On the other hand, accelerating inflation has begun to tear at the fabric of Yugoslav society.

As an example we may note the rash of strikes which occured in 1985, notably the strike of 2,000 miners at Stari Trg in Kosovo on 13–14 August, while at Koper in Slovenia eight workers were sacked and fifteen demoted for leading 500 dockers out on strike on 12 July. Two faced expulsion from the party. Less dramatic and hardly reported – but more widespread – are the so-called 'white-strikes' where workers turn up for work but simply don't work, or work counter-productively, in response to a situation in which, in May 1985 for example, nearly 10,000 workers in 463 enterprises received reduced wages due to enterprise illiquidity. And in 1985 also, the Communist Party is reported to have lost membership among blue-collar workers for the first time. Labour unrest became widespread in the late 1980s, in the face of a continual decline in living standards, which was only briefly arrested in 1986. In Serbia, in particular, dissatisfaction was harnessed into a political movement promoting Serbian nationalism which threatened to encourage a further regional fragmentation of an economy which has already lost much of its internal cohesion. The province of Kosovo in particular became a focus of nationalistic dissent with claims of discriminatory practices being hurled between Serbs and Albanians on the basis of little more than unsubstantiated newspaper reports and rumour, despite the scarcity of any firm evidence for discrimination in, for example, the labour market (Bartlett, 1990). This economic and political fragmentation also exacerbated the poor foreign-trade performance as each republic vied for scarce foreign currency, the duplication of production facilities reduced the nation's comparative advantage in trade through specialization, and trade opportunities were diverted away from other republics towards the overseas market in a reversal of the benefits which could be expected to be gained from a customs union.

In addition, there were signs of some confusion over the underlying rationale for the stabilization measures. For example, one of the government's three special experts appointed to negotiate with the IMF was reported as saying that both an extension of market forces *and* more central planning would be needed before economic restructuring could take effect. Confusion over the economic basis of the stabilization policy is not to be wondered at, however, since, as is shown below, there exists a potential conflict between the various policy measures applied, in particular between the exchange rate and the interest rate policies, conflicts which emerge uniquely in the context of a self-managed economy. It will be shown, in other words, that it is not sufficient in devising policies of economic stabilization, that is policies to deal with chronic balance of payments deficits (supposing they could ever be effective on an unco-ordinated national basis alone), without making a careful economic analysis of the system-specific features of the economy to which they are to be applied.

Issues of Stabilization Policy in a Self-managed Economy

If the rapid growth and associated balance of payments crisis and debt problem was the cause of the introduction of the stabilization programmes of the 1980s, so, it is argued in this chapter, was the stabilization programme itself at least partly responsible for the economic difficulties of the 1980s. This view contrasts with that of Robinson and Tyson (1985) whose work has been adopted by the World Bank as the basis of its latest report on Yugoslavia (World Bank, 1984), and was apparently being used as a basis of some planning models inside Yugoslavia. Robinson and Tyson estimated a computable general equilibrium model to simulate the effects of various policy options. For example, they estimated that in 1980 the dinar had been overvalued by some 20 per cent with respect to its equilibrium level. This, however, as subsequent events have shown, was a wildly inappropriate estimate since a depreciation of more or less 90 per cent has actually been required to bring about current account equilibrium in convertible currency transactions. Even granted that over such a long period *ceteris paribus* conditions could not hope to be maintained, a model which yields estimates which seem to be so much at variance with observed outcomes should be considered vulnerable to substantial criticism. The criticism which is relevant in the present context is that the Robinson–Tyson model takes no account of the particular systemic features of the Yugoslav economy, that is its self-managed structure. Although this structure is deeply embedded in the economy, Robinson and Tyson avoid the issue and prefer to model Yugoslav firms as pursuing an objective of constrained profit maximization, the constraint being the achievement of a minimum target growth rate of wages. Whilst it is possible to trace this line of argument back to the work of Horvat (1967), one loses much of the peculiar character of Yugoslav self-managed socialism as the resulting behaviour of the system becomes theoretically akin to that of a capitalist economy with strong unions. However, it is possible to build upon the extensive literature which has emerged over the past twenty years on the economics of the labour-managed firm (see Bartlett and Uvalić, 1986, for a review),[3] and attempt to make applications on issues of trade, employment and inflation in Yugoslavia. The successful application of this line of theory to the issue of income distribution in Yugoslavia (Estrin, 1983) encourages the further pursuit of this theme in the present context.

The first feature of the stabilization policy which I wish to examine in the context of labour management theory is the effect of a devaluation on the supply response of firms engaged, or potentially engaged, in export trade. Since a devaluation or depreciation of the dinar involves in the first instance an increase in dinar-denominated export prices, it seems at first glance as though we may apply the classic theorem due to Ward (1958) on the supply response of an income-per-head maximizing labour-managed firm. This theorem states that in the short run, with labour the only variable input, the supply function will be characterized by an inverse relation between supply and price. In the long run, with both labour and capital variable, the supply response is indeterminate, although in the restricted case of a homothetic technology supply can be shown to be completely inelastic with respect to price changes (Ireland and Law, 1984).[4] All this could cause very serious problems for balance of payments stability in the face of a devaluation.

A standard method for the analysis of balance of payments stability is the 'elasticities approach' (see, for example, Alexander, 1959; Bronfenbrenner, 1956). The approach hinges upon the as-

<hr>

3. The 'self-managed' firm of Yugoslav reality can be distinguished from the 'labour-managed' firm of pure theory. The latter is of course designed as a model of the essential system-specific features, abstracting from the full, confusing, detail of reality.
4. Recently Ireland has produced an example of a technology which induces a positive long-run supply response on the part of a labour-managed firm, see Ireland (1985).

sumptions made concerning the values of some of the key elasticities of demand and supply in the foreign trade market. If at least two of these can be reasonably assumed to be infinitely large, then it is possible to derive an explicit condition showing the expected effect of a currency devaluation on the trade balance, for any values of the other two elasticities. For example, let e_m and e_x (measured positively) stand for the demand elasticities for imports and exports respectively, and s_m and s_x for the corresponding supply elasticities. If we follow the conventional assumption that the supply elasticities for exports from the domestic economy, and for the imports from the rest of the world into the domestic economy are very large, and in the limit are infinite, then it is easy to show (see Appendix I), that devaluation will improve the trade balance so long as the demand elasticities sum to a value greater than, 1, that is:

$$(e_m + e_x) > 1 \qquad (7.1)$$

This condition has become known in the trade literature as the 'Marshall-Lerner condition' and is commonly used without much attention being paid to the underlying assumptions.

But if the supply elasticity for exports is very small or even actually negative then the Marshall–Lerner condition is invalid. In the present context, Ward's labour-management theorem indicates that the supply elasticity of exports cannot be taken to be very large, whilst, on the other hand, the position of Yugoslavia as a small country relative to the size of the world market means that we may assume the demand elasticity for Yugoslav exports to be very large. Under these assumptions it can be easily shown (see Appendix I) that the condition for a balance of trade improvement following a devaluation should be that the sum of the export supply elasticity and the import demand elasticity should be greater than zero, that is:

$$(s_x + e_m) > 0 \qquad (7.2)$$

Clearly, if e_m, is small and s_x is negative, then this condition may be violated and devaluation may be unstable, and produce a perverse balance of payments reaction. That this may be a real possibility for the Yugoslav case is indicated by empirical estimates of the short-run elasticity of import demand which has been calculated by Tyson and Neuberger (1979) to be about 0.3, a figure whose order of magnitude is supported by other studies surveyed by Burkett (1983).[5]

The Labour-managed Economy in the Face of a Foreign Trade Opportunity

It is, however, insufficient to consider the export response of a labour-managed firm or sector in isolation from the impact of the devaluation on the supply decisions to the domestic market. An appropriate way to analyse the behaviour of a labour-managed economy with a foreign trade sector is through a model which treats the socialized sector as if it were a single labour-managed firm, faced with two distinct markets. The domestic market is characterized by a downward sloping demand curve for the output of the sector, whilst on the overseas market demand is perfectly elastic, since there are many alternative sources of supply readily available. Such a situation is characteristic of the Yugoslav case since the self-managed industrial sector is highly imperfect (Estrin and Bartlett, 1982) and is afforded a degree of protection by the foreign exchange allocation system.[6] (The OECD report of 1984 also mentions the

5. Tyson and Neuberger (1979) report a failure to obtain significant estimates of the price elasticity of export demand. A summary of all the work done on estimating import and export functions up to about 1982 is presented in Burkett (1983), most of which, to varying degrees, supports the research findings of Tyson and Neuberger. He also reports an equation for the export price index due to Fair (1981) which gives a coefficient of exactly 1.00 to the dinar/dollar exchange rate with a t-statistic of 42. As Burkett remarks, this implies that 'devaluation is futile as a means to increase the competitiveness of exports' (Burkett, 1983, p. 107). Burkett reports for his own estimates a negative (but insignificant) estimate of the elasticity of export supply, and an elasticity of import demand of about 0.26. Within the range of the reported standard errors of the estimates, therefore, the true figure for the export supply elasticity, assuming there are no serious simultaneous equation biases, could be either small and positive, or small and negative.

6. Under this system firms were allowed to retain a portion of their own hard-currency export earnings, and surrender the rest to local republican governments or the federal government. The regional CIFERs acted as auctioneers of bids and offers of foreign currencies, a process which took place under the aegis of the CIFER and took the form of self-management agreements. The proportion of foreign exchange earnings retained by the enterprises and either used for their own purposes or sold at a mark-up to other enterprises through the CIFER system, varied from time to time as amendments to the 1977 Law were introduced in 1982 and 1983, but was generally around 40 per cent. In this way, a dual system of rationing of foreign exchange was implemented which Robinson and Tyson (1985) dub as fix-price and flex-price systems. Under the fix-price system, firms could import at the official rate up to their foreign exchange quota set by the plan, whilst under the flex-price system, firms could import outside those limits, but usually paying a premium over the official rate. Whilst the foreign exchange retention system was designed as an export-promotion measure, the regionalization of the resale market organized through the

249

existence of some import quotas but little information is available.) Since the labour-managed sector is a price-maker on the domestic market, and a price-taker on the export market, the model is akin to models of price discrimination which have been developed elsewhere,[7] but which require substantial modification in the present context.

The Yugoslav socialized sector is therefore modelled here as a composite labour-managed firm, which allocates labour between production for the export market and production for the domestic market and sets domestic prices, given the demand elasticity, in such a way as to maximize income per worker. As is shown in Appendix 2, this requires that the labour-managed firm equates marginal revenue product in each market. Given this equilibrium condition, the reaction of the sector to a change in the exchange rate can be worked out. We require only one more new concept, namely that of the 'domestic viability' of the economy. By domestic viability is meant a situation where domestic sales (i.e. sales to the domestic market) are, on their own, sufficient to cover fixed costs of production. In contrast the economy may be 'domestically unviable' and yet may still support a positive level of income per head through export earnings. So long as the economy was domestically viable, currency depreciation would tend to induce a shift of labour resources into the export sector and lead to an increase in the volume of exports. Domestic viability could be problematic if fixed costs were raised so high, say through a sudden sharp increase in interest costs, or if there was a sufficiently large drop in labour productivity, say through a drop in investment or through a decrease in work motivation, that the labour-managed firms in the socialized sector became increasingly unprofitable. Eventually the economy would become domestically unviable, and then the direction of the export response to a currency depreciation would be reversed.

To see these effects, suppose initially that the economy is domestically viable. Equilibrium is attained where marginal revenue

---

republican CIFERs was a prime cause of the break-up of the domestic market into semi-independent sub-markets. This fragmentation of the Yugoslav market has led to multiple inefficiencies (Uvalić 1983) and the CIFERs and associated system of retention quotas were abolished at the beginning of 1986.

7. A model of a price-discriminating capitalist firm in the context of foreign trade has been developed by Basevi (1970), whilst an earlier attempt to apply the technique to the case of a labour-managed firm was made by Katz and Berrebi (1980). However, some technical flaws in the latters' analysis prevented them from deriving the general results, which are contained in the present paper.

product is equated in each market. This equilibrium is preferred to an autarchic equilibrium because fixed costs are diluted across the workers employed in the production of exports. Should a devaluation take place, that is the exchange rate rise, then the initial increase in income per workers permits a reduction output for the domestic market (along the lines of the Ward theorem) to take advantage of the inelasticity of domestic demand. However, this involves a reduction in the total number of employed workers and leads to an intensification of fixed costs per worker. Further dilution of fixed costs per worker may then be obtained by shifting workers *into* the export sector (*contra* the Ward theorem), whilst the infinitely elastic demand of the overseas market ensures that dollar prices do not need to change as a result of the increase in supply of exports.

Suppose, on the other hand, that domestic production is unviable. Then production for the overseas market plays the role of diluting fixed costs to such an extent that that production as a whole is viable. As the dinar depreciates this role for overseas production becomes less urgent and employment in the export sector can be reduced in the usual way for a labour-managed firm faced with a price increase. The increase in average revenue simultaneously permits a reduction of employment for the domestic market, as average costs can be covered at a lower level of output and a correspondingly higher price.[8]

The predictions of the effects of a devaluation or depreciation of the currency following from the model are therefore as follows:

1. In each case domestic price rises, irrespective of any feedback effect from higher import prices.

2. In each case the volume, though not necessarily the value, of domestic sales falls.

8. The point can be expressed more precisely by focusing on equation (A5) from Appendix 2:

$$y = ep_2q_2{}'$$

whilst from equation (A1): $y = (ep_2q_2 + [p_1q_1 - c] / (l_1 + l_2))$
Let $[p_1q_1 - c] = \theta(l_1)$
then $y = (ep_2q_2 + [\theta(l_1)]) / (l_1 + l_2)$
Considering variations in l_2 alone, $\theta(l_1)$ acts like a fixed cost. For $\theta(l_1) < 0$ we have the standard case that as the price e rises, so y rises more than proportionately to ep_2q_2' so the equilibrium value l_2^* falls. However for $\theta(l_1) > 0$, y rises less than proportionately to ep_2q_2' and so the equilibrium value l_2^* rises.

3. In the case of 'domestic viability' the volume and value of exports rises.

4. In the case of 'domestic non-viability' the volume of exports falls, as does the value in foreign currency, although its value in domestic currency may rise or fall.

Should domestic fixed costs rise (say due to an increase in the interest rate or an increase in the domestic price of essential imports), then, although there would be no effect on any given established equilibrium, the elasticity of export supply will be reduced.

A corollary of the model is that the stability implications of the modified Marshall–Lerner condition developed above depend crucially upon whether the economy is in a regime of domestic viability or one of domestic non-viability. In the former case the spectre of an unstable response to devaluation or depreciation vanishes, since the elasticity of export supply has been shown to be positive. However when the economy is in the regime of domestic non-viability, the possibility of an unstable trade balance response to a devaluation or a depreciation is a very real one.

The Consequence of Stabilization Policy in Yugoslavia

Table 7.7 shows the evolution of the foreign trade position after the introduction of the stabilization policy after 1980. The really startling thing about this table is the sharp fall in import values, from US$15 billion in 1980 to US$12 billion in 1985, implying a more than 20 per cent reduction in value terms alone.[9] The nominal value of imports did not return to the 1980 figure until the end of the decade. Exports showed much less response to the stabilization policy, at any rate after 1981. The trade balance consequently improved and the current account balance entered into a small surplus in 1983 which has been subsequently maintained. A similar picture emerges with respect to trade with the convertible currency area which is affected most directly by the devaluation (although some trade with Council for Mutual Economic Assistance (CMEA) countries is conducted in convertible currencies – but the account-

9. That a large part of the reduction was due to the fall in imports of machinery from the EEC area is shown in Bartlett and Uvalić (1985).

Table 7.7 Foreign Trade in the 1980s (US$m)

	1980	1981	1982	1983	1984	1985	1986	1987	1988	1989
Exports	8,977	10,929	10,241	9,913	10,254	10,622	11,084	na	12,779	13,560
Imports	**15,064**	**15,757**	**13,334**	**12,154**	**11,996**	**12,223**	**13,096**	na	**13,329**	**15,002**
Trade balance	**6,086**	**4,828**	**3,093**	**2,241**	**1,742**	**1,601**	**2,012**	na	**550**	**1,442**
Current account balance	2,291	750	464	274	504	833	**1,100**	na	2,487	2,427

Note: Bold figures indicate negative values.

Source: National Bank of Yugoslavia Quarterly Bulletin, No. 2. 1985; Vanous (1985); OECD, Economy Survey of Yugoslavia, 1987–88; OECD, Economic Survey of Yugoslavia, 1988.

ing exchange rate used for these transactions has been frozen at least for some of the period – but there will be indirect effects too). Table 7.8 shows the details.

As can be seen from these tables there has been considerable success in reducing the dollar-denominated trade balance,[10] and even creating a surplus on current account transactions as a whole. It is no doubt for this reason that there is a certain optimism in financial circles, and the Western banks are prepared to continue rescheduling the outstanding debt so long as the IMF stewardship is in force.[11]

Real export volumes have been increasing since 1983 (following a fall from 1981 to 1983) as the effects of the devaluation have begun to work through. The supply response of exporting firms has been positive suggesting that the economy is in the regime of domestic viability. The increase in export volumes was around 10 per cent in 1984 and around 5 per cent in 1985 (Vanous, 1985). Initially, foreign indebtedness continued to increase, with gross foreign debt exceeding US$20 billion for the first time in 1987 (OECD, 1988), but began to fall thereafter.

However, as can be seen from Table 7.1, domestic sales fell continuously from an index of 100 in 1980 to one of 89 in 1984. At the same time the price level rose rapidly and by 1989 inflation had accelerated to a hyper-inflation, reaching 500 per cent in the middle of the year, and over 2,000 per cent by its end. Both these features of the stabilization period are predicted by the model.

Despite the recent improvements in export performance which has followed the depreciation of the dinar, the increased illiquidity of the enterprise sector due to the increase in interest rates which has accompanied the stabilization policy created a danger that the economy would enter the regime of domestic non-viability. By 1987, some 7,031 enterprises employing 1.6 million workers were operating at a loss (Lydall, 1989, p. 87). According to a recent report (Economist Intelligence Unit, 1985) enterprise funds have been squeezed dramatically. The report questions whether the government would 'have the nerve to persevere with the IMF programme in the face of an increasing danger of a collapse in the enterprise financial system'. If the economy *were* to enter the regime of

10. The trade deficit had been reduced from –9% of GSP in 1980 to –2.8% in 1985.
11. For an analysis of the Yugoslav foreign debt problem see Bartlett (1987) and Cemović (1985).

Table 7.8 Trade Balances with the Convertible Currency Area (US$bn)

	1980	1981	1982	1983	1984	1985	1986	1987	1988	1989
Exports	5.66	6.44	5.85	6.27	6.59	na	7.2	8.5	9.6	10.5
Imports	**11.32**	**11.74**	**9.63**	**8.07**	7.76	na	**9.8**	9.6	**10.5**	**12.0**
Trade balance	**5.66**	**5.30**	**3.78**	**1.80**	1.17	**0.8**	**2.6**	1.1	0.6	**1.5**
Current account balance	**2.20**	**1.82**	**1.42**	0.3	0.87	0.2	0.2	1.0	2.2	2.0

Note: Bold figures indicate negative values.

Source: National Bank of Yugoslavia Quarterly Bulletin, No. 2. 1985; OECD, Economic Survey of Yugoslavia, 1988.

domestic non-viability, the export response would reverse and the volume of exports and the dollar denominated export revenue would fall as depreciation continued. Then, even the relative success of the improvement in the foreign trade balance would be endangered.

Eventually it became apparent that the medicine was not working. The main visible results were hyper-inflation, and almost total loss of the international value of the dinar, dramatic falls in living standards and production, and an increasing danger that civil unrest would spread from containable clashes between Serbs and Albanians in Kosovo into a much bloodier break-up of the federal system.

A U-turn was called for. It came in January 1990, when a new economic policy was introduced, building on a series of constitutional reforms which had been passed through the Skupština during the previous year, and were designed among other things to encourage the development of new forms of enterprise organization, such as joint-stock companies, partnerships and sole-proprietorships. The policy of depreciation of the dinar was abandoned and the value of the dinar was pegged in relation to the Deutschmark at 7 dinars to the mark. Import restrictions and quotas were lifted on 87 per cent of goods, and the dinar was made convertible. A tight monetary policy was introduced designed to impose a credit squeeze and penalize inefficient enterprises with a real threat of bankruptcy. Since the international value of the dinar was pegged, the trade balance instability associated with non-viability of the self-managed sector economy should have been avoided.

Some initial success was claimed for the policy. Inflation was reduced dramatically reaching a zero level by May, although at a severe cost in terms of a large number of bankruptcies and a continued fall in industrial production. The long-term success of the new policy depends upon the ability of the federal government radically to reform the system, and reinvigorate the productive enterprise of the economy through stimulating the creation of new private or cooperative enterprises. The short-term difficulties and costs involved in such an exercise in restructuring should not be underestimated.

Conclusion

The foregoing analysis demonstrates that the exchange rate and interest rate instruments of a stabilization policy in a labour-managed economy are potentially in conflict with each other. This analysis has been shown to be of relevance to the actual experience of stabilization policy which has been implemented in Yugoslavia under IMF guidance throughout the 1980s.

In contrast to previous analyses I have explicitly modelled the impact of the self-management environment on the outcome of the stabilization policy. The classic Ward theorem on the supply response of a labour-managed firm suggests that the elasticity of export supply might be negative or at best highly inelastic. A modified version of the traditional Marshall–Lerner condition was developed to cope with this situation and it was shown to carry the implication that devaluation would be likely to produce an unstable response of this type and could be expected to be observed in practice. Then a more sophisticated model of the labour-managed firm facing an export opportunity was developed, taking account of the impact of domestic demand upon the export supply decision. This analysis demonstrated that so long as the economy was in a regime which was referred to as one of 'domestic viability' then the possibility of an unstable reaction to a devaluation was removed. However, an over-sharp increase in the interest rate which pushed such an economy into a regime of 'domestic non-viability' would recreate once again the possibility of an unstable reaction to the exchange rate policy.

The attempt to induce developing countries to shoulder the burden of adjustment to the malfunctioning of the international economic system through a unilateral stabilization policy designed apparently to achieve the impossibility of a positive balance of payments surpluses in every country has been dubbed the 'political economy of overkill' by Sidney Dell (1982).[12] The accompanying reduction

12. In the first issue of the Oxford Economic Papers in 1949 Sir Hubert Henderson wrote: 'The idea that exchange rate variations balance of payments is not only . . . fundamentally impractical. It misconceives the attributes of exchange rates; it overlooks their special fitness for a function of real importance. They are one of the few things in the economy which can be definitely fixed; and it is as well that something should be fixed', since, he asserts, they provide a focus of stability. 'For the much larger task which faces us today, deliberate policy, using such instruments as systematic import programmes and trade arrangements, is not only indispensible for the time being, but will remain indispensible in my judgement for many years to

in domestic activity and employment are exacerbated in a self-managed economy by the simultaneous encouragement of hyper-inflation. In addition to this internal instability by the pursuit of an over-ambitious interest rate policy, combined with other measures of the stabilization programme had threatened the Yugoslav self-managed economy with future instability of its external balance too, an event which would impart a sinister resonance to Dell's amusing characterization.

Recent economic reforms and the return to a fixed parity for the dinar hold out the prospect for a renewal of the Yugoslav economy, and a return of the promise of a prosperous alternative path of economic development based on an attenuated model of 'market socialism' similar to that which had appeared so attractive and successful in the later 1960s and early 1970s. However, the economic policies which were adopted in the 1980s have put a severe strain on the political cohesion of the country and resulted in powerful tendencies towards regional fragmentation. This political cost is likely to be their long-term legacy.

---

come . . . the British balance of payments deficit could only be corrected by price-system forces at the cost of huge, unnecessary, and impractical lowering of the standard of life.' (Henderson, 1949, p. 16). This may be more relevant advice for the Yugoslav policy-makers today.

Bibliography

Alexander, S. S. (1959), 'Effects of a Devaluation: A Simplified Synthesis of the Elasticities and Absorption Approaches', *American Economic Review*, Vol. 49, pp. 22–42

Bajt, A. (1984), 'Una reconsiderazione dello svillupo economico jugoslavo', *Rivista di politica economica*, Vol. 74, No. 3, pp. 231–59

Bartlett, W. (1987), 'The Problem of Indebtedness in Yugoslavia: Causes and Consequences', *Rivista internazionale di scienze economiche e commerciali*, Vol. 34, Nos. 11–12, pp. 1179–95

—— (1990), 'Labour Market Discrimination and Ethnic Tension in Yugoslavia: The Case of Kusovo', in M. Wyzan (ed.), *The Political Economy of Ethnic Discrimination and Affirmative Action*, New York, Praeger

Bartlett, W. and M. Uvalić (1985), 'Yugoslavia and EEC Trade Relations: Problems and Prospects', *EUI Colloquium Papers*, 133/85 (Col. 47)

—— (1986), 'Labour-Managed Firms, Employee Participation and Profit-Sharing: Theoretical Perspectives and European Experience', *Management Bibliographies and Reviews*, No. 20, No. 1, pp. 1–67 (special issue)

Bartlett, W. and G. Weinrich (1985), 'Instability and Indexation in a Labour-Managed Economy: A General Equilibrium Quantity Rationing Approach', *European University Institute Working Paper*, No. 85/186

Basevi, G. (1970), 'Domestic Demand and the Ability to Export', *Journal of Political Economy*, Vol. 38, pp. 33–7

Brera, P. (1984), 'L'economica jugoslava dalla reforma del 1965 alla stabilizazione', *Quaderni dell'Instituto di studi economici e sociali*, Vol. 3, pp. 67–140

—— (1984), Self-management and economic development: Jugoslavia's growth patterns in the Seventies and their crisis in the Eighties, *Rivista Internazionale di Scienze Economiche e Commerciali*, Vol. 31, No. 1, pp. 77–96

Bronfenbrenner, M. (1956), 'Exchange Rates and Exchange Stability (Mathematical Supplement)', *Review of Economics and Statistics*, Vol. 32, pp. 12–16

Burkett, J. P. (1983), *The Effects of Economic Reform in Yugoslavia: Investment and Trade Policy, 1959–1976*, Research series, no. 55, Institute of International Studies, Berkeley, Calif., University of California

Cemović, M. (1985), *Zašto, kako i koliko smo se zadužili*, Ljubljana, Institut za unapredjenje robnog prometa

Dell, S. (1982), 'Stabilization: The Political Economy of Over-Kill', *World Development*, Vol. 10, No. 8, pp. 597–612

Dornbusch, R. (1984), 'On the Consequences of Muddling Through the Debt Crisis', *The World Economy*, Vol. 7, No. 2, pp. 145–61

Economist Intelligence Unit (1985), 'Yugoslavia', *Quarterly Economic Review*, No. 2

Estrin, S. (1983), *Self-Management: Economic Theory and Yugoslav Practice*, Cambridge, Cambridge University Press

Estrin, S. and W. Bartlett (1982), 'The Effects of Self-Management in Yugoslavia: An Empirical Survey', in D. Jones and J. Svejnar, *The Economic Performance of Participatory and Self-Management Firms*, Lexington, Mass., Lexington Books

Fehr, E. and I. Zloch (1983), 'Die wirtschaftskrise Jugoslawiens: falsche Wirtschaftspolitik oder Systemfehler?', *Quartalshefte der GZ*, Vol. 18, No. 4, pp. 71–90

Flaherty, D. (1982), 'Economic Reform and Foreign Trade in Yugoslavia', *Cambridge Journal of Ecònomics*, Vol. 6, pp. 105–43

Horvat, B. (1967), 'A Contribution to the Theory of the Yugoslav Firm', *Economic Analysis*, Vol. 1, Nos. 1–2, pp. 288–93

Ireland, N. (1985), 'An Illustrative Production Function for Labour-Managed Firms', University of Warwick, mimeograph

Ireland, N. and P. Law (1984), 'On the Labour-Managed Firm with a Homothetic Technology', *Economic Analysis and Workers' Management*, Vol. 18, No. 1, pp. 1–13

Katz, E. and Z. M. Berrebi (1980), 'On the Price-Discriminating Labour Cooperative', *Economics Letters*, Vol. 6, pp. 99–102

Killick, T. (1984), *The Quest for Economic Stabilization: The IMF and the Third World*, London, Heinemann

Lydall, H. (1984), *Yugoslav Socialism: Theory and Practice*, Oxford, Clarendon Press

—— (1989), *Yugoslavia in Crisis*, Oxford, Clarendon Press

OECD (1984), *Economic Survey of Yugoslavia*, Paris, Organization of Economic Cooperation and Development

Robinson, S. and L. D'A. Tyson (1985), 'Foreign Trade, Resource Allocation and Structural Adjustment in Yugoslavia: 1976–1980', *Journal of Comparative Economics*, Vol. 9, No. 1, pp. 46–70

Sapir, A. (1980), 'Economic Growth and Factor Substitution: Whatever Happened to the Yugoslav Miracle?', *Economic Journal*, Vol. 90, No. 3, pp. 387–402

Skulić, M. K. (1982), *Uzroci Sadašnje Ekonomski Krize u SFRJ*, Belgrade, Zapis

Tyson, L. D'A. and E. Neuberger (1979), 'The Impact of External Economic Disturbances on Yugoslavia: Theoretical and Empirical Explorations', *Journal of Comparative Economics*, Vol. 3, No. 4, pp. 346–74

Uvalić, M. (1983), Il problema del mercato unitario jugoslavo, *Estovest*, 14 (4): 7–44

Vanous J. (1985), 'Yugoslav Foreign Trade Performance and Payments Situation in 1984', *Wharton Econometrics: Centrally Planned Economies Current Analysis*, No. 5, pp. 35–6

Ward, B. (1958), 'The Firm in Illyria: Market Syndicalism', *American Economic Review*, Vol. 48, No. 4, pp. 566–89

World Bank (1984), *Yugoslavia – Adjustment Policies and Development Perspectives*, Washington DC, World Bank

Appendix 1

Following devaluation the extent of change in the balance of trade depends upon the initial level of imports, M, and exports, X, and their responses to the devaluation, which in turn depend upon the demand and supply elasticities for imports and exports. Letting e_m and e_x be the demand elasticities for imports and exports respectively, and s_m and s_x be the corresponding supply elasticities, the general condition for an improvement in the trade balance following a small devaluation (known in the foreign trade literature as the Bickerdike–Metzler–Robinson condition) is:

$$X[s_x (e_x - 1) / (s_x + e_x)] + M[e_m (s_m + 1) / (s_m + e_m)] > 0$$

Conventionally it is assumed that both supply elasticities are very large. Applying L'Hospital's rule to take the limits for $s_m \to \infty$ and $s_x \to \infty$ gives:

$$X.(e_x - 1) + M.e_m > 0$$

and if trade is initially balanced we arrive at:

$$(e_x + e_m) > 1$$

which is the Marshall–Lerner condition. If, however, the elasticities are such that it is e_x rather than s_x which is very large, so that we take the limits as $s_m \to \infty$ and $e_x \to \infty$, then we arrive at the very different result that:

$$(s_x + e_m) > 0$$

which is equation (7.2) in the text.

Appendix 2

Here we consider the self-managed sector as a composite self-managed firm which produces output q_1 by means of labour input l_1 for the domestic market at a dinar price p_1, and output q_2 for export, by means of labour input l_2, at a given world dollar price p_2, converted into dinars through the exchange rate e (dinars/dollar). The firm seeks to maximize income per worker where, given fixed costs c:

$$y = \frac{p_1(q_1[l_1]).q_1[l_1] + ep_2q_2[l_2] - c}{l_1 + l_2} \tag{A1}$$

The domestic demand curve is assumed to be linear and downward sloping so that:

$$p_1' < 0, p_1'' = 0 \tag{A2}$$

while production conditions are such that:

$$q_1' > 0, q_1'' < 0 \tag{A3}$$

First order conditions are given by:

$$y = p_1'q_1'q_1 + p_1q_1' \tag{A4}$$

$$y = ep_2q_2' \tag{A5}$$

As the labour-managed firm equates marginal revenue product in each market, (A4) and (A5) can be combined to give:

$$p_1 q_1' \{1 + 1/\varepsilon\} = ep_2q_2' \tag{A6}$$

Considering a small devaluation, which is equivalent to an increase in e, the comparative statics are given by:–

$$\frac{\delta l_1}{\delta e} = \frac{p_2q_2}{(l_1 + l_2)[2p_1'(q_1')^2 + q_1'' (p_1'q_1 + p_1)]} \tag{A7}$$

But from (A4):

$$(p_1'q_1 + p_1) = y/q_1' > 0$$

therefore:

$$\frac{\delta l_1}{\delta e} < 0 \qquad (A8)$$

Additionally:

$$\frac{\delta l_2}{\delta e} = \frac{p_2 q_2 - p_2 q_2' \ (l_1 + l_2)}{(l_1 + l_2)(e p_2 q_2'')} \qquad (A9)$$

but from (A1) and (A5):

$$p_2 q_2 - p_2 q_2' \ (l_1 + l_2) = \left(\frac{c - p_1 q_1}{e} \right) \qquad (A10)$$

Hence:

$$\frac{\delta l_2}{\delta e} = - \left[\frac{p_1 q_1 - c}{e(l_1 + l_2)(e p_2 q_2'')} \right] \gtrless 0 \qquad (A11)$$

$$\text{as } (p_1 q_1 - c) \gtrless 0 \qquad (A12)$$

since $q_2'' < 0$. When $(p_1 q_1 - c) > 0$, we call the economy 'domestically viable'. This means that domestic sales are, on their own, sufficient to cover fixed costs. In contrast, the economy may be 'domestically unviable' and yet may still support a positive level of income per head through export earnings.

8

Relations Between Britain and Yugoslavia, 1945–1987*

Andrew Wood

It may in retrospect have been rash to agree to present this paper on Anglo-Yugoslav relations since the war – rash to venture among professional historians, as an amateur with little or no time for research, and rash because the canvas to be covered is so large. But a promise is a promise. What follows is based partly on general reading and partly on the accounts sent by my predecessors to London during the past forty years. Some, but only the earliest of the latter, are now available for scrutiny at the Public Records Office. I have not, of course, been able to research official Yugoslav sources, and there are severe limits to my knowledge of other relevant Yugoslav material. The end product is purely personal. The slant is British.

Background

Since the war my own country has been through changes in their way as revolutionary as those in Yugoslavia. In 1945 we were not merely the most powerful Western European country with, it seemed, the strongest economy. We also had an Empire, and formed our foreign policies, in close alliance with the United States, on the basis of these facts. Since then we have implemented fundamental social changes and gone through a period of relative econ-

---

* An earlier version of this paper was presented to an Anglo-Yugoslav seminar in Kragujevac, Yugoslavia (September 1987), held to commemorate '150 Years of Diplomatic Relations with Serbia/Yugoslavia'. The proceedings of the seminar were subsequently published by the Institute for Contemporary History, Belgrade, in November 1988.

omic decline, followed by times of very real difficulty, to emerge today, after painful economic restructuring, with much more buoyant prospects, regaining our rightful place as a major European economic and political force. We have retained our intimate friendship with the United States but have seen the former Empire develop into independent countries, most of whom are members, like us, of the Commonwealth, and have moved steadily closer to our partners in Western Europe. We are today a European power among others, embarked on the adventure which is the European Community, while remaining like our friends and allies conscious of our wider foreign interests and obligations.

All that is clear enough, as it is also clear that similarly profound and fundamental changes have taken place in Yugoslavia, but a reminder at the outset of what we have been through over the past forty years may help to make the constants in the Anglo-Yugoslav relationship clearer. We also need to recall the changes that have taken place in East–West relations, which form an essential part of the background.

Markers

All ambassadors are in favour of good bilateral relations. Sometimes, indeed, their home governments may suspect them of leaning over backwards to avoid unpleasantness. Reading what ours have said from Belgrade about Anglo-Yugoslav relations over the years fixes a certain pattern in the mind. The ups and downs in the relationship were especially marked at the start, but have gradually settled down over time. It would be against human nature to expect them to disappear altogether. Even in the bad times, however, a basic affection for the peoples of Yugoslavia comes through – to quote Sir Charles Peake, writing in October 1951 and surveying the bilateral relationship at the end of a distinguished period as ambassador: 'I have been constantly impressed by the warm and underlying friendliness of the great majority of the Yugoslav people.' His successors have felt the same. Sir Duncan Wilson, for example, wrote a life of Vuk Karadžić as well as a book called *Tito's Yugoslavia*, and I learned much in this vein from my own first mentor, Sir Dugald Stewart. Many here at this seminar will in any case know of this general sympathy and regard through direct personal experience, so I need not labour the point.

Because the swings were more marked at first, it is easier to put dates on them. Merely to write 1945–48, followed by 1948–53 establishes a pattern. I propose to look now a little more closely at those first years with the idea of drawing out some themes which may help us through succeeding swings of the pendulum or, perhaps better, phases of the cycle (the latter allowing for more local difficulties.) Future dates might include 1953–60 or so. Thereafter it is probably best to think in decades, with the caveat that attempting to award retrospective marks for up or down in the bilateral relationship becomes steadily less useful.

The Early Years

The three determining, and interlinked, parameters for the British of the 1945–53 period were Yugoslavia's position within the overall East–West relationship, Yugoslav determination to preserve their country's independence, and the course of Yugoslav internal and ideological development. I have listed them in what now seems to me to have been their order of importance for the British governments of the time, given the possibilities as they then appeared, but it is nevertheless perhaps worth stressing that Yugoslavia's determination to be responsible for herself has always been the bedrock of our relationship, from the time of Colonel Hodges's arrival in Serbia in 1837, through both world wars up until the present. We have never had ambitions to dominate here, despite misinterpretations of the so-called Churchill–Stalin percentage deal. We have always had the most obvious national interest in seeing Yugoslavia as an independent actor on the European stage. That was indeed the interest which seemed to us most directly threatened between 1945 and 1948, when Yugoslavia appeared to be the closest possible ally of a malevolent Soviet Union under Stalin. The British Government did not welcome the changes introduced by the new regime in Yugoslavia after the war and did what it could to make good its obligations to the exiled government it had sheltered in 1941 by promoting the agreement whereby Dr Šubašić and others joined the post-war coalition. But the British made no attempt to interfere with internal Yugoslav processes even though they feared their effect was to bind Yugoslavia more and more closely to the Soviet Union, and despite a number of disquieting incidents, to say nothing of major differences over Trieste and events in Greece. We saw the matter in balance-of-power, not ideological, terms.

Our fears of Yugoslavia becoming merely a Soviet dependency were, of course, confounded by events, however soundly based they seemed at the time. Even then, there were some counter-notes. On 8 August 1945 Tito told the Third Session of the Anti-Fascist Council for the Liberation of Yugoslavia (AVNOJ): 'We desire and will see to it that our cooperation and contacts . . . are as firm in peace as they have been in war . . . we want our relations to become still more heartfelt than at present.' Sir Charles Peake reported that 'nothing could have exceeded the cordiality of Marshal Tito on my first visit to him' in 1946. Despite Yugoslavia's refusal to participate in the Marshall Plan, it was evident that the Yugoslavs, too, very much wanted to maintain and expand trade relations. A British Council exhibition of books in Belgrade and Zagreb in 1947 was opened by Mr Noel-Baker, at that time Secretary of State for Air. Tito came, gave a major reception and hosted a lunch (at which he spoke in English). Later the same year the British Commander-in-Chief in Austria visited Tito in Bled to sign an agreement (later denounced) concerning Yugoslav nationals held in various post-war British camps. Both these events apparently caused strong displeasure to the Soviet government.

As 1948 began, however, Western representatives in Belgrade felt more isolated than ever, and felt the West to be the object of suspicion and mistrust. There were, none the less, useful talks in May that year with Deputy Foreign Minister Bebler in London, and we now know this difficult atmosphere arose from a natural reaction on the part of the authorities to the impending rift with the Soviet Union, which became public on 28 June that year. Sir Charles Peake noted the coincidence with Vidovdan, reporting that on that date 'Soviet Russia initiated open political action against Yugoslavia and helped it perhaps decisively to find its soul.' That is an apt summary of the importance of 1948 when seen through British eyes.

Two points are worth stressing, reinforcing as they do a comment I have already made, that practical balance-of-power politics, rather than ideology, were of the essence in the close relationship that now began to develop between the Yugoslav and the British (as well as the American) governments – a comment that, while true, is nevertheless perhaps truer of the British than the Yugoslav side. The first point is that the Yugoslav Communist Party under Tito's leadership acted in defiance of Stalin without making any prior attempt to secure themselves new friends elsewhere, a course of notable moral and political courage. The second is that my country, along with the United States, came rapidly to Yugoslavia's aid, with the conclusion in our case of a short-term trade agreement and an agreement on compensation for British property nationalized in Yugoslavia by the end of 1948, and a longer-term trade agreement involving very substantial credits by the end of 1949. This was the beginning of a period of extensive, and probably vital, support for Yugoslavia from the United Kingdom, the United States and, in due course, other Western governments. It started at a time when most outside observers saw Yugoslav internal policies as still very much designed to give the lie to Cominform accusations of heresy, the increased push for collectivization being the most obvious case in point. The stress was on the community purity of the Yugoslav government and the prospect of an eventual readjustment of the relationship with the East. A British–Yugoslav marriage of convenience had nevertheless begun – and marriages of convenience are often the most durable.

That relationship developed rapidly in 1949, and more especially 1950, leading to still closer cooperation from 1951 to 1953. Cominform pressure on Yugoslavia and the Stalinist menace increased. In November 1949 Yugoslavia was nevertheless elected to the United Nations Security Council. In June 1950 the North Korean Army attacked South Korea and was condemned for its invasion by the Yugoslav Minister for Foreign Affairs on 5 September. The disastrous drought of that summer led the Yugoslavs to consider economic aid from the Western world, aid which was quickly and generously supplied. Kardelj reported to the National Assembly on 29 December 1950 that British help had been given 'on her own initiative and without any political conditions'. The Yugoslav Foreign Minister visited Britain in early 1951 to seek further economic help and military supplies. Western military equipment was in the pipeline soon thereafter and a tripartite agreement on economic aid was reached with Britain, France and the United States at Bled the same year. Parliamentary delegations exchanged visits during 1951 (the Yugoslav delegation being led by Moše Pijade), and the then Minister of the Interior, Ranković, paid a private visit to the United Kingdom. By 1952 Anglo-Yugoslav foreign policy views were close on a whole range of essential issues of peace and war, including the vital necessity of preserving Yugoslav independence and the need for West German rearmament, a fact recorded during the visit paid by the then British Foreign Secretary, Sir Anthony

Eden, to Yugoslavia in September 1952. The process was highlighted by the state visit paid by Marshal Tito to the United
Kingdom in March 1953 (and returned by Her Majesty The Queen
in 1972) and symbolized in another way by the Treaty on Balkan
Cooperation ratified by Yugoslavia on 23 March the same year.

A last quotation from Sir Charles Peake is in order: 'It has never
been the policy of His Majesty's Government to proselytise the
Yugoslav Government, but rather to leave them free to work out
their own salvation.' (Just as well, really, considering the luck of
those who have tried the opposite tack.) The connection between
ideological and political development in Yugoslavia and Anglo-
Yugoslav relations is nevertheless important, and complex. The
primary British state interest in the question has been whether or
not such developments might compromise Yugoslavia's non-bloc
position, but there has also been a natural British public interest in
the development of Yugoslav socialism and a natural welcome when
it has seemed to the public to be moving in a democratic and liberal
direction. The first Workers' Councils set up in late 1949, leading to
the construction of a framework of a decentralized self-managing
system, as well as the 1951 slow-down and eventual modification of
the collectivization effort, therefore, helped develop Yugoslavia's
relationship with the West. But for all the closeness of that friendship there was never any illusion in London that Yugoslavia's
leaders were about to abandon their socialist orientation or to
change the ideological spectacles through which they viewed the
world, a perspective which defined Britain as capitalist, and therefore to a degree alien, just as much as currently friendly. A major
speech by Kardelj in January 1951 stressed the socialist nature of
Yugoslavia's foreign policy and the country's antagonism to capitalism. Tito emphasized in March 1952 that Yugoslavia stood firmly
by Marxist–Leninist positions and had never made any concessions
in internal or foreign policy. He also underlined the need to fight
'petty bourgeois' influences at home. The Sixth Congress of the
Yugoslav Party in November 1952, while introducing a whole series
of seminal ideas whose general thrust answered to many British
hopes, seemed also to the British grudging about Western aid to
Yugoslavia and unhelpful over colonial problems. Its warnings over
the dangers of Westernization were also duly noted in London.
These forces, coupled with serious differences over Trieste (Sir
Anthony Eden commented to the Yugoslav Ambassador on 1 April
1952 that our efforts to hold the ring there seemed to earn us

nothing but abuse from both Italy and Yugoslavia) meant that once the extreme tensions of the Cold War, as focused on Yugoslavia, were changed by the death of Stalin in 1953, so, too, Anglo-Yugoslav relations were bound to alter.

Some General Themes Apparent in Later Phases

I previously said that I hoped, by discussing the early post-war years, to draw out some themes which might help in an analysis of the later phases of the Anglo-Yugoslav relationship. I do not propose to go through the years since 1953 in detail, but rather to treat the principal areas thematically before attempting some general conclusions.

The first and most obvious point to be made is that we were bound, especially during the pre-*détente* era, to see Yugoslavia very much through the general prism of East–West relations. There were particular troubles over Trieste soon after Stalin's death, involving demonstrations and damage to British premises in Yugoslavia, and the possible threat of worse. The June 1953 meeting on the island of Brioni seemed to modify the outcome of the Sixth Congress in calling for tighter ideological and political discipline within the League of Communists of Yugoslavia. The first steps were taken in 1953 to restore Yugoslav links with the countries of Eastern Europe and the Soviet Union, leading rapidly towards the restoration of close state and party relations on the bases of the 1955 Belgrade and 1956 Moscow declarations. This process was seen on the Yugoslav side as one of normalization but inevitably raised question marks in Western minds as to where it would end. Such doubts were reinforced by particular developments such as Yugoslav statements as to the 'necessity' of Soviet intervention in Hungary in 1956 and Yugoslav recognition of East Germany in October 1959. There were, of course, major counter-notes, like the differences over the Programme of the League of Communists, or the relationship between individual parties on the one hand, and the communist movement as a whole on the other. There was also the withdrawal of Soviet credits in 1958 (as in 1948). This is not the place for an analysis of Yugoslav–Soviet relations – especially as we have authoritative accounts to hand such as Veljko Mićunović's *Moskovske godine: 1956–58* (trans. D. Floyd, *Moscow Diary* (London, Chatto & Windus, 1980)) and his subsequent *1969–71*. But the question of whether or not Yugoslavia might somehow return to the Soviet fold (as the West would see it) was clearly a vital preoccupation for Britain and her allies in the 1950s and 1960s, with consequences for later years too.

The record shows that the British displayed a commendable steadiness of judgement. Sir Ivor Mallet reported at the outset that he did not believe Tito had any illusions about the then Soviet leaders or that he would willingly endanger the independence of his country by breaking with the West or risking again becoming dependent on Moscow. The British Government consistently held to that view, and were given to understand that the Yugoslav Government welcomed the understanding shown for the sincerity of their policy of 'normalization'. It of course helped that the Trieste problem had been resolved in 1954. On the other hand, British and other Western press speculation as to Yugoslavia's future could sometimes have upset official judgement, especially as the Yugoslav press's habit – as British observers saw it – of adopting two standards, one of criticism for the United Kingdom and the West and the other of praise or silence concerning the Soviet Union, tended to work in the same direction.

There was a further, major, issue which troubled Anglo-Yugoslav relations for many years after 1953: the question of colonialism and the direction of the non-aligned movement. The issues were important and difficult in their own right. They also fed speculation about the extent and direction of Yugoslav–Soviet rapprochement. This, along with the 'normalization' of Yugoslav–Soviet relations, served to undermine some of the more naive hopes (not reflected in British government thinking of the time) that Yugoslavia and the West would be able to sustain or even further develop the mutual interdependence and intimacy of the period immediately before Stalin's death. Yugoslav reactions to the invasion of Suez in 1956 were notably vitriolic – as, for that matter, were those of many in Britain, or in the United States and elsewhere too. There were, of course, also many in the British Labour Party and beyond it who shared the general Yugoslav perception of the need to move as rapidly as possible into a post-colonial era, and such sympathies were buttressed by personal ties too. The latter could produce cross currents, most notably in the case of Milovan Djilas. But whatever the resonances between the general Yugoslav stance on colonial questions and the aspirations of parts of the British political spectrum (and it is fair to remind ourselves in parenthesis that the basic aim of all British governments after the war was to wind up the Empire as soon as appeared practical), there were always bound to be major differences of perception over how far and how fast to go at any particular stage. The British Government not unnaturally felt, as governments will, that it was doing its best, and did not always take criticism from those without the day-to-day responsibilities particularly kindly. The British also distinguished between individual members of the non-aligned movement, and had their differences with some of Yugoslavia's particular friends of that era, such as President Sukarno of Indonesia, whose policy of armed confrontation with Malaysia the British Government actively helped to oppose. There were also special cases, like that of Cyprus. It was, lastly, not always easy during the 1960s to distinguish between the general Soviet and Yugoslav lines on colonial issues, a fact which tended to play into the hands of those who tried to argue that Yugoslavia was moving back towards a special relationship with the Eastern bloc.

As time passed, however, a number of developments meant that some of the preoccupations of the 1950s and 1960s got pushed more into the background. First of all, the colonial problem (if one can generalize about a complex series of historical processes by lumping them all together as a 'problem') was a temporary one. No one can now speak of British imperialism and expect to be taken very seriously. Second, the non-aligned movement made it clear in the 1970s it was not prepared to see itself as anyone's 'natural ally'. President Tito's stand in Havana in 1978 was especially important here. The two governments in any case find themselves on the same side on crucial issues like Afghanistan and Cambodia. And even where they differ, that is often because they have something real to say to each other, not merely the pleasure of exchanging attitudes. Third, the whole East–West context has changed so thoroughly there is less temptation on the part of British or other Western observers to extrapolate from a coincidence of Yugoslav and Soviet views. The development of socialism in the world has been such – and the Yugoslav part in this has been crucial – as fatally to undermine the possibility of the re-emergence of a single directing centre for the communist version of socialism. Events of 1968 showed that if there were any revival in the possibility of outside, ideologically motivated pressure being put on Yugoslavia, we would both react as we always have in the past. Although practical systemic differences between Yugoslav self-management and British democracy remain, founded ultimately on different ideas as to how societies can best be organized, basic ideological differences between us, and to a lesser degree between East and West, have become attenuated.[1]

While the international context has changed in the last two decades, substantial forces have been at work bringing our peoples closer together. These have operated both when our governments have felt relatively pleased with each other and when they have been less close, for economic, commercial, cultural and sociological life goes on whatever our immediate political preoccupations. Our shared wartime experiences gave us a solid basis from which to work, and cooperation in defence matters remains important. Our trade is now well balanced, and growing – though I could wish it greater. Much of the Embassy's effort is devoted to helping it increase, thereby providing everyday substance to the Anglo-Yugoslav relationship. Our two governments have recognized the need for close coordination and established a network of regular political consultations which we are keen to maintain and develop. The British Council plays a notable role in promoting British–Yugoslav cultural and scientific ties, a task made easier as well as more congenial by the fact of the importance of the English language, and by the existing texture of personal ties between our intellectual communities. Our churches are close. The relationship between our trade unions has been fruitful. Some 700,000 British voted with their feet and visited Yugoslavia in 1987. The freedom of Yugoslavs to travel has meant they too have acquired, like the British, the West-European habit of looking at our continent, not just their country, as part of their birthright.

Some Conclusions

President Tito described his last visit to the United Kingdom, in 1978, as 'a pleasant stay among tested friends, in contact with whom we have always found particular cordiality, high esteem, easy

---

1. Footnotes are to be avoided, except in learned papers, but a quotation from a letter of Turgenev to Tolstoy, written in 1856, struck me when preparing this as too good to miss: 'Would to God your horizon may broaden every day! The people who bind themselves to systems are those who are unable to encompass the whole truth and try to catch it by the tail: a system is like the tail of truth but truth is like a lizard; it leaves its tail in your fingers and runs away knowing full well that it will grow a new one in a twinkling.'

communication . . . It is a rare historical phenomenon for two such different countries, with so many different customs, to share such understanding.' Heads of State are usually cordial on such occasions, but I think he described an important truth. Anglo-Yugoslav mutual sympathy is firmly founded on experience and joint interest in each other's stability, cohesion and independence as well as a realistic recognition and acceptance of differences between us.

At the same time, the Anglo-Yugoslav relationship has become more and more like that between Yugoslavia and other West European countries. That has been partly the result of the changes in the British context I referred to at the beginning of this paper, and partly because of the way Yugoslavia, too, has developed. The overall effect is to leave us free to concentrate on the immediately practical. That means:

1. Working together on the commercial and financial relationship, at least as much as nurturing our political friendship. The record shows long-standing British concern, both moral and practical, for Yugoslavia's economic and financial health, expressed in concrete help over the past forty years or so. Yugoslavia's exports to the United Kingdom almost tripled between 1982 and 1986. We have been closely involved, in support of the aims of the Long-Term Economic Stabilization Programme, with doing what we can to ease Yugoslavia through the problems of the 1980s, confident from our own experience that there is a way through; a hard one, certainly, but only the one way, using market disciplines.

2. Working together as partners in Europe. The rise of the European Community is in its way a challenge to countries like Yugoslavia who are not members, just as it was to the Britain of the 1950s, 1960s and 1970s. A unique and fruitful relationship between Yugoslavia and the Community has developed, founded on the Belgrade Declaration of 1976 and the Cooperation Agreement of 1980, under which Yugoslavia received preferential treatment for exports to the European Community. Yugoslav exports to the Community increased by 70 per cent in 1982–86, and the potential for further increase is there. The Community is also a political institution and will play an increasing role in the bilateral Anglo-Yugoslav context.

3. Recognizing that the practical, systemic and ideological limits to the Anglo-Yugoslav relationship will change (and, I hope, continue to diminish) over time, and that they also affect the broader Yugoslav–Community picture. The history of the Anglo-Yugoslav relationship shows we have consistently welcomed moves towards the democratization of Yugoslav society and the introduction of market-oriented mechanisms into the Yugoslav economy, as enlarging the opportunities for us to work together productively. At the same time, of course, we continue to recognize, as Sir Charles Peake put it, that it is up to Yugoslavia to work out its own salvation.

A Final Comment

I said at the beginning it was perhaps rash of me to attack so broad a canvas, and there are obvious constraints, not least those of space, which I have had to observe. But an account of Anglo–Yugoslav events in the narrowest sense over the past forty-odd years would have been tedious, and it seemed better to range, on a purely personal basis, rather more widely.

9

Rhetorics of Nationalism in Yugoslav Politics*
John B. Allcock

Introduction

The purpose of this paper is to explore dispassionately the sociological significance of nationalism in Yugoslavia, and in the process
to produce a conceptual re-evaluation of this problem. Press coverage of Yugoslav affairs (certainly in Britain, and probably more
generally) has reported the recent history of the country largely in
terms of a succession of conflicts in which nationality has featured
strongly. The Croatian upheavals of 1970–71 were followed a
decade later by the Albanian disturbances in the province of Kosovo. The rise of Slobodan Milošević as the leader of a distinctively
Serbian populism, and the violent clashes with the Albanian population over the revision of the Serbian constitution in 1989, once
again concentrated attention on issues of nationality. Most dramatically and most recently, the effective disintegration of the League of
Communists of Yugoslavia, precipitated by the walk-out of Slovene
delegates from its Extraordinary Congress in January 1990, confirmed the general picture of a country chronically riven by national
differences. Indeed, if one confined one's reading about Yugoslavia
to press reporting one could be forgiven for thinking that the
principal cause of Yugoslavia's difficulties is nationalism, which
threatens to wreck the system. The task which this more popular
level of discussion does not address is that of providing an explanation as to why such problems arise, and why they appear to be so
intractable. This chapter does not set out to provide either a com-

* This is a revised and extended version of paper which has appeared in the *Third
World Quarterly*, Vol. 11, No. 3, October 1989.

plete historical account of the nationalities question in Yugoslavia, nor to offer an exhaustive theory within which to place the phenomenon of nationalism. It takes on the more limited task of exploring the interest of the concept of 'political rhetorics' within these wider ventures, in specific relation to a limited number of illustrations taken from recent Yugoslav political life, adding thereby to the kit of theoretical tools which are available to us in political sociology and comparative politics.

The ideas examined here are not confined in their relevance to Yugoslavia, however: and the experience of Yugoslavia could be instructive as a point of comparison both with other countries of Eastern Europe and with other relatively new states. My general contention, in brief, is that in many cases the phenomenon of nationalism can be understood in terms of the process of institutionalizing a common political discourse.

Nationalism and Political Instability

Why have we come to accept that nationalism is so central to the explanation of the Yugoslav crisis?[1] Political sociology certainly gives us no warrant for associating national diversity with inherent political instability. In fact, what seems to have happened is that the ideological self-definitions of the Yugoslav regime have been allowed to feed those images which circulate in the press, where they have become entrenched largely because of the lack of any serious challenge to them on the part of those with an academic engagement with Yugoslav affairs.

The ruling dogma in Yugoslavia (often echoed in similar terms elsewhere in Eastern Europe) is that nationalism, given its head, will naturally and necessarily lead back to the horrors of inter-ethnic strife experienced in the Second World War. The League of Communists has represented itself as being the only force able to rise

---

1. In passing I would like to suggest that in part we see here a reflection of British ethnocentrism. It is an assumption which has been taken for granted in Britain since the days of the Tudors that the hegemony of a strong state is necessary for the successful operation of political life. Anything which challenges this central authority is disruptive, debilitating and therefore to be deplored. (It is interesting that most British people do not distinguish between citizenship and nationality.) This negative view is qualified with respect to the Eastern European countries, in so far as British commentators have tended to look positively on anything which serves to destabilize communism.

above national particularism, to secure both a harmonious state and the overthrow of the class enemy. The problem is posed in terms of stark oppositions. Nationalism is divisive: communism unifies. Nationalism is internally unstable: communism has made for internal institutional stability. Nationalism was unable to defend Yugoslavia against external aggression: communism has done so. The principal objections to this argument are that it does not fit the observed facts of history, and that it is incapable of bearing the theoretical weight of explanation which is often placed upon it.

The supposed simple, dichotomous opposition between nationalism and communism, is plainly ill-founded. The League of Communists of Yugoslavia (LCY) has been as often associated with the political use of nationality as with its suppression. It was King Alexander between 1929 and 1934, after all, who tried unsuccessfully to impose a common Yugoslav nationality, at the expense of historical forms of national identity. From the time of the royal dictatorship the party has offered itself as the champion of national differences, recognizing these and enshrining the facts of diversity in a succession of post-war constitutions. As Paul Shoup has argued effectively, however, the LCY has never been able to develop a coherent theoretical stance with regard to nationality. Typically it has treated the question through a succession of *ad hoc* responses to tactical needs; and the much-vaunted respect for national identity in Yugoslavia has consisted rather of a tacit agreement to 'bracket' the issue, removing it from intellectual controversy instead of attempting a proper analysis of the problem.[2]

Arguably, communism has been associated in Yugoslavia with the creation of three nationalities which – with varying degrees of probability – might not exist today without its ministrations: Macedonian, Muslim and Montenegrin (for a discussion of 'Muslim' nationality, see below pp. 282–3). It seems closer to the historical truth to portray communism as the most powerful force creating and legitimating national identity in post-war Yugoslavia. That it has done so, and the manner in which this has been achieved through the formulae adopted by *Anti-fašističko vijeće narodnog oslobodeje Jugoslavije* (Anti-fascist Council for the National Liberation of Yugoslavia: AVNOJ) in 1943, are to the credit of the regime's capacity at that time for pragmatic adaptation to the

2. Paul Shoup, *Communism and the Yugoslav National Question* (New York and London, Columbia University Press, 1968).

complexities of a historical situation rather than a reflection of any superior theoretical grasp. The great irony of the Yugoslav situation is that these same formulae, which were rhetorical and reactive in origin, should subsequently have been elevated to the status of dogmas.

Theories of Nationalism

Turning to the putative association between communism and stability: one is forced to ask what are the continuing springs of contemporary nationalism? If communism does make for stability, why is nationalism able to take hold to disturb that situation? Three equally unsatisfactory solutions are sometimes proffered.

The role of external agitators is sometimes appealed to in the case of Albanian nationalism (as it was also in the case of Croatia in the 1970s). This cannot offer an acceptable general explanation of the phenomenon, even if it contains a limited truth in these specific cases. The suggestion has never been entertained seriously in relation to the current events in Serbia. Sociologists are always sceptical about too ready a reliance on exogenous causes; but it is not just fashion in sociological explanation which has prevented this from being adopted within academic circles more generally.

Another alternative, more plausible possibly in the case of Serbia, seems to envisage nationality as a purely natural attribute of human consciousness which, as in Freud's view of sexuality, can only be repressed at a cost. Such views are the obvious inheritors of the Romantic tradition, and where they surface in social science the task of 'explaining' nationalism is interpreted in terms of *éclaircissement* rather than explication. The latter is scarcely necessary if the existence of the phenomenon can be taken for granted. In this way Fred Singleton's otherwise excellent survey, *A Short History of the Yugoslav Peoples*, manages to avoid altogether confronting the question of why contemporary Yugoslav do see themselves as members of a particular set of 'peoples'.[3] In common with many other historical commentators, the problem is taken to be how the several (naturally occurring) nations of the region managed to secure recognition of their inherent qualities of being nations.

Although this is the most widely accepted interpretation of the

---

3. Fred Singleton, *A Short History of the Yugoslav Peoples* (Cambridge, Cambridge University Press, 1985).

existence of nationalism (in the last analysis: nationalism exists because there are nations) it can be shown to have its deficiencies with respect to each of Yugoslavia's national groups. Its weaknesses are particularly clear, for example, in the case of Macedonia. The Romantic theory, favoured by the post-war political and cultural elite of the republic, portrays the struggle for national autonomy as a natural result of there being a Macedonian nation, and its expected form of self-expression. Any close inspection of Macedonian history, however, will reveal that the contemporary existence of the nation is the result of that process of struggle, rather than its cause and precondition.

The third possibility is to see nationalism within the Marxist paradigm, as an ideological reflection of underlying economic conflicts. The primary reality is the economy: nationalist disorders simply reflect economic disorder. The oddity is that this view is frequently adopted by writers who in other respects would not dream of associating themselves with the Marxist tradition. Harold Lydall's recent work is a case in point.[4] There certainly is an economic dimension to the problems of Yugoslavia; but there are good reasons for demanding a further explanation as to why the specific form of that crisis should give rise to nationalist manifestations such as those which we see. The link is far from obvious.

In fact, in spite of extensive academic and lay discussion of nationalism in Yugoslavia, we still lack an answer to the question as to why conflicts in Yugoslav political life should be expressed specifically in national terms. How does nationalism function? More particularly, what does it mean?

Nationalism as Political 'Rhetoric'

An adequate answer to these very large questions is certainly not possible within the compass of a single article: and indeed a more limited objective will be attempted on this occasion. Its purpose is to make a preliminary move in the direction of recasting our appreciation of the nature and role of nationalism in Yugoslav political life by placing the question on a distinctive theoretical footing. I want to examine it in terms of the characteristics of

4. Harold Lydall, *Yugoslav Socialism: Theory and Practice* (Oxford, Clarendon Press, 1984); *Yugoslavia in Crisis* (Oxford, Clarendon Press, 1989).

political 'rhetoric'. A word of explanation is needed here. Although many aspects of this approach are more familiar under the guise of 'ideology', this term is deliberately eschewed because its use typically aligns one directly with Marxist theory. Similarly, contemporary social theory makes a great deal of 'discourse analysis'. This term too seems unsatisfactory, as 'discourse' carries with it unavoidable – and unsuitable – echoes of Cartesian rationalism. My preferred option is the term 'rhetoric', in the use of which I follow the great American critic, Kenneth Burke.[5]

In different ways, the importance of a political rhetoric has been acknowledged in sociology. Whether one describes the problem in terms of the Weberian concept of 'legitimation', or Gramsci's 'hegemony', the idea is generally accepted that any stable political order requires a generally diffused and widely accepted linguistic and symbolic medium. There must be ways in which political actors – rulers or ruled – give accounts of their own and each other's actions. The hypothesis which I propose here is that, for one reason or another, there has not developed in Yugoslavia a stable 'rhetoric' of this kind. The following argument sets out in a simplified and highly schematized form the reasons why I believe this has not taken place, leaving the field of political culture open to varieties of nationalism.

The Failure of Political Rhetoric in Yugoslavia

An important reason for the failure to develop an effective political rhetoric in Yugoslavia is the failure of alternatives. An acceptable rhetoric must simultaneously include the parties to political struggle while enabling them to articulate the variety and specificity of their contending interests. The view of conflict adopted here depends heavily on that of Georg Simmel, who insisted that it should be treated as a form of 'sociation' – positively, as a type of structured human interaction, and not as the absence of society.[6]

---

5. I have taken the term from Burke: but I am clear about the fact that I do not write within the very specific framework of general theory which he erects. See Kenneth Burke, *A Rhetoric of Motives* (New York, Prentice Hall, 1950); also William H. Rueckert, *Kenneth Burke and the Drama of Human Relations* (Minneapolis, Minn., University of Minnesota Press, 1963).

6. Donald N. Levine (ed.), *Georg Simmel on Individuality and Social Forms* (Chicago, Ill. and London, Chicago University Press, 1971).

Religion, although possibly a *prima facie* candidate for consideration here, could never provide an acceptable political medium in Yugoslavia. Religion in the history of Yugoslavia is heavily freighted with oppositions which are just too deep, and would create a succession of exclusions, without defining a symbolic community. For Orthodox and Catholic populations alike the story of their struggle for independence includes episodes in which 'freedom' has come to be defined in terms of liberation from Islam – from 'the five hundred years of Turkish night'. Between Catholic and Orthodox, on the other hand, falls the dreadful shadow of the so-called 'Independent State of Croatia' (the puppet created by the Axis powers after the fall of the first Yugoslav state in 1941) in which the ostentatiously Catholic regime of Ante Pavelić sought to solve the problem of its large Orthodox Serbian population along lines reminiscent of Hitler's 'final solution' to the Jewish question. Any workable political rhetoric in Yugoslavia must of necessity, for these reasons, bracket issues of religious identity in so far as this is possible.

An important test of this hypothesis can be found in the creation, since 1945, of a 'Muslim' nation in Yugoslavia. (The ethnogenesis of the 'Muslim nation' in Yugoslavia has historically deeper roots than this, and encompasses the creation of specifically confessional parties in the inter-war period. Only in the post-war years, however, has Muslim identity come to be designated specifically in national terms.)[7] During the early centuries of the Ottoman Empire, in the Balkans substantial numbers of indigenous Slavs converted to Islam, especially in the region of Bosnia. Since 'Serb' and 'Croat' national identity have been historically inextricably intertwined with religion (Orthodoxy and Roman Catholicism respectively) the question of the national provenance of a Serbo-Croat-speaking Islamic population presented modern Yugoslav politics with a puzzle. In the fascist state of Pavelić they were assiduously courted as 'Muslim Croats', by a regime anxious to secure their compliance in the elimination of the Serbs. In the post-war period, however, the policy of 'bracketing' controversy over nationality has led to the

7. See Pedro Ramet, 'Religion and Nationalism in Yugoslavia', in Pedro Ramet (ed.), *Religion and Nationalism in Soviet and East European Politics* (Durham, NC and London, Duke University Press, revised and expanded edition 1989), esp. pp. 308–11. The journal *L'Autre Europe* has also devoted a useful special edition to this topic: see especially Stevan Pavlowitch, 'En Yougoslavie – la religion totem du clan', Nos. 21–2, pp. 245–62.

curious result that Muslims have been designated as a particular nationality. The reason for this, of course, is that if they can be demonstrated to be a nationality *sui generis* this removes them from the competition to demonstrate their 'real' identity as either Serbs or Croats, and helps to neutralize the territorial aspirations of either with respect to Bosnia.

Here the 'bracketing' strategy is exemplified probably in its clearest form. In this process the specifically *religious* connotation of the term 'Muslim' has been played down: they are officially referred to as *Muslimani u etničkom smislu* – 'Muslims in the ethnic sense'. Precisely what is the content of 'Muslim' identity in this 'ethnic' sense, however, remains (deliberately?) unclear, as linguistically they are not distinguishable from either Serbs or Croats, and they are quite explicitly not people of Turkish descent, from whom they are distinguished in the census returns. What is more, religious practice is deemed to be irrelevant to the question of whether or not one is a 'Muslim'. The use of this device has been quite important if not in the resolution at least in the amelioration of nationality conflicts in Bosnia. 'Muslim' identity has been able to function acceptably in this way within the secular Yugoslav state precisely because it has been explicitly evacuated of all specifically religious significance.[8]

This has been a high risk strategy, of course, in that there is no guarantee that at some future date Yugoslav Muslims (in this ethnic sense) will not strive to reintegrate their broader cultural identity with Islam. The consequences of such a development would be considerable, although it is inappropriate to speculate about them in this context.

One might generalize the significance of this illustration for the possible development of a pluralistic politics in Yugoslavia. Explicitly confessional parties of any kind, in all probability, would stand ultimately upon incompatible theological and philosophical views about the nature of the state. The recent process by which both in Serbia and Macedonia the Orthodox Churches have begun to move once again into the foreground of politics must therefore be viewed with concern by those with an interest in the future stability of Yugoslavia. Although the history of church–state relations in

8. For a lucid and concise discussion of Islam in Yugoslavia, see Alexandre Popović, 'L'Islam en Yugoslavie', *Cadmos*, Vol. 11, No. 41, spring 1988, pp. 63–77; 'Les musulmans sous souveraineté non-musulmane: le cas de la Yugoslavie (1945–1985)', *L'Autre Europe*, Nos. 21–2, pp. 129–41.

John B. Allcock

Yugoslavia has been far from untroubled in the post-war years, one element of the post-war pattern appears to constitute a precondition for any reasonably successful prescription for the future of Yugoslav politics: namely, there must be a general acceptance of the secular character of the state.

Class, similarly, has limited value as a central rhetorical category in a supposedly socialist society. Having eliminated the exploiting class, the rhetoric of class can only serve to define the boundaries of the political community *vis-à-vis* real or imaginary outsiders. Hence at different times reference to the dangers of the 'restoration of capitalism', or the threat of the 'technocratic deformation' of self-management, in different ways have served as levers for political mobilization in defence of the regime. They have done so in such a way as to mark out those (actual or fictitious) enemies whose class interest is alleged to pose a threat to the secure development of self-managing socialism. One cannot, however, legitimately formulate the issues in the political struggle within such a community in class terms.

One might mention here a couple of clear illustrations of the hazards which attach to any attempt even to acknowledge the utility of 'class' for the sociological analysis of Yugoslav society. The first, and best known, is the fate of Milovan Djilas. His outspoken identification of a 'New Class' of political officials as the principal moral and political obstacle to socialism was the most significant factor precipitating his expulsion from the inner circle of leadership in the 1950s.[9] Less visible has been the persistent distortion within sociology of the analysis of stratification in Yugoslav society, which has been forced on occasions to tie itself into intellectual knots over the question of how to conceptualize inequalities in Yugoslavia – especially those which relate directly to political engagement – without intimating the possibility that processes of class formation are afoot.[10]

The heart of the matter appears to be the failure of the Yugoslav regime to institutionalize a distinctive rhetoric of 'self-management', which would provide ways of identifying and expressing

9. Abraham Rothberg (ed.), *Anatomy of a Moral: The Political Essays of Milovan Djilas* (London, Thames & Hudson, 1959); Milovan Djilas, *The New Class: An Analysis of the Communist System* (New York, Harcourt Brace Jovanovitch, 1957).
10. For two recent reviews of the literature, see Marija Bogdanović, *Društvene Nejednakosti* (Belgrade, Institut Društvenih Nauka, 1988); Zagorka Golubović, *Kriza Identiteta Savremenog Jugoslavenskog Društva* (Belgrade, Filip Višnjić, 1989), pp. 136–43.

interests, and mobilizing parties to conflict, legitimately within the system. Self-management has been trumpeted as the distinctive badge of the 'Yugoslav road to socialism'. It has been held to provide an ideological and institutional lynch-pin which secures both the external legitimacy of a socialist regime which turned its back on the leadership of Moscow, and the internal legitimacy of a communist party which affirms its own 'leading role', while attempting to accommodate itself to the exigencies of a country containing a range of social and economic interests which is exceedingly diverse. In spite of all that has been written and spoken about the unique interest of the system of 'socialist self-management' both inside and outside of Yugoslavia – and its real achievements at many levels – it is necessary to recognize that it has not succeeded in fully institutionalizing itself as the source of a taken-for-granted rhetoric of Yugoslav politics. The language of self-management has remained, on the whole, an opaque and mystifying externality to which ordinary Yugoslavs have not turned when seeking for ways in which to communicate their own concerns and aspirations. It is for this reason that some critics of the country have seen in the current economic reforms the start of a process of abandonment of self-management, and one which will be largely unresisted by the Yugoslav population who have been its supposed beneficiaries. To date it is too soon to assess this hypothesis.

In the absence of the opportunity to demonstrate that point fully, two casual illustrations will have to suffice. Over the past two decades industrial life has seen a growing number of occasions on which the workers have resorted to strikes – 'against themselves' – as a means of highlighting their collective grievances and as a form of communal action. Also, throughout the late 1980s, the massive street demonstration has time and again been the resort both of the citizenry and of populist leaders, who have completely by-passed the institutions of self-management and the delegate system in order to state demands and secure results. A much fuller study of these processes is needed; but it does seem to be the case at first sight that self-management may have failed at this rhetorical level. It is possible to suggest two reasons for this.

An image of society which sees itself as composed of an undifferentiated 'working people' of Yugoslavia will necessarily tend to represent political problems in terms of a bland series of 'adjustments', achieved through 'social compacts', 'self-managing agreements' and 'communities of interest', rather than through honestly recognizing, naming and legitimating conflict and its bases.

Complex (and occasionally imaginative) as the peculiar language of self-management is, it simply fails to offer anything which could stand a remote chance of succeeding as a political rhetoric, because its very essence is to obscure the character of social conflict. It has come to provide a *partial* rhetoric, the distinctive feature of which is that it specifies in every one of its core concepts a normative inclusion, while remaining silent about conflict (with the exception of the propensity of politicians to rail about the enemies and perverters of self-management).

The regime emerged from the period of war and revolution with a considerable fund of legitimacy, which it has proceeded to spend prodigally over the post-war years without commensurate reinvestment. This is a point on which previous commentators on Yugoslav affairs have sometimes been seriously misleading, although it is easy to understand how this misjudgement could have come about for as long as the stage was occupied by the charismatic figure of President Tito. With his passing, and in the light of more recent historical research, we are able to appreciate just how serious has been the strain on the regime's claims to legitimacy in the past.[11] Without in any way denying the significance of the economic difficulties which now face Yugoslavia, I suggest that one important reason for the exceptional severity of the country's current problems is that it now also faces a major legitimation crisis.

The failure of self-management to generate a legitimating rhetoric has left a vacuum in the political life of the country, into which nationalism has moved. It has been able to do so because it has been sanctioned by the regime as the only (although semi-legitimate) rhetorical vehicle for the expression of conflict. The current political structure of the country, including the six republics and two autonomous provinces, was created as a solution to the post-war problem of creating a legitimate alternative to the Serbian hegemonism of the Karadjordjević monarchy. The self-determination of its own nations and nationalities has been a vital component of the regime's self-definition. So although the officially sanctioned account of Yugoslav history does oppose 'nationalism' and 'communism' along the

11. In his recent study of the importance of the Cominformists, Ivo Banac has documented fully the scale, persistence and severity of the challenge to Tito's leadership offered by those who sided with the Soviet Union after 1948. See Ivo Banac, *With Stalin Against Tito: Cominformist Splits in Yugoslav Communism* (Ithaca, NY and London, Cornell University Press, 1988).

lines mentioned above, and there has been a constant series of attacks on 'chauvinism', 'irredentism' and 'nationalism', the regime itself has elevated the republics and provinces to the status of the only legitimate bearers of openly competing interests within the system. In this way it has prepared for itself a major contradiction within which it has become ensnared. Consequently, during the process of creating a party-pluralist system in the early 1990s, although rhetorics of religion and class are emerging as media for defining interests and articulating conflicts in Yugoslavia, typically these are both subordinated to rhetorics of nationality.

The Diversity of Yugoslav 'Nationalisms'

At this point it is important to acknowledge a central feature of nationalism, and that is its vacuity. The terms 'nationalism' and 'nationality' imply no specific intellectual or symbolic content. They are portmanteau terms which can be used to accommodate virtually anything. Clearly in Yugoslavia (as elsewhere) 'nationalism' does not mean the same thing in different regions. It is evident from an examination of Yugoslav history, as still today, that to speak of Serb or Slovene, Croat or Albanian nationality is to refer to different types of political culture. A thorough treatment of this issue is not possible within the confines of a brief essay, but it is possible to give a brief indication of the ways in which the concept of 'nation' functions quite differently in political discourse in different regions of Yugoslavia. To this end I will comment briefly on some important contrasts between the rhetoric of nationality in Slovenia and Serbia.

The Slovenes have never had anything resembling a national state of their own, unlike the other South Slav peoples. The creation of a Slovene national identity has always taken place within the context of larger and more inclusive political units. Although one does hear mention of Slovene separatism, their historical tradition has emphasized typically the creation of a succession of institutions which stand between the state and the individual, acting as the focus for common action and common identity. The precise form of these has varied. During the nineteenth century, under the Habsburg monarchy, where the cities of the region had become thoroughly germanized, these forms were typically tied to the patterns and processes of peasant culture – principally the parish and rural cooperatives. These continued to be of vital importance during the inter-war years, when they were supplemented by educational institutions, banks and – very significantly – the Slovene Popular Party, a clerical-led party of the Christian Democrat variety.

Throughout the history of Yugoslavia Slovenes have cooperated with the state, and in both pre-war and post-war regimes have been centrally identified with it. This was particularly the case between the wars, when the leader of the Slovene Popular Party, Mgr Antun Korošec, held cabinet positions in every parliamentary government, in alliance with the dominant Serb parties. The strategy has been that of 'render to Caesar the things that are Caesar's'; and within the wider framework of Yugoslavia, through the medium of their distinctive language, they have sustained and indeed developed a sense of identity by building institutions at a sub-state level. Among the latest in this series of ventures have been the creation of a Slovene Agrarian Union, together with a Slovene Union of Agrarian Youth, and the emergence of a peace movement.

The importance of this often passes unrecognized among commentators on Yugoslav affairs. In his otherwise excellent review of the relationship between religion and nationality in Yugoslavia, Pedro Ramet presents the reader with a discussion of every aspect of this question with the exception of the Slovenes. His remarks in this respect are confined to a single sentence: 'The relation of the Catholic church to Slovenian nationalism was passed over chiefly because Slovenian nationalism has been fainter, so that aside from making a few declarations ruling out Slovene secession, the Catholic hierarchy in Slovenia has concentrated on the defense of human and ecclesiastical rights.'[12] Ramet's mistake is to think that there is any basis here for believing that Slovene nationalism is 'fainter' than other Yugoslav nationalisms (a view which would come as a surprise to any Yugoslav!). Far from indicating that the kinds of activities to which he refers mark either an absence of nationalism, or a failure of the church to become involved in it, they seem to be of the essence of a very highly developed nationalism, but one which takes a very specific form.

This approach is marked in Slovene political rhetoric by an emphasis on the importance of the concept of 'civil society', and the affirmation that 'society' is not co-terminous with the state. It is illustrated very well by events during the early summer of 1988,

---

12. Ramet, 'Religion and Nationalism in Yugoslavia', p. 327.

when two journalists and a serving military NCO were arrested, tried and sentenced for possession and dissemination of a secret military document. The events were accompanied by a massive and general outcry in the republic, by very large public demonstrations, and by a petition which bore the signatures, not only of many individuals but also of representatives of more than a hundred organizations.[13] The document in question had given reason to believe that the Yugoslav Army had prepared plans for the arrest of a large number of people, who were known (or alleged) to have an active commitment to various forms of political opposition, in the event of any large-scale civil disorder. The grounds for defence advanced by those who had leaked it were those of the right of the public to know facts of such central political importance.

Two related aspects of the case appear to have excited the greatest concern. The first was the fact that the trials took place before a military tribunal, and not the civil court. The specifically military aspect of the process meant that access to the accused by lawyers, relatives and others directly concerned with the welfare of the prisoners was greatly restricted, as was press coverage of the trial itself. The second was the linguistic dimension to the conflict. The language of command in the Yugoslav People's Army is Serbo-Croat. Consequently procedure in a specifically military court was also conducted in that language, and not in Slovene – the native language of the defendants.

Within the context of our discussion of political rhetoric, an important feature of the episode was the way in which events came to be conceptualized in Slovenia in terms of a problematic process of 'the militarization of society'. The issues in question were the extent to which it was proper that the military desire for secrecy should be allowed primacy over the need for an informed democratic political debate, the conditions under which military law could claim a degree of priority over the institutions of civil law, and the thinking apparently exposed by the leaked document, which allowed the military the role of determining the parameters within which permissible limits of political dissent were to be determined.

13. Press coverage of these events has generally mentioned 200 such organizations. The statement about the 'Foundation of a Committee for the protection of the rights of Janez Janša', published in *Independent Voices from Yugoslavia*, Vol. 4, No. 2, June 1988, pp. 8–10, lists only 108 organizations by name. This issue of *Independent Voices* carries a very full account of the events preceding the trial itself.

The role of language in this process is of particular interest here, as it focused attention very directly upon the problematic relationship between the state (Serbo-Croat) and civil society (Slovene). The use of language emerged as a potent symbol of the nature of the underlying structural conflict. The strength of the political protest can be explained in terms of the stark contrast between the peremptory demands of the (Yugoslav) state – especially in that these emanated from the armed forces – and the independence of republican (Slovene) institutions, which had a measure of public accountability. It is upon the integrity of the latter (expressed in terms of the concept of 'civil society') that the future of Slovene national independence was seen to depend. An important consequence of this feature of Slovene political culture is that one finds in the republic the greatest advance towards real political pluralism in Yugoslavia (and possibly also in Eastern Europe more generally).

It is within the context of these events that it is possible to see why a peace movement should have emerged as such a prominent element of Slovene oppositional politics. To Western European and North American ears mention of a peace movement draws attention to issues of international relations, disarmament and especially nuclear disarmament. It is fundamentally puzzling why Slovenia should give rise to a peace movement at at time when the Cold War is apparently a thing of the past, and Yugoslavia has no possibility of becoming implicated in the nuclear weapons race. The fact of the matter, however, is that the focus of this movement is the *demilitarization of Yugoslav society*, and the strengthening of 'civil society'; and it is precisely this feature which marks it out as such a typical expression of Slovene national consciousness.[14]

The contrast with Serbia is remarkable. Here there is a very weak tradition of political pluralism.[15] The Serbs acquired early in the nineteenth century a state even before they acquired a sense of nationality, in the modern sense. Serbian politics and political aspirations, therefore, always have been bound up intimately with

14. The argument developed in this section of the paper has been emphatically and quite independently vindicated in a paper which was not available to me when it was first drafted. Tomaz Mastnak, 'The Slovenian Spring: The Triumph of Civil Society', presented to the panel 'Civil Society under Communism', Fourth World Congress for Soviet and East European Studies, Harrogate, July 1990.

15. Much of the diversity of Serbian politics between the wars is accounted for by the activity of Serbs resident outside the former Kingdom of Serbia, principally in the former Habsburg lands. In this respect there were marked contrasts between the political culture of Serbs from Serbia itself, and the *prečani*.

statehood. There has been also a close identification between the state and the Serbian Orthodox Church, and throughout the nineteenth century the Serbian state played a strongly interventionist and paternalistic role in the economy. To a large extent it is these traditions which lay behind the 'hegemonism' of the inter-war period. In the post-war years it has been in Belgrade that one has found – on the whole – the lowest levels of toleration of expressions of political opposition. The wider student movement, which in 1968 appeared in all the Yugoslav universities, was met with greater official hostility in Belgrade than in any other city.[16] The innocuous and scholarly endeavours of the *Praxis* group of philosophers in the 1960s similarly resulted in their uncompromising ejection from the University of Belgrade.

Against this background it seems hardly surprising to find that innovation in Serbian politics has recently taken the form of a populist leader emerging within the League of Communists itself.[17] No full or serious analysis of the emergence of Slobodan Milošević and the style of politics which he embodies has yet been attempted either in Yugoslavia or elsewhere. My remarks here will be suggestive and programmatic rather than a digest of established academic wisdom.

Obsessed as they have been with the figure of Tito, both press and scientific commentators on Yugoslav affairs have tended to focus upon Milošević in highly personalized terms. They have either hoped or expected to find another figure endowed with charismatic powers – a new 'strong man' to lead Yugoslavia. It has taken some time to dissipate these expectations, which have been fed by the extraordinary personal adulation with which he has been received in Serbia. One encounters in Milošević, however, the paradox of a man who has been elevated as the individual embodiment of Serbian nationalism, but who lacks conspicuous personal

16. A very full account of these events has recently been published: Nebojša Popov (ed.), *Contra Fatum: Slučaj Grupa Profesora Filozofskog Fakultata u Beogradu* (Belgrade, Mladost, 1989).
17. For a full discussion of the concept of 'populism', see John B. Allcock, '"Populism": A Brief Biography', *Sociology*, Vol. 5, No. 3, 1971, pp. 371–87. See also M. Canovan, *Populism* (London, Junction Books, 1981). A recent attempt to apply the concept to Balkan politics is contained in Nicos P. Mouzelis, *Politics in the Semi-Periphery: Early Parliamentarism and Late Industrialisation in the Balkans and Latin America* (London, Macmillan, 1986). The analysis of Serbian politics in terms of 'populism' merits further discussion, especially in view of the disconcerting historical fact that populisms have ranged widely across the political spectrum, from the most extreme left to the equally far right.

charisma. It is in a study of the rhetoric of Milošević's politics, and not in his person, that one finds the explanation of his effectiveness. A reading of the articles and speeches of the man who in five years rose from obscurity to the presidency of the Serbian republic (and notoriety throughout Yugoslavia) reveals a very clear and consistent picture of a rhetoric which may be interpreted as deeply symptomatic of Serbian politics rather than one that is purely personal and idiosyncratic.

Two features of Milošević's political rhetoric are especially worthy of comment in this context: his political language and the understanding which emerges from his public pronouncements of the relevant actors in the drama of politics. The notion of 'rhetoric' is particularly apt in relation to Milošević, as his language stands in sharp contrast to that which is typical of Yugoslav political life. With few exceptions it is devoid of the flat jargon of socialism which often makes attention to political reporting in Yugoslavia so unrewarding. He speaks and writes something very closely akin to the language of the ordinary person – simply constructed, direct and for the most part concrete in reference.[18]

A surprising feature of his language, in view of the way in which he has come to be associated with a specifically nationalist standpoint, is the relative scarcity in his discourse of recourse to the more heavily laden emotional symbols of the former strength of the Serbian state and the glory of its ecclesiastical past. If he is concerned to argue the need for the rightful claims of a Serbian state to be justly acknowledged within the framework of the Yugoslav federation, his case is couched in terms of the greatness of the Serbian people, rather than the historical attributes of their state. More typically, his language makes reference to homely popular moral values, traditionally conceived.

One very striking illustration of this aspect will suffice here. At a time when there was great controversy over the personal security of the declining number of Serbs and Montenegrins still residing in the predominantly Albanian province of Kosovo (particularly focused upon the allegedly high incidence of sexual assaults) Milošević addressed the issue during a visit to a factory in the town of Uroševac, in April 1987:

---

18. The following discussion of the political language of Slobodan Milošević is based on his collected speeches and articles: *Godine Raspleta* (The Years of Dénouement), 4th edn (Belgrade, BIGZ, 1989).

It is just and moral that every nation, and its own most progressive people before all others, should struggle against their own nationalism: against all those terrible and inhuman actions which offend and degrade others. For these terrible and inhuman things, in the end, offend and degrade that nation itself, and those of its members who perpetrate them.

The Albanian nation must defend not only Serbs and Montenegrins from the shame of those things which its nationalists do, but themselves.

With every assaulted Serbian child a stain falls on every Albanian who has not prevented such a shameful thing.

The safety of Serbian and Montenegrin children, here in Kosovo, ought rather to be the concern of every Albanian mother and father, than that of the police.[19]

The significant thing about this passage is not principally that the speaker fails to question whether the alleged incidents have taken place or not, but rather that he deals with the issue by placing it centrally within the language of traditional Balkan values dating back to a pre-industrial age – the collective responsibility of kin for the defence of moral values, and shared responsibility for the avoidance of shame.

This resort to common language and the appeal to popular values is entirely consistent with the other principal feature of the rhetoric of Milošević. I refer to his characterization of the actors in the political scene in terms of a simple opposition between 'the people' and 'the bureaucracy'. This second feature is, if anything, more obvious and well-developed than the first. Milošević presents himself as the spokesman of ordinary folk – 'the people', 'working people', and (very frequently) 'honest people'. (Note that in Serbo-Croat the word *narod* can be translated both as 'the people' or as 'the nation'.) To their legitimate interests and aspirations is opposed a bureaucracy which is 'conservative', self-serving, preoccupied with 'theoretical' issues and beset by 'opportunism'. Asked in a press interview in *Večernje novosti* in January 1989 to explain his own vision of a way of escape from the current crisis, Milošević listed as first among the necessary tasks 'renewal of the administration' (*kadrovska obnova*).[20] The ordinary people are the repository of good sense and the traditional virtues, but the nation has been betrayed by the weakness and moral sterility of their leaders.

In pursuit of the 'renewal' of Serbian (and consequently of

19. Ibid., pp. 147–8.
20. Ibid., p. 307.

Yugoslav) public life, Milošević appeals over the heads of all established political institutions to the Serbian people. In this respect his version of nationalism contrasts very plainly with that current in Slovenia. He has no sense of the need for a network of intermediate institutions which will provide a flourishing 'civil society' within which the nation can find its own identity, protected from the intervention of the state. If anything, his demand is for a closer union between the state and the people, in which the standards of conduct of the former – and above all, of the Communist Party itself – are more closely conformed to the needs and values of the latter.

In this respect, Milošević is no more of a novelty in Serbia than the peace movement is in Slovenia. Both are entirely coherent within a language of politics which has been an integral part of the culture of their regions for a very long time. In certain very important respects, Slobodan Milošević is the inheritor of the mantle of pre-war Serbian agrarian radicalism, with its image of the eternal opposition between the *opanci* (moccasins – or symbol of the peasantry in general) and the *kaputaš* (the man who wears a city coat). Similarly, it is possible to see a basic cultural continuity linking the youthful peace movement activists of Slovenia with the thriving cooperatives of the Slovene People's Party under Antun Korošec.[21]

Conclusion

When one encounters the varieties of nationalism within Yugoslavia in such extreme instances as Vuk Drašković's public commitment to the wholesale deportation of Albanians, or the uncomfortable echoes of Pavelić's Ustaše which emanate from Tudjman's Hrvatska Demokratska Zajednica (Croation Democratic Union: HDZ), then it is tempting to turn away from all expressions of nationalism and to look with sympathy on the view that it is necessarily retrograde, destabilizing or even dangerous. However bizarre or repellent the

---

21. For additional information on the historical development of the various forms of nationalism among the South Slavs see Ivo Banac, *The National Question in Yugoslavia: Origins, History, Politics* (Ithaca, NY and London, Cornell University Press, 1984). For a briefer discussion, see Ivo J. Lederer, 'Nationalism and the Yugoslavs', in Peter F. Sugar and Ivo J. Lederer (eds.), *Nationalism in Eastern Europe* (Seattle, Wash. and London, University of Washington Press, 1969); also Singleton, *A Short History*.

manifestations of nationalism might seem to the outsider, it is nevertheless important that we try to make them intelligible.

In recent years it has become a commonplace of the discussion of Yugoslav politics to depict the process of decentralization, and the rise of a close association between the republics and various nationalisms, in terms of a process of 'refeudalization'.[22] The metaphor of feudal society is a compelling one in many respects, but it does carry with it one danger. The focus of the established sociological analysis of the process of feudalization, going back to the work of Max Weber, focuses on the emergence of smaller units as the loci of power during a period when the centre is weak. The barons (republics) emerge as rivals to an enfeebled crown (the federation). What this analysis leaves out of account is the possible diversity in the nature of those units. Functionally they may be equivalent, but their internal culture remains unexplored. If we are going to understand the present character or future development of Yugoslavia, however, it will be necessary to add to such a purely formal analysis of power an appreciation of this cultural level. Two conclusions can be drawn from the foregoing analysis of political culture in Yugoslavia.

The first conclusion of this argument is that by its failure to institutionalize a common political rhetoric based upon socialist self-management the Yugoslav regime has, quite unwittingly, kept in being the possibility of developing rhetorics, which are alternatives to that of self-managing socialism, through which a wide variety of issues over which there is conflict can be articulated. Whether or not at an official level political developments continue to be rationalized in terms of the vocabulary of socialist self-management, at a deeper level the success of the wide-ranging economic reform which is currently being attempted by the Yugoslav government will depend critically upon the ways in which these measures are seen to be intelligible within a series of rhetorics based upon nationality.

To those who see the need to tackle Yugoslavia's economic problems as its most serious test, debate about vocabularies of politics may seem to be a diversion from the important issues. Until recently, however, an insurmountable obstacle to economic change in many respects has been the lack of any real debate, not so much

---

22. This debate has been summarized in Blažo Perović, *Jugoslovenstvo i Nacional-Feudalizam* (Belgrade, Gardoš, 1988).

about the issues, as about the interests involved and the available alternatives at the level of political institutions, through which economic change might be guided and made accountable. In very significant measure the fact that there have been no legitimate means of organizing political opposition around competing courses of action has been a result of the rather stifling embrace of the League of Communists, which until 1990 managed to stave off challenges to its 'leading role' in politics.

In some ways, nationalism has operated as a kind of political Trojan horse, by which it became possible to smuggle a significant measure of pluralism into the system. Both of the illustrations which have been considered here introduced standards of value into political debate which relativized the historical claims of the League of Communists. From these, in each case, flowed forms of political action which have permitted organization around competing interests and political goals.

Second, the analysis of nationalism in terms of political rhetoric helps to make clear and to underline one of the key features of contemporary Yugoslav politics, namely, the mutual unintelligibility of many sections of Yugoslav society. Study of the succession of events throughout 1989 which flowed from Slovene criticism of Serbian policies in Kosovo – the demand for a 'Rally of Truth' to be held in Ljubljana, its banning by the Slovene authorities, the subsequent mutual economic and political boycotting of the two republics, culminating in the secession of the Slovenes from the LCY – reveals clearly that to each side the position of the other was (quite literally) incomprehensible. This chapter by no means provides a complete analysis of this problem, but it does point the way towards a fuller and more careful examination of the real diversity of political culture between the Yugoslav regions, of which the question of Serb–Slovene relations is only one facet.

There appears to be an emerging consensus among students of Yugoslav affairs that the end result of the political processes under way in Yugoslavia will be a new, looser form of confederal association between the component units of the state. This development, if it comes, will provide a vivid illustration of the extent and seriousness of those differences in political rhetoric which now separate the Yugoslav peoples.

10

Yugoslav Health Care: Is the Cup Half Empty or Half Full?

Donna E. Parmelee

Introduction

For Yugoslav area specialists, the 1980s have been a sad period indeed. We have witnessed the deepening political and economic crisis in Yugoslavia which has come in the wake of Josip Broz Tito's death in May 1980. We have shared heartfelt concerns over the outcome of this current and ongoing crisis with Yugoslav colleagues and friends. In this context, it is useful, though, to think of the special meaning of the Chinese character for the word 'crisis'. For the Chinese, 'crisis' joins together two separate characters, one meaning 'danger', the other 'opportunity' (Sidel and Sidel, 1983, p. xvii). For Yugoslavia, there is clearly both danger and opportunity in current developments, and which of these will prevail remains yet to be seen.

Yugoslav watchers have also been saddened by the death of Fred Singleton in 1988. For those of us who have relied heavily upon his studies of Yugoslavia in our own research and teaching, who have had the good fortune to know him personally and who share his basic 'optimism and hope for the future' of Yugoslavia (Singleton, 1985, p. 285), his death represents a great loss. His voice on the unfolding events in Yugoslavia will be sorely missed.

I am honoured to contribute to this *festschrift* for Fred Singleton, a fitting memorial to the man and to his work, and a timely occasion to take stock of recent developments in Yugoslavia. In the chapter which follows, I offer a 'progress' report on Yugoslav health care. First, I identify the major health policy objectives of socialist Yugoslavia. Then, as someone who firmly believes (like Fred

Singleton) that the present bears the imprint of the past, I sketch the broad outlines of the organizational structure of the Yugoslav health sector during the inter-war period as well as its transformation over the post-Second-World-War years. I next turn to an evaluation of socialist Yugoslavia's achievements in the health sector relative to three sets of benchmarks: the record of inter-war Yugoslavia, the experience of other countries and socialist Yugoslavia's own self-proclaimed policy objectives. To anticipate this evaluation, I would note that along with some impressive gains one also finds some troubling shortcomings, particularly relative to the experience of other countries and to the Yugoslavs' own objectives. In the final section, I examine some of the dilemmas confronting Yugoslav health care in the 1980s, looking at possible policy options to address these dilemmas and at likely constraints on policy choices in the immediate future.

Health Policy Objectives Under Yugoslav Self-Managing Socialism

Although I have not seen a formal statement of Yugoslavia's health policy objectives under self-managing socialism, the following would seem to be among the most important objectives which can be gleaned from various legal documents and discussions of the health care system in Yugoslav sources:

1. According to Article 185 of *The Constitution of the Socialist Federal Republic of Yugoslavia* (1974), 'everyone shall be entitled to health care'. In effect, health care has been defined by the Yugoslavs as a right, and creating the conditions for fulfilling this entitlement is deemed a collective responsibility (based on 'solidarity and reciprocity', to use the Yugoslav parlance).
2. While accepting inequalities based on the socialist principle of 'to each according to his (or her) work', the Yugoslavs have declared their intentions to transcend differences stemming from economic underdevelopment and other unequal conditions of life and work (*Constitution*, 1974, Section V). By implication, health inequalities are among those social differences which the Yugoslavs seek to prevent and eliminate since they are not (or should not be) based on application of the principle of distribution according to work performed. At the same time, certain

categories have been singled out for special attention in the area of health given the important role they play in the country's biological and socioeconomic development. In particular, special protection is guaranteed for children and young people, women, workers and war veterans (Feliks, 1978).

3. In contrast to socialist societies based on the Soviet model of state socialism characterized by centralized, bureaucratic state-controlled health sectors, the Yugoslavs envision decentralized, de-etaticized[1] and democratized health delivery and health insurance systems. Under the general rubric of self-managing socialism, the aim has been to give users and providers of health services a greater and more direct role in health policy making and planning. While there is some redistribution of funds for health above the commune level, emphasis has been placed on local control and financing of the health sector, such that the needs of particular communes are to be satisfied using local 'material' (i.e. financial) possibilities (Popović and Škrbić, 1979).

The Organizational Structure of the Yugoslav Health Sector

As part of broader efforts of institution restructuring and innovation in post-Second-World-War Yugoslavia, the health sector has undergone major reforms designed to achieve these various health policy objectives.[2] I would argue, though, that the organization of the health sector in post-liberation Yugoslavia reflects both discontinuity *and* continuity with the past. For although the ongoing socialist revolution has brought with it important changes in the formal organizational and ideological bases of the health sector, many of these changes were actually superimposed on developments which occurred in the pre-revolutionary years. Thus, as a backdrop to my discussion of Yugoslav health care under socialism, I shall first sketch the broad outlines of the organization of health services during the years of the inter-war monarchy.

1. 'De-etaticized' is an admittedly awkward rendering of the Marxist 'withering away of the state'. The Yugoslavs have borrowed from the French (*état*) to create the Serbo-Croatian word, *de-etatizacija*. I have merely Anglicized their word.
2. Unless otherwise indicated, materials in this section are from Parmelee (1983, 1985, 1988).

Donna E. Parmelee

Health Care Under the Inter-war Monarchy

The founding of the Kingdom of the Serbs, Croats and Slovenes in 1918, in effect, marked the beginning of *Yugoslav* health care. As a largely agricultural and underdeveloped country, the new Kingdom was plagued by major health problems typical of the developing world: the predominance of mass infectious diseases, high infant mortality, low levels of nutrition and hygiene, etc. Like most developing countries, especially those emerging from long periods of foreign domination, health resources were limited and extremely maldistributed in favour of the wealthy members of a small urban population. With the exception of traditional practitioners and a few categories of health workers such as midwives, available health personnel had to study abroad (primarily in Austria, Germany, France and Czechoslovakia), and local capabilities for medical training were just beginning at newly established medical schools in Zagreb (1917) and Belgrade (1919). Add to this the fact that the country was recovering from the ravages of the First World War, and it is clear that the South Slav Kingdom faced enormous tasks in the area of health.

Following the lead of other European countries, the monarchy proclaimed its intentions to address the country's health needs. Article 21 of the 1921 Royal Constitution (quoted in Štampar, 1925, p. 7) declared that: 'It shall be the duty of the Government to endeavor to improve general and social hygiene: to safeguard public health, extend special protection to mothers and children, protect the health of all citizens, fight chronic and acute diseases and alcoholism, and provide free medical care and medicine for the poor.' Moreover, Articles 23 and 31 of the 1921 Constitution called for special legislation to guarantee the health and safety of industrial workers and public employees, who then constituted less than one-quarter of the population, and to provide material assistance to workers in the event of illness, disability, old age and death (SGKJ, 1929, p. 89).

Over the course of the inter-war years, a three-part health system combining a public or state health service, social insurance for workers and private medical practice was established to address the country's health needs. The state health service's principal activities were in traditional public health work, such as infectious disease control, basic hygiene and sanitation measures, and health education. In addition, a small number of state health facilities (out-

300

patient clinics, dispensaries, health centres and most of the country's hospitals) provided free medical treatment for specific disease conditions (e.g. infectious diseases, mental disorders) and categories in the population defined as particularly at risk (e.g. mothers and infants, school children).[3] It is worth noting that the head of the Kingdom's public health service during the 1920s, Dr Andrija Štampar, played an instrumental role in shaping the basic policies and organization of the state health service, and in supplementing meagre domestic government funding for health with aid from such sources as the Rockefeller Foundation. A strong proponent of socialized medicine, Štampar reportedly became somewhat of a folk hero to the rural population towards whom many of his efforts were directed and a prophet to health workers who shared his ideals, as well as an enemy to those whose interests were threatened by anything resembling socialized medicine (Adamic, 1934, pp. 309–23; Grmek, 1966). Among other things, Štampar called for the integration of preventive and curative medicine, an ideal he attempted to realize in some fifty-one state health centres called 'Homes of People's Health' (*Domovi Narodnog Zdravlja*) which were opened under his leadership. Although Štampar would be 'retired' under the royal dictatorship in 1930, his health ideology as well as the *Domovi Narodnog Zdravlja* would be retained in post-Second-World-War Yugoslavia, when he went on to head the University of Zagreb, the Yugoslav Academy of Sciences and Arts and the Zagreb School of Public Health which now bears his name. In addition, Štampar's ideas were influential in shaping the goals of the World Health Organization, which he helped to found in 1948.

Along with the state health service, several state and private social insurance carriers administered medical and disability benefits for specific categories of wage- and salary-earners and members of their respective families. Building upon earlier efforts to provide social insurance coverage for workers in the South Slav territories which were united in 1918, legislation was first passed in 1922 to create a comprehensive system of insurance against sickness and physical injury for wage-earners, salaried employees and their respective dependents. The more than three-quarters of the population who

---

3. By 1939, there were 159 health stations, 51 'Homes of People's Health' (see below), 76 miscellaneous outpatient clinics, 152 state and municipal hospitals and 10 Hygiene Institutes (SGKJ, 1941, pp. 380–1).

were peasants remained uninsured. Although this and subsequent inter-war social insurance legislation called for equalization of rights and benefits for all workers and for unification of the separate social insurance carriers, these provisions were never fully implemented. Of the various carriers, the state-sponsored general insurance programme for workers was by far the largest, and would serve as a prototype for social insurance administration under the communists. In addition, during the inter-war years there were separate insurance carriers for state transport workers, a seaman's trade union sickness fund, four social insurance funds for miners and several small private carriers for white-collar workers ('Health Insurance in Yugoslavia', 1961). As of 1939, some 2.62 million employed persons and their dependents (around 17 per cent of the Yugoslav population) were covered by these various insurance carriers, with primarily curative medical care delivered to them in the small number of outpatient clinics, hospitals and other facilities owned by the carrriers themselves, or on a contract basis with state facilities or private physicians ('Social Insurance', 1960).[4]

In addition to the state and social insurance health services, during the inter-war monarchy Yugoslavs who could afford to do so could also obtain medical treatment from private physicians and in a limited number of private or religious-sponsored health facilities. Information on this private sector tends to be rather sketchy, although there is some evidence that it tended to be concentrated in the larger urban areas. For example, Štampar (1946, p. 100) reports that immediately before the Second World War around one-quarter of all physicians served the less than 4 per cent of the Yugoslav population living in the country's two major urban areas, Belgrade and Zagreb. Moreover, by 1938, only 20 per cent of the 4,747 physicians were exclusively engaged in private practice (Tomasevich, 1955, p. 597). According to Tomasevich (ibid.), despite the very great need for medical care and the relatively small number of physicians (around one physician for every 3,300 persons), the country's low level of economic development did not create enough effective demand for services to support a larger contingent of private practitioners. As a result, most physicians combined public service with private practice, some for humanitarian reasons, but

4. In 1939, the following facilities were owned by the social insurance carriers: 162 outpatient clinics, six health stations, nine hospitals and eleven other inpatient institutions (convalescent homes, health spas, tuberculosis sanitoria) (SGKJ, 1941, p. 409).

many to guarantee themselves a minimum income and a pension in old age through government practice.

Finally, a small but none the less interesting experiment in the application of cooperative principles to health on a private or voluntary basis was also recorded in inter-war Yugoslavia. I refer here to health cooperatives (*zdravstvene zadruge*) which were formed in some of the wealthier rural areas. An outspoken advocate for the cooperative movement, Dr Gavrilo Kojić, is credited with organizing the first health cooperative in 1921. Kojić argued that a private cooperative organization would be more acceptable to the rural population than a government-sponsored health service and would encourage greater involvement of the people in health care activities in their local communities. Moreover, he contended that there would be less bureaucracy in a private rather than a state service. The basic model was one in which rural residents paid a contribution into a common fund used to build a health centre and hire the necessary staff (Sigerist, 1939). It should be noted, however, that while the number of health cooperatives increased throughout the inter-war years, the portion of rural inhabitants included still remained quite small. In 1938, for example, there were 117 active health cooperatives with 68,745 members (not counting family members) (SGKJ, 1941, p. 398). Even including family members, this represented only a small percentage of the almost 12 million Yugoslavs engaged in agriculture at that time. Furthermore, the cooperatives were not self-supporting but relied on government subsidies and even foreign assistance (e.g. from the United States) to continue their work (Sigerist, 1939).

Transformation of the Yugoslav Health Sector
Under Socialism

Coming to power in a war-torn and devastated country in 1945, the Yugoslav communists soon took steps to reorganize the three-part health system which they inherited from the inter-war monarchy. With the Soviet Union at that time *the* model of proper socialist development, state intervention and centralized regulation of the health sector were strengthened. By 1948, for example, the social insurance facilities and personnel were merged with those of the state health service, and the few remaining private health institutions were nationalized. As in the early years after the Bolshevik Revolution, private practice was permitted to continue given the great need for care, and indeed did so until it was formally abolished by federal legislation in the late 1950s.[5] Federal and republic Ministries of Health began to plan the expansion of health personnel and facilities under the First Five-Year Plan (1947–51). Furthermore, in a policy which encountered resistance until it was abandoned in the early 1950s, Ministries of Health could assign health workers to areas where mass infectious diseases were rampant and shortages of health workers most acute (i.e. in the least developed regions of the southeast: Bosnia–Hercegovina, Kosovo, Macedonia and Montenegro). In contrast to the Soviets who fairly quickly abandoned an insurance mechanism for financing its social security programme in favour of general tax revenues (Navarro, 1977, p. 18), the Yugoslavs would retain the social insurance concept inherited from the inter-war period, albeit with greater centralized state control. Thus, in 1946, state social insurance offices at the federal, republic and district levels assumed responsibility for administering the programme of social insurance (including health, disability and pension insurance), which was made compulsory for all blue-collar wage-earners and white-collar salaried employees and their respective dependents – categories in the population expected to increase rapidly through the country's ambitious industrialization plans. Despite their important contributions to the war of national liberation, peasants were not initially guaranteed social insurance coverage.

As in the broader society and economy, Yugoslavia's break with Stalin and the Cominform in 1948 led to a break with its early fascination with state or administrative socialism in the health sector. After some initial floundering, the Yugoslavs began to develop their own model of socialist society, self-managing socialism, a model which they intended to be clearly distinguishable from that of the Soviet bloc. With varied emphasis and not without

5. Private medical practice was made illegal through federal legislation in 1958, although older practitioners were allowed to continue to practice beyond that date. Then, in the wake of a fiscal crisis in the late 1960s and growing unemployment among physicians and dentists, Croatia and Slovenia reintroduced private practice on a very limited scale. In the 1970s, Slovenia again abolished private practice, and through a new health law passed in Croatia in 1980, it appeared that private practice would be gradually phased out there, too. However, when I was in Yugoslavia in 1986, plans to abandon it in Croatia had been put on hold, and Serbia was in the process of reintroducing private dental practice, again in the context of an economic crisis and a surplus of unemployed health workers. To date, the numbers of private practitioners have remained quite small relative to those employed in the socialized health sector.

occasional setbacks, constitutional and legislative reforms after 1950 have called for the transfer of health decision-making prerogatives from the federation to the republics–provinces and communes (decentralization), and from government authorities at any level to health facilities themselves (Marx's 'withering away of the state', or de-etatization, as the Yugoslavs call it). Simultaneously, there have been attempts to secure greater and more direct participation of health workers and citizens in the management of various aspects of the health sector (democratization).

These reforms aimed at the creation of a self-managed health sector can be illustrated by changes in the status of health facilities and health workers, and in the sources and administration of funding for health services and capital expenditures. With regard to the status of health facilities, in contrast to the early post-war years when they were under the direct jurisdiction of the central state administrative apparatus, health facilities gradually became relatively autonomous *vis-à-vis* the state and acquired the status of socially owned institutions managed ('self-managed') by their employees and community representatives. In the 1950s, federal and republic Ministries of Health were replaced by councils (and in the late 1970s, by committees) of Public Health, their name changes and reduced staffing reflecting their more limited jurisdiction over the operations of health facilities (e.g. regulating the legislative framework of the health sector, supervising matters of common interest such as the supply and quality of pharmaceuticals and implementing international health conventions).

As to the status of health workers under self-managing socialism, by the 1960s health workers were no longer state employees, and have since then been free to apply for positions as they become available and are advertised. Like their counterparts in all Yugoslav socialized work organizations, these employees participate in the management of their workplaces directly as members of 'assemblies of workers' (all employees) and through referenda, and indirectly through their elected delegates in workers' councils. Initially mandated at the level of the entire health facility only, since the 1974 Constitution these assemblies and councils are also formed for separate departments or clinics which are organized as 'basic organizations of associated labour' (or OOURs, to use the Serbo-Croatian acronym). Since the 1960s, these self-management bodies have acquired increasing responsibility for the organization of work, hiring and firing of the institution's director and employees, allocation of revenues and setting of pay scales. Unlike the case in Yugoslav enterprises which are formally self-managed by their employees only, community delegates have been included in self-management bodies in health (and other social service) institutions since their inception in the 1950s, ostensibly to ensure representation of 'broader social interests'. However, in the 1960s, these community representatives lost their majority membership in these bodies and, while democratization via community participation has been weakened, democratization via health worker self-management has been enhanced.

Concomitant with these developments in the administration of health facilities, sources of funding for health services and capital expenditures have also changed. In the immediate post-war period, health facilities were funded through government budgets, compulsory social insurance contributions for blue- and white-collar workers in the socialized sector and direct patient fees (primarily from the large but declining number of private agricultural producers who were not provided insurance coverage until 1959). However, as part of broader processes of decentralization during the 1950s, republics and especially local areas (districts and communes) assumed greater responsibility for financing health services. To illustrate, local budgets provided only 17 per cent of the combined expenditures for health and social welfare from 1947 to 1951; by 1960, this share had increased to over 54 per cent. By the 1960s, the share of total health expenditures financed from government budgets at any level had been reduced to a minimum. In 1965, for example, with virtually the entire population by then at least partially covered by compulsory health insurance, less than 5 per cent of total health expenditures came from government budgets, whereas 80 per cent was financed through local workers' and farmers' insurance associations (with the remainder coming from direct 'out of pocket' payments, enterprises and other unspecified sources). And, while government budgets had been the major source of capital investment funds during the 1950s, they accounted for only 20 per cent of these funds in 1965.

Trends towards decentralization, de-etatization and democratization also affected the administration of the health insurance programme. During the 1950s, the social insurance programme (including health insurance) was removed from the competence of the state administrative apparatus, and acquired the status of a semi-autonomous public service managed by assemblies of insurees. The word 'State' was dropped from the title of existing Social

Insurance Offices which continued to implement the insurance provisions. After extension of compulsory insurance coverage from workers in the socialized sector to other categories of insured persons (to private farmers in 1959 and to self-employed craftworkers and professionals during the 1950s), Communal Insurance Associations for each category were founded in 1962. Communal (or at times intercommunal associations) were given autonomy to determine insurance benefits above and beyond minimum standards prescribed by federal law until 1974 and by republic law thereafter, provided they agreed to collect the necessary funds. (Federal grants and republic-level 'solidarity funds' assisted regions and communes unable to afford the basic level of services.) In addition to a professional staff, each communal association had an assembly composed of insuree-representatives formally charged with health planning and programming in the commune, negotiating contracts with provider institutions and determining the level of contributions from insurees and the types and range of benefits. In the 1974 Constitution, these insurance associations were re-renamed 'self-managing communities of interest' (or SIZs, to use the Serbo-Croatian acronym) to reflect the fact that they would henceforth be co-managed by assemblies of user *and* provider delegates, and therefore settings where the interests of different social actors could be 'harmonized', in theory with minimal state involvement.

Evaluating Yugoslav Health Care Under Self-Managing Socialism

By its very nature, evaluation is a problematic endeavour. For what is defined as an 'achievement' or a 'failure' lies very much in the eye of the beholder, and depends upon the often arbitrary benchmarks against which something, in this case a health system, is judged. Moreover, measures typically used to evaluate health systems are often very crude. To illustrate, various measures of health resources such as physician-to-population ratios, or of health service utilization such as physician visits per capita, tell us something about the quantity of medical care but tell us nothing about the quality of that care. And, health status indicators such as infant mortality rates reflect not only the quantity and quality of specific biomedical interventions but also, and some would say more importantly, such social and environmental factors as sanitation, housing and nutrition, as well as the overall standard of living in a society (Dubos, 1959; McKeown, 1971).

With these caveats in mind, I shall none the less attempt an evaluation of Yugoslav health care under self-managing socialism. First, I shall compare measures of health and health resources in inter-war and post-Second-World-War Yugoslavia. Then, employing classifications used by the World Bank (1983b, pp. xix–xxi), I shall compare Yugoslav health care in the 1980s with the experience of other 'Southern European Developing Economies', several 'East European Nonmarket Economies', and various 'Industrial Market Economies'.[6] Finally, I shall consider Yugoslav health care in the 1980s relative to the proclaimed health policy objectives of the Yugoslavs themselves which were discussed at the beginning of this chapter.

Pre- and Post-Revolutionary Yugoslav Health Care

To compare achievements of socialist Yugoslavia relative to those of the interwar monarchy, I shall look at two categories of measures. The first category concerns the accessibility of medical services as evidenced by the availability of health resources (personnel and facilities) and in the removal of financial barriers to obtaining medical care. The second category embraces various measures of health or health status which reflect changing patterns of morbidity and mortality.

As can readily be seen from the data presented in Table 10.1, socialist Yugoslavia has clearly outpaced royalist Yugoslavia in terms of the supply of health resources, the removal of financial barriers via insurance coverage and in the health status of the Yugoslav population. With regard to health personnel, the total number of physicians has increased more than eightfold, and the number of inhabitants per physician decreased by more than 80 per cent in the period from 1938 to 1985. This illustrates the substantial investment the Yugoslav communists have made in developing medical education. For whereas there were three Yugoslav medical schools which produced just over 2,500 graduates during the inter-war years, by the mid-1980s there were twelve medical schools which had graduated over 53,000 physicians from 1945 to 1985. Indeed, by the 1980s, Yugoslav medical schools on average pro-

6. Yugoslavia is classified as a Southern European Developing Economy by the World Bank.

Table 10.1 Health Resources, Health Insurance Beneficiaries and Health Status in Pre-and Post-revolutionary Yugoslavia

	Pre-revolutionary 1939	1952	1961	Post-revolutionary 1971	1981	1985
Health Resources						
Physicians						
Number	4,747[a]	6,256	12,699	21,902	33,514	40,329
Population per physician	3,241	2,685	1,461	937	669	573
Number of medical schools	3	5	8	9	12	12
Total graduates	2,511 (1923–39)			53,115 (1945–85)		
Percent women	22.3			43.7		
General outpatient clinics[b]		1,227	3,163	3,747	4,151	4,537
Specialist clinics and polyclinics[b]		80	156	629	2,993	3,366
Occupational health units			804[c]	1,257	1,501	1,694[d]
Hospital beds						
Number	29,000[e]	61,000	97,000	120,000	137,000	141,000
Population per bed	531	275	191	171	164	164
Insurance Beneficiaries						
Workers' Insurance						
Number (in thousands)	2,616	4,387	9,002	12,969	17,137	18,172[f]
% of total population	16.8	26.1	48.5	63.2	76.4	78.1[f]
Farmers' Insurance						
Number (in thousands)			7,583	6,118	4,754	4,671[f]
% of total population			40.9	29.8	21.2	20.1
Health Status						
Infant mortality[g]	132.3	105.1	82.0	49.5	30.8	28.4[h]
Life expectancy at birth[i] Male	48.6[j]	56.9	62.3	65.4	67.7	
Female	53.0[j]	59.3	65.4	70.2	73.2	

Notes: [a] 1938; [b] Comparable data for the inter-war period are not available; [c] 1966; [d] 1984; [e] 1938; [f] 1986; [g] Infant deaths per 1,000 live births; [h] Preliminary data; [i] Post-revolutionary data presented are for the following periods: 1952–54; 1960–62, 1970–72, 1980–81; [j] 1948.

Sources: SGJ (various years); SGKJ (various years); SGNZ (various years); Kesić (1983); Vajs and Feliks (1986).

duced about as many physicians per year as had graduated during the entire inter-war period (SGJ, 1985)! Moreover, although not shown on the table, there has been a consistent trend towards specialization in the post-revolutionary period, so that by 1985 some 57 per cent of physicians were classified as specialists (compared with only 33 per cent in 1952) (Federal Statistical Office, 1973; SGJ, 1987). With medicine still considered a relatively prestigious and highly paid profession at least into the 1970s (Denitch, 1976; Hammel, 1969), I would also note the increasing share of women among medical faculty graduates (see Table 10.1). While women constituted just over 22 per cent of medical faculty graduates in pre-revolutionary Yugoslavia, they accounted for over 43 per cent of graduates between 1945 and 1985.

Paralleling this increase in the number of physicians (and other health workers) in the post-war years, there has also been a substantial expansion in the network of health facilities. To illustrate, in contrast to the fairly small number of outpatient facilities operated by the state at the end of the inter-war period (51 'Homes of People's Health' and 235 other miscellaneous clinics or health stations), by 1985 there were over 4,500 general practice outpatient clinics, over 3,300 specialist clinics and over 1,600 occupational health units in Yugoslav enterprises operating as part of a broader network of socially owned, locally controlled outpatient facilities.[7] Similarly, the supply of hospital beds has been expanded by the Yugoslav communists, particularly in the first two decades of their rule, with the rate of increase relative to population growth moderating over the past two decades (see Table 10.1).

Thus, in terms of the sheer quantity of facilities and personnel, it would seem fair to say that medical services have become more accessible to the Yugoslav population in the post-revolutionary period than had been the case under the monarchy. Financial barriers to services have also been reduced significantly relative to the inter-war monarchy as a result of the expansion of obligatory health insurance coverage to virtually the entire population. Whereas only around 17 per cent of the Yugoslav population was covered by the various public and private workers' insurance funds on the eve

7. For data on the inter-war period, see notes 3 and 4 above. Data for the inter-war and post-war periods are not exactly comparable, since outpatient care was also provided during the inter-war period by private practitioners and by physicians employed by municipalities or the social insurance funds or who worked on contract with the state to treat the poor (Federal Institute of Public Health, 1975, p. 50).

of the Second World War, by 1985 over 98 per cent of the population was insured through publicly sponsored workers' or farmers' insurance associations (SIZs), with most of the residual share of the population (e.g. veterans, recipients of public assistance) receiving health care subsidized directly from state budgets.

Finally, in terms of health status, the post-revolutionary regime can report impressive gains. As noted earlier, the Yugoslav monarchy came to power in a society marked by health underdevelopment. That is, they inherited a whole series of health problems including rampant infectious diseases, high infant mortality rates, poor nutrition and sanitation, etc. Although the inter-war monarchy had made some efforts to address these problems, it would not be until after the Second World War that significant progress would be made. For example, with regard to the patterns of morbidity and mortality, it was not until after the Second World War that Yugoslavia made the epidemiologic transition from diseases of underdevelopment to those of the developed world. To a large extent, infectious diseases such as malaria and tuberculosis were brought under control, only to be replaced by such health problems as cardiovascular diseases, cancer and accidents as the leading causes of death (Feliks, 1978). Furthermore, concomitant with post-revolutionary Yugoslavia's more rapid socioeconomic development, the infant mortality rate declined substantially. Whereas the infant mortality rate dropped only modestly in the inter-war years (from around 145 deaths per 1,000 live births in 1924 to 132 in 1939), progress thereafter has been much more noteworthy (from 105 in 1952 to an estimated 28.4 in 1985) (see Table 10.1 and Parmelee, 1983, p. 235). And, as a result of improvements in the standard of living, medical care and infant mortality rates, life expectancy at birth increased by 19.1 years for men and 20.2 years for women between 1948 and 1981 (see Table 10.1).

In sum, without denying that the inter-war monarchy did make some improvements in the country's health system and in the people's health, the post-revolutionary regime has made far more substantial gains in the area of health than its predecessor even taking into account socialist Yugoslavia's advantage of longevity. In defence of the monarchy, it is worth reporting that such renowned observers of the international health scene in the first half of the century as Brockington (1958, pp. 180–7) and Sigerist (1939) acknowledged that certain developments in the inter-war health sector were fairly advanced for that time. These include the extension of social insurance coverage to workers, the progressive ideas and activities of people like Dr Andrija Štampar, as well as the small experiment in rural health cooperatives. However, as Štampar's own forced retirement from public service in 1930 so well illustrates and as post-war Yugoslav observers are often wont to say, conditions in the inter-war period were not yet ripe for full development of these progressive ideas and organizational forms.

The Yugoslav Health Care System in Comparative Perspective

Having argued that socialist Yugoslavia has made significant gains in the health sector relative to the inter-war monarchy, I shall now turn to an evaluation of these achievements *vis-à-vis* the experience of other countries. For this comparison, I have selected nine countries which have historically controlled parts of Yugoslavia (Austria, Hungary, Turkey), which share Yugoslavia's history of foreign-domination or which have a roughly similar level of socioeconomic development but have contrasting sociopolitical and economic systems (see Table 10.2). I have also included the United Kingdom, the United States and the USSR as points of reference. I shall not attempt a thorough comparison of the health sectors of these various countries, but shall instead simply present and discuss some basic quantitative economic and health indicators against which the Yugoslav case can be judged. Using a World Bank (1983b) scheme which classifies these countries by economic system/level of development, I offer relevant data for 1984 in Table 10.2 for three Southern European Developing Economies, five East European Non-market Economies and three Industrial Market Economies.

Looking first at our crude measures of health outcomes, infant mortality and life expectancy, one can see that praise of socialist Yugoslavia's achievements compared to the inter-war monarchy needs to be qualified. On the one hand, only Albania and Turkey have higher infant mortality rates than Yugoslavia (41 and 93 infant deaths per 1,000 live births, compared with 29), although the Soviet Union is not too far ahead of Yugoslavia with its infant death rate of 26. On the other hand, although the life expectancy at birth in Yugoslavia (70 years) equals or approaches that found in the East European Non-market Economies, it still falls short of that found in the Industrial Market Economies and only Turkey has a shorter life expectancy than Yugoslavia among the Southern European Developing Economies.

Table 10.2 Yugoslav Health Policy in Comparative Perspective, 1984

	GNP per capita in US$	Public health expenditure as % of GNP[a]	Public health expenditure per capita US$	Population per physician	Population per hospital bed[b]	Infant mortality per 1,000 births	Life expectancy at birth
Yugoslavia	2,990	4.1	123	626	166	29	70
Southern Europe							
Greece	4,273	3.6	156	353	157	14	74
Portugal	2,340	3.0	71	418	189	17	72
Turkey	1,460	0.7	10	1,452	506	93	63
East European Non-market Economies							
Albania	1,655[c]	2.6	43	617	156	41	71
Bulgaria	5,018	4.0	198	356	115	16	72
Hungary	5,915	2.8	164	340	114	20	70
Romania	3,571	2.0	72	583	109	23	71
USSR	7,095	3.2	227	243	82	26	70
Industrial Market Economies							
Austria	9,245	4.7	430	559	89	11	73
UK	8,616	5.4	470	729	120[d]	10	74
USA	15,541	4.3	674	474	159	11	75

Notes: [a] Private expenditures for health care are not included. For countries shown here, private expenditures would be largest in the USA, which in 1984 spent a combined public and private 10.3 percent of its GNP, or $1,595 per capita on health care (National Center for Health Statistics, 1986); [b] 1980; [c] In 1982 and 1983, the GNP per capita for Albania was reportedly $950 and $993, respectively (Sivard, 1985, 1986). I am unable to explain the large increase for 1984; [d] England and Wales only; for the Scotland and Northern Ireland, the ratio is 88 and 89, respectively.

Sources: Kurian (1984); Sivard (1987); United Nations Statistical Office (1988).

Similarly, when we look at physician and hospital bed density measures, we see that Yugoslavia lags behind most of the other countries chosen for comparison. As shown in Table 10.2, among the Southern and East European countries, only Turkey has a higher population-to-physician ratio than Yugoslavia (1,452 versus 626 inhabitants per physician, respectively). Perhaps somewhat surprisingly, in 1984 Yugoslavia actually had fewer inhabitants per physician than the United Kingdom. In terms of hospital beds, Yugoslavia only fares better than Portugal and Turkey, although again it is interesting to note that Yugoslavia actually approaches the ratio found in such wealthier countries as the United States and Greece. (I shall return to these two anomalies in a moment.)

At this point, one might well ask: how can one account for Yugoslavia's relatively poor showing on these health care resource and health status measures? Of course, some of this advantage for other countries can be explained by their headstart relative to post-Second-World-War Yugoslavia. For example, countries such as Austria, the United Kingdom, the United States and Greece already had lower infant mortality rates and longer life expectancies on the eve of the war than did Yugoslavia. However, at least some of the countries which had similar or higher infant mortality rates and comparable or shorter life expectancy in the late 1930s such as Portugal, Bulgaria, Hungary and Romania have none the less managed to outpace Yugoslavia on these measures (United Nations, 1949, pp. 53–8; 1953, pp. 44–5).

In addition to the effects of a headstart, Yugoslavia's still modest level of wealth compared to that of most of the other economies shown here must also be taken into consideration. As reported in Table 10.2, only Portugal and Turkey (among Southern European Developing Economies) and only Albania (among East European Non-market Economies) had a lower Gross National Product (GNP) per capita in 1984 than Yugoslavia's US$2,990. And only Portugal, Turkey, Albania and Romania had lower per capita public health expenditures than Yugoslavia's US$123. Although there are exceptions, those countries which are poorer than Yugoslavia and/ or which spend less on health care than Yugoslavia are the only ones which perform worse on these measures of health care resources and health status, and vice versa.

A third factor which helps to explain Yugoslavia's performance relative to other countries would be country-specific social policies. I shall offer two examples. First, several of the East European

Non-market Economies (such as the USSR, Bulgaria, Hungary and, more recently, Albania) have committed themselves to a very rapid increase in the supply of physicians, so much so that some observers have suggested that quantity has been sacrificed for quality, with a corresponding deprofessionalization of medical practitioners (e.g. Kaufmann, 1981; Kurian, 1984; Letica, 1987). While Yugoslavia has not pushed this 'hyperproduction' of physicians as far as, say, the Soviet Union, it, too, moved quickly after the Second World War to increase the number of physicians. And, in the context of the country's political decentralization and the rather autarchic development of the republics and provinces, by the late 1970s Yugoslavia had twelve medical schools – at least one in every republic or province with the exception of Montenegro. The United Kingdom offers an interesting contrast in that opportunities for medical education have not opened up as in these other countries, as evidenced by its somewhat higher physician-to-population ratio relative to the countries presented in Table 10.2 (and to other European countries, too) (Sivard, 1987).

A second example of the impact of specific social policies can be seen in the similar population-to-hospital-bed ratios for Yugoslavia and the United States in 1984. Namely, the current figures for the United States reflect the sharp decline in the number of psychiatric beds in the United States which accompanied moves towards the de-institutionalization of mental patients in the 1960s. Furthermore, given different medical philosophies and varying levels of efficiency and cost containment pressures, the mean lengths of stays at somatic (short-term) hospitals tend to be considerably shorter in the US than in Yugoslavia (and in other European countries, for that matter) (Berg *et al.*, 1976; OECD, 1985). As such, the fact that Yugoslavia's hospital bed density approaches that of the US does not necessarily mean that ease of access to available beds is the same in both countries. (This point also illustrates some of the shortcomings of 'hospital bed density' as a measure typically used to compare and evaluate health systems.)

While such factors as the headstart advantage, greater wealth and social policies help us to interpret the data in Table 10.2, I would contend that perhaps the most important explanation for Yugoslavia's low ranking relative to the other European countries lies in the country's striking regional gaps in level of socioeconomic development which overlap with its ethnic divisions. As Fred Singleton (1985, p. 269) so aptly put it, within its borders Yugoslavia has the dilemmas 'of having in microcosm the North/South problem which faces the world at large – of having India and West Germany within the same country'. I shall discuss the issue of regional economic and health inequalities in a moment when I assess post-war Yugoslavia's accomplishments relative to the regime's own health policy objectives. For now, suffice it to say that the gap in economic development between the most developed region, Slovenia, and the least developed region, Kosovo, is far greater than in most West European countries (e.g. Kiljunen, 1983) and, I would surmise, in the East European economies, too.[8] Moreover, on such indicators as per capita income, the development gap between Slovenia and Kosovo continues to increase. As a result, the data for Yugoslavia as a whole conceal significant regional variations within the country.

Overlapping with this gap in economic development, one must also consider the effects of ethnic diversity. With the exception of the USSR, the European countries included in this comparison are essentially ethnically homogeneous (with 80 per cent or more of each country's population constituted by members of a single ethnic group) (World Almanac, 1989). However, like the USSR, Yugoslavia has a markedly heterogeneous population. In each case, several ethnic groups have experienced centuries of Western European influence, while other ethnic groups trace their cultural heritage to influences from the East, in particular, the Muslim populations of southern Yugoslavia (and those of the Central Asian republics in the USSR). It is precisely these Muslim-influenced regions which 'lag behind' all other regions in these two countries on basic measures of socioeconomic development such as income per capita, infant mortality, nutrition, etc. Given fairly traditional cultural attitudes about contraception, the roles of women, and the like, birth rates in the Muslim regions continue to be quite high, and populations tend to be relatively younger (see Table 10.3 for relevant demographic indicators for Yugoslavia). As a result, data on per capita measures for these regions tend to 'pull down' the average for the country as a whole, with no immediate prospect for improvement so long as birth rates remain high.

8. Kiljunen (1983) presents regional data for the following European countries in the 1970s: Yugoslavia, Italy, France, Finland, the Netherlands, Belgium, Sweden, Great Britain, Denmark and West Germany. The ratio of per capita income between the most developed and least developed regions of Yugoslavia was 7.3:1; for all other countries, the corresponding ratio was less than 3:1. Among the East European Non-market Economies, the most developed Soviet republic had a per capita national income in 1970 which was 2.6 times larger than that of the least developed republic (Dellenbrant, 1986, p. 56).

Table 10.3 Demographic Indicators, by Region

	Population (in thousands)	Percent of population below age 20		Natural growth rate[a] (per 1,000)		Crude birth rate (per 1,000)	
	1981	1981		1952	1984	1952	1984
More developed regions[b]							
Slovenia	1,892	30.6		12.4	3.2	22.8	13.7
Croatia	4,601	28.2		12.3	2.3	23.4	14.0
Serbia proper	5,694	27.5		16.6	3.7	27.4	13.7
Vojvodina	2,035	26.7		11.7	1.4	23.8	13.6
Less developed regions							
Bosnia–Hercegovina	4,124	38.0		27.7	10.6	40.2	17.4
Montenegro	584	37.3		22.7	10.3	32.0	17.4
Macedonia	1,909	38.4		25.9	12.4	39.9	19.5
Kosovo	1,584	52.3		27.3	26.0	44.7	32.1
Yugoslavia	22,425	32.7		18.0	7.1	29.8	16.4

Notes: [a] The crude natural growth rate equals the crude birth rate minus the crude death rate; [b] Regions are ranked from highest to lowest by national income per capita in 1952.

Sources: SGJ (various years).

Thus, when juxtaposed to the record of other European countries, Yugoslav achievements in health care are not quite as impressive as they appeared in the comparison with those of the inter-war monarchy. Indeed, despite improvements over the post-war years, Yugoslavia still ranks near the bottom of European countries on the various measures of health care resources and health status. Whether this can be taken as an indictment of Yugoslavia's efforts to create a self-managed society, in general, and a self-managed health sector, in particular, is a highly debatable issue. For even though their efforts to decentralize, de-etaticize and democratize the health sector have not been without certain 'costs' (which I shall discuss later in this chapter), successes and failures of the Yugoslav system have to be judged in the context of the economic disparities and cultural diversity which the Yugoslav communists (*and* their predecessors) inherited with the creation of Yugoslavia as a unified country. Such disparities and diversity would likely place constraints on development under *any* health system.

Evaluating Achievement of Yugoslav Health Policy Objectives Under Self-Managing Socialism

In this section, I shall look at Yugoslav achievements in the health sector relative to the objectives they have set for themselves. As I have noted earlier, socialist Yugoslavia has declared that (a) health care is a right of citizenship; (b) inequalities in the area of health should be transcended, while at the same time promising that certain categories in the population should be given special treatment (women, children, workers and veterans); and (c) the health delivery and insurance systems should be self-managed by users and providers of health services in each commune, with minimal state–bureaucratic interference. To what extent have these objectives been met?

Health Care as a Right Through extension of health insurance to virtually the entire population by 1960, Yugoslavia has taken an important first step towards meeting its promise of health care for all. Living in a country which has yet to make health care an entitlement of citizenship, I find this first step to be no mean accomplishment. Of course, in promising that 'everyone shall be entitled to health care', the Yugoslav Constitution does not specify 'how much' or 'which kinds' of health care the population is to be guaranteed. As noted earlier, until 1974 the extent and range of health insurance benefits were prescribed by federal legislation and, since then, through republic–provincial laws and contracts negotiated by the communal health insurance association (SIZ) assemblies. Following federal legislation in 1969, all categories of insurees (workers, farmers and privately employed craftspeople and professionals) have been guaranteed health insurance for certain 'obligatory forms of health care', with republic-level solidarity funds used to ensure this basic level of coverage in poorer communes unable to finance it themselves. These benefits include: prevention, control and treatment of tuberculosis, venereal and other infectious diseases; care and treatment of patients with mental disorders, malignancies, rheumatic fever and muscular dystrophy; total care for women during pregnancy and postnatal care for one year; total care for children up to the age of fifteen, young people in school up to the age of twenty-six and persons over sixty; and various health education and environmental sanitation activities. Communal SIZs can, and most do, also provide supplemental health benefits besides this basic obligatory coverage, including outpatient general practitioner and specialist examinations, hospital care, laboratory tests, dental work and prescription drugs. In addition, cash reimbursement is provided for travel expenses for referrals to health providers in other communes, as well as funeral benefits, compensation for lost income in the event of temporary illness or injury, maternity leave and when caring for a sick family member (Federal Committee of Labour, Health and Social Welfare, 1979, p. 7; Pejovich, 1979, pp. 31–3).

It is, of course, one thing to *promise* health insurance coverage for these various disease categories and risk groups, and another thing actually to be able to satisfy the need or demand (from patients and providers) for such coverage. While I cannot quantify the degree to which the Yugoslavs have fulfilled this promise, I can illustrate some of the difficulties they have encountered in trying to do so. For example, in health service research publications and the popular media, throughout the post-war years one finds not-infrequent reports about such problems as shortages of essential pharmaceuticals, overcrowded waiting rooms, deficits in the health insurance funds, and health institutions which have already delivered the quantity of services agreed to under annual contracts with SIZs before December, and which then have to absorb the costs of additional care provided until the new year (e.g. Džadžić, 1986; Parmelee, 1983; Trklja, 1988). One also finds repeated attempts to control consumption of health services and rising health expenditures through such measures as federally determined freezes on the level of contributions for health insurance, introduction of small user fees (known as *participacija*, or participation payments) to be made at the point of delivery, increases in the share of sick leave compensation paid out directly by work organizations in the hope that this will reduce unjustified sick leaves, as well as exhortations to workers that they should more vigilantly oversee how their own contributions are being spent by health SIZs (often depicted in the popular media as greedy institutions with overpaid professional staffs) (see Parmelee, 1983; 1988). In essence, as other countries have discovered, need and demand for health services have proven to be elastic and seemingly insatiable, expanding faster than increases in available personnel, facilities and financial resources. Moreover, the Yugoslavs' clearly ambitious package of health insurance benefits would likely strain the resources of far wealthier, more economically secure countries, let alone one with a per capita annual GNP of less than US$3,000. Add to this the deepening economic crisis of the 1980s, during which the share of the country's stagnating social product allocated to health care has actually declined from 6.2 per cent in 1979 to 4.2 per cent in 1986, and it is little wonder that health care for all remains out of reach (Letica, 1987).

The Redress of Health Inequalities The issue of health inequalities in Yugoslavia could be a separate study in and of itself. For such a study one would need to examine inequalities in access to health services and health status among the different categories of insurance beneficiaries and, given decentralization of responsibility for organizing and financing health care to the republics and communes, both inter-regional and intercommunal disparities. Here, I shall only comment briefly on the first and third of these dimensions, giving more attention to inter-regional inequalities. For it is these latter disparities which are especially politically sensitive in Yugoslavia's multi-ethnic context, albeit less so with respect to health *per se* than for overall economic development. I would add that no society has yet to produce a fully equitable health system (Anderson, 1972), so that my main concern here will be to evaluate the extent to which inequalities are at least diminishing.

By singling out certain categories in the population for special treatment, a certain measure of inequality was built into the Yugoslav health insurance system from the start. I would note especially the distinction in coverage between workers in the socialized sector and private farmers. As I discussed earlier, blue- and white-collar workers in the socialized sector were given preference over farmers during the first fifteen years of communist rule. Indeed, workers' health insurance was used as an enticement to help bring the excess rural population to the cities and factories of industrializing Yugoslavia (a process which has led to a sharp decline in the share of the population whose livelihood is based on agriculture from 67.2 per cent in 1948 to 19.9 per cent in 1981) (SGJ, 1985, p. 450). Even with the introduction of health insurance coverage for farmers in 1959, the range of benefits as well as the utilization of health services remained lower than for workers in the socialized sector (e.g. Hrabač, 1968; Berg *et al.*, 1976). With the merger of workers' and farmers' insurance associations in several of the Yugoslav republics in the 1970s and 1980s, some of these inequities are declining, at least in terms of coverage for medical care and travel reimbursements for services outside one's home commune. However, farmers still do not receive cash compensation for sick and maternity leaves.

Similarly, when looking at inter-regional health inequalities, one can report both good and bad news (see Tables 10.4 and 10.5). On the one hand, in terms of relative physician distribution measured by indexes of physician-to-population ratios (Yugoslavia = 100), regional inequalities have declined by roughly half over the post-war period (Table 10.4). Even though the least developed region, Kosovo, still lags behind the other regions, its relative position at least has continued to improve. There likewise have been some gains in the regional distribution of general hospital beds since 1952, although the relative position of three of the less developed regions (Montenegro, Macedonia and Kosovo) has actually worsened in the most recent period (Table 10.4). Inter-regional disparities on two measures of health service utilization (physician visits per capita and per cent of births in health institutions) and in life expectancy have also greatly decreased, with impressive gains in absolute terms (Table 10.5). On the other hand, significant gaps in infant mortality rates persist, with two of the less developed regions (Kosovo and Macedonia) lagging far behind the rest of the country (Table 10.5). Although improving up until around 1980, infant mortality rates in Montenegro, Macedonia and Kosovo actually increased slightly during the 1980s (SGJ, 1987, p. 447). And, at the extremes, the *relative* position of Kosovo on this measure is worse in 1985 than it was in 1952!

Table 10.4 Indexes of National Income, Workers' Health Insurance Expenditures,[a] Physicians and General Hospital Beds, by Region

(Yugoslavia = 100)

	National income per capita			Workers' health ins. expenditures per capita			Physicians per 100,000[b]			General hospital beds per 10,000		
	1952	1970	1985	1963[c]	1970	1986	1952	1970	1985	1952	1970	1985
More developed regions (MDRs)	104	120	124	113[c]	112	125	125	119	114	115	111	112
Slovenia	168	190	205	148	137	195	151	122	112	145	164	132
Croatia	114	123	128	114	119	122	132	118	111	137	113	111
Serbia Proper	98	98	94	99	98	105	122	120	121	103	99	114
Vojvodina	85	108	122	94	97	107	96	115	102	77	91	89
Less developed regions (LDRs)	77	63	61	74	75	57	45	65	77	66	80	80
Bosnia–Hercegovina	89	67	70	80	81	65	41	62	77	57	75	84
Montenegro	83	76	73	80	74	64	57	74	80	89	96	91
Macedonia	68	70	64	68	71	44	59	89	101	90	98	90
Kosovo	44	34	31	60	58	47	30	39	48	49	63	57

Ratios of indexes

MDRs:LDRs	1.4	1.9	2.0	1.5	1.5	2.2	2.8	1.8	1.5	1.7	1.4	1.4
Slovenia:Kosovo	3.8	5.6	6.6	2.5	2.4	4.1[d]	5.0	3.1	2.3[e]	3.0	2.6	2.3

Notes: [a] . Excluded are cash benefits covered under workers' health insurance (e.g. sick and maternity leave pay, funeral benefits, etc.) and insurance administration costs;
[b] Including stomatologists;
[c] Data for earlier years are unavailable;
[d] In 1986, Macedonia ranked below Kosovo on per capita workers' health insurance expenditures. The ratio of highest to lowest (Slovenia:Macedonia) was 4.4;
[e] In 1985, Serbia Proper ranked higher than Slovenia on physicians per 100,000 inhabitants. The ratio of highest to lowest (Serbia Proper:Kosovo) was 2.5.

Sources: SGJ (various years).

Table 10.5 Health Status Indicators by Per Capita GNP, Workers' Health Insurance Expenditures[a] and Selected Health Service Utilization Measures, by Region

	GNP per capita US$ 1987	Workers' health insurance expenditure per capita, US$ 1986	Physician visits per capita[b] 1952	1985	Percent births in health institutions 1956	1984	Infant mortality 1952	1985[c]	Life expectancy at birth 1952–54 M	F	1981–82 M	F
More developed regions[d]												
Slovenia	5,127	187	2.1	3.7	61.4	99.6	64.3	13.6	63	68	67	75
Croatia	3,171	117	1.8	4.8	41.6	98.7	102.3	16.0	59	63	67	74
Serbia Proper	2,304	101	1.1	4.4	39.2	96.4	87.0	25.1	59	61	69	74
Vojvodina	3,022	102	1.5	5.2	50.7	98.0	113.2	11.2	58	62	67	74
Less developed regions												
Bosnia–Hercegovina	1,759	63	1.0	2.5	19.7	90.9	113.9	22.9	53	55	68	73
Montenegro	1,883	62	.9	2.8	33.5	95.2	80.4	20.6	58	60	72	76
Macedonia	1,585	42	.7	3.7	28.2	82.0	129.8	47.7	55	55	69	72
Kosovo	743	45	.5	3.0	12.6	61.9	145.9	57.1	49	45	67	71
Yugoslavia	2,480	96	1.3	3.9	33.9	89.5	105.1	28.4	57	59	68	73

Notes: [a] See note 1, Table 10.4. Conversion to US$ based on exchange rate of $1 = 457.18 dinars (SGJ, 1987, p. 792);
[b] Includes visits to general and specialist outpatient clinics;
[c] Preliminary data;
[d] Regions are ranked from highest to lowest by national income per capita in 1952.

Sources: SGJ (various years); World Bank (1989).

Thus, even with the decentralization of administration and financing of health services, there are promising trends towards lessening inter-regional inequalities. These trends are particularly heartening given the increasing inter-regional gap in per capita health care expenditures and even greater disparities in per capita national income (Table 10.4). Accordingly, it would appear that federal policies to establish medical faculties in the less developed regions (in Bosnia–Hercegovina in 1946, Macedonia in 1947 and Kosovo in 1969) and to provide supplemental grants for social services in these regions have had ameliorative effects.[9] However, the inability of federal policies to mitigate broader disparities in standard of living, an overall decline in standard of living in the context of the current economic crisis, together with differences in the quality and utilization of health services, would seem to account for persisting inter-regional variations and, indeed, recent increases in infant mortality rates. As I have pointed out earlier, the higher rates of population increase and younger populations in the less developed regions do not bode well for an early resolution of regional disparities in development (see Table 10.3).

Finally, I shall consider intercommunal variations in access to health services. Although in part due to disparities inherited from the past, these inequalities have also been perpetuated by the decentralized financing of health services via communal insurance associations and, to a lesser degree, by the reluctance of physicians to work in the 'provinces'. Like public education in the United States, wealthier communes have been able to develop their health facilities and expand their insurance coverage beyond that possible in poorer communes. And physicians, like their counterparts elsewhere, have tended to be disproportionately located in urban areas, particularly in the capital cities of the different regions (Dimitrijević, 1984). On balance, republic-level solidarity funds do mitigate some of these disparities by assuring coverage of a basic level of health services. Moreover, as a result of the increase in the number of physicians, intercommunal disparities in physician-to-population ratios have improved over the past two decades (Kunitz, 1980; Dimitrijević, 1984). And, some degree of concentration of expensive

9. Data on the actual amounts redistributed to individual less developed regions as federal grants for health care are not readily available. Total supplemental financing of social services, in general, for the 1966–84 period amounted to around 150 billion dinars (current prices). For the 1976–80 period, this represented 0.93 per cent of the social product of the socialized sector of the economy (Federal Statistical Office, 1986, pp. 194–5; World Bank, 1983a, p. 243).

technology and specialist services is clearly desirable provided, of course, that the services are geographically and financially accessible to people beyond a given communal boundary. While difficult to measure, one nevertheless hears enough reports of higher prices being charged for services rendered in one commune to patients from other communes, or of efforts to keep health insurance funds within the commune (e.g. by limiting access to care elsewhere or by developing the commune's own capacity despite unused capacity in a neighbouring commune), to realize that the problem of intercommunal inequalities has not yet been completely resolved.

Towards a Self-managed Health Sector Through numerous constitutional and legislative reforms, the Yugoslavs have attempted to transform central state bureaucratic control over the health sector into more decentralized, de-etaticized and democratized control in accordance with their evolving ideology of self-managing socialism. Stated alternatively, they have experimented with various mixes of state, professional and lay control over health service delivery institutions and the health insurance programme. What have been some of the outcomes of these experiments?

Of the three 'Ds' (decentralization, de-etatization, democratization), decentralization appears to have gone the farthest. Although the federal and republic authorities do continue to intervene in local health policy decision-making, (e.g. by setting limits on the annual rate of contribution for health insurance, by prescribing the legislative framework for the health sector and the obligatory forms of care), communes do exercise considerable control over the financing and development of health care on their territory. For example, communal health SIZs develop their own annual programmes of care which must be approved by their assemblies composed of users and providers of health services, as well as through referendums among insurees. Similarly, communal referendums are held to approve financing of local capital construction projects through *samodoprinosi* (voluntary local taxes).

By contrast, I would argue that efforts at de-etatization and democratization have been somewhat less successful. As I have suggested above, federal and republic authorities continue to orchestrate many of the broad parameters of the health sector. And, although there has been a reduction in the prerogatives of the federal government since 1950, the prerogatives of government authorities at the republic–provincial and communal levels have been strengthened. As Sekulić (1983) has put it, 'central statism' has been replaced by 'pluralistic statism'. For example, even though negotiations between the health SIZs and health facilities are the subject of so-called 'self-management agreements' which explicitly exclude state involvement, local governmental authorities do have the legal right to intervene in the event that an agreement cannot be reached or if its contents are deemed 'socially harmful' (Pejovich, 1979). Likewise, any major policy change of either the health SIZ or health facility (e.g. to introduce direct 'out of pocket' payments for services or to call for a referendum to underwrite capital construction projects) must have the support of various communal political structures, in particular, the commune assembly and the local sociopolitical organizations (the trade union council, the Socialist Alliance and the League of Communists) (Parmelee, 1983).

Finally, the Yugoslav health sector is democratized only in a qualified sense, despite the creation of numerous self-management bodies in health facilities and the health insurance programme, and despite the involvement of thousands of Yugoslavs in their membership. In addition to the ongoing involvement of the state (or, better to say, states) in health policy making, professional insurance administrators continue to play an important role in shaping health SIZ activities through their responsibility to set assembly agendas, draw up often complex contracts between provider institutions and the health SIZs, and formulate and present most proposals for assembly consideration, which tends to be largely *pro forma* (Parmelee, 1988). Moreover, membership in the various self-management bodies in the health sector has consistently been biased in the direction of highly educated and male white-collar workers (Parmelee, 1983). And, to the extent that any others share control over health decision-making with political elites, these 'others' are generally health professionals, in particular, physicians (e.g. Milanović and Stambolović, 1985; Himmelstein *et al.*, 1984). In effect, if one can speak of the Yugoslav health sector as democratized at all, it would appear to be limited to a form of 'expert' democracy.

Yugoslav Health Care in the 1980s: Is the Cup Half Empty or Half Full?

Through this examination of Yugoslav health care under self-managing socialism *vis-à-vis* the inter-war monarchy and other countries, as well as some of the Yugoslavs' own health policy objectives, one cannot help but conclude that any praise of socialist Yugoslavia's health sector must be qualified praise. As I have attempted to demonstrate, post-war Yugoslavia has made significant gains in terms of health resources and health status relative to the inter-war monarchy. Yet, despite these achievements, the country still lags behind most other European countries and has been only partially successful in fulfilling its own promises of guaranteeing health care for all, transcending health inequalities and establishing a genuinely self-managed health sector. Whether one concludes that the cup is half full or half empty would thus seem to depend on the particular benchmark one might choose to emphasize. While I shall leave that judgement to the reader, I would nonetheless venture to say that the Yugoslav health 'cup' appears, as it were, to have sprung a leak in the 1980s. In this final section, I shall review some of the major problems confronting the Yugoslav health system. I shall also consider possible policy options available to the Yugoslavs for addressing these problems, as well as some of the constraints on these policy choices.

I have already alluded to a few of the difficulties in the Yugoslav health sector in the 1980s, some of which are actually ongoing rather than new problems and some of which are certainly not unique to the health sector or, for that matter, to Yugoslavia. Organizationally, the health sector has become extremely atomized or, as some prefer to call it, 'feudalized'. That is, as a result of the various self-management reforms which devolved most responsibility for health care to the republics and communes, it has become increasingly difficult to coordinate the activities and development of the various levels and parts of the health sector. For example, since each republic determines its own requirements for specialist training, there is considerable variation in the length and, presumably, quality of such training among the various republics, and efforts to achieve any uniformity have yet to succeed (Mičeta, 1988). At the communal level, each commune tends to look after what it perceives to be its own interests (e.g. keeping its own health funds within the commune or developing its own facilities as much as possible), thus making intercommunal cooperation to minimize duplication of expensive technology difficult to achieve. This tendency towards atomization is also reproduced within communes, as individual health facilities or parts of these facilities organized as basic organizations of associated labour (OOURs) likewise act like feudal fiefdoms and pursue their own interest at the expense of the others. Even Yugoslav medical supply firms contribute to the atomization, as illustrated by the case of several firms which bought licences from Western companies to manufacture a quantity of kidney dialysis units many times beyond what Yugoslavia could absorb itself and without many marketing possibilities elsewhere (Brkan *et al.*, 1982).

Furthermore, in the context of the current economic crisis and requirements to reduce social service expenditures imposed by the international lending agencies as a condition for debt rescheduling, the share of the country's social product which is allocated for health care declined during the 1980s (from 6.2 per cent in 1979 to 4.2 per cent in 1986) (Letica, 1987). Therefore, it has become increasingly difficult to finance the ambitious health insurance programme that the Yugoslavs have established. Among the variety of specific problems which this fiscal crisis in the health sector and in the economy more generally has entailed, I would highlight the following:

1. Increasing complaints from patients about the care they receive, along with increasing reliance on *veze* (connections) and the proverbial 'blue envelope' (bribes) to get access to care (e.g. Ćirić, 1987; Letica, 1987).

2. Recurrent shortages of pharmaceuticals and other essential medical supplies such as surgical thread and anesthetics (e.g. Simić, 1987; Trklja, 1988).

3. Decreasing morale among health workers, given declining funds for personal incomes and for maintaining existing health facilities, let alone for keeping abreast of technological and other medical advances occurring elsewhere in the world (e.g. Džadžić, 1986; Letica, 1987; Trklja, 1988).

4. Increasing numbers of unemployed physicians and other health workers despite unmet health needs (e.g. Letica, 1987; Milošević, 1988).

5. Persistent regional disparities as well as declines in health status, as illustrated by recent increases in infant mortality in Montenegro, Macedonia, Serbia Proper and Kosovo (Tables 10.4 and 10.5 above; SGJ, 1987, p. 447).

On the basis of my own research in Yugoslavia, and from recent dialogues with Yugoslavs in the health sector, I can identify four basic options the Yugoslavs might pursue to address these problems. At the extreme, they could abandon or at least significantly reformulate the meaning of self-management in the health sector, opting either for a more centralized or a more privatized health system. In an earlier paper (Parmelee, 1985), I came out in favour of a certain measure of recentralization in order to counter the problems of persistent regional health inequalities and an organizationally atomized health sector. By contrast, some fairly high-level Yugoslav health officials have told me that perhaps it might be better simply to let the Yugoslav people keep their health insurance contributions and fend for themselves in an open, and presumably private, health care marketplace. A somewhat less extreme variant of the reprivatization option would be to expand already existing moves to restrict benefits covered under the health insurance programme, to increase 'out of pocket' payments for health services (*participacija*), and to reintroduce legalized private medical and dental practice (see Letica, 1987).

Alternatively, the Yugoslavs might institute further reforms aimed at a more genuinely self-managed health sector in which workers and citizens would have proportionately greater control and the state, insurance bureaucrats and health professionals proportionately less control. This would appear to be the policy recommended by Professors Milanović and Stambolović of the Belgrade Faculty of Medicine in their critique of my own proposal for a return to greater central state coordination of the health sector (see Milanović and Stambolović, 1985; Milanović, 1987; Stambolović, 1987). In their view, such recentralization would only exacerbate current problems in the health sector, which they attribute to too little rather than too much self-management. Like some Western Marxists (e.g. Navarro, 1976; Waitzkin, 1983), Milanović and Stambolović retain their faith in genuine worker and citizen control over the health sector.

Finally, the Yugoslavs could continue to tinker with the existing organizational and financial arrangements, hoping to keep the health sector – indeed the entire society – afloat until better economic times. Such tinkering with the system is illustrated by three strategies that health delivery facilities and/or health SIZs have already used to respond to the current fiscal crisis: marketization, rationalization and externalization (Svetlik, 1989). Marketization entails the identification of potential patients with funds and the attempt to sell them services directly without the involvement of the health SIZs (e.g. the sale directly to enterprises of preventive examinations for workers; the marketing of Yugoslav health facilities to people in the Third World or of health tourism in the country's hotels and spas to people in the First World). The strategy of rationalization, or the attempt to use available labour and capital more efficiently, can be seen in efforts since the late 1970s to place greater emphasis on primary health care[10] (rather than the more costly secondary and tertiary care), in the development of detailed time norms against which to assess the quantity and quality of care, and in moves to create common administrative staffs for health SIZs in neighbouring communes. Finally, externalization, according to Svetlik (1989), involves shifting the responsibility for provision of services away from health institutions, or the responsibility of payment for these services via the health SIZs, to individuals and enterprises. For example, this has taken the form of calls for greater individual responsibility for preventing disease and maintaining health through self-care activities or in discussions to increase enterprises' liability for sick leave benefits before the health insurance funds take over. In effect, each of these three strategies is aimed at either reducing health expenditures *per se* or at finding alternative sources of funding beyond the health insurance mechanism, while simultaneously leaving the basic health delivery and health insurance systems intact.

Which of these options are the Yugoslavs likely to pursue in the immediate future? In the political and economic context of early 1989, I would expect that tinkering around the edges of existing organizational and financial arrangements may be the Yugoslavs' best and, indeed, only option. For barring any sort of military takeover and in the absence of central leadership acceptable to the entire country, the immediate prospects for recentralization do not seem very likely. Moreover, as repeated debates over the reintro-duction of legalized private practice since the 1960s would seem to suggest, any significant moves towards reprivatization would go against the country's socialist ideology and would likely encounter stiff resistance from a public which has come to accept the promise, if not always enjoying the reality, of a right to health care. And, while *genuine* worker and citizen control of the health sector might

10. Primary health care refers to services provided by community-based phys-icians, whereas secondary care is provided by specialists on an outpatient or inpatient basis, and tertiary care is provided in specialized hospitals or by highly specialized or sub-specialized personnel.

have some salutary effects in bridging the gap between the theory and practice of self-managing socialism, I believe that most Yugoslavs, preoccupied with the political and economic challenges of recent years, do not see this as a top priority. Nor do I believe that further reforms claiming to bring genuine self-management would be an experiment that the country can currently afford to undertake. Given these various political, economic and ideological constraints, continued tinkering or, if you prefer, muddling along, would seem to be about the only option the Yugoslavs have left, and one that I regret to say may keep Yugoslav health care on the critical list for some time to come.

Postscript 1990

It is with amazement and cautious optimism that I have watched the dramatic developments of the past several months in the communist world, in general, and in Yugoslavia, in particular. Apart from their domestic and international significance, these developments have reminded us of the limits of social science prognostications. Who among us could have anticipated the pace and direction of change? Ideas which seemed unimaginable a year ago – the end of communist hegemony, multi-party elections, German reunification – are now ideas whose time has come.

Do these developments alter the picture of the Yugoslav health system's current situation which I have painted above? No and yes. On the one hand, it is clear that the Yugoslav health system remains in critical condition, particularly with regard to the country's ability to finance a health insurance programme which is satisfactory to both users and providers of services (e.g. Letica, 1989; Milinović, 1989; Nikolić, 1989a, 1989b). Moreover, given the past experience of Yugoslavia and other countries, the effects of economic restructuring and debt rescheduling are likely to make the problem of underfinancing of health care worse before it gets better.

On the other hand, in the wake of the flood of East German health workers to West Germany and in anticipation of German reunification, I would expect additional pressure to expand legalized private practice from Yugoslav physicians working abroad and unemployed health workers at home for whom the safety valve of foreign employment is being restricted. While complete reprivatization still would not seem to me to be a viable option, the weakening of ideological constraints and greater openness of debate should expand the range of possible options beyond merely tinkering around the edges. Indeed, Croatian physicians and health organizations have already called upon the Croatian *Sabor* to abandon tinkering and to come up with a new system for organizing and financing health services (Nikolić, 1989b). Finally, given the heightened ethnic tensions within Yugoslavia, especially the growing chasm between the Slovenes and Croats versus the Serbs, I am left wondering whether this will be the final paper I shall write on *Yugoslav* health care.

Bibliography

Adamic, Louis (1934), *The Native's Return*, New York, Harper

Anderson, Odin (1972), *Health Care: Can There Be Equity?*, New York, Wiley

Berg, Robert L., M. Roy Brooks, Jr and Miomir Savičević (1976), *Health Care in Yugoslavia and the United States*, Fogarty International Proceedings No. 34, Washington, DC, US Government Printing Office

Brkan, Božica, Jovo Paripović and Radmila Stanković (1982), 'Ako Nema Dijalizator, Ima Tvornica', *Vjesnik*, 13 December

Brockington, Fraser (1958), *World Health*, Baltimore, Md, Penguin

Ćirić, Aleksandar (1987). 'Simptomi Smrti', *NIN*, 18 October, pp. 24–5

The Constitution of the Socialist Federal Republic of Yugoslavia (1974), Belgrade, Secretariat of the Federal Executive Council for Information

Dellebrant, Jan Ake (1986), *The Soviet Regional Dilemma*, Armonk, NY, M. E. Sharpe

Denitch, Bogdan Denis (1976), *The Legitimation of a Revolution: The Yugoslav Case*, New Haven, Conn., Yale University Press

Dimitrijević, Dušan (1984), 'Physicians', *Yugoslav Survey*, Vol. 25, No. 1, pp. 131–40

Dubos, Rene (1959), *Mirage of Health*, New York, Harper and Row

Džadžić, Toma (1986), 'Ofanzivno Zdravstvo', *NIN*, 12 January, pp. 18–20

Federal Committee of Labour, Health and Social Welfare (1979), *The System of Health Planning in Yugoslavia*, Belgrade

Federal Institute of Public Health (1975), *The Public Health Service in Yugoslavia*, Belgrade

Federal Statistical Office (1973), *Materijalni i Društveni Razvoj SFR Jugoslavije 1947–1972*, Belgrade

Donna E. Parmelee

——— (1986), *Jugoslavija 1945–1985*, Belgrade

Feliks, Radmilo (1978), 'Public Health, Health Care and the Health Services', *Yugoslav Survey*, Vol. 19, pp. 137–56

Grmek, M. D. (ed.) (1966), *Serving the Cause of Public Health: Selected Papers of Andrija Stampar*, Zagreb, Yugoslav Academy of Sciences and Arts

Hammel, Eugene A. (1969), *The Pink Yo-Yo: Social Prestige and Occupations in Yugoslavia*, Berkeley, Calif., Institute of International Studies, University of California

'Health Insurance in Yugoslavia' (1961), *Yugoslav Survey*, Vol. 2, pp. 827–32

Himmelstein, David U., Slobodan Lang and Steffie Woolhandler (1984), 'The Yugoslav Health System: Public Ownership and Local Control', *Journal of Public Health Policy*, Vol. 5, No. 3, pp. 423–31

Hrabač, Tomo (1968), 'Osnovna Zdravstvena Zaštita u Bosni i Hercegovini', *Socijalna Politika*, Vol. 23, Nos. 2–3, pp. 36–40; Vol. 23, No. 5, pp. 29–31

Kaufmann, Caroline L. (1981), 'The Right to Health Care: Some Cross-National Comparisons and U.S. Trends in Policy', *Social Science and Medicine*, 15F, pp. 157–62

Kesić, Branko (1983), *Život i Zdravlje*, Zagreb, Stvarnost

Kiljunen, Kimmo (1983), 'Comments on "Regional Disparities in Yugoslavia"', in Dudley Seers and Kjell Ostrom (eds.), *The Crises of the European Regions*, New York, St Martin's Press, pp. 62–7

Kunitz, Stephen J. (1980), 'The Recruitment, Training, and Distribution of Physicians in Yugoslavia', *International Journal of Health Services*, Vol. 10, No. 4, pp. 587–609

Kurian, George Thomas (1984), *The New Book of World Rankings*, New York, Facts on File Publications

Letica, Slaven (1987), 'Kako Lečiti Zdravstvo', *NIN*, 24 May, pp. 22–5

——— (1989), 'Komunisti Živi Duže', *Danas*, 4 July, pp. 26–7

McKeown, Thomas (1971), *The Role of Medicine: Dream, Mirage or Nemesis*, London, Nuffield Provincial Hospitals Trust

Mičeta, Luka (1988), 'Kasnimo za Svetom', *NIN*, 1 May, pp. 26–7

Milanović, Vladimir (1987), 'Humanism and Medicine', *Social Science and Medicine*, Vol. 25, No. 1, pp. 35–7

Milanović, Vladimir and Vuk Stambolović (1985), 'The Prescription for Yugoslav Medicine'. *Social Science and Medicine*, Vol. 21, No. 7, pp. 730–2

Milinović, Zdravko (1989), 'Bolnica Na Rubu Zapada', *Danas*, 7 November, pp. 68–9

Milošević, Milan (1988), 'Upisani i Otpisani', *NIN*, 3 July, pp. 26–9

National Center for Health Statistics (1986), *Health United States–1984*, DHHS Pub. No. (PHS) 87–1232, Washington, DC: U.S. Government Printing Office

Navarro, Vicente (1976), *Medicine Under Capitalism*, New York, Prodist
—— (1977), *Social Security and Medicine in the USSR: A Marxist Critique*, Lexington, Mass., D.C. Heath
Nikolić, Zorica (1989a), 'Siromašna Medicina Želja', *Danas*, 7 February, pp. 67–8
—— (1989b), 'Oprostite, Morate Umrijeti', *Danas*, 10 October, pp. 85–7
OECD (1985), *Measuring Health Care: 1960–1983*, Paris
Parmelee, Donna E. (1983), *Medicine Under Yugoslav Self-managing Socialism*, Ann Arbor, Mich., University Microfilms International
—— (1985), 'Whither the State in Yugoslav Health Care?', *Social Science and Medicine*, Vol. 21, No. 7, pp. 719–28
—— (1988), 'Yugoslavia: Health Care Under Self-managing Socialism', in Mark G. Field (ed.), *Success and Crisis in National Health Systems*, London, Tavistock, pp. 165–91
Pejovich, Svetozar (1979), *Social Security in Yugoslavia*, Washington, DC, American Enterprise Institute for Public Policy Research
Popović, Boško and Milan Škrbić (1978), 'The Health Care System in the Socialist Federal Republic of Yugoslavia', Paper presented at the International Postgraduate Training Course: Planning and Management of Basic Health Services in Developing Countries, Andrija Štampar School of Public Health, Zagreb
Sekulić, Duško (1983), 'Planning, Self-Management and Crisis', Paper presented at the International Sociological Association Research Committee 10, Workshop on Future Prospectives of Industrial and Economic Democracy, Dubrovnik
SGJ (various years), *Statistički Godišnjak Jugoslavije*, Belgrade, Federal Statistical Office
SGNZ (various years), *Statistički Godišnjak o Narodnom Zdravlju i Zdravstvenoj Zaštiti u SFR Jugoslaviji*, Belgrade, Federal Institute of Public Health
SGKJ (various years), *Statistički Godišnjak Kraljevine Jugoslavije*, Belgrade, State Printing Office
Sidel, Victor W. and Ruth Sidel (1983), *A Healthy State*, New York, Pantheon Books
Sigerist, Henry E. (1939), 'Yugoslavia and the Eleventh International Congress of the History of Medicine', *Bulletin of the History of Medicine* Vol. 7, January, pp. 99–147
Simić, Zvonko (1987), 'Ima Leka za Lekove', *NIN*, 15 March, pp. 22–4
Singleton, Fred (1985), *A Short History of the Yugoslav Peoples*, Cambridge, Cambridge University Press
Sivard, Ruth Leger (various years), *World Military and Social Expenditures*, Washington, DC, World Priorities
'Social Insurance' (1960), *Yugoslav Survey*, Vol. 1, pp. 65–72
Stambolović, Vuk (1987), 'Comments on "Humanism and Medicine"', *Social Science and Medicine*, Vol. 25, No. 1, pp. 37–40

Štampar, Andrija (1925), *Organisation of the Public Health Services in the Kingdom of the Serbs, Croats and Slovenes*, Geneva, League of Nations Health Organisation

—— (1946), *Liječnik, Njegova Prošlost i Budućnost*, Zagreb, Ministarstva Narodnog Zdravlja Narodne Vlade Hrvatske

Svetlik, Ivan. 1989. 'The Social Welfare System in Yugoslavia', Lecture, Ljubljana, 13 November

Tomasevich, Jozo (1955), *Peasants, Politics, and Economic Change in Yugoslavia*, Stanford, Stanford University Press

Trklja, Milivoje (1986), 'Funding of Public Services, 1975–1984', *Yugoslav Survey*, Vol. 27, No. 3, pp. 101–10

—— (1988), 'The Relationship between Economy and Non-Economy in the National Income Distribution', *Yugoslav Survey*, Vol. 29, No. 2, pp. 49–62

United Nations Statistical Office (1949), *Statistical Yearbook – 1948*, Lake Success, NY

—— (1953), *Statistical Yearbook – 1953*, New York

—— (1988), *1986 Demographic Yearbook*, New York

Vajs, Vera and Radmilo Feliks (1986), 'Health Status and Health Care of Workers', *Yugoslav Survey*, Vol. 27, No. 1, pp. 115–36

Waitzkin, Howard (1983), *The Second Sickness*, New York, Free Press

World Almanac (1989), *The World Almanac and Book of Facts – 1989*, New York, Pharos Books

World Bank (1983a), *Yugoslavia: Adjustment Policies and Development Perspectives*, Washington, DC

—— (1983b), *World Tables*, 3rd edn, Vol. 2, Baltimore, Mass., Johns Hopkins Press

—— (1989), Yugoslav Regional GNP Per Capita Income Data-1987, personal communication with the World Bank Yugoslavia Desk

11

Ecology and Self-Management: A Balance-Sheet for the 1980s

Barbara Jančar

Introduction

The 1980s will doubtless be viewed as one of the most momentous ten years in the history of post-war Yugoslavia. The decade started with the first revolts in Kosovo and ended with the Kosovo question unresolved. In 1981, Yugoslavia was just entering its long crisis that forced constitutional and economic reforms in 1988, but did not end the search for a viable Yugoslav perestroika. By the end of the decade the country's severest critics were calling for an end to one-party rule, while some still hoped that the Yugoslav self-management system could be retained. While the Yugoslav crisis exemplifies the political and economic crisis which have occurred in all communist societies, it is more than that. For thirty years or more, Yugoslavia has boasted of a special kind of socialism, more democratic than those in the neighbouring communist countries and hence more economically efficient. Despite some solid political and economic gains during the 1980s (Remington, 1987; Seroka, 1988; Singleton, 1985), the persistent crisis has suggested to thoughtful and frustrated Yugoslavs that Yugoslavia's way may have been little more successful than the Stalinist system in providing efficient economic growth and political stability. The inability of the country's leaders to offer a way out of the economic and political impasse has undermined government and Communist Party (LCY) authority. As Yugoslavia's civil society has found the state increasingly irrelevant to its needs, it has developed alongside the formal instruments of political discourse, an informal civil politics analogous to what Hernando de Soto has described for the Third World in the economic sphere, as the 'other path' (De Soto, 1989).

While environmental issues have not been at the forefront of the crisis, they nevertheless have been bellwethers of its progress. By the end of the 1980s, Yugoslavs had developed an environmental consciousness. Prominent academics were warning of the ecological dangers of modern civilization and calling for a change in lifestyle (Glavas, 1988), and an environmental agenda figured prominently in the programmes of the newly formed alternative associations operating within the official party front organization, the Socialist Alliance. The emergence of a grassroots environmental movement has been largely the work of students and young people. However, like environmental movements everywhere, its activities are supported, justified, and in some cases led by an ever-growing number of environmentally concerned scientists and experts.

The current environmental activism may be compared to the virtual environmental apathy that I observed in Yugoslavia in 1981. At that time, there was not one mass environmental organization which cut across republican borders with the exception of the Gorani Movement. This movement was directed at elementary and secondary school students and its primary purpose was to recruit young people for much needed reforestation projects throughout the country. The then Secretary of the Council for the Preservation and Improvement of the Environment, Milivoje Todorović, was busy promoting campaigns such as '100 Roses for Tito' with the aim of educating people to the country's rising environmental problems and enlisting popular support in combating them.

What happened during the decade to turn apathy into activism? The immediate answer is Chernobyl, when the Yugoslav public realized that Yugoslavs were not, in the word of Zagreb socialist Slavenka Drakulich-Ilić, 'ecologically independent' (Drakulich, 1987a, p. 177), and that events could occur over which they had no control. But the answer is more complex than that. Chernobyl was the culmination of a series of environmental events that raised serious questions as to the ability of the Yugoslav self-management system to protect the environment. The current concern over environmental issues must be seen within the context of three related developments. During the 1980s, self-management proved too parochial to handle the scope and number of environmental problems which overwhelmed it. Pollution control could no longer be set aside as a luxury. Second, as in the rest of Eastern Europe and the Soviet Union, a large number of the Yugoslav public, especially members of the country's most educated social strata, became convinced that environmental protection could only be effective if the public participated in management decisions. Behind the environmental issues lay a democratic agenda. Finally, the 1980s saw the first generation of Yugoslavs reach adulthood which had no personal memory of the Second World War, many of whose standards and values were shaped by its easy access to Western Europe.

Yugoslavia's Environmental Problems

Unlike Poland and Czechoslovakia (Singleton, 1987), Yugoslavia's environmental problems are not yet catastrophic. Rather they reflect a steady deterioration in environmental quality over the past forty years. Until recently, there was little systematic effort to collect environmental data. The first and only thorough study of environmental conditions throughout the country was completed and published in 1978 under the auspices of the Council for Environmental Protection and Land Use Management, an advisory council attached to the Federal Executive Council and the republican and provincial executive councils.

The study graphically documented the rapid shift of population from the rural areas. In 1948, around 70 per cent lived and worked in the countryside. In 1971, only 38 per cent did so, while urban growth averaged 10 per cent each decade. The results of urbanization need not be elaborated on. Expansion of urban areas (65 per cent in Slovenia alone) increased water consumption. Energy use went from 126 KWh per inhabitant in 1950 to 1,860 KWh in 1976. Transportation by automobile increased dramatically. In 1951, automobile use represented 13 per cent of all transportation. In 1976, it represented 86 per cent. Use of railways was reversed by almost exactly the same percentages. The impact upon the environment of these rapid changes was predictable. The amount of land under cultivation dropped from 15 million hectares in 1961 to under 10 million in 1976. The amount of forested area fell from 10,322,000 to 9,125,000 hectares in 1976, a drop of approximately 1 per cent annually. By 1971, there were only two rivers in Yugoslavia with a Quality I rating, and these had become Quality II by 1976. During this period, the Sava alone had gone from a rating of II to IV when sampled at Sremska Mitrovica, 46 miles west of Belgrade. Most noticeable was the increase in soil erosion, as the young abandoned family farms too small to yield a profitable return for work in the city, leaving the old to till the fields with no material interest in practising conservation. By 1976, erosion of the seriousness of categories I, II, and III covered 54 per cent of the territory of Yugoslavia, with excessive erosion (category I) occurring in 14 per cent of the eroded areas ('Savet Za Čovekovu Svedinu', 1978, pp. 13–34, 37–8, 41, 50–1).

The situation had further deteriorated in 1985. The urban population now represented over 46 per cent of the total population, with variations between republics ranging from a high of 60 per cent in Serbia and Macedonia to 36 per cent in Slovenia. Between 1975 and 1980, the average annual population urban migration of 2.8 per cent was the highest in Europe with the exception of Albania. Land under cultivation had dropped to 7,784,000 hectares. Although forests had increased by a modest 2.3 per cent, reversing slightly their downward trend, acid precipitation had started to take its toll. In 1986, 39 per cent of the coniferous forests were reported damaged, and 23 per cent were characterized as moderately to severely damaged. Per capita consumption of energy had increased 74 per cent since 1970, with the largest rate of change in the consumption of natural gas. The only other European countries with a larger increase in per capita energy consumption were Greece, Portugal and Malta (World Resources Institute, 1988, pp. 265, 267, 290, 307). Yugoslavia now had nuclear power from a Westinghouse reactor that went on line at Krško outside of Zagreb in 1981. The rapid growth of cities caused breakdowns in the already inadequate urban infrastructure and brought with it two major urban environmental problems, air pollution and noise. Of a total of fifty-four cities selected by the World Health Organization and United Nations Environment Programme, Zagreb stood fifteenth from Milan, the city on the list with the highest average recording of sulphur dioxide levels in 1980–84 (World Resources Institute, 1988, p. 166). A 1980 study of exposure to traffic noise in Novi Beograd, a district of Belgrade, found that apartments on the higher floors of apartment buildings were exposed to day-long noise levels of 70 dBa and over (OECD, 1985, p. 99).

In 1981, the public-at-large was largely unaware of these problems. But the authorities and the scientific community already knew about them and were taking the first steps in the organization of a global environmental management system. During the 1970s, Yugoslavia followed the lead of the industrialized countries, and developed a corpus of environmental legislation. Each of the constituent republics and autonomous provinces passed its own regulations as did the major regions and cities (Todorović, 1983). By the end of the decade, the environment was regulated by over 130 statutes. While the legislation was a welcome step, little or no attention was given to standardization or legislative correspondence. The 1980–85 plan called for the development of nationwide standards in environmental methodology and permissible levels of pollution but these have yet to be realized (Jančar, 1987, p. 208). A self-management centrepiece was the creation in 1974 of a system of advisory councils on the human environment and territorial planning attached to the government administration. The system went from the opština level all the way to the Federal Executive Council. A corresponding socio-political organization under the aegis of the Socialist Alliance was also created. The role of the Council for the Protection and Improvement of the Human Environment, as it was called, was to coordinate government *akcije* in the environmental area and to mobilize the population to support them.

During the 1970s, Yugoslavia futher embarked on comprehensive land-use planning, the setting aside of conservation areas and the development of a national park and reserve system. At the municipal level, city councils drew up comprehensive urban plans. These often conflicted with procedures and standards set forth in the republican plans, and lengthy bureaucratic negotiations over land use made many plans obsolete by the time they were adopted. Throughout Yugoslavia, cities grew chaotically. Attempts were made to control local environmental effects like noise and air pollution, but the dictates of self-management tended to benefit the more economically developed republics and rich cities with their concentration of scientific and technological resources at the expense of the less developed republics and poorer municipalities.

Yugoslavia's self-management system was launched in 1952. It acquired its present organization with the adoption of the post-Tito Constitution in 1974. The lengthy and cumbersome document decentralized government administration, provided for self-management at every level of government and vested effective political power in the six republican governments. The League of Communists of Yugoslavia (LCY) was also decentralized. Self-management meant that every enterprise and/or organization in principle was self-financing, self-sustaining and autonomous in decision-making.

The flaws in self-management were not slow to appear. The main flaw was the inability of the individual enterprises to develop their own investment capital. The workers preferred to put what profits that were made back into their own earnings rather than in the capital development of the enterprise. Through the medium of 'self-managing compacts', an organization could go outside itself to seek funds, either through establishing purchasing agreements for its services or products, or through borrowing 'compacts' with financial institutions. These compacts operated within the framework of a decentralized, one-party, administrative system. Without a *bona fide* market to impose performance criteria, the economy fell apart. The course of environmental protection followed the overall economic pattern, and indeed provides a barometer of the rise and fall of the self-management system.

Notable environmental successes of self-management in the 1970s have been described elsewhere (Jančar, 1987), but some should be mentioned here. Two of the most significant were the reclamation of Lake Palić near Subotica in the Vojvodina and the development and implementation of the first stage of a sewerage system for Lake Ohrid on the Greek, Albanian and Yugoslav borders in Macedonia. Lake Palić was a fashionable turn-of-the-century summer resort which was virtually dead by the 1960s. The principal of a local high school in nearby Subotica was a chemist by training and head of the Subotica Council for the Protection and Improvement of the Human Environment. He aroused public opinion and mobilized area scientists to develop a plan for the draining and cleaning of the lake. The plan was presented to the town council and the local authorities persuaded to implement it. Since self-management requires self-financing, a referendum was held on whether to increase taxes for local residents to raise the necessary funds. The referendum passed. The lake was drained, cleaned and stocked with fish. By the beginning of the 1980s, it was once again a popular summer vacation spot, attracting Hungarians from over the border.

The sewerage system at Lake Ohrid was a more complex and expensive project. Both in terms of design and construction and financing, it required material assistance beyond the capabilities of local government. Lake Ohrid, however, had a higher visibility than did Lake Palić. Because of its age and unique system, it has been called the 'Lake Baikal' of Yugoslavia and is under the protection of the United Nations Man and the Biosphere (MAB) programme. The deepest body of fresh water in the Balkans, Ohrid shares with the Siberian lake the distinction of harbouring unusual aquatic life which has survived from the prehistoric era. In addition, the lake has a Mediterranean climate, making it attractive to tourists virtually all year round. In antiquity, Ohrid was a stopping place on the Via Appia from Byzantium to Rome and is a treasurehouse of archeological artifacts. On its shores are monasteries and churches from the tenth century, the most notable of which is the Church of St Naum. Many of the interiors retain their original frescoes, untouched by renovation or restoration, witnesses to the journey of Eastern Christianity from Greece to Kiev and Moscow.

These many unique features made the protection of Lake Ohrid an object of international concern, and it was the international community which helped draft and finance the project for the construction of a sewerage system on the Yugoslav side of the lake. Self-management applied. The poverty of the region ensured that local government would be unable to raise even half of the money locally. Eventually, a compact was reached whereby 80 per cent of the project would be funded through international sources and the Yugoslav federal government, while the local communities would raise 20 per cent. The amount to be raised locally was substantial. Thus before the referendum to increase taxes was held, proponents of the project visited the voters personally to explain why Ohrid was unique and what would be the benefits to them in preserving it. The referendum passed and the first stage of construction began in the early 1980s. Today, Ohrid is the only lake in Macedonia where strict environmental regulations are enforced. In a similar way, residents of Sarajevo voted to raise their share of the funds locally to improve the water system in that city in preparation for the winter Olympics in 1980 (Jančar, 1987, pp. 185–8).

Nature conservation is the area where self-management has functioned at its optimum. Croatia has two nature reserves that are among the best maintained anywhere in the world: Plitvice Lakes and Kopački Rit. The first, under the protection of MAB, is an extraordinary mix of clear aquamarine pools of water and ever-changing waterfalls descending over limestone and aquatic life formations. As the falling water wears away new areas of these formations, the main thrust of the falls moves to occupy the eroded places. The waterfalls the tourist sees at Plitvice one year may be in a different place upon his or her return five years later. Self-management has meant the park must raise its own revenues to maintain and preserve the natural attraction. Visitors pay a modest entrance fee. In addition, the park owns and maintains a motel and other facilities in the area. With these monies, the park management has built wooden boardwalks across water and swampy areas to make it possible for tourists to get closer to the different falls without eroding the ground underneath. Trails criss-cross the reserve. Management personnel have done a careful study of the habits of foreign tourists to identify peak areas of park use and maximum capacity for each park facility. From the analysis of tourist flow, a mobile transport system was built to carry visitors through the park. Some park scientists believe that Plitvice's delicate ecological structure is gradually being broken down from overuse, but others argue that monitoring of tourist traffic will prevent that eventuality and that the revenues brought in by tourists are vital to preserving the park's natural equilibrium.

Kopački Rit is a *zoo reservat*, or wildlife and hunting reserve. The reserve is important to the conservation of European wildlife, as it lies on one of the great migratory bird flyways and contains more than fifty species of deer, wild boar and smaller animals. Originally a Habsburg hunting preserve, it became Tito's private reserve during his lifetime. Upon his death in 1981, local pressure increased rapidly to open the reserve to the public. Much of this demand came from the tourist organizations in nearby Osijek, which saw an opportunity for growth and development. As a public reserve, Kopački Rit fell under the jurisdiction of the local government in Belje. Local self-management was installed under the regulatory supervision of the Ministry of Economic Planning, Agriculture and Forestry of the Republic of Croatia. Hunting in the reserve is organized and managed by the local hunting 'family' or association, *Jelen*. Under the guidance of a director with a doctorate in forestry, the 'family' develops plans for wildlife conservation and management which include artificial culling of herds by local residents and tourists. Fees are charged to hunt in the preserve. The red deer's antlers are considered among Europe's most coveted trophies and hunters may pay up to US$80,000 to hunt these animals and bring the rack home (Ricciuti, 1987). Given this kind of income, it is understandable why self-management should be successful.

Two final examples of environmental self-management in practice involve projects that local residents turned down. The first was a proposed nuclear power plant on Vir Island, an island north of the Croatian port of Zadar on the Adriatic. As in the case of Kopački Rit, the tourist organizations supported the public demand. The local authorities at first hesitated but anti-nuclear protest reached such proportions that they withdrew their approval of the proposal. The plant was later built at Krško near Zagreb, where public and scientific opposition failed to generate sufficient pressure to stop construction. Environmental protest in the city of Ulcinj near Bar on the Adriatic coast also caused a reversal of an approval for plant construction. This time, public concern was focused on the building of an offshore plant to obtain ferromagnesium out of seawater. Here, too, the local tourist industry aided and encouraged the public protest, even though the plant was backed by French and American capital. The local council hesitated, and the investors withdrew their application. Eventually, Split agreed to permit the plant's construction (Jančar, 1987, pp. 300–2).

These cases where self-management has been successful have several features in common. The first is the localization of the problem at issue. Whether it be the building of a plant, or the maintenance of an important natural monument, the project is contained within well-defined local boundaries. Construction of the sewerage system at Lake Ohrid, it is true, demanded the agreement of three towns, but the project itself was confined to the lake area. In addition, the amount of money to be raised locally was broken down and each community was only responsible for raising its own amount. In the other cases, the conservation area came under a single commune.

Second, self-management worked where the environmental issue was conservation of a natural area with little or no established polluting industry, or a one-time project like development of a water purity system at Sarajevo which would have become necessary some time anyway. Third, in all the cases, there was a powerful economic incentive for protection: tourism. In each case, if popular opinion was not mobilized by the local or regional tourist organizations, it was certainly supported and encouraged by a vocal 'tourist lobby'. The return on the ecological investment was perceived as virtually risk free.

Finally, ecological awareness on the part of the local community went hand-in-hand with international interest. Croatia, Slovenia and the Vojvodina participated in the conservation movements which developed at the end of the nineteenth century in the Austro-Hungarian Empire. This history has given them an environmental sensitivity which the southern republics did not acquire under Ottoman rule (Todorović, Interview, 1983). Hence the special importance of international support for the preservation of Lake

Ohrid. The fact is, however, that the Croatian towns on Yugoslavia's Adriatic coast, and the residents of Belje (near Kopački Rit), or Bihac and neighbouring communities near Plitvice Lakes make their living from foreign tourists. Over 50 million come to Croatia's Adriatic coast annually. Lake Palić attracts Germans, Hungarians and other Central Europeans. And Sarajevo has become a winter sports centre attracting skiers from all over the world. The international community has an interest in maintaining the environmental quality of these areas, and comes, in large part, because of their ecological attractiveness.

There were other instances in the 1970s and 1980s where none of these factors applied and where self-management proved incapable of handling the problem. Where many communities had to agree, self-management tended to get bogged down in area politics. And when republics had to agree, self-management broke down altogether. In the early 1980s, there was a proposal to make the Una River a wild river with similar restrictions to a wild river in the United States. The designation required the agreement of the communes along the length of the shoreline covered by the proposal. Many communes could not see an economic advantage in adopting the wild river restrictions. Others saw direct economic disadvantages. The result was that the proposal lapsed. The proposal to establish a national park on Murter Island also fell foul of intercommune politics and the proposal was dropped. Throughout the country, where international visibility was less, local communities evidenced less interest in environmental conservation, and management activities were either non-existent or much less comprehensive. At the end of the 1980s, for example, few of Yugoslavia's other national and republican parks had either a permanent administration or adequate personnel to maintain them.

The most serious examples of the failure of self-management came in the area of the effects of human economic activity. Primary among these was the rising pollution in all the major cities. There are many winter days in Belgrade, Zagreb and other Yugoslav metropolitan areas where pollution indicators go well above the levels recommended by the WHO. The levels are published daily in the press. But the public perceives that little is done to change them. In Belgrade, the smell of coal hangs heavy in the winter air, particularly in the older residential districts, and black chunks fall out of the sky. In Skopje, daily measurements showed that in some parts of the city, pollution was so severe that normal breathing was difficult (*Vjesnik*, 27 October 1979, p. 27). Land-use planning produced well-drawn maps and charts in the institutes, but broke down because agreement could not be reached between municipal, regional and republican agencies. Kosovo had experienced only twenty years or so of industrialization, but by 1979 there was not a single river in the province that could be classified as safe for drinking (*Privredni Pregled*, 29 March 1979, p. 8).

Nowhere were the harmful effects of man's activity more evident than in the pollution of the Sava River, the only major tributary of the Danube to lie entirely within Yugoslavia's borders. In 1985, water quality had deteriorated so far that the Sava was called 'the river of death' by Belgrade newspapers. The problem was attributed to polluting industries upstream in neighbouring Croatia. Croatia denied the allegations but refused to allow Serbian environmental officials to monitor stations in Croatia (Jančar, 1985a). Pollution was exacerbated by the nuclear power plant at Krško, which initially was denied a licence to operate by the International Atomic Energy Authority because it failed to satisfy criteria of environmental safety, among which was a guarantee of water temperature in the Sava. The water temperature of Krško remains 2° C warmer than it should be ('From Coal to the Atom . . .?', 1986). In 1980, the communities along the river signed a Sava River Compact but the agreement had no republican commitment and remained largely symbolic. A weak central government with no ability to require or enforce the standardization of environmental norms and heightened inter-republican rivalry further stalemated efforts to clean up the river. The demonstrations of the summer and autumn of 1988 did little to cool nationality passions and while these remain high, the chances for cooperation through new self-managing agreements are slim.

The Sava was not the only victim of republican 'misuse', to borrow Singleton's word (Singleton, 1976). One of the most beautiful stretches of wild gorge in Europe, the canyon of the Tara River in the Durmitor Mountains, barely escaped inundation. The canyon's unique beauty caused the Yugoslav federal government to place it under the protection of MAB. However, in the 1980s, Serbia, Montenegro and Bosnia–Hercegovina (BiH) became critically short of energy, particularly in the area of electric power generation. The shortages may be traced to a complex of factors: the absence of an inter-republican market, inefficient utilization of Yugoslavia's domestic reserves and fuel imports. On the one hand, experts have

pointed out that Yugoslavia spends precious hard currency import-
ing refined fuels while the country's own petroleum refineries are
being used at 50 per cent capacity (Nedeljković, 1986). In 1970, fuel
imports represented 4.8 per cent of Yugoslavia's commodity imports. In 1985, fuel imports were at their highest point (27.2 per
cent) and stood at 22.3 per cent in 1986 (OECD, 1988). On the
other hand, Yugoslavia has developed only 40 per cent of its
hydroelectric power reserves as compared with 80–90 per cent in
most West European countries (Djurić, 1986).

The Tara forms an important part of the Drina River system
which has been the object of study for hydroelectric power generation for some time. Montenegro, which is energy-poor, has only
two rivers where hydroelectric power can be generated, the Tara--
Drina system and the Morača, a short precipitous river which rises
and falls within the republic. The severe winter of 1983 provided the
impetus for moving forward with plans for a dam on the Tara.
Belgrade residents experienced a major power shortage and the
Serbian press was strong in complaints about existing power conditions and demands that the situation be remedied. Bosnia–Hercegovina (BiH) and Serbia sought federal approval for a hydroelectric
project that foresaw the construction of a chain of dams on the
Drina river system. Because of the federal water law regulating the
exploitation of inter-republican rivers, Serbia and BiH needed
Montenegro's agreement in order to build dams on their part of the
river system. The three republics united around a project to build
dams on the Drina and the Morača river systems. The enabling law
was passed in May 1984.

The legislation brought an outcry from concerned scientists, who
charged that the three republics and the energy industry had deliberately concealed information and manipulated the public's fears for
heat and light. The scientists were able to organize themselves into a
'lobby' through the professional and environmental associations
within the Socialist Alliance, such as the clean water organization. But
although the environmentalists generated strong pressure among the
intellectual community to review the whole project, the law could
not be changed, only amended. The protected canyon of the Tara
was saved, but a dam would be built elsewhere in the wild section of
the river (Jančar, 1987, chapters 5 and 6).

The Sava and Tara River examples highlighted the flaws of
self-management in the environmental area. Inter-republican cooperation comes easier when the economy is at issue than when

environmental protection is the question. There is marked reluctance on the part of republican and *opstini* administration to undertake environmental objectives with no short-term economic return, because economic decisions are central to the maintenance of the self-management system and local party authority. Thus, the Sava River Contract has become, like much of Yugoslav environmental regulation, essentially a dead letter. Self-management's creation and promotion of autonomous territorial entities has proved to be a liability. Each unit, and particularly the republics, exploits regulation to strengthen and expand its own independence *vis à vis* the other units in the system.

A positive result of the Tara River controversy, however, was that it brought together for the first time a supra-republican, pro-environmental scientific lobby. Scientists had gradually been developing a pro-environmental network through the environmental associations organized under the Socialist Alliance and through contacts with environmentally inclined party officials. The saving of the canyon was clear indication that party-sponsored organizations could be used as vehicles to promote and sustain an environmental agenda. It further demonstrated that the environment could be a rallying point for individuals interested in promoting 'Yugoslav', as opposed to 'South Slav nationalist' politics. This tactic was to be developed more completely in the anti-nuclear power movement at the end of the decade.

As the 1980s drew to a close, the flaws of the self-management system in the environmental area became increasingly evident. Most of the major papers now ran a special section on environmental protection. The mass media also carried environmental news reports and environmental programmes. The news was almost always bad. Despite a comprehensive land-use plan, and numerous regulations and agreements, pollution of the Adriatic was increasing. Acid rain was attacking the beautiful forests of Gorski Kotar on the Mediterranean (Rušan, 1988). Water quality was further deteriorating everywhere. Chemical waste had become a problem (Mikulićić, 1988). One of the saddest reports was of the death of Lake Dojransko, the third and smallest of the three lakes in Macedonia which have a common border with Greece. The other two are Lakes Ohrid and Prespansko. In the words of the *Danas* reporter: 'ecological catastrophe is happening "here" and not only "there"'.

The death of Lake Dojransko was only one of a series of pollution episodes to have struck Macedonia in the late 1980s. In 1988, residents of Skopje could no longer be sure they were drinking safe water, when news of the dumping of chemicals into water sources by the giant chemical plant, Ohis, became public. At Štip in central Macedonia, chemically polluted water in water systems caused an outbreak of dysentery. A huge cement works at Šare in southern Serbia poured some 40 tons of *mažut* into the Lepenac River above Skopje, and the leather plant in Komanovo was found to be dumping pollutants into the Pčinja River, one of the principal tributaries of the Vardar River (Rusi, 1988). In all cases heavy industry was at fault, and in all cases, weak local or republican enforcement, or inadequate environmental regulations had contributed to the problem.

By the end of the decade, a large part of the Yugoslav public knew that all was not right with the Yugoslav environment and that in some places the situation was comparable to disasters that had occurred elsewhere in the industrialized world. With the exception of Lake Ohrid and a few other localized examples, commune, regional and republican governments had been remiss in carrying out environmental regulations. Laws might be on the books, but were not implemented or enforced. Like the economic situation, environmental protection in Yugoslavia had surpassed the ability of the political system to implement an efficient and effective management programme.

Chernobyl provided the catalyst to turn vague fears and uneasiness into a mass demand for more popular participation in environmental decision-making. The accident followed on a three-month heated public debate in the press over the construction of more nuclear power plants in Yugoslavia. In December 1985, the Federal Executive Council approved the purchase of four new plants costing billions of dollars. A round-table discussion organized soon after by Yugoslavia's Union of Engineers and Technicians revealed divisions among the experts on the virtues of nuclear energy and of Yugoslavia's overall energy future. The press raised questions about the wisdom of borrowing billions of dollars given the current level of foreign debt. But more significant than the published discussion was the popular anti-nuclear outcry. In Serbia, young people initiated a petition demanding the end of nuclear energy in Yugoslavia and succeeded in getting 120,000 signatures to it. The petition was circulated during elections to the Federal Parliament in April. However, the debate and petition had little impact on the new government which shortly after assuming office went ahead and voted the purchase of one of the four reactors.

The nuclear accident at Chernobyl occurred on 26 April 1986. On 10 May hundreds of young people under the auspices of the Slovenian League of Yugoslav Communist Youth (SOJ) demonstrated in Ljubljana against further construction or production of nuclear power in Yugoslavia. They also demanded reparation from the Soviet government of damages occurring to the Yugoslav economy from the accident (Jančar, 1987, chapter 9). Protest flowed over republican borders, generating the first trans-republican popular movement in the history of post-war Yugoslavia.

The Anti-Nuclear Movement and the Democratic Agenda

The anti-nuclear protests focused attention in Yugoslavia on an emerging social phenomenon which the Yugoslavs call 'alternative movements'. The movements generally came into being around a single issue and many operated openly within the Socialist Alliance. Slovenia has been the most vocal proponent of political pluralism as a solution to the country's economic problems and alternative movements of all kinds are most active there. In October 1988, some of the more non-conformist Slovenians associated with these movements joined together to form an independent Social Democratic Alliance outside the auspices of the official Socialist Alliance.

The attempt to establish an open political opposition in Slovenia closes a chapter in the development of alternative groups that began with the anti-nuclear protests after Chernobyl. Observers in the West have tended to emphasize nationality conflict and inter-republican rivalry as a seminal factor in Yugoslavia's continuing crisis. But nationalism is only one manifestation of the crisis, reflecting traditional attitudes and behaviour. The new cleavage in the 1980s has been the increasing polarization of interest between the vested political and economic interests of self-management and the 'little people': ordinary workers, young people and disaffected intellectuals. According to official sources, in 1987 the number of strikes increased over eightfold since 1982 while the number of participants has increased twenty-two times. In 1987, there were over 1,500 strikes involving some 365,000 workers and occurring in every republic. Huge strikes took place in Skopje (*Politika*, 2 December 1987), in Ljubljana, in the Labin coal mines in Croatia, and in the huge Zenica Coal and Iron and Steel Works in Bosnia

(Bavčar, 1987). By 1988, strikes were attracting tens of thousands of participants and had become common throughout the country.

The main cause of the strikes was low wages and an inflation rate that had drastically reduced the buying power of a worker's pay. As the strikes proliferated and grew in numbers of participants, they became increasingly politicized. In November 1987, the strikers at the Skopje Mining and Iron and Steel Works called for the resignation of top officials in the Macedonian leadership for 'having eaten our money', and demanded the confiscation of the possessions of what they termed 'the red bourgeoisie' (*Danas*, 24 November 1987). At the Zenica works in Bosnia, workers reportedly formed an independent trade union because they were 'fed up with the state labour unions' (*Večernje novosti*, Belgrade, 25 and 26 November 1987).

Important as the economic issues were, they were able to forge a worker's alliance across republican borders. On the contrary, 1988 saw the attempt by republics, particularly Serbia, to utilize worker discontent to fan the flames of nationalism. While workers forced the resignation of republican leaderships, their activities remained confined within republican borders. Economic health, wealth and experience with political pluralism vary so greatly across the Yugoslav republics that economic demands have not readily been transferable across frontiers. The common denominator is that workers blame the official trade unions along with the party and enterprise management for the collapse of the Yugoslav economy.

Young people were among those most affected by the economic crisis. *Danas* reported in 1986 that in 1985, the number of unemployed grew three times faster than the employed and that young people constituted the largest unemployed sector: 77 per cent of all those between the ages of twenty and thirty had no jobs (*Danas*, 11 November 1985, 24–6). According to Drakulich-Ilic (Drakulich, 1987b, p. 602), young people experience an average wait of up to three years for a job. The situation is particularly hard on university graduates. Up until the middle of the decade, young people could compensate for not having a job by living at home with their families. But as inflation rose and living standards deteriorated, there were fewer and fewer families which did not feel the pinch of the economic crisis. In their increasing frustration, young people turned to the streets and to the formation of independent organizations through which to express their grievances. However, as was the case with labour unrest, youth disaffection has varied from republic to republic and has been most marked in the economically most advanced and most Western-oriented republics of Slovenia and Croatia. Young people's grievances, like labour's, do not translate easily across republican frontiers.

Like the workers, young people turned their energies against what they perceive as the establishment. In the late 1970s, a feminist movement began among young scholars and students in the universities at Ljubljana and Zagreb (Jančar, 1985b, 1988a). Significantly, when they decided to organize ten years later, the feminists did not organize by themselves. In both Slovenia and Croatia, they merged into the newly formed peace and ecology movement. The draft became a prominent issue. In addition to the anti-nuclear demonstrations in 1986, there were also demonstrations against a proposal for compulsory military service for women, and against military service in general. In 1986, Ivan Češko, a Jehovah's Witness from the Slovenian city of Maribor on the Yugoslav–Austrian border, was sentenced to five years in prison for refusing to be drafted. He was subsequently released, after the Slovenian SOJ mobilized public opinion against the sentence (Drakulich, 1987b). Slovenian youth then stepped up their attacks on the military. In March, 1988, the official journal of the Slovenian Zveza Mladina Jugeslavije (ZMJ), *Mladina*, published an article describing the Minister of Defence, among other things, as a 'merchant of death'. The article brought a storm of protest from veterans, and party and government officials, particularly when *Mladina* subsequently published fourteen demands to end the 'moral corruption' of the League of Communists, including 'public control of the Yugoslav People's Army'. The magazine was put under temporary ban only to re-emerge in print with new allegations against the army, the most serious being the charge that the army planned to move against Slovenian reformers. These and other allegations led to the arrests first of the journal's managing editor, Franc Zavrl, and then of the chief reporter on military affairs, David Tasić (Andrejevich, 1988).

Such radical activity was characteristic only of Slovenia. Significantly, the 1986 demonstrations against compulsory military service for women were not reported in the main Croatian and Serbian papers. While young people in other republics, particularly university students, doubtless felt the same way about the party and the military, the political climate in other parts of Yugoslavia was not yet as open as in Slovenia, and young people did not feel they could vent their views so publicly. Moreover, in Serbia and Kosovo, young people's frustrations channelled into the nationality conflict. Indeed, Kosovo loomed so large in Serbia that it obscured other serious issues.

The emergence of the ecological movement must be set against this background, which Zagreb social ecologist, Ivan Cifrić, has defined as 'a confrontation between the masses and leadership'. In July of 1986, he gave an interview with the press, which deserves to be quoted at some length. Asked whether there exists a 'socialist ecology', Cifrić responded:

> Of course not . . . the problems are the same in both East and West. Socialism which should cultivate all human values cannot be without ecology, but in our country one can count on one's fingers the theoreticians who deal with ecology, and very little literature has been translated into our language. Noninstitutional, alternative movements are . . . arising in our country today because of the ineffectiveness of the present system. If the League of Communists remains deaf to ecological problems, a movement will develop outside the system. It will expand and be fully justified historically. I think a broad democratic discussion is needed on the current questions of protecting the environment and there should be a party conference on this topic. One should listen to these initiatives because if they are not accepted as reality, we will have an 'opposition' which we ourselves have created and which will be justified. Silence is the worst thing. (*Danas*, 8 July 1986, pp. 65–6).

In this passage, Cifrić provides the main reasons for the emergence of informal, alternative politics in Yugoslavia: the ineffectiveness of the current system, the refusal of the authorities 'to listen' and accept initiatives from below 'as reality', and the 'deafness' of the party to environmental problems. Further into the interview, Cifrić elaborated on the theme of confrontation between people and leadership. Calling the official youth organization, the League of Yugoslav Youth a 'typical copy' of the party, he explained that young functionaries had similar privileges as their adult counterparts in the party (apartments, official cars, high pay). Because of this gap of privilege, the interests of the Union of Socialist Youth of Yugoslavia (SSOJ) rank-and-file and the Youth League functionary cannot be the same. If the party-sponsored organizations did not overcome this gap, and not listen to the rank-and-file, the official organizations would break up. In other words, formal politics was unresponsive to the real needs of the country.

The anti-nuclear movement differs from the nationality, labour and youth protests that developed parallel with it in its transnational political capability. Until the anti-nuclear movement, youth groups were divided by republican borders. Since Slovenia was the most advanced republic economically, and had the closest ties with Austria and Western Europe, it was not surprising that restructuring of the official youth organization should have first occurred in Slovenia. In 1985, the Slovenian ZMJ was opened up to alternative ecology and peace groups. One group which organized under the ZMJ was the Ljubljana Peace Group. The group first came to public notice in the spring of 1985 when 200 of its members demonstrated against the 9 May military parade in Belgrade commemorating the end of the Second World War. Subsequently, the group became increasingly outspoken on domestic and military issues. It was responsible, for example, for the demonstration in 1986 against compulsory military service for women.

The philosophy of the Ljubljana Peace Group argued the relevancy of the new alternative politics to the Yugoslav political scene by drawing a distinction between state and society. There are two kinds of peace, the group said: 'state peace' guaranteed by state dictatorship over society, and 'civil–social peace', which is the demolition 'of the boundaries between civil societies or the "internationalization" of civil society'. The group established contacts with like-minded groups in both Eastern and Western Europe, believing that links with the West were critical to the achievement of its domestic goals.

The Peace Group had an avowed political purpose. Sociologist Tomas Mastnak, fellow of the Institute for Marxist Studies of the Slovenian Academy of Arts and Sciences and a spokesperson for the group stated that given Yugoslavia's federal composition and national rivalries, an independent peace and environmental movement might be the only type of movement that could unite people across Yugoslavia's many boundaries. Ties with the West were essential because 'we lack a democratic tradition and popularly shared memories of a strong and independent civil society. Issue-oriented campaigns . . . fill this gap "and help produce" a democratic culture in Yugoslavia'. Mastnak believed that it was necessary to invent new forms of democratic activism which were appropriate to domestic conditions, and not imitate Western or Eastern experiences, such as Solidarity (*From Below*, 1987, pp. 181–5).

The Slovenian experience was initially transmitted to youth in the other republics mainly by word of mouth, but it provided a model for the movement for a nuclear moratorium, which at its beginning was a Serbian youth initiative. The story of the movement is a lesson in Yugoslav alternative politics.

The idea of a petition against further construction of nuclear plants was started by Aleksandar Knezivić, a high school student at the Moše Pijade High School in the Belgrade district of Stari Grad. Knezivić obtained the consent of his high-school principal to present a proposal to the district Sovez Omladuria Jugoslavije (SOJ) conference. The conference enthusiastically supported the idea and resolved that the cost of printing and distributing the petition be borne by all the schools in the district of Stari Grad. Then the conference president was replaced and the incoming president did not want to get involved in controversy so early in his tenure. Support for the project quickly died. Knezivić began getting phone calls at night, some threatening him with two months in jail, others predicting his parents would lose their jobs. Knezivić's principal was called to the Stari Grad Communist Party (LYC) municipal committee. The committee rejected the idea of a petition, but approved the reading of a letter in all the schools of Serbia. Each class could decide whether to support the proposal to cease construction of the proposed nuclear power plants. According to *NIN* (13 April 1986), of 464 schools in Serbia, 110 responded and letters came from schools in three towns in Croatia. There were 70,000 signatures in all.

The success of the petition raised the objections of officials involved in the planning and management of the nuclear power industry. Specialists from the Machine-Building Faculty of Belgrade University invited themselves to the Mŏse Pijade School to lecture the students on the benefits of nuclear power. At the beginning, the Serbian SOJ was uneasy about the iniative. Then, the Ljubljana Peace Group issued its statement calling for the Soviet Union to pay reparations for damage done, and demanding a moratorium on nuclear power and a referendum on the construction of a second plant.

Throughout the summer of 1986, the anti-nuclear movement gathered momentum, as more people joined in protests. Youth groups were not the only ones concerned about the dangers of nuclear power. Chernobyl occasioned much soul-searching among the scientific community and many scientists who had previously been in favour of it, changed their minds. As one told me: 'If the Soviets and Americans with all their experience with nuclear energy cannot avoid accidents, how can an underdeveloped country like Yugoslavia? It only takes one man coming to work drunk.' The press ran many articles by experts expressing doubts as to whether the cost was worth the benefits and challenging the need for nuclear power.

In June 1986, the veterans' organization, SUBNOR, indicated its support of a moratorium on nuclear energy until the year 2000. That same month, the first Congress of the Anti-nuclear Movement was held in Belgrade. At the meetings, professors, experts and journalists elaborated the strategy and tactics for achieving the moratorium, including a possible sit-in at the construction site for the proposed new nuclear power plant (*Danas*, 17 June 1986, pp. 60 and 65). In a press interview during the Congress, writer Mijana Robie said it was 'the little people' of Yugoslavia who were protesting against nuclear power. Moreover, she continued, 'this is the first time a truly important and strong public opinion in the real sense of the word has been expressed which seeks for itself the right to speak, think, and inquire' (*Danas*, 17 June 1986, p. 60). In July, a group promoting ecology, peace and the feminist movement called SVARUN was formed along the lines of the Ljuljbana Peace Group within the Croatian SOJ. SVARUN's slogan was: 'Today in the consciousness, tomorrow in the councils; more salt in the head, less iodine in the grass.' (*Danas*, 8 July 1986).

In the autumn of 1986, an environment and peace group formed in Belgrade, called the Committee for the Protection of Man and the Environment. Its members were primarily intellectuals, and its president, Biljana Jovanović, belonged to the Serbian Writers' Union. The Committee energetically wrote environmental articles for both Serbian and Slovenian journals, notably *Mladina* and *Tribuna* in Slovenia (*From Below*, pp. 186–93), and helped mobilize adult support for the moratorium. Unlike the Tara River case, questioning of official decisions had now gone beyond a narrow band of intellectuals or experts to encompass a broad spectrum of the population.

In November, the Ljubljana Peace and Ecology group organized a campaign to defeat a referendum on a proposed increase in the environmental protection tax in Ljubljana, arguing that a different policy would make an increase unnecessary. The referendum went down ('The Stirrings of Yugopluralism', 1987, p. 55).

The mass outcry was evidently unexpected by the authorities, who launched a not very convincing counter-attack. The defenders of nuclear power became known as the 'nuclear lobby', and included top government leaders. Two former Prime Ministers, Milka Planinc and Branko Mikulić, who resigned at the end of 1988, exerted their influence on behalf of the nuclear industry. The lobby defended nuclear energy with the standard arguments: the existing plant at Krško ranked high on the list of high quality power stations according to the IAEA (TANJUG, Belgrade, 7 December 1986). Nuclear plants were cleaner than fossil-fuel plants and cheaper to run. Moreover, a moratorium would decimate Yugoslavia's nuclear community and severely undermine any further commitment by young people to study nuclear physics (Petrović, 1987). In Slovenia, the government organized public meetings to deal directly with people's concerns. Planinc and Mikulić took the case for nuclear energy before the LYC Central Committee (Jovanović, 1988). In response, the anti-nuclear movement produced expert studies of its own. Milan Djurić (1986) argued that Yugoslavia's energy requirements up to the year 2010 did not need nuclear power plants, while Dragoslav Nedeljković (1986) noted the inefficiencies and discrepancies in Yugoslav energy planning that resulted in poor use of existing capacity.

The debate continued through 1986 and 1987. The anti-nuclear movement became better organized and solidified its contacts with West European peace and environmental groups. For its part, the government did not stop its plans for the further development of nuclear power. In January 1987, the residents of Osijek and adjacent towns demonstrated against a proposal by Elektroslavonija to build a nuclear power plant on Tanja Island in the Danube (*Vjestnik*, 29 January 1987, p. 6). In April, the Presidium of the youth organization at the federal level, the SSOJ, invited Mikulić to a meeting to address the merits of nuclear power. Mikulić declined to come and sent an official from the Ministry of Energy and Industry instead (Jovanović, 1988). On 10 May 1987, *Mladost*, the journal of the Slovenian KMJ, printed an article endorsing the moratorium. In July 1987, the SSOJ annual conference formally approved a legislative proposal for a moratorium on nuclear energy until the year 2000 ('I zakonom protiv nuklearki', 1987). The 1974 Constitution gives socio-political organizations the right to recommend legislation and the proposal was duly forwarded to the Yugoslav federal legislature, the *Skupština*. In November 1987, in a rare recognition of popular opinion, the *Skupština* voted for the moratorium (*New Scientist*, 19 November 1987). Almost a year later to the day, the

Federal Executive Council signed the moratorium into law (Jovanović, 1988).

The story of the anti-nuclear movement supports Mastnak's contention that environmental and peace issues are capable of crossing Yugoslavia's republican frontiers and uniting people for action. In contrast to the anti-nuclear protests which developed elsewhere in Europe after Chernobyl, including Western Europe, the movement was able to build the initial spontaneous popular reaction to the accident into an organized sustained battle for legislation. For the first time, Yugoslavs in different republics coordinated their actions against a common enemy, the 'nuclear lobby'. For the first time, unofficial groups were seen by functionaries in the party and government-sponsored organizations as truly representing public opinion, and the government gave in. And for the first time, a non-government-supported initiative was successful at the federal level. The success further broadened what Yugoslavs call 'their democratic space', setting a precedent for further initiatives.

The success of the movement revealed the depth of the gap between the young and the old, and between the 'little people' and the Yugoslav *nomenklatura*. From this revelation, it was but a short step to the formation in more radical Slovenia of the Socialist Democratic Alliance. Although neither Mastnak nor Cifrić condemned self-management, they believed that an independent 'opposition' is necessary and that this opposition must be based on non-violence and democracy. The alternative movements could only engage in the new informal politics if violence were kept at bay. The peace and ecological movement opened up the possibility for the development of a trans-republican democratic opposition. To bring about this eventuality is the hidden agenda of the ecological groups.

In the 1980s, the ecological movement was active mainly in Yugoslavia's three most modern cities, Ljubljana, Zagreb and Belgrade. Environmental groups were forming in other localities. Republican autonomy and the limited range of the national languages impeded the development of a trans-national press which would have helped speed up the process. Residents of Skopje learn of happenings in Slovenia primarily from their home papers. Information transmission is thus constrained by the reporting and financial limitations of the local media, as well as by the range of local censorship. With their larger income, greater number of reporters and greater openness to controversy, newspapers like *Politika* and *Vjestnik* can keep their readers informed of happenings all over the country. Nevertheless, pollution in Macedonia affected so many people and received such exposure in the Macedonian press that the formation of an ecological group became inevitable there (Rusi, 1988). The lesson of the anti-nuclear movement was that environmental protection was impossible without active democratic participation.

The Generation Gap

The generation gap was not the product of the anti-nuclear movement. The movement served to dramatize that gap. The current generation of young people has no memory of pre-war Yugoslavia, of the Nazi occupation and civil war, or of the early years of socialist industrialization. Brought up in the era of self-management, this generation takes easy trips to the West for granted, and was the first group of children to receive environmental education in grade school. Most Yugoslavs see Slovenia as the most Western of the republics, and young people especially look to Ljubljana for what is new, and beyond Ljubljana to Western Europe. Of all the republics, only Slovenia produced an independent youth culture before 1980. Although there were attempts to repress it, the culture persisted through time and became the source of the alternative movements which emerged in the 1980s.

The Westward-orientation of young people was well expressed by the editor-in-chief of *Mladina*, Robert Bettori. In his words, every significant achievement in Yugoslavia, including the industrial revolution and Marxism, came from the West, while from the 'Eastern steppes' had come Yugoslavia's lone negative development, the communist party. 'Democracy is our motto and our mission,' he said. To achieve democracy, 'we have begun to destroy various taboos, publishing articles that other newspapers did not want or dare to publish . . . This is how we have come to the conclusion that newspapers have always been able to spread the ideas generated by young people throughout the country "from below".' The alternative movements would have stayed 'below', he concluded, if it had not been for journals like *Mladina* (*Intervju*, Belgrade, 23 October 1987).

In the 1980s the younger generation rejected the authorities' accusation that the new movements were 'an extended arm of capitalism' in Yugoslavia. According to the opinion of young people, the older generation was always looking back. The younger generation looked forward. To go forward, they must observe and adapt modern Western political movements to the Yugoslav setting. Adaptation did not necessarily mean the import of the political party system. Most important, from young people's viewpoint, was the development in the West of single-issue politics which did not attack a political system as a whole, but attack one problem at a time. The anti-nuclear movement was an example of this kind of politics. Once the moratorium had become law, the anti-nuclear movement could fade from the Yugoslav scene to regroup around other environmental or peace issues.

Like all generations before them, Yugoslav young people saw moral decadence and spiritual emptiness in their elders. Young activists like Bettori do not necessarily reject Marxism, but they would like to transform the League of Communists from an instrument of power into some kind of moral or educative force. The older generation of leaders saw a combination of political naivety and a threat to its power in such a change, and quite naturally resisted it. The gap then is not only one of ideals but of power. Young people view the economic institutions of self-management much as the Greens or the environmental movement in the United States tend to perceive big business: as corrupted entities, intent on corporate or personal gain, in league with big, or in the Yugoslav case, monopolist government. The tangible indication of big-business corruption is spoliation of the environment.

In the 1980s the environment for the younger generation was thus not merely a cause for action in itself alone. It became a symbol of a global agenda to end what was perceived as the moral bankruptcy of the self-management system. The younger generation of Yugoslavs shared the Greens' belief that if the environment is to be saved, there have to be fundamental changes in the political system in both West and East. However, contrary to the Greens who emphasize the economic dimension, and attack nuclear power because it represents to them the epitome of the military–industrial contract (Capra and Spretnak, 1984, pp. 57–81), the stress of Yugoslavia's young people was on a new Yugoslav way to democracy: the promotion of alternative movements outside the official system which through interaction with organizations such as the SSOJ inside the system can slowly bring about changes from within.

Barbara Jančar

Conclusion

The record of environmental protection in the Yugoslav self-management system is mixed. Self-management has played a positive role where projects have been limited in scope and contained within one self-management unit, or where there has been strong international interest as in the case of Lake Ohrid. The clearest successes are in nature conservation where the tourist industry has had a vested interest in environmental protection. Self-management has been far less successful in tackling inter-republican trans-boundary pollution, or environmental degradation within one republic, where the local polluter has been a major industry necessary to the local and republican economy.

Whether one agrees with the moratorium or not, the emergence of an independent environmental movement capable of surmounting national rivalries and concentrating popular pressure to modify leadership decisions, was a hopeful sign in the turmoil of Yugoslav politics. It suggested that the environment had now found a permanent public defender in Yugoslavia. When the issue was of sufficient seriousness, that defender would speak out loudly and strongly. Second, the apposition of an environmental lobby against the traditional industrial lobby was a positive step forward in the development of *federal* political pluralism in a *confederated* political system. While other dissidence remained fragmented within republican boundaries, the environmental movement was able to project its message to the country as a whole. In institutionalizing political conflict above and beyond republican concerns, the environmental movement positioned itself to make a positive contribution to the development of trans-republican interest-group politics. Such a development would have introduced a much needed centrifugal element into Yugoslavia's fractured political discourse.

The success of the anti-nuclear movement indicates that the expansion of group pluralism was not necessarily perceived as a threat by the Yugoslav political leadership and that alternative trans-republican politics could become a permanent part of Yugoslavia's way. However, with the dramatic collapse of communism in Eastern Europe in 1989, nationalism proved stronger than environmentalism. The desire for national independence overran federalism, relegating the trans-republican efforts of the 1980s to history.

Bibliography

Andrejevich, Milan (1988), 'Some Aspects of the Slovenian Situation', Radio Free Europe, *Situation Report*, No. 6, 6 July 1988, pp. 11–16

Bavčar, Igor (1987), 'Strikes in Yugoslavia', *Across Frontiers*, Vol. 3, No. 4, pp. 22–3

Capra, Fritjof and Charlene Spretnak (1984), *Green Politics: The Global Promise*, New York, E. P. Dutton

Cicmirko-Pokrajčić, Zdravka, 'From Coal to the Atom . . . To the Candle?', interview with James Dular, General-Director of the Krško Nuclear Power Plant, *Privredni Pregled* (Belgrade), 8–10 November 1986, p. 3

De Soto, Hernando (1989), *The Other Path: The Invisible Revolution in the Third World*, translated by June Abbott, foreword by Mario Vargas Llosa, New York, Harper & Row

Djurić, Milan (1986), 'Nuclear Power Plants Without Foundation', *Ekonomska politika*, 2 June 1986, pp. 26–8

Drakulich, Slavenka (1987a), 'Hard Rain Falls on Yugoslavia', *The Nation*, 14 February, pp. 177–8, 180

——(1987b), 'Yugoslav Youth Stir it Up', *The Nation*, 9 May, pp. 601–3

From Below, Independent Peace and Environmental Movements in Eastern Europe & the USSR, A Helsinki Watch Report, October 1987, New York, Helsinki Watch

Glavas, Davor (1988), 'Razgovor:Zvonimir Devide: "Svjedoci vlastitog uništenja"' (A Conversation with Zvonimir Devide: 'witnesses to our own destruction'), *Danas*, 10 April, pp. 69–72

'I zakonom protiv nuklearki' (Legislation Against Nuclear Reactors), *Zvjestnik*, 2 August 1987, p. 3

Jančar, Barbara (1985a), 'Environmental Protection – The Tragedy of the Commons', in Pedro Ramet (ed.), *Yugoslavia in the 1980s*, Boulder, Colo., Westview Press, pp. 224–46

——(1985b), 'The New Feminism', in Ramet (ed.), *Yugoslavia*, pp. 201–23

——(1987), *Environmental Management in the Soviet Union and Yugoslavia*, Durham, NC, Duke University Press

——(1988a), 'Neofeminism in Yugoslavia: A Closer Look', *Women and Politics*, Vol. 8, No. 1, pp. 1–30

——(1988b), Testimony before the US Commission on Security and Cooperation in Europe, Washington DC, 25 April 1988

Jovanović, Dragan (1988), 'Konačno – Moratorijum' (At last – A Moratorium), *NIN*, 11 December, p. 70

Mikuličić, Damir (1988), 'Kemija po glavi stanovnika', *Danas*, 4 November, pp. 70–1

Nedeljković, Dragoslav (1986), 'Fortune-Telling Instead of Planning', *Ekonomska politika*, 30 June, pp. 27–8

OECD (1985), 'Urban Environmental Issues in Yugoslavia', *Ekistics*, Vol. 53, Winter, pp. 96–101

Remington, Robin Alison (1987), 'Nation versus Class in Yugoslavia', *Current History*, Vol. 86, November 1987, pp. 365–8

Petrović, Boris (1987), 'Što donosi 26 prosinca?' (What does 26 December Bring?), *Viestnik*, 6 December, p. 6

Ricciuti, Edward R. (1986), 'Tito's Wilderness', *Audabon*, Vol. 88, Summer, pp. 24–26, 31

Rušan, Rajka (1988), 'Olovni usud šuma' (The Leaden Fate of the Forests), *Danas*, 10 October, pp. 72–3

Rusi, Iso (1988), 'Makedonske mutne' (Macedonian Muddles), *Danas*, 25 October, pp. 70–2

Savet za čovekovu sredinu i prostorno uredjenje Saveznog izvrsnog veča i izvrshnih veča republika i pokrajina (1978), *Čovekova sredina i prostorno uredjenje u Jugoslaviji: Pregled stanja* (The Human Environment and Land Use Management in Yugoslavia: A Status Survey), Belgrade, OOUR Izdavačka delatnost

Seroka, Jim (1988), 'Prognosis for Political Stability in Yugoslavia in the Post-Tito Era', *East European Quarterly*, Vol. 22, No. 2, June 1988, pp. 173–90

Singleton, Fred (1976), *Environmental Misuse in the Soviet Union*, New York, Praeger

——(1985), *A Short History of the Yugoslav People*, New York, Cambridge University Press

——(1987), *Environmental Problems in the Soviet Union and Eastern Europe*, Boulder, Colo., Lynne Reinner

'The Stirrings of Yugo-pluralism' (1987), *Economist*, 21 February, pp. 55–6

Todorović, Milivoje (1983), *Moguca resenja u sistemu covek – drustovo – zivotna sredina* (The Possibility of a Solution in the System: Man – Society – The means of Life), Belgrade, Mladi istraživače Srbije

World Resources Institute (1988), *World Resources 1988–89*, New York, Basic Books

12

Yugoslav Foreign Direct Investment in the West

Patrick Artisien and Alan Brown

Introduction

This study focuses on the phenomenon of Yugoslav direct investment in Western markets. The main objective is to discuss the origin, development, specific characteristics, motivation and success of Yugoslav multinationals in the West. The focus is on four issues: first, what are the major historical, economic and political variables behind the growth of Yugoslav foreign direct investment in the West? Second, what are the motives for these investments? Third, how successful have Yugoslav firms been in establishing subsidiaries in the West? Finally, what factors account for the ownership pattern of Yugoslav foreign direct investment?

The data were collected from twenty-one subsidiaries and four parent companies, covering twenty-five firms with Yugoslav equity participation in the United Kingdom, Germany, Austria, Italy, the Netherlands and the USA. Interviews were based on a structured questionnaire and conducted with senior executives in charge of overseas operations. Company reports and other statistical sources from the Federal Secretariat for Foreign Economic Relations, the Social Accounting Service and Yugoslav chambers of commerce abroad complement the interview-based data.

The background

Amongst the few studies conducted to date of East European firms investing abroad, McMillan (1979; 1987) has linked the growth of East European multinationals in the 1960s and 1970s to a new perception by the Comecon countries of the need to break out of their regional isolation and engage more actively in the mainstream of international economic relations. The growth of Comecon-based multinationals sanctioned the transition from the post-war period of 'extensive' growth which laid the industrial foundations for the extensive mobilization of labour and capital, to the emergence of a more 'intensive' growth strategy intended to rely on qualitative improvements in industrial products and processes through a more efficient use of resources and new technology. The growth of Soviet and East European foreign investment into manufacturing and financial and transport services resulted in a significant qualitative change in the East European economic 'presence' abroad (McMillan, 1979). The motivation of Comecon-based multinationals bears many similarities to that of their Western counterparts in the immediate post-war years: the search for markets, raw materials and lower production costs are major objectives. McMillan (1987) suggests further that the ownership structure of Comecon companies abroad is not significantly different from that of the subsidiaries of Western multinationals; there is a clear preference for majority ownership, and expansion and diversification are financed mainly through reinvested profits and local borrowing rather than through capital exports from the home country.

Studies of Yugoslav multinationals abroad have concentrated on investments in less developed countries (LDCs) (Svetličič and Rojec, 1985, 1986; Artisien, Rojec and Svetličič, 1991). These studies link the emergence of Yugoslav foreign direct investment (FDI) to the post-1965 Economic Reform period in Yugoslavia which spurred enterprises to integrate more fully with the world economy. Economic decentralization provided Yugoslav enterprises with the necessary incentives and independence to intensify direct economic links with foreign firms. Unlike their Western counterparts, Yugoslav multinationals do not manufacture new or exclusive products, but instead rely on adaptations of standard technologies. This explains the under-representation of Yugoslav investors in manufacturing ventures in Western markets, where they lack the necessary firm-specific advantages to internalize operations (Artisien, Rojec and Svetličič, 1991).

The origin of Yugoslav direct investment in the developed market economies (DMEs) dates back to the immediate post-war years: in 1947 the Anglo-Yugoslav Shipping Company was established in the United Kingdom, and the following year BSE-Genex was set up in

London. During this period the German market also became a target of Yugoslav investments: in 1951 the electronics conglomerate Iskra set up a subsidiary (Cefra) in Munich, whilst the Zagreb-based enterprise Exportdrvo established a subsidiary (Omnico) in Landshut for the assembly of furniture and related products. Up until the mid-1950s Yugoslavia's readiness to engage in foreign investment activity was constrained by ideological and financial factors. Ambitious domestic industrialization programmes restricted the volume of funds available for foreign investment. This was exacerbated by the country's expulsion from the Cominform in 1949, which cut off sources of aid and capital from the Soviet bloc. Moreover, the latent xenophobia which persisted in those years was another impediment to innovative forms of industrial cooperation, which remained limited to traditional exports and imports.

The initial surge of Yugoslav outward investment in the West occurred in the mid to late 1950s when the authorities initiated a network of licensing and long-term industrial cooperation agreements with major Western trading partners with the objective of establishing qualitatively new relationships as a source of foreign technology. Yugoslavia's participation in the Marshall Plan contributed to the strengthening of these economic links.

This was followed in the 1960s by the emergence of a new foreign economic policy which formed the basis of the 1965 economic reforms. The Reforms opened the Yugoslav market to foreign competition with the objective of increasing the industrial efficiency and competitiveness of Yugoslav enterprises. They also strengthened the economic profile of the enterprise, which became the main vehicle through which to intensify direct industrial cooperation with foreign firms.

Traditionally, the foreign subsidiaries of Yugoslav enterprises in the DMEs have been trade-oriented. This reflected Yugoslavia's relatively undeveloped industrial base in the 1960s which prompted firms to concentrate on trade activities rather than on the more capital and technology intensive manufacturing sectors. Moreover, the establishment of subsidiaries in the West has generally been preceded by the setting up of representative offices and small business units as ways of minimizing risks. Finally, Yugoslav investment in the DMEs has been undertaken primarily in support of exports to those markets.

The significance of Yugoslav enterprises abroad is illustrated further by the share of exports and imports realized by these firms in Yugoslavia's overall foreign trade. The shares of total Yugoslav exports handled by marketing subsidiaries and affiliates abroad rose from 25.6 per cent in 1983 to 35.8 per cent in 1988, whilst the corresponding shares of imports trebled from 7.1 per cent to 21.7 per cent (see Table 12.1 for details).

Profile of External Investments by Yugoslav Firms

According to the Social Accounting Service of Yugoslavia, at the end of 1988 there were 372 wholly or partly owned Yugoslav subsidiaries abroad. Table 12.2 shows that 308 (or 82.8 per cent) are located in the DMEs, and 64 (17.2 per cent) are established in the LDCs. Of the 664 representative offices established abroad at the end of 1988, 194 were located in the DMEs.[1]

From the Federal Secretariat for Foreign Economic Relations in Belgrade, it was possible to identify 287 Western susidiaries with Yugoslav equity paricipation. Table 12.3 shows the distribution of these companies by country of location and principal activity.

The geographical distribution of companies with Yugoslav equity participation in the West is very broad. Table 12.3 shows that, of the 287 companies identified in our survey, the principal investment targets have been those DMEs with which Yugoslavia has traditionally maintained close commercial relations: Germany, Italy, Austria and Switzerland host 163 subsidiaries (or 56.8 per cent) of Yugoslav firms in the West. The UK with twenty-two firms (7.6 per cent of the total) illustrates the importance of London as a financial and commercial centre. The concentration of Yugoslav investments in the neighbouring countries of Austria, Italy, Germany and Switzerland confirms the importance of geographical proximity and historical links. Our evidence is broadly in line with Wells's observation that LDC firms[2] have a preference for investing in neighbouring countries (Wells, 1983).

1. For the purpose of this study, a *foreign subsidiary* has been defined as a domestic firm over which the Yugoslav investor has operational control. A *representative office*, on the other hand, does not have a legal identity separate from the Yugoslav parent company, and is therefore treated as a foreign, rather than as a domestic, firm by the host country.
2. McMillan (1987) has used the terminology 'Multinationals from the Second World' to describe the relatively new phenomenon of foreign direct investment from the Comecon countries. McMillan's definition is exclusive to the systemic characteristics of the planned state–socialist economies of the Soviet Union and Eastern Europe. In its present state of decentralized self-management, Yugoslavia does not

Table 12.1 Foreign Trade Conducted by Foreign Subsidiaries and Affiliates of Yugoslav Firms, 1983–88

	1983	1984	1985	1986	1987	1988
Exports (US$ millions)	2,534.4	2,256.8	2,891.4	3,388.2	4,398.8	4,702.9
Handled by subsidiaries/affiliates in DMEs (%)	93.2	92.8	87.4	94.1[a]	95.1[a]	92.6[a]
Handled by subsidiaries/affiliates in LDCs (%)	6.8	7.2	10.3	3.3[a]	4.9[a]	7.4[a]
Handled by subsidiaries/affiliates in East European countries (%)			2.3	2.6[a]	–	–
Share of total Yugoslav exports (%)	25.6	22.0	27.2	32.7	36.1	35.8
Imports (US$ millions)	865.4	1,040.8	1,479.6	2,084.5	2,459.2	2,991.2
Handled by subsidiaries/affiliates in DMEs (%)	96.2	96.2	96.9	91.6[a]	92.5[a]	86.8[a]
Handled by subsidiaries/affiliates in LDCs (%)	3.8	3.8	3.1	5.4[a]	7.5[a]	13.2[a]
Share of total Yugoslav imports (%)	7.1	8.7	12.2	17.4	18.1	21.7

Notes: [a] Includes wholly-owned and majority-owned Yugoslav enterprises abroad only. Minority-owned Yugoslav joint ventures abroad are excluded.

Source: Social Accounting Service of Yugoslavia.

Table 12.2 Number of Yugoslav Economic Entities Abroad, end of 1988

	Developed Market Economy Countries	East European Socialist Countries[a]	Less Developed Countries	Total
Number of Countries	25	12	60	97
Number of Entities–Total	623	558	1,044	2,225
Subsidiaries	308		64	372
Wholly (Yugoslav) Owned	224		27	251
Majority (Yugoslav) Owned	30		3	33
Minority (Yugoslav) Owned	54		34	88
Entities for Construction Works[b]	103	244	754	1,101
Representative Offices	194	275	195	664
Business Entities[b]	18	39	31	88

Notes: [a] Includes China and Mongolia;
[b] Entities for construction works and business entities are both set up to undertake construction projects abroad. Business entities, however, are not legally bound to draw up their balance sheet reports for the Yugoslav authorities.

Source: Social Accounting Service of Yugoslavia.

Wells argues further that some subsidiaries are established primarily to service a local community, which is related to an ethnic group in the investor's home country. Such projects account for a significant number of 'upstream' investments targeted at industrialized countries (Wells, 1983). Our evidence confirms that Yugoslav FDI has a bias for Germany, Italy and Austria, and thus mirrors the country's overall pattern of international economic relations.

Our sample also identified 35 subsidiaries in the USA, which has become a major market for Yugoslav cars and furniture products. In some cases, subsidiaries have established their own branches, either in the country where they are themselves situated, or in other countries. The sport equipment manufacturer, Elan, set up the Elan Holding company in Austria in 1987 which owns all of Elan's other foreign subsidiaries in Austria, the USA, Canada, Switzerland, Sweden and Germany.

Table 12.3 also reveals the wide range of economic activities of Yugoslav FDI in the West. Of the total of 287 companies, 179 (62.3 per cent) are primarily engaged in trading, marketing and distribution activities; another 51 (17.8 per cent) are located in other service industries, including transport companies, tourist agencies and banks. Only 57 of the 287 firms are engaged in manufacturing and processing. The low profile of manufacturing investments points to the relatively higher unit costs of production in the West as well as to the lack of hard currency capital inputs, which such investments would entail. This suggests that Yugoslav firms, in the absence of the necessary firm-specific advantages referred to above, are more likely to give preference to exports than to manufacturing investments, thus avoiding the need to collect as much information and minimizing financial risks.

Of the 51 companies in the service industries, approximately half are engaged in consumer services (namely airline and travel agencies); the remainder are fairly evenly distributed among technical, transport

---

easily espouse the above definition. While it is understood that Yugoslavia-based multinationals originate from a country whose socioeconomic system sets it apart from the rest of the world, the main sources of advantage of Yugoslav multinationals bear many similarities to those of the newly industrializing countries of the Third World. As this study will illustrate, Yugoslav multinationals show strength mainly in the use of low- and small-scale technology; they have a comparative advantage in the production and export of labour-intensive commodities; Yugoslav foreign investments are comparatively limited and on a small scale by the international standards of multinational activities, and there is a clear preference for trade and marketing investments in the DMEs, but for manufacturing and construction in LDCs.

Table 12.3 Number, Location and Distribution by Principal Activity of Western Subsidiaries of Yugoslav Companies (as of 1987)

Host Country	Activity					Total
	1 Trading	2 Manufacturing	3 Services	4 Banks	Combination of 1, 2, 3, 4	
EUROPE						
Austria	21	10	6		9	37
Belgium	1	3				4
Denmark	3		2			5
France	12	1	1	1	4	15
Germany	30	19	10	1	9	60
Greece	5				2	5
Italy	28	9	4		6	41
Liechtenstein	6					6
Netherlands	3	2	4		1	9
Portugal	1					1
Spain	1		1			2
Sweden	6		1			7
Switzerland	18	1	6			25
Turkey	2				1	2
United Kingdom	10	4	7	1	5	22

NORTH AMERICA						
Canada	2	2	1		1	5
USA	26	4	4	1	5	35
PACIFIC REGION						
Australia	2	2			1	4
Japan	2					2
TOTAL	179	57	47	4	44	287

Source: Federal Secretariat for Foreign Economic Relations, Belgrade.

(predominantly shipping) and financial services. A number of representative offices have also been set up abroad, with Germany, Italy and the UK the major recipients. These are concentrated predominantly in the financial, transport and travel services. Table 12.4 shows that, of the 241 representative offices identified by the Federal Secretariat for Foreign Economic Relations, 112 are engaged in services and 47 in banking and insurance. The latter trend is to a large extent attributable to the regionalization of the Yugoslav banking system: each republic and autonomous province has its own bank with its own network of branches overseas. The predominance of Yugoslav banks in the UK and Germany also confirms the pulling influence of London and Frankfurt as leading European financial centres. The second largest group of representative offices is directed to the provision of transport services (mostly airlines) which complement the burgeoning tourist market in Yugoslavia and its importance as a hard currency earner.

Motivation for Investment

This section examines the motivating factors behind the growth of Yugoslav enterprises in the DMEs. Wells (1983) has identified five major factors that have prompted the growth of LDC firms abroad: these include the search for cheaper markets, risk diversification, the defence of export markets, offshore production and the existence of ethnic ties. Diversification has clearly been an important factor for Yugoslav firms setting up activities in the West: the 287 subsidiaries listed in Table 12.1 span 19 European, North American and Australasian countries. Generalexport, whose activities include international trade, tour operating, hotels and catering and air transport, has some 35 overseas operations in the DMEs; INA has set up 11 subsidiaries in 6 countries (many of which are travel agencies), whilst Interexport, Iskra, UNIS and Gorenje have each established five or more subsidiaries in at least five countries. Ethnic ties with neighbouring countries and investments in support of exports to Western markets are two other principal motives for Yugoslav firms abroad.

A similar pattern of diversification emerges in the banking sector. Two major banks – Ljubljanska Banka and Udružena Beogradska Banka have 13 and 9 offices respectively operating in 10 and 9 Western countries. Wells (1983) has observed that the overseas banking operations of LDC firms reflect closely the trade flows of the parent countries, whilst McMillan (1979; 1987) has found that the trading, marketing and manufacturing functions of Soviet companies abroad have been supported by a well-established banking infrastructure. This complementarity of investment and banking functions is pertinent to the Yugoslav experience, where the close inter-relationship between enterprises and banks on a republican basis has often been duplicated in overseas operations. Examples include Koprodukt and Vojvodjanska Banka in the UK; Macedonia Steel and Stopanska Banka in the UK; Intertrade and Ljubljanska Banka in Japan; and Interco Handel and Stopanska Banka in Germany.

As Tables 12.3 and 12.4 illustrate, Yugoslav banks have employed different forms of organization overseas: the most popular route is the branch office, followed by the setting up of subsidiary banks. A handful of joint banking ventures have also been entered into with foreign banking partners.

Yugoslav banks abroad serve a variety of purposes: they provide a channel to Western money markets for the financing of Yugoslav trade, as well as advice and financial data for Yugoslav exporters. A significant volume of export business is also conducted through the foreign affiliates of the banks' customers.

In our survey the 25 sample firms were asked why they invested abroad. Table 12.5 reports the responses of Yugoslav managers which are ranked in a descending order of importance. The prevalent motive has been to boost export promotion, with 12 firms citing the objective of export-marketing as 'very important' or 'important'. Traditionally Yugoslav firms have lacked the incentives and flexibility to respond to changes on external markets. The ongoing programme of modernization and restructuring of the Yugoslav economy is partly based on liberalizing imports of technology with a view to creating greater competition for domestic industries, which often enjoy a monopolistic position in the domestic market. The objective of export promotion can therefore be seen as an important stimulus to economic reform; the firms interviewed thought that the establishment of foreign subsidiaries provided a more effective marketing technique than local agents in promoting the exports of increasingly diversified products and services. Trade missions and chambers of commerce in the West are increasingly seen as lacking in specialized knowledge to identify the needs of Western customers, a function gradually taken over by

Table 12.4   Number, Location and Distribution by Principal Activity of Representative Offices of Yugoslav Companies in the West (as of 1987)

Host Country	Activity				Combination of 1, 2, 3, 4	Total
	1 Trading	2 Manufacturing	3 Services	4 Banks		
EUROPE						
Austria		2	9	4	2	15
Belgium	1	3	1			5
Denmark	1	1	1			3
France	2	2	5	4		13
Finland	1					1
Germany	5	4	25	8	3	42
Greece	2	1	8			11
Italy	6	5	15	6	2	32
Liechtenstein	1					1
Netherlands	–	2	1	1		4
Norway	2		1			3
Portugal	1					1
Spain	2	1	2	1	2	6
Sweden	1	1	3	2		7
Switzerland	1	1	1	1		4
Turkey	2	2	1		1	5
United Kingdom	3	4	8	8	1	23

NORTH AMERICA

Canada	10		3	2	5	
USA		9	19	8	46	

PACIFIC REGION

Australia	1	2	4	2	9	
Japan			5		5	
TOTAL	42	40	112	47	10	241

Source: Federal Secretariat for Foreign Economic Relations, Belgrade.

Table 12.5 Motivation for Foreign Investment by Yugoslav Firms

Motivation	Average score[a]	Ranking of motives	Total number of responses
Export promotion	1.50	1	12
Source of hard currency	1.59	2	17
To supply the host country market	1.64	3	14
To facilitate access to international financial markets	1.71	4	14
Access to higher levels of technology	1.85	5	13
To increase profitability	1.86	6	14
To defend existing markets	2.08	7	12
Product diversification	2.17	8	12
To circumvent tariff and non-tariff barriers	2.25	9	12
To reduce transport costs	2.27	10	11
As a point of entry into the EC	2.36	11	11

Notes: [a] Average scores were derived as follows: (i) very important, (ii) important, (iii) unimportant.

Source: Cardiff University Business School, Yugoslav Foreign Investment Data Bank.

some marketing subsidiaries acting as *in situ* purchasing agents for their Yugoslav parents.

Access to hard currency has been another significant motive for Yugoslav investments in the West (mentioned by 17 respondents). Trading companies earning capital through foreign subsidiaries have been able to finance their expansion and diversify through reinvested profits and local borrowing. Other market considerations for the investment included the desire to supply the host-country market (14 firms) and to facilitate access to international financial markets (14), the latter explaining the relatively high concentration of subsidiaries in the London and Frankfurt areas. Differences in levels of development between Yugoslavia and DMEs also explain why Yugoslav investors have placed emphasis on gaining access to higher levels of technology. Profitability and the defence of existing export markets are also major motivations. Access to raw materials, whilst an important motive of Yugoslav investors in LDCs (Artisien, Rojec and Svetličič, 1991), has not been an incentive to invest in the DMEs.

To sum up, our sample has illuminated two distinctive characteristics in the motivation of Yugoslav enterprises in the DMEs: first, market-related factors (including the growth of an export base and the potential accessibility to host-country markets) have prevailed. Second, financial objectives, including closer proximity to financial markets and the availability of hard currency have produced a concentration of investments in the European Community's leading financial centres, London, Frankfurt, Milan and Paris. Finally, to a large extent, foreign investments have been targeted at host countries in parallel with existing trade patterns.

Scale of Operations

The broad geographical and functional distribution of Yugoslav direct investments in the West referred to above provides only a partial picture of the scale of operations to which these investments have given rise. Hence, other measures of investment activity are examined below.

Systematic data on employment levels in the Western affiliates of Yugoslav companies have proved difficult to assemble. The Centre for International Cooperation and Development in Ljubljana has estimated that, at the end of 1986, Yugoslav enterprises abroad employed 10,684 people, of which 4,800 (45 per cent) were employed in the DMEs.

Table 12.6, which provides employment figures for 42 companies, shows that 22 firms (52 per cent of the sample) have between 1 and 9 employees; 9 (21 per cent) have 10–19 employees; 5 firms (12 per cent) employ between 20 and 29 people, and only 6 firms (14 per cent) more than 30. Firms employing fewer than 20 employees are engaged mainly in trading activities, whilst those with more than 20 employees are concentrated in the more labour-intensive service

Table 12.6 Number of Employees in Forty-two Western Subsidiaries

Employee size	Number of respondents	Percentage representation (%)
1–9	22	52
10–19	9	21
20–29	5	12
over 30	6	14
Total	42	100

Source: Cardiff University Business School, Yugoslav Foreign Investment Data Bank.

sector, particularly banking. Thus, in terms of employees, the scale of Yugoslav operations in the West is quite small.

However, the value of the equity capital invested in the banking sector is not negligible, ranging from £5 million for UK-based banks to Schillings 80 million in Austria and DM90 million in Germany. The operations of some firms contacted in our survey are also quite extensive: the London-based trading company, BSE-Genex, is ranked 266th among Britain's largest 500 companies with sales in 1987 of £300,000, a rate of return on capital of 20 per cent and a workforce of 47.

An analysis of profit as a percentage of turnover is presented in Table 12.7 and suggests that few of the sample companies have performed well: over 50 per cent reported a profit/turnover ratio of 1 per cent or less, and another 20 per cent of respondents between 1 per cent and 2 per cent. Only one company reported a profit margin of more than 4 per cent. It appears, therefore, that Yugoslav companies in the West are operating at comparatively low levels of business performance, well below the average profitability levels of Western firms. Such a low profit-margin is consistent with the defensive activities of firms seeking to penetrate new markets in a highly competitive environment, rather than with the consolidation strategy of a market leader in possession of a differentiated product. Our findings also depart from the conventional view that firms attempting to maximize sales revenue do so subject to a profit constraint (normally a satisfactory return on the shareholders' investment). In the case of Yugoslav firms abroad, a targeted profit margin of 1 per cent seems indeed to be an unlikely profit constraint. Thus, the Western subsidiaries of Yugoslav firms attempt to maximize sales revenue to enable them to continue in operation, a strategy prompted both by competition levels on Western markets

Table 12.7 Profit Margins of Western Subsidiaries During 1987

Range of profit/ Turnover ratios (%)	0	0–1	1–2	2–3	3–4	over 4%
Number of companies	2	12	5	2	2	1

Source: Cardiff University Business School, Yugoslav Foreign Investment Data Bank.

and the lack of competitiveness of Yugoslav products. It is probably safe to conclude that Yugoslav parent firms do not view their Western subsidiaries as a means of securing high profits, but as vehicles of market penetration.

Success

This section addresses itself to the sample firms' perception of the fulfilment of expectations: the underlying premise being that the companies concerned are better equipped than any external observer to determine what constitutes success in their particular situation. The results are summarized in Table 12.8.

First, sample firms were asked to compare the results of their overseas operations with their expectations. Ten of the 12 respondents were satisfied with the outcome, which ranged from 'satisfactory' to 'very successful'. This finding was strengthened by 8 of the 9 respondents declaring to be satisfied with the *financial* objectives achieved. The next set of questions relating to the comparative profitability of operations in the West and in Yugoslavia revealed that 77 per cent perceived their activities in the West as either more profitable than, or as profitable as, their home-based operations. This evidence reinforces the argument that non-profit objectives played an important part in the firms' assessment of performance. Moreover, given the aforementioned low levels of profitability, two further sets of observations suggest themselves: first, expectations regarding financial performance were set at a low level; second, profit margins, albeit low, were deemed satisfactory by the firms concerned. Although conclusions drawn from a relatively small sample must remain tentative, the relatively high level of satisfaction described by a majority of respondents prompts the observation that the sample is tilted towards success rather than failure. The

Table 12.8 Success Indicators

Response		Number of firms	%
Actual outcome met expectations		10	83
Actual outcome did not meet expectations		2	17
Financial objectives met expectations		8	89
Financial objectives did not meet expectations		1	11
Host country is more profitable than Yugoslavia		5	38.5
Host country is as profitable as Yugoslavia		5	38.5
Host country is less profitable than Yugoslavia		3	23
Have operations been	Yes	10	71.5
expanded in host country?	No	4	28.5

Source: Cardiff University Business School, Yugoslav Foreign Investment Data Bank.

profit/turnover figures further suggest that, although the Western subsidiaries of Yugoslav firms are less profitable than wholly Western-owned companies, they are regarded primarily by their Yugoslav parents as channels to secure hard currency, with sufficient profits to stay in business or even generate expansion (this finding is corroborated by Malcolm Hill's survey of Comecon companies in the UK, Ireland and Sweden, 1986). It is pertinent to note that 10 out of 14 sample firms expanded the physical capacity of operations in the host countries.

Ownership Patterns

Yugoslav companies in the West are in the main wholly- or majority-owned. Table 12.2 indicated a strong preference for sole ownership, with 224 firms (72.7 per cent) wholly-owned by the Yugoslav parent, and 30 firms (9.8 per cent) majority-owned. In the remaining 54 firms (17.5 per cent) the Yugoslav parent has a minority share of the equity. This contrasts with the ownership pattern of Yugoslav firms in LDCs, where minority-owned enterprises were prevalent (34 out of a total of 64, or 53.2 per cent). A number of reasons suggest themselves: first, DMEs generally impose fewer ownership restrictions on foreign firms in an attempt to encourage inward investment. Second, the structure of ownership is

Table 12.9 Ownership Structure of Yugoslav Investments in the West

Period of Investment	Majority Yugoslav ownership		50–50 ownership split	Minority Yugoslav ownership	Representative Offices	Total
	Single	Joint				
1945–59	5	2	0	0	3	10
1960–75	17	4	1	2	2	26
1976–	4	2	2	0	11	19
Unknown	3	0	0	2	7	12
Total	29	8	3	4	23	67

Source: Cardiff University Business School, Yugoslav Foreign Investment Data Bank.

often determined by the nature of the activity in which the investment is made (McMillan, 1987). Our survey has established that wholly- and majority-owned Yugoslav enterprises are associated with trade, retailing and services, which by their nature tend to require clear control. Third, trading subsidiaries, unlike their manufacturing counterparts, minimize the amount of equity capital required, thus reducing the financial constraints on Yugoslavia's scarce hard currency reserves. Moreover, regardless of the extent of its equity holding, the Yugoslav partner can exercise effective control through the functional as much as the organizational structure of its subsidiary, as the latter's assets are often of secondary importance to the supply of goods by the Yugoslav partner. As McMillan (1987) observes, the East European partner's 'key role as the source of technology, capital and other major inputs to the operation provides in most instances the basis for its controlling influence, regardless of the degree of its formal ownership'.

Our survey results of 67 respondents in Table 12.9 confirm that the majority of firms (84 per cent) are majority-owned; 9 per cent are minority-owned, and 7 percent consist of 50–50 split ownership. Majority-owned companies are divided between single majority, where the Yugoslav parent holds a majority stake of the equity, and joint majority, where a conglomerate of Yugoslav companies have invested jointly, but not necessarily in equal shares, in setting up the subsidiary. Single-majority-owned subsidiaries predominate and range from small units to very large organizations, which operate with a considerable degree of autonomy.

Although subsidiary companies abroad are generally preferred to representative offices, the latter have been used to test the host-market potential for expansion and to provide a service, particularly in banking and transport. Not infrequently, representative offices have been established by the foreign subsidiaries of Yugoslav parents as means of promotion and information gathering.

Concluding Remarks

An attempt has been made in this paper to raise and answer a number of questions about direct investment by Yugoslav firms in the Western economies. In response to the first question – what are the major determinants behind the growth of Yugoslav FDI in the DMEs? – we noted that the process of economic decentralization initiated by the 1965 reforms had spurred enterprises to integrate more fully with the world economy. However, unlike their counterparts in the West, Yugoslav multinationals do not manufacture new or exclusive products, but rely on adaptations of standard technologies. This explains the under-representation of Yugoslav investors in the manufacturing sector, where they lack the necessary firm-specific advantages to internalize operations. Instead, investments have been channelled into the trade and service industries, with the principal objective of promoting the export marketing of the parent companies.

Our second question addressed itself to the motives of Yugoslav investments in the DMEs; the primary motive was to service markets directly rather than at arm's length or through intermediaries. Another important motive was to use the subsidiaries as a source of hard currency in order to finance their expansion. Few of these companies have extended their operations beyond trading on behalf of their Yugoslav parents. However, because the parent companies tend to be multi-product enterprises, most subsidiaries trade in a diversified range of goods and services, including banking and tourism. Trade promotion has been supported by investments in financial services: Yugoslavia's republican banks have established operations in the major Western financial centres. The desirability of partnerships with local Western firms was acknowledged by most interviewees, not only as a means of improving marketing techniques, but also with a view to setting up technological linkages for their back-up producers at home.

The third question – related to the scale of operations and their success – established that the subsidiaries were quite small by international standards (both in terms of employees and turnover), and that profitability levels, albeit low, sufficed the parents' objectives of market diversification and slow growth.

Fourth, it was suggested that Yugoslav multinationals in the West, like their Comecon counterparts, had a preference for majority ownership. This reflected both the open door policy of the host countries *vis-à-vis* inward investment, and the concentration of subsidiaries in the trade and service industries, which tend to require clear control.

Finally, there is little doubt that the realization of the Single European Market in 1992 should stimulate long-term growth and encourage exports and investment from non-member states, such as Yugoslavia. The proximity of the Single Market offers scope for the more competitive Yugoslav firms (in particular those prepared to engage in the production of sophisticated products and services) to intensify their import-substituting outward investments among EC member states, particularly those countries with which Yugoslavia shares a longstanding trading tradition (Germany and Italy). The potential for establishing a base in the EC in order to take full advantage of new opportunities brought about by standardization and harmonization measures will, however, ultimately depend on the speed with which Yugoslav investors can increase the tempo of modernization in their industries, and by implication raise their international competitiveness.

Bibliography

Artisien, P., *Yugoslavia to 1993: Back from the Brink ?*, Economist Intelligence Unit, London, 1989

Artisien, P., M. Rojec and M. Svetličič (1991), 'Yugoslav Foreign Direct Investment in Less Developed Countries', in P. J. Buckley and J. Clegg (eds.), *Multinational Enterprises in Less Developed Countries*, London, Macmillan

Artisien, P., C. H. McMillan and M. Rojec (1992), *Yugoslav Multinationals Abroad*, Macmillan, London

Hill, M. R. (1986), 'Soviet and Eastern European Company Activity in the

United Kingdom and Ireland', in G. Hamilton (ed.), *Red Multinationals or Red Herrings?*, London, Frances Pinter

McMillan, C. H. (1979), *Soviet Investment in the Industrialised Western Economies and in the Developing Economies of the Third World*, Joint Economic Committee, US Congress, Washington DC

——(1987), *Multinationals from the Second World*, London, Macmillan

Svetličič, M. and M. Rojec (1985), *New forms of Equity Investment by Yugoslav Firms in Developing Countries*, Paris, OECD

——(1986), *Investment among Developing Countries and Transnational Corporations*, Ljubljana, Research Centre for Cooperation with Developing Countries, and Harare, Zimbabwe Institute of Development Studies

Wells, L. T. (1983), *Third World Multinationals*, Cambridge, Mass., MIT Press

13

Economic Development and Institutional Underdevelopment: Tourism and the Private Sector in Yugoslavia*

John B. Allcock

Introduction

Although in many respects Yugoslavia had made huge strides in the transformation of its economy and society over the post-war period, it is important to recognize that in some areas of the economy there has been a distinct lag in the creation of appropriate institutional structures. This means that whereas Yugoslavia is able to maintain the superficial appearance of being a quite highly developed country, not far beneath the surface there are still indicators of its underdeveloped status.[1]

The focal concern of this chapter is this 'institutional underdevelopment'; and this concept needs to be understood in relation to the more common sociological term 'institutionalization'. The latter refers to the emergence in the society of taken-for-granted and routine ways of conducting relationships between participants, and to the creation of established models of acceptable conduct for

* This paper reports some of the work done towards a wider study of tourism in Yugoslavia. It has been financed in part by the exchange scheme between the British and Yugoslav Academies, and in part by the cultural exchange scheme between the two countries administered by the British Council. The author would like to thank in particular Dr Ante Kobašić of the Fakultet za turizam i vanjsku trgovinu (Faculty for Tourism and Foreign Trade), Dubrovnik, for his assistance.

1. Good general introductions to the post-war transformation of the Yugoslav economy are found in: Fred Singleton and B. Carter, *The Yugoslav Economy* (London, Croom Helm, 1982); H. Lydall, *Yugoslav Socialism: Theory and Practice* (Oxford, Clarendon Press, 1984); H. Lydall, *Yugoslavia in Crisis* (Oxford, Clarendon Press, 1989); D. Dyker, *Yugoslavia: Socialism, Development and Debt* (London, Routledge, 1990).

which people spontaneously reach when faced with the need to undertake some task or another.

The problems of 'institutional underdevelopment' dealt with in this chapter are not lags which arise because of the persistence of traditional, or 'pre-modern', elements of values or social organization. They are contradictions which relate largely to differences in the conception of development and its desirable direction, held by various groups in Yugoslav society. Change, development, modernity, however one likes to term it, are not in question. What is in question is the kind of society which Yugoslavia should and can be, and the routes by which these ends are most appropriately achieved. These various concepts of development, which probably reflect contests of real interest between groups in Yugoslav society, become encapsulated in institutional forms. This is not a rapid process, however; and precisely because there is conflict over the institutionalization of certain arrangements in society, it is possible for the superficial aspects of economic change to have gone a long way while these less obvious, but in many ways nevertheless basic issues, remain unresolved beneath the surface.

Economic development can thus coincide with institutional under-development. These general ideas are in no way confined in their relevance to Yugoslavia; and the intention of this chapter is in part to suggest their general utility while concerning ourselves directly with a specific aspect of institutional change in Yugoslavia. These ideas are important for the understanding of several aspects of contemporary Yugoslavia, but we will simply illustrate them by reference to some facets of the growth of tourism in the post-war years. Before taking up this central task, however, it will be useful to place the discussion within the context of several central features of the recent history of the country (dealt with more fully in other contributions to this volume), and to sketch in very shortly the general shape of the development of its tourist industry.

Some characteristics of contemporary Yugoslavia

Of particular relevance for our present concern is the way in which the post-war regime has sought to pursue a socialist path of development, or possibly more accurately, the ways in which it has been compelled to adapt its aspirations in this respect, to the exigencies of both internal and external conditions.

Yugoslavia emerged from the Second World War with its leadership full of confidence in their own power to push through a radical and strongly centralized form of socialism closely modelled on the Soviet system of planning. The divisions which opened up in the late 1940s between the Yugoslavs and the rest of the socialist bloc pushed Yugoslavia initially into a position of isolation. Two important consequences are generally held to have followed from this: a rapid movement towards greater reliance on the capitalist countries for both trade and technical cooperation, and the creation of the famous system of 'workers' self-management'. Although in the course of the world economic crisis following the 'second oil shock' of 1979 Yugoslavia found that the balance of its trade began to shift once more towards the CMEA countries, generally speaking throughout the post-war period its stance has been one of close involvement with Western Europe and economic openness to the forces of the world market. In this respect the country's observer status with the OECD and its special relationship with the European Economic Community are indicative of the general pattern.

Self-management emerged in the 1950s largely as an answer to the needs of the regime for a distinctively socialist legitimation both at home and abroad. The expansion of the system beyond its specifically industrial beginnings provided – in theory at least – for a very radical decentralization of ownership, control and administration. It matched well, ideologically speaking, the emphasis on decentralization which also emerged as the political response to the continuing problems posed by the existence of Yugoslavia's numerous nationalities and national minorities.

Along with economic and political decentralization there went, not surprisingly, a decline in the capacity of central bodies to plan, and dictate courses of action to the component elements of the system. This did not involve a simple replacement of planning by market forces. Within the space vacated by central planning and control negotiation emerged, in the shape of 'social compacts' and 'self-managing agreements', as the chief means of political and economic coordination. In large measure these have served, along with more informal controls, to ensure that the movement towards a market economy has been a very imperfect and incomplete one, giving ample scope for continuing political interference in the economic process, if not for planning in its more conventional sense.

Critics of the Yugoslav system frequently claim that these devices have created as many problems as they have solved; and in some respects this point has been conceded by the provisions of several of the statutory reforms which are under discussion. In particular, far greater emphasis is being placed upon the market as a principal mechanism for coordination and the allocation of resources, and a clearer disengagement of political influences from the economy is envisaged. A more precisely defined role is sought for those institutions and mechanisms, such as the banking system, through which a central policy for the management of the economy might be implemented. It is central to my present interest to emphasize the importance of this tense balance between political control and market forces within the Yugoslav economy, and of the continuing political sensitivity of everything which bears on these questions.

Yugoslavia's tourist industry: an overview

The growth of tourism in Yugoslavia can be summarized conveniently in six phases.[2] Tourism in the area now included in Yugoslavia has quite a long history. The Istrian Peninsula and several towns in the Julian Alps, together with parts of the Adriatic coast, were developed as luxury resorts, largely funded by Austrian or Hungarian interests, before the First World War. This came to play quite an important part in preserving the country's balance of trade before 1939.

The years after 1945 saw a marked contrast in the type of tourism which was developed. Under the regime of administrative socialism, democratization, state control and extensive subsidization became central features of the new tourism serving a principally domestic clientele. Following the break with the Cominform in 1948, it was realized once again that the sector could play an important part in the solution of the country's balance of payments problems. There was a gradual reorientation, by which trade was placed once more on a commercial footing, subsidies were phased out, and efforts made to attract the foreign visitor.

2. See Ante Kobašić, 'Lessons from Planning in Yugoslavia's Tourist Industry', *International Journal of Tourism Management*, December 1980, pp. 233–9; Tomislav Hitrec, Ante Mandosić, Boris Pirjavec and Boris Vukonić, *Pride and Problems of Tourism in Yugoslavia*, Zagreb, Papers presented to the 32nd Congress of AIEST, September 1982; John B. Allcock, 'Yugoslavia's Tourist Trade: Pot of Gold or Pig in a Poke?', *Annals of Tourism Research*, Vol. 13, No. 4, 1986, pp. 565–88; Ante Kobašić, *Turizam u Jugoslaviji* (Zagreb, Informator, 1987).

Table 13.1 The Growth of Yugoslavia's International Tourist Trade, 1948–89

Years	Three year averages (000s)		Percentage of foreign tourists	Balance of earnings in US$
	No. of tourists	No. of foreign tourists		
	(1)	(2)	(3)	(4)
1948–50	2,019	45	2	
1951–53	2,823	358	5	
1954–56	3,258	400	12	
1957–59	4,076	644	16	
1960–62	5,253	1,065	20	24,517
1963–65	7,059	2,213	31	76,397
1966–68	9,348	3,667	39	173,133
1969–71	11,990	4,911	41	325,568
1972–74	13,888	5,583	40	606,576
1975–77	19,927	5,676	36	803,861
1978–80	18,010	6,254	35	962,933
1981–83	18,666	6,176	30	1,036,300
1984–86	21,542	8,041	31	1,146,967
1987–89	22,033	8,954	41	1,794,000

Sources:
Cols. (1) and (2):
  1948–60, *Statistički Pregled Jugoslavije: 1945–65*, Belgrade, SZS, 1965
  1961–80, *Tourism in Yugoslavia*, Belgrade, Tourist Association of Yugoslavia, 1981
  1981–89, *Statistički Godišnjak SFRJ*, Belgrade, SZS, relevant years
Col. (4):
  1960–78, *Tourism in Yugoslavia*
  1979–89, OECD, *Tourism Policy and International Tourism in OECD Member Countries*, Paris, OECD, relevant years

The most important period of growth in international tourism took place following the economic reform of 1965. The expansion of tourism became a priority of both federal and republican planning, and a battery of fiscal, credit and other measures were instituted in order to speed up the process of expansion. The effects of these policies are reflected clearly in Table 13.1.

The 'first oil shock' in 1973 introduced the fifth phase of the process. In the years of economic crisis which followed, Yugoslavia maintained its place in the international league table of tourist destinations. Development policy remained hesitant and confused with respect to tourism, however, and the process of economic reorganization set in motion by the new Law on Associated Labour, in 1976, also posed some structural problems for the sector.

The critical review of the Yugoslav economy by the International Monetary Fund in 1983, and the stringent requirements which were laid down in that period by the country's foreign creditors, herald the final phase of tourist development. Once again, the need to boost export earnings turned the attention of policy makers to the importance of tourism, which has become for the second time a planning and investment priority.

The importance of tourism for the Yugoslav economy can be measured in a number of ways. Currently, arrivals from abroad fluctuate at around the 8 million mark per annum, recording somewhere in excess of 50 million overnight stays. Yugoslav official sources make much of the fact that foreign currency earnings from this source for the first time in 1987 exceeded US$1,500 millions, and for many years the sector has been the largest contributor to Yugoslavia's balance of 'invisibles'.[3] Tourism and catering now employ about 250,000 Yugoslavs (excluding seasonal labour), which means that they embrace more than 4 per cent of the employed labour force. (Seasonal employment may add between a quarter and a third to that total.)[4]

Against the background of these considerations it is now possible to address specific examples of 'institutional under-development' in Yugoslavia. For this purpose two closely related illustrations have been chosen which give a point of entry into broader issues of policy and values arising in the transformation of Yugoslav society. I shall consider first of all the problematic status of private enterprise within the socialist framework of the Yugoslav economy. Second, I shall focus on the more specific issue of the significance of the underdevelopment of the taxation system of that country. These will be discussed specifically in relation to tourism.

---

3. Note the problem of estimating correctly figures both in relation to numbers of tourists and earnings from tourism in Yugoslavia (as in other countries). Yugoslav statistics do not separate 'tourists' in the narrower sense from any other type of traveller or visitor. Regarding estimates of foreign currency earned, the figures quoted in this paper are all based on OECD sources, which are generally lower than other estimates. No attempt is made to adjudicate between them.

4. Figures from *Statistički Godišnjak SFRJ*, 1988. On the significance of seasonality, see John B. Allcock, 'Seasonality', in Stephen F. Witt and Luiz Moutinho (eds.), *Tourism Marketing and Management Handbook* (London, Prentice Hall, 1989), pp. 387–92. The estimation of numbers is particularly difficult in this area, which is so heavily involved in the 'grey economy'.

The private sector in Yugoslav tourism and catering

The position and role of private ownership of the means of production have always been, not surprisingly, surrounded by difficulties in Yugoslavia. Although in many respects the situation of the entrepreneur has been easier in Yugoslavia than in the other socialist countries the match between the overall strategy of socialist development pursued by the state and the interests of the private business proprietor has remained awkward.[5]

The constitution of the Federal Republic unambiguously permits the establishment of private businesses. Article 64 of the Constitution of 1974 guarantees 'the freedom of independent, individual work with the means of work in the possession of the citizen', and declares the right of citizens to associate with each other, and with cooperative and social sector enterprises, in pursuit of legitimate business aims. It is specified that this must take place in such a way that it is not 'in contradiction with the principle of obtaining income according to one's work', which is taken to be the foundation of other aspects of socialist social organization. By Amendment XXI of the Constitution, of November 1988, this commitment is strengthened.[6] The details of the application of this are left to specific legislative provision. Up until the revision of the law in 1989 this was taken to mean that any individual proprietor could employ up to five people other than members of the immediate family. Under the package of recently introduced economic reforms this number was expanded.[7]

5. For an interesting, though by now somewhat dated, comparison of the private sector in Yugoslavia and some CMEA countries, see Tatjana Globokar, 'Le Rôle des entreprises privées en Pologne, RDA, Tchecoslovaquie, Yougoslavie', *Le Courrier des pays de l'est*, No. 281, February 1984, pp. 3–23. The entire number is devoted to this general theme.

6. 'Ustav Socijalističke Federativne Republike Jugoslavije' (Constitution of the Socialist Federal Republic of Yugoslavia), *Službeni List SFRJ*, No. 9, 21 February 1974. See articles 64–8, esp. art. 64. The place of the self-employed is also acknowledged in the *Programme of the League of Yugoslav Communists* (London, ISSS, 1959, pp. 106–9), while at the same time, ambiguously, committing the League to continued struggle against the 'remnants of the bourgeoisie' and their 'harmful influence'. See also comment by Catherine Samary, *Le Marché contre l'autogestion: l'expérience Yougoslave* (Paris, Le Breche, 1988), pp. 88–90.

7. In the case of tourism and catering enterprises the relevant regulations for the republic of Croatia are set out in: 'Zakon o ugostiteljskoj i turističkoj djelatnosti (prečišćeni tekst)' (Law on Catering and Touristic Activity (Revised Text)) *Narodne novine: Službeni List SRH*, 1981, pp. 537–54, articles 4 and 36–62, esp. art. 58. There are some differences between provision in the various republics, but these need not concern us here. For the recent legal changes relating to the private sector, see: 'Zakon o poduzećima' (Law on Enterprises), *Službeni List SFRJ*, 77/88. Under the new legislation the precise numbers which any private employer may take on are left to be determined by the republics.

A review of the growth and importance of the private sector in Yugoslavia is not easy. Official statistics are meagre, and there has been little systematic study of the area undertaken by Yugoslav social scientists. Two important exceptions to this are to be found in the work of Čedo Grbić, whose discussion is by and large restricted to the descriptive level, and Andrija Gams, whose principal concerns are philosophical and juridical in character.[8] Neither can be said to have provided us with an adequate economic or sociological appraisal of the role of private property in post-war Yugoslavia. This is hardly surprising since, as in other socialist countries, the topic has been guaranteed to bring to the surface a variety of phenomena of a dubious, if not semi-legal character, which have rendered detailed study unwelcome on the part of both the business community and the state. There have been obvious incentives for concealment of the real extent of development, which will to some extent be considered below. Bearing in mind the fact that there are serious limitations in the information which is available to us, however, it is possible to put together some kind of picture of this section of Yugoslavia's tourist industry.

The private sector in the Yugoslav economy has always been dominated by the small agricultural producer, who cultivated (in 1987) about 8 million of the country's 9.8 million hectares of agricultural land.[9] It is, however, by no means confined to farming. Building, transport, the servicing and repair of motor vehicles and electrical appliances, together with catering and a variety of other personal services, are all heavily represented. In 1987, the individual producer provided 59.1 per cent of the social product in craft industry, 15.6 per cent in construction, and 14 per cent in tourism and catering.[10]

There has been a general decline in the importance of the small-holding in agricultural production, reflecting the general processes of urbanization and industrialization at work in the country, and an expansion of the various types of non-agricultural enterprise. (It is,

8. Čedo Grbić, *Socijalizam i rad privatnim sredstvima* (Socialism and Work with Private Means) (Zagreb, Biblioteka Socijalističko Samoupravljanje i Suvremeni Svijet, 1984); Andrija Gams, *Svojina* (Property) (Belgrade, Center za filozofiju i društvenu teoriju, 1987). The most thorough discussions dealing with this field available in English are: Singleton and Carter, *Yugoslav Economy*, Chapter 16; Lydall, *Yugoslav Socialism* (1984), Chapter 13; Dyker, *Yugoslavia*.
9. *Statistički Godišnjak SFRJ*, 1988, p. 240.
10. Ibid., p. 166. It is necessary to stress the approximate nature of these figures, and the importance of the 'grey economy'.

of course, too early to say what effect, if any, the recent changes in the law relating to the maximum permitted size of private land holding will have on this trend.) The pattern varies considerably from region to region.

Turning specifically to tourism, the expansion of trade generally in Yugoslavia has been reflected in the private sector in two particular ways – in the growth of the number of catering establishments and in the provision of accommodation. In the case of the former, the rate of growth is indicated by the figures for the numbers of establishments, numbers employed and turnover, for the whole Yugoslav federation, given in Table 13.2. These data should be treated with a measure of caution (as should all others which have been presented in this chapter), since there is reason to believe that the trend they portray may be more apparent than real, and may reflect the growth in the registration of private businesses rather than their increasing real numbers.[11]

The principal impetus toward the expansion of private enterprise probably came with the economic reform of 1965. This not only ushered in a period of (generally) more liberal economic policy, but also for the first time raised the expansion of tourism to the first rank of economic priorities. The private entrepreneur was explicitly expected to play a role, which was given public definition in both the Five-Year Plan inaugurated in that year, and the new law dealing with the catering activities of private citizens.[12] According to Dulčić, this law was quite specifically formulated with the intention of stimulating individuals to move into the provision of tourism and catering services.[13] This stimulation was backed by the limited

11. See Krešimir Tadej, 'Samostalno ugostiteljstvo u sadašnjem razvoju' (Independent Catering in Contemporary Development), *Turizam*, Vol. 16, No. 1, 1968, pp. 23–5. Prior to the law of 1965 the licensing of private enterprise was at the discretion of the commune. There was widespread illegal development which became legitimated by the new statutory provisions. Tadej suggests that these figures may reflect a transfer of some establishments previously registered as socially owned.
12. 'Osnovni zakon o ugostiteljskoj djelatnosti' (Basic Law on Catering Activity), *Službeni List SFRJ*, No. 8, 1965. See also Stjepan Čudina, 'Uloga i značaj ličnog rada u turizmu', Savjetovanje: 'Turizam kao faktor razvoja zemlje, Conference organized by the Društvo Ekonomista, Zagreb, Hvar, 24–7 October 1968. (Hereafter referred to as the 'Hvar Consultation'.) See *referat* No. 5, esp. p. 3. (The unpublished papers of this consultation are held in the Centre for Documentation, Fakultet za turizam i vanjsku trgovinu, Dubrovnik.)
13. Ante Dulčić, 'Mogućnost razvoja sitnih turističkih i ugostiteljskih djelatnosti na području Srednje Dalmacije' (The Possibility of the Development of Small Tourist and Catering Businesses in the Area of Central Dalmatia), in Ivan Petrić (ed.), *Uključivanje radnika u inozemstvu u proces privrednog i društvenog razvitka Srednje Dalmacije* (The Incorporation of Workers Abroad in the Process of the Economic and Social Development of Central Dalmatia) (Institut za Pomorsku,

Table 13.2 Participation of the Private Sector in Catering in Yugoslavia, 1961–87

Year	Business establishments			Numbers employed			Total turnover (millions of d.)		
	Total SFRJ	Private sector	(b) as % of (a)	Total SFRJ	Private sector	(d) as % of (c)	Total SFRJ	Private sector	(f) as % of (e)
	(a)	(b)		(c)	(d)		(e)	(f)	
1961	13,676	3,490	26	87,103	829	1	151,306	6,827	5
1971	25,286	11,958	47	147,096	9,745	7	11,479[a]	1,642[a]	14
1981	30,734	16,318	53	239,474	21,972	9	112,970	14,702	13
1987	39,030	23,266	60	293,266	29,160	10	2,508,680	345,865	14

Note: [a] 1 New dinar = 100 Old dinars: the currency was revalued in 1965.

Sources: Statistički Godišnjak FNRJ, 1962, pp. 214–15, Tables 213–14.
Statistički Godišnjak SFRJ, 1972, pp. 239–40, Tables 115–16 and 115–19.
Statistički Godišnjak SFRJ, 1982, p. 339, Tables 123–7.
Statistički Godišnjak SFRJ, 1988, p. 342, Tables 124–3 (Adapted).

expansion of credit facilities to those wishing to improve their property to meet the needs of the tourist trade.[14]

Between 1963 and 1968 the number of private catering firms in the Republic of Croatia grew from 865 to 3,461. (It is important to note that in the year before the introduction of the new law the reported number actually fell to 825.) By the end of this period more than a third of all catering establishments in the republic were in private hands. Dulčić's study of the Split region records that between 1966 and 1970 there was an expansion of the number of these establishments from 323 to 705, or a growth of 118 per cent in the four-year period.[15] This trend apparently continued throughout the 1970s and 1980s. By 1987 there were some 23,000 catering firms in private hands throughout the Yugoslav federation, employing more than 29,000 people in addition to the members of the proprietors' families.[16] It is noticeable that after the initial period of very rapid expansion, the rate of advance of private enterprise measured in terms of its share in both employment and the total volume of business has slowed, although there has been a steady advance in the absolute numbers of such firms.

A corresponding process can be documented for the emergence of the private citizen as a supplier of Yugoslavia's holiday accommodation, the proportion of which provided by private citizens has remained constant at roughly 40 per cent of the total for a long time now. Capacity has steadily expanded, however, from just over

---

Turističku i Obalnu Privredu, Split, Institut za Geografiju Sveučilišta u Zagrebu, Book II, *Mogućnost razvoja sitnih djelatnosti*, Split, 1972), pp. 287–365; see p. 304.

14. Credit support for the building or improvement of private accommodation to let for tourist purposes antedates the legislation discussed above. Measures were introduced in 1962, making available loans of up to 75,000 dinars per family. In the first two years of the scheme individual citizens took up 3.2 million dinars of such credit. The limit was raised after 1967 to 150,000 dinars per family. See Čudina, 'Uloga i značaj', p. 7; A. Božićević, 'Mjesto i uloga privatne zanatske inicijative u razvoju turizma' (The Place and Role of Private Craft Initiatives in the Development of Tourism), *Turizam*, Vol. 14, No. 5, 1965, pp. 2–4; esp. p. 3.

15. Dulčić, 'Mogućnost razvoja', pp. 316–17. See also his article, 'Sitne turističke i ugostiteljske djelatnosti u Srednjoj Dalmaciji' (Small Tourist and Catering Businesses in Central Dalmatia), *Turizam*, Vol. 22, Nos. 7–8, 1974, pp. 11–16. His figures indicate that by 1970 roughly 45 per cent of the turnover in catering in the region covered by his research was handled by private firms. See also Čudina, 'Uloga i značaj', p. 4.

16. See Franjo Radišić, *Turizam i turistička politika* (Tourism and Tourism Policy) (Pula, Istarska Naklada, 1981), pp. 89–90. It is likely that the employment role of the private sector is underestimated in these figures. Not only could there be a failure to register employment, but the author does not indicate the extent to which seasonality is considered in his figures. Also there is considerable room, with respect to the part played by members of the proprietor's family, for confusion over the status of 'employment'.

125,000 beds in the year before the reform of 1965, to more than 288,000 ten years later, and to around 449,000 in 1987.[17] Official figures relating to accommodation are far less reliable than those for catering, and it is generally acknowledged that they provide a considerable underestimation of the importance of the private sector in this respect. There is believed to be a considerable under-reporting of private accommodation through the official registration scheme; and these figures leave out of account entirely the use of private weekend cottages by the proprietors, their friends and families.[18]

The private sector also participates very significantly in the provision of other types of service in tourist areas, such as the manufacture and sale of souvenirs, the provision of guides, the running of taxi services and water excursions. Some of these activities may be quite important (for example, as is probably the case in most Yugoslav resorts, there are only privately owned taxis in Dubrovnik) though there is probably no way of making meaningful estimates of the total volume of trade accounted for in this manner. Such an estimate would, in any case, add nothing to our overall argument.

The controversial status of private enterprise

Several groups and individuals both within the academic and the business worlds in Yugoslavia have argued over the past two decades (sometimes quite strongly) for a more positive effort to be made to expand the part played by private initiative in the development of the country's tourist trade. The case has been made on many grounds.

17. *Statistički Godišnjak SFRJ*, 1988, p. 344.
18. The inaccuracy of Yugoslav official statistics (of which this is only one aspect) was emphasized to me in an interview with Professor Srdjan Marković (Zagreb, 23 June 1983), one of the authors of a report presented by a group of prominent Croatian economists to the Economic Chamber of Croatia (Privredna komora Hrvatske), in which it was estimated that there were at the time on the Adriatic coast as many as 1,000 unregistered private *pansioni* – not to mention other types of unregistered activity. See Peter Vidaković (ed.), *Turizam i ekonomska stabilizacija: Prilog za dugoročnog programa ekonomske stabilizacije* (Tourism and Economic Stabilization: A Contribution to the Long-Term Programme of Economic Stabilization) (Zagreb, Studeni, 1982), p. 98. See also Nenad Grozdanović, 'Uloga i značaj individualnog rada u turizmu' (The Role and Significance of Individual Work in Tourism), *referat*, No. 10, Hvar Consultation, p. 6. This discussion leaves out of account altogether the interesting question of the role of the *vikendica* (private weekend cottage).

It has been stated that a more freely developing individual economy would be more flexible than the socialist sector, which has in the past demonstrated a tendency to concentrate resources into large units.[19] One author has castigated this sector for its:

> orientation towards the building of large, often gargantuan capacities (offering) relatively low quality, in which organization and control are hindered by the failure to incorporate these into the functioning of a definite system. Large capacities certainly constitute for us the skeleton, in the economic sense, of the tourist economy; however, the inclusion into that economy of numerous smaller units is not only possible but also essential if we want to adjust our supply to the demand.[20]

The development of these complementary small units he sees as the particular forte of the individual proprietor.

The second reason which has been advanced for the expansion of the private sector is the effect which this is expected to have upon employment. Levels of unemployment have been rising for a long time in Yugoslavia, and it is agreed that the true level is disguised both by the large number of Yugoslav workers who have found temporary work abroad, and by the inefficient retention of surplus labour. The tourist trade is identified as one of the areas of the economy in which there would be room for the effective stimulation of private employment.[21]

Finally, the point has been made that there is insufficient opportunity for the useful economic investment of small savings, too much of which find their way into projects of conspicuous consumption. The encouragement of citizens to construct accommodation for private rent to tourists not only satisfies their desire to improve their own standard of living, but also puts that investment to productive use.[22]

---

19. See, for example, Vidaković, *Turizam i ekonomska*, pp. 78–9; also Ivan Strgačić, 'Mogućnost razvitka sitnih djelatnosti na području Srednje Dalmacije - Opći' (The Possibility of Developing Small Businesses in the Area of Central Dalmatia), in Petrić, *Uključivanje radnika*, pp. 102–4. Similar points are reported by Lydall, *Yugoslav Socialism*, pp. 276–7.

20. Dulčić, 'Mogućnost razvoja', p. 297.

21. See Vidaković, *Turizam i ekonomska*, pp. 69–72; Dulčić, 'Mogućnost razvoja', p. 340. See also Ante Dulčić, 'Ekonomski efekti poslovanja ugostiteljskih radnja i privatnog smještaja' (The Economic Effects of Employment in Catering Establishments and Private Accommodation), *Turizam*, Vol. 22, No. 9, 1974, pp. 12–15. The point was made in several of my interviews.

22. See Vidaković, *Turizam i ekonomska*, p. 79. The problem of the inadequate utilization of personal savings is also emphasized forcefully in George Macesich,

A series of interviews conducted by the author with business people, officials and academics in Croatia, who were in one way or another associated with tourism, revealed a wide measure of support for these views even among those employed in the social sector. The small private trader was seen as having a definite, complementary role to play, and not as an illegitimate competitor with socially owned firms. Those criticisms which were voiced related on the whole to the conditions under which private businesses operate (as we shall see below) and not to the legitimacy in principle of such activities.

The recently enacted reforms suggest that these pleadings on behalf of the individual proprietor may have received a certain amount of sympathy among policy makers. That this may well have been part of a trend is suggested by the announcement in 1984 of measures liberalizing the customs burden on the import of tools and equipment intended to constitute the capital of small businesses, on the part of those migrant workers returning to Yugoslavia.[23] Attempts have been made also to stimulate the involvement of small business firms in cooperative arrangements with larger, socially owned enterprises.

In spite of these affirmative measures, and the constitutional rights to which reference has already been made, the overall position of the individual proprietor in the Yugoslav economy remained difficult. It has been possible in the past to point to discouragement, and even to harassment, of such individuals; and the whole question of the nature and extent of the private economy remains surrounded by ambivalence, and even by a continuing sense of its 'semi-legality', which has not yet been definitely dissipated by the current trend towards economic liberalization.[24]

The controversial nature of the private sector is readily apparent

---

'Monetary–Financial Organization and Policies: Yugoslav Post-1970 Experience', Paper read to the conference, 'Open socialism': A Balance Sheet of the Yugoslav Experiment, University of Bradford, March 1983. This important issue is understudied, as commentators tend to deal with institutional under-saving, but neglect the individual level.

23. See 'Carinske Olakšice' (Customs Concessions), *Vjesnik* (Zagreb), Wednesday, 1 February 1984, p. 1.

24. See Vidaković, *Turizam i ekonomska*, p. 28. Globokar, 'Le Role des entreprises', pp. 4–6 and 20, also comments on the atmosphere of 'semi-legality'. Illustrating the formal difficulties which surround the operation of private businesses she comments: 'To obtain permission to operate a private business it is necessary to get together 47 different documents which require on average 13 months of preparation' (p. 22). This is a significant point on which it will be interesting to see whether recent legal changes do have any impact.

from a scrutiny of the Yugoslav press. Against the general background of the apparent official toleration of self-employment, in January 1984 the Croatian Sabor (Parliament) debated the possibility of forbidding private practice in medicine. It was pointed out that the situation with respect to health care was untypical of self-employment in general, and in any case the result of the debate was to extend the provisions for private health care for another five years. The occasion served to highlight, however, the fact that in one respect or another the private sector was still under scrutiny.[25] It was thought by some to be anomalous in a socialist society, and its existence might be interpreted as a matter of toleration and the pressures of pragmatic adaptation to circumstance, rather than of right.

In July 1983, *Vjesnik* (the principal Croatian daily) carried a half-page investigation into the mushroom growth of the small *bife* (bar).[26] Referring to the huge growth in the numbers of these establishments, the authors questioned whether any real social or commercial need was served by them while (paradoxically) attacking the excessive profits which it was said were made from them. The proprietors were said to be living like *bubrezi u loju* (pigs in clover). The 'false glitter' of the *kafić* (café) was said to conceal low standards of service – 'worse than the worst *krčma* (dive)'. Such places operated on the margins of legality, and encouraged undesirable social habits. The authors of the article regretted the lack of adequate means of inspection, which would allow the enforcement of controls on quality, conditions of operation and taxation of these establishments. A letter to the same paper in January 1984, from an aggrieved individual proprietor, asked whether it was now 'open season' for hunting the *privatnik*.[27] It would not be difficult to multiply illustrations of this kind.

In case it should be thought that the explicit market-orientation heralded by the installation of the Marković government in 1989

25. 'Novi rok za privatne ordinacije' (A New Period for Private Practice), *Vjesnik* (Zagreb), Friday, 13 January 1983, p. 3. The proposal for a new 'Law on the Abolition of Medical Practices' was not accepted on the recommendation of the Presidency of the Republic. The reasons had to do with the shortage of medical practitioners in Croatia, and nothing to do with the rights of the self-employed. At the time of writing it is not known whether this permission has been extended.
26. 'Jesu li bifei mala privreda?' (Are Cafés Small Businesses?), *Vjesnik* (Zagreb), Saturday–Monday, 2–4 July 1983, p. 17; also, 'Lažni sjaj oltara današnjice' (The False Glitter of the Altar of Fashion), ibid.
27. 'Lov na privatnike' (Hunting the Self-Employed), *Vjesnik* (Zagreb), Tuesday, 31 January 1984, p. 3

spells the end of such attitudes, it is worth noting that the debates on the need for economic change, and the causes of the country's difficulties, have featured calls for greater economic 'discipline' as well as demands for enhanced freedom. There are many misconceptions current in this respect among commentators on Yugoslav affairs. The fact that Slobodan Milošević, whose meteoric rise to political prominence in Serbia has drawn such attention, comes from a banking background has often been assumed to imply a commitment on his part to the ideals of 'market socialism' and some sympathy for the expansion of private enterprise. This hardly squares with his public pronouncements on the matter. He has repeatedly insisted that Yugoslavia's crisis is at root a 'social' rather than an economic crisis, and has grouped demands for the expansion of 'private property' along with 'political pluralism' and a 'multi-party system' as badges of 'anti-communist' opposition, against which it is necessary to preserve party unity.[28] His continuing capacity to resist the collapse of support for the League of Communists – bucking the trend in the rest of Yugoslavia – does not hold out the promise of a stable commitment to the development of the private sector from that quarter.

'Institutional underdevelopment' and the private sector

An examination of the limited discussion which has taken place in the Yugoslav literature, together with the brief series of interviews conducted by the present writer, suggests that the problematic position of the individual proprietor may be understood at three levels. Each of these relates in a crucial way to the question of the degree of institutionalization of the private economy in Yugoslavia. First of all, there is the theoretical, or more generally, conceptual confusion over the terms of the discussion. Then there is the matter of the socially acceptable level of differentiation which may be bound up with the growth of private enterprise. Finally, there is the practical political question of the ways in which 'official' views on policy matters actually articulate with the realities of local political and economic structures in the highly decentralized state which is Yugoslavia.

28. Slobodan Milošević, *Godine raspleta* (The Years of Denouement) (4th edn, Belgrade, BIGZ, 1989); see esp. p. 203.

At the first of these levels, the investigator rapidly becomes aware of the multiplicity of partly overlapping and partly exclusive terms in which discussion of this area of problems has come to be framed.[29] There has been real confusion here, covering a problem which is of central theoretical significance for the ideological legitimation of policy within an overtly socialist system. In many respects the Yugoslav constitution is relatively clear, in that what it explicitly permits is 'individual work with one's own means', while challenging the right to extract surplus *from the work of others*. Private *property* thus has had a recognized place within Yugoslav social and political life, whereas *alienated labour* was ideologically unacceptable.

The key practical and theoretical problem therefore hinges upon the extent to which the individual *proprietor* may be allowed legitimately to develop as a private *employer*. Whereas the situation of the former is unambiguously secure within Yugoslav constitutional and, more generally, social thought, the status of the latter is not.[30] Neither the previous nor the present general limits on private employment have any theoretical or principled underpinning: they provide purely arbitrary, pragmatically determined boundaries. Hence, there is at one and the same time no basis for resisting pressure either to increase the limit still further, or for permitting *any* such employment at all.

The confusion is compounded repeatedly both in academic and political literature, where the focus of discussion, as often as not, is on the nature and role of the 'small economy', or 'small business' (*mala privreda*). Such discussion necessarily leaves untouched the thorny problem of whether there are and can be within the socialist system any *rights* either to purchase the labour-power of others or to sell one's own. Theoretically and ideologically (and therefore *politically* in a society in which ideology counts for so much in politics) the basis for the institutionalization of a private sector in the Yugoslav economy remains up in the air. In all probability it will rest there, in spite of the excitement with which in non-Yugoslav circles the recent legal changes have been met. The Law on Enterprises enacted in January 1989 still preserves the technical

---

29. For stylistic reasons I too have permitted a good deal of laxity in this discussion. It is interesting that Gams conceptualizes the issue in terms of 'responsibility'. Gams, *Svojina*, p. 340.

30. See, Grbić, 'Socijalizam', chapter 2; also Gams, *Svojina*. The particular position of tourism is discussed in, Krešimir Car and Čedo Grbić, 'Privatni sektor u turizmu' (The Private Sector in Tourism), *Turizam*, No. 5, 1986.

distinction between 'social', 'mixed' and 'private' enterprises, and thus does not clarify at all, as far as I am able to determine, the existing ambiguities about the status of types of property in Yugoslav law.[31] Whatever else may have changed in Yugoslavia, the theoretical confusion over the nature of property has not.

The second level of problems – those associated with the process of differentiation in Yugoslav society – is best introduced by an extract from a speech by the later President Tito, in 1972.

Today we are waging a struggle also against enrichment (*bogaćenje*). Plainly it would be wrong if we were to attack those who achieve something by means of their own work . . .

Yugoslavia is planning, by the middle of the next decade, for two billion dollars on the tourist account, relying in this respect on the private sector in tourism for very firm support. If we don't want these plans to come to nothing, we will have to be very sure of our definition of private enterprise (*privatništvo*). Changing the criteria from day to day could be disastrous in its consequences. In any case, neither campaigning against the 'undergrowth', nor neurotic prattling about alleged enrichment, is going to do anything for tourism. To fight against social differences doesn't mean to fight for uniformity in poverty, but quite the reverse.

It is impossible to cram into the same basket those who have earned something by honourable work (even though this is above the 'average') and that which is gained by speculation and fraud. But we do have a tendency to do that. Society can and must always find a way to 'dock' (*potkusi*) that which is gained from work, if it departs significantly from confirmed principles; but that must be done without neurosis and campaigns – but by another route. We are seriously counting upon the investment in tourism of our workers abroad, but we are obliged to let them know conscientiously what possibilities are open to them.[32]

The heart of the matter here is the concept of 'enrichment' (*bogaćenje*). References to 'campaigns' and 'neurotic prattling' are an open acknowledgment of the fact that there has been public harassment of the private employer. The reassuring noises about

31. The Deputy Federal Finance Secretary, commenting recently on the economic reforms, has pointed out that they establish a system of 'pluralism in ownership' in Yugoslavia. In other words, several different types of property relationship, and hence presumably several different judicial theories of the nature of property relations, are allowed to co-exist. (See Vuk Ognjanović, 'Money and the Economic Reform in Yugoslavia', *Review of International Affairs*, Vol. 41, No. 960, pp. 1–4.)
32. Quoted in Strgačić, 'Mogućnost razvitka', p. 110. (Original in *Novi list* (Rijeka), 22–3 April 1972, pp. 2–3.)

the seriousness with which the state welcomes the support of the individual investor are intended to be noticed: but there remains here a serious measure of ambiguity. How does one define *bogaćenje*, and just what is the limit beyond which the yield from private enterprise can be permitted to go beyond 'the average' before it becomes politically contentious?

The question of the degree of acceptable differentiation within a socialist society is a complex one, and it is certainly a controversial one in Yugoslavia. Clearly the emergence of private property in the means of production is by means the only factor at work in the creation of such differences. These notions remain subjective, and probably must necessarily remain so. There is little doubt that the growth of the private sector *does* contribute to the process of differentiation, and to the increasing steepness of the gradient of inequality between strata.[33] What is in some respects more important than the actual effects of this process, however, is the emergence of a *mythology* of differentiation which has come to surround the individual proprietor. This is an area in which rumour is more powerful than any directly politically motivated campaign against *bogaćenje*.

During my visit to Zagreb in 1988, I heard a rumour circulating freely that there were sixty dollar-millionaires living in the city. It was never possible to identify the basis for this belief – if such there was. The important thing is that it was relayed as a matter of fact. True or untrue, these beliefs add to what has been called the air of 'semi-legality' which surrounds the private economy.[34] They contribute in no small way to the difficulties which lie in the path of the institutionalization of the private sector.

33. This general contention cannot be argued here. The issue has been rather neglected until recently by Yugoslav sociologists, largely because of its politically contentious nature. See, however, Mihailo V. Popović, Silvano Bolčić, Vesna Pešić, Miloslav Janićijević and Dragomir Pontić, *Društveni slojevi i društvena svest* (Social Strata and Social Consciousness) (Belgrade, Institut društvenih nauka, 1977). On the particular significance of tourism in the differentiation process, see Simo Elaković and Vlaho Brangjolica, *Efekti i posljedice ekonomskih, socijalnih i drugih promijena pod utjecajem turizma na Jadranskom području* (The Effects and Consequences of Economic, Social and Other Changes under the Influences of Tourism in the Area of Dalmatia) (Dubrovnik, Fakultet za turizam i vanjsku trgovinu, 1985).

34. The role of rumour is stressed here because the actual size of the personal fortunes which are revealed in the occasional cases of criminal prosecution for tax evasion are rather lower than those credited in popular stories about the amounts to be made in the private sector. Tales of 'millionaires' persist, even though the title of the following news item belied the substance of the article which followed it. 'Milionerite ne gi plakaat danocite' (Millionaires Don't Pay Taxes), *Nova Makedonija* (Skopje), Saturday, 3 September 1983, p. 3.

In many respects the ambiguities surrounding the position of the private sector in the Yugoslav economy stem directly from the decentralized structure of politics in the country. The operation of policy is made effective at the local, communal level, so that there is no necessary or straightforward process of transmission between the pronouncements of politicians (or academics) who move in federal – or even republican – circles, and conditions which actually prevail 'on the ground', where the situation may be very variable indeed.[35] Several factors in the local situation may be relevant here.

First of all, although tourism has been affirmed as a priority in economic development within federal and republican plans, that commitment is by no means uniformly shared. There may well be perceived conflicts between the interests of tourism and those of industrial organizations.[36] Where private economic initiatives come to be identified with the growth of tourism, then even without there being specifically ideological elements in the conflict, its freedom to develop may become a pawn in a wider political game.

In spite of the official and constitutional sanction given to private enterprise, local party functionaries may still cling to 'conservative' ideological definitions of the businessman as by definition the 'class enemy'. Ample opportunity exists within the framework of the law – and even outside it, through informal pressure – for such officials to engage in harassment of private-sector businesses.

Their tendency to do so is enhanced by shifts in the social and economic status of those involved. Generally speaking, since the war political office has guaranteed high status and relatively high income within the local community. As time has passed, however, not only has this situation been altered by the overall advance of industrial and commercial incomes, but it has become possible for quite substantial sums to be made in self-employment. The press stories of 'millionaires' may be exaggerated, but such evidence as there is does suggest that the owner of a small business concern is likely to be better-off than the average Yugoslav.[37] Where opportunities do arise for the discouragement, obstruction or open har-

35. See Čudina, 'Uloga i značaj', p. 3; Božičeviç, 'Mjesto i uloga privatna', p. 3. The same point was made strongly in several interviews. On inter-republican differences, see Kobašić, *Turizam u Jugoslaviji*, pp. 58–9.

36. See J. Alan Coley, 'The Development of the Triglav National Park, Slovenia', *Bradford Studies on Yugoslavia* (University of Bradford, Postgraduate School of Yugoslav Studies), No. 8, 1985; F. B. Singleton, 'The Triglav National Park in the 1980s', *Slovene Studies*, Vol. 10, No. 1, 1988, pp. 39–49.

37. See, for example, Dulčić, 'Mogućnost razvoja', pp. 349–50.

assment of the individual proprietor, therefore, these may be seized upon under the stimulus of a simple sense of economic relative deprivation as much as out of a feeling of ideological offence.

An important factor to be borne in mind here is that these attitudes are not only based upon the situation and outlook of party officials, and hence likely to be brushed aside easily as an immediate consequence of the current political upheavals and the decline of party influence. As David Dyker has emphasized, there is ample evidence in the work of Yugoslav sociologists that the hostility to *bogaćenje* stems from a widespread and frequently vocal egalitarianism in Yugoslav culture, which is likely to prove much more durable.[38] The economic law may have become much more 'liberal' in Yugoslavia, but in the economic difficulties currently being endured the constant pressure on the income of citizens is likely to ensure that the private entrepreneur remains a focus for sentiments of relative deprivation.

The aim of this discussion is not to demonstrate that development in Yugoslavia is dependent in some way upon the growth of private enterprise – that the way to prosperity only lies through the restoration of capitalism. The focus of this chapter is on the process of *institutionalization*. Although the foregoing discussion has remained somewhat general and even speculative, it is my contention that even now institutionalization, in the sense in which it was defined above, cannot be said to have taken place with respect to the status of private economic initiative and the role of private property in the means of production in Yugoslavia.

The Yugoslav taxation system and the private sector

The general points made above can be illustrated by reference to a problem about which it has been possible to gather some detailed information – namely, the system of taxation. In this task the limited amount of published information has been supplemented by interviews with several Yugoslav academics and public officials.

Our concern in this section is not to give a systematic and exhaustive account of the Yugoslav taxation provisions, but to examine the ways in which their operation illustrates our general problem, of exploring the institutional underdevelopment of

38. See Dyker, *Yugoslavia.*

Yugoslavia with special reference to the emergence of the private sector in tourism. In this case, the overall political uncertainty which surrounds the existence of private business is reflected in the confusion and controversy which have surrounded the taxation system, certainly over the past twenty-five years.

In common with other aspects of Yugoslav administration, the fiscal system is extremely complex, and that complexity relates in large measure to the degree of decentralization which has been adopted.[39] The Federation has little direct role in fiscal affairs, its income as of right being confined to yield from customs and excise duties, a fixed percentage of the general sales tax and a stamp duty on all administrative and judicial transactions. In effect there are six quite separate taxation authorities – one for each of the republics. Unlike in Britain, and indeed any other country with which this author is familiar, the key to the exactions of the fiscal system is not central government, but the municipality. Even though taxation policy is shaped principally at the level of the republics, the *općina* (or *opština* – the commune) is the major unit both of administration and of account. In the first instance, money is collected within the commune; and the needs of the state are met, paralleling the system of delegation, by payments passed upwards from the locality to higher levels of government.

The principal component in tax receipts is the sales tax on goods and services. This has been steadily growing in its relative importance for the funding of all levels of government, and from 45 to 50 per cent of budgetary income in the early 1970s, this proportion has now reached approximately 70 per cent.[40] Correspondingly, the role of personal income tax has been steadily falling. In contrast to many other countries, individuals are not generally assessed directly

39. For general discussion of the taxation system and fiscal policy in Yugoslavia, see the following: Aleksandar V. Perić, *Finansijska teorija i politika* (Financial Theory and Policy) (Belgrade, Savremena Administracija/Institut za Ekonomska Istraživanja, 1979), part 2, chapter 7; Pero Jurković, *Fiskalna politika u ekonomskoj teoriji i praksi* (Fiscal Policy in Economic Theory and Practice) (Zagreb, Informator, 1977), part 2 ; Alojz Rozmarić, *Javne financije* (Public Finance) (Zagreb, Informator, 1973), chapter 4. I have also relied heavily on an unpublished account of the system prepared by Ante Kobašić, for which I would like to record my thanks. A rare discussion in English of the Yugoslav taxation system is found in Lydall, *Yugoslavia in Crisis*, pp. 144–53.

40. Published information about the yield from various kinds of tax is not systematically available. See, however, Rozmarić, *Javne financije*, p. 280; Perić, *Finansijska*, p. 417. For the contemporary situation I have relied upon information obtained from an official of the Služba Državnog Knjigovodstva (State Accounting Service), Dubrovnik.

for taxation purposes. For the most part the point of both assessment and collection is the work organization. It is not normally individuals who pay income tax, but their place of employment, which pays out of its collective income. Only if personal income exceeds a certain limit, determined from time to time by the republic, is the individual then liable to pay personal income tax, directly to the commune.

The most notable exception to this general pattern is the self-employed person, who is directly responsible to the commune. All self-employed persons are required by law to register their business with the municipality, and they are individually assessed for taxation purposes by local officials.

Whereas one might expect that in a socialist state the burden of taxation would fall with special severity, through the operation of a discriminatory mechanism, on the self-employed, this does not appear invariably to be the case.[41] In fact the most frequently aired criticism of the arrangement is not its harshness but its arbitrariness and extreme variability. Kobašić has castigated the 'inconstant . . . and extremely hesitant taxation policy (which) induces in particular private entrepreneurs unbusinesslike and even delinquent behaviour'.[42] Such are the irregularities of the system that they surface, not only in academic discussion, but also in the press. With regard to the private sector these irregularities become controversial as often as not because of the ways in which they can be said to provide direct incentives to fraud and evasion. Two issues are worth mentioning here, both of which bear upon our interest in 'institutional underdevelopment': the local differences in levels of exaction, and the variations in the method of payment.

The variation in the amounts which individual proprietors may be expected to pay in taxes is considerable. These sums extend, according to one author, from the 'symbolic' to the burdensome. The published data which have been obtained refer only to the late 1960s, when the range for small businesses in general appeared to lie between 20,000 and 60,000 dinars annually. More recent information has not yet appeared which would enable us to update these figures systematically, but interviews indicate that the range is still very considerable.[43]

41. Information from the above-mentioned sources suggests that the direct yield from personal direct taxation may be as little as 5 per cent of total budgetary income.
42. See Kobašić, *Turizam u Jugoslaviji*, p. 60.
43. See Tadej, 'Samostalno ugostiteljstvo', p. 24; Božićević, Mjesto i uloga pri-

There are two main reasons for the unevenness of the tax burden on the small private business. First, the policy of taxation in this area is not founded upon impersonal, objective or standardized criteria, but usually on rather subjective notions. The political attitudes of local officials (whether or not they entertain rooted ideological oppositions to the petty capitalist) or their commitment to using the private sector as a stimulus to the tourist trade, will influence their decisions.[44] Thus similar enterprises can be treated very differently in adjacent localities, and in the same commune traders in different lines of business may find themselves favoured or penalized.

Furthermore, the commune only determines its needs from year to year: there seems to be little attempt at long-term planning with respect to finance. Hence levels of taxation are likewise only announced annually. Because of the variability also in the level of demand from the republican government, the commune itself may be expected to pass on sums which can only be determined in the short term. Under these circumstances it is very difficult for the individual proprietor to anticipate from year to year the likely burden of taxation, and it is very difficult for those engaged in business to develop any rationally adjusted cash flow.

Turning to the question of the methods by which tax obligations may be paid, it seems that here too there is considerable variation, and in ways which encourage similarly a sense of the unfairness of the system. Because of the fact that practice is determined locally, there are a variety of regimes in operation.[45] Tax assessments for the self-employed may be paid in a lump sum (*paušalno*), or in instalments due at intervals – monthly, or weekly. The assessment may be based on a flat rate for all similar businesses, or may be adjusted to take account of turnover.

Each of these practices produces its own crop of protests, as the

---

vatna', p. 3. I was told of one *bife* proprietor in Zagreb who expected to be able to pay his monthly taxation demand from the sale of only two kilos of coffee, which may be said to illustrate the 'symbolic' end of the scale. Kobašić, however, reports proprietors who have surrendered their licenses because of the tax burden (Kobašić, *Turizam u Jugoslaviji*).

44. Tadej, 'Samostalno ugostiteljstvo' suggests that the levels of taxation are systematically lower in coastal areas.

45. With the addition of information gathered in interviews, this section is based on: Stevo Mraović, 'Doprinosi i porezi od izdavanja soba i pruženja usluga prehrane' (Contributions and Taxes from the Letting of Rooms and the Provision of Meals), *Ugostiteljstvo i turizam* (Catering and Tourism) (Zagreb), No. 5–6, 1966, pp. 15–20; Ćudina, 'Uloga i značaj', pp. 5–6; Božićević, 'Mjesto i uloga privatna', passim; Tadej, 'Samostalno ugostiteljstvo', p. 24.

system is felt to bear unevenly upon different types of individual or branch of trade. The lump-sum system, especially where the level of taxation is heavy, has been criticized strongly as a considerable disincentive to the growth of private initiative. On the other hand, where it is light in its exactions, it has been attacked as a public subsidy to the private trader. (In an economy which was regularly undergoing high rates of inflation – reputedly exceeding 2,000 per cent at the time of the introduction of the Marković reforms in 1989 – depending upon its conditions of payment, a lump-sum payment may be accused of being unreasonably lenient, where social sector enterprises had to bear the brunt of inflation-adjusted periodic payments.)

It is not possible – and neither is it our intention – to provide a systematic survey of the extent of these different taxation practices in Yugoslavia, or to gather detailed data regarding responses to them. The point is simply, however, that after twenty-five years of controversy which has surrounded the present system, the whole topic of taxation of the private sector remains contentious, and has become more so as the growth of the tourist trade has stimulated the growth of private business. The present arrangements are experienced as capricious and inequitable: they are accused alternately of providing the mechanism for *bogaćenje* on the part of the individual business proprietor, and of acting as a destimulating influence on the much-needed growth of small enterprise.[46] Moreover, it seems likely that the existing system gives a massive stimulus to the misrepresentation of turnover, and to the evasion of payment, adding force to the charges of 'semi-legality' which are regularly levelled at the individual business proprietor.

If evasion is encouraged by the arbitrariness of the taxation system, the situation is made worse by the ineffectiveness of the means of enforcement. An inspection service is attached to the tax office of each commune, but this is acknowledged to be quite inadequate to the task it faces, especially in the larger municipalities, and in those areas such as the major tourist resorts where private enterprise has expanded with unusual rapidity and flourishes in particularly large numbers. The situation is summed up in a press interview with Srdjan Kliska, City Secretary for Finance in Zagreb:

46. See 'Milionerite ne gi plakaat danocite'. This article is a serious attempt at investigative journalism, and not at witch-hunt, in spite of its sensational title. The author points out that in 1976 the individual sector of the Macedonian economy contributed 7.7 per cent to the budgetary income of the republic: by 1982 this had declined to 6.2 per cent, in spite of the growth of private business.

> Apart from that [the possibility of a visit by the inspector] caterers aren't particularly afraid of inspection. First of all, there are 61 inspectors in the city who have 13,000 tax cases in 14 communes, and who must carry out 6,000 controls in the course of a year. If . . . the inspectors have to come back several times to some places, the others can calculate that the inspectors might visit them once in every five years![47]

The behaviour of individual traders is especially difficult to police in tourist areas, and above all in the case of those offering accommodation in their own homes. Although the law requires them to register their business with the commune, to have their rooms rated according to the official categories, and to charge standard prices, there is widespread evasion. Touting for custom outside of the recognized tourist agencies; the failure to declare all guests (especially Yugoslavs) to the authorities; the provision of services (such as meals) the income from which is not reported; negotiation of prices for rooms which do not accord with the official rates (especially for payment in hard currencies); all these – and many other – devices enable the providers of holiday accommodation to earn far more than they declare for taxation purposes.

Of particular significance has been the differential access of some private traders to foreign currency. Before the currency reform of 1990 this was a very important factor in tourist areas, and especially so in a period of high inflation and depreciation of the dinar. It has been impossible to determine the extent to which such currency transactions were handled according to the official regulations. It is impossible to say at this stage whether the reform of the foreign exchange regime has improved the degree of supervision here.

There are occasional orgies of prosecution, well covered in the press; but these in general can not make a deep impression on the situation.[48] Even where inspectors do call, the standard of book-keeping is often so poor that it is extremely difficult for them to make any serious attempt at an audit, and where tax evasion is discovered, the penalties provided in the law are sufficiently light as to make the risk of prosecution one which large numbers of individuals are willing to bear.[49]

47. See 'Jesu li bifei mala privreda?'.
48. See, for example, 'Milionerite ne gi plakaat danocite'.
49. 'Milionerite ne gi plakaat danocite' reports that there is no known case of a private establishment being closed down as the result of prosecution for tax evasion, although this is provided for in the law. This could be an illustration of the way in which the value attached to the protection of the livelihood of the individual has become institutionalized in a labour-managed economy.

Conclusions

Since the economic reform of 1965, both federal and republican planning documents in Yugoslavia have given prominent place to the role which tourism can play in the country's development strategy. As the review which we have presented earlier suggests, in many respects this effort has been successful, and there is no doubt that tourism does indeed make a substantial contribution to the overall economic survival of the country. Within the general framework of that development strategy there has been repeated emphasis on the active part which could and should be played by the individual proprietor, investor or entrepreneur, in the provision of goods and services to tourists. Indeed, the private sector has come to play a significant role in Yugoslavia's tourist trade, and recent legal changes suggest that it is expected that this role will be enhanced in the future.

The contention has been, however, that these changes exhibit a condition of 'institutional underdevelopment'. The position of the individual proprietor is still both ambiguous within the framework of the law, and uncertain and vacillating both within the context of ideology and at the level of practice. The situation is well illustrated by the anomalies within and controversies surrounding the fiscal system of the country. These may be interpreted both as a reflection of the political and ideological conflict within Yugoslavia, and reciprocally, as fuel which continues to sustain that conflict. In spite of the widely acclaimed current process of economic reform, within the frame provided by the system of socialist self-management there are still many respects in which it is true to say that the private sector exists in a twilight of 'semi-legality': in other words, it has not yet become fully institutionalized.

Given the positive, indeed high, expectations which are currently being placed upon this segment of the Yugoslav economy, by the country's development planners and foreign observers alike, it is clear that this failure of institutionalization must be regarded as an important outstanding problem lying in the path of the future execution of development strategy.[50]

50. Research currently being conducted at the University of Bradford by Milford Bateman investigates in greater depth and generality the development of policy with respect to small businesses in Yugoslavia.

14

The Role of the Press in Yugoslavia

Sabrina P. Ramet

Introduction

In the years since President Tito died (that is, since May 1980), the Yugoslav press has figured as a fairly precise barometer of the broader institutional and political context. Like Yugoslavia itself, the press has been dramatically decentralized, and all efforts to achieve a 'unified information system' have proved unavailing. Like Yugoslavia itself, the press experienced a period of 'release' after the death of Tito; during this period, in the absence of the helmsman, the press shared in the general exploration of new paths, in particular in launching the general discussion of the Goli Otok prison camp.[1] As in the case of the Yugoslav system more broadly, subsequent attempts (1983–85) to rein-in the press by and large failed[2] – and, indeed, the press continued to report the dissatisfaction of responsible agencies with its work. And like Yugoslavia itself, the press reflects the more general chaos which afflicts Yugoslavia on both the *inter*-republican and *intra*-republican level and which results in a measure of sometimes unintended liberalization. And, as journalists have repeatedly discovered in Yugoslavia, if it proves impossible to publish something in one periodical outlet, regardless of the reason, it may be a simple matter to get it published in a different periodical: the youth press has often provided this kind of service as an 'alternative' outlet; other times it is a matter of crossing inter-republican borders and taking one's story to a periodical based in another federal unit.

---

1. Interview with magazine editor, Belgrade, July 1982; and interview with newspaper editor, Ljubljana, July 1982.
2. See Pedro Ramet, 'The Yugoslav Press in Flux', in Pedro Ramet (ed.), *Yugoslavia in the 1980s* (Boulder, Colo., Westview Press, 1985).

It is often said that Yugoslavia, unlike the other communist countries of Eastern Europe, did not have a censorship *office*. Strictly speaking, this was true – at least formally. But there were various levels and ways in which censorship *activity* was carried on, and in which political authorities attempted to assure that the general contents of publications accord with what they considered acceptable. To an outside observer this may seem incomprehensible in view of the intense polemics which frequently rage in the Yugoslav press, in view of the repeatedly demonstrated ability of the Catholic weekly, *Glas Koncila*, to defend itself against mudslinging, and in view of the 'alternative outlet' syndrome. The explanation of this complexity is to be sought in three sources: first, as previously mentioned, the press lies within the jurisdiction of republican authorities, and hence, the evolution of Yugoslavia after 1963 into a set of eight often warring republican–provincial power centres has been accompanied, necessarily, by a republicanization of the press; second, even within a single republic, the authorities appreciate that the press must be diverse if it is to operate effectively, and hence that the youth press, the women's press, even the pornographic press, must have sphere-specific areas of leeway if they are to reach their audiences and function effectively; and third, the authorities simply have not had the resources or the will to assert bloc-style control (and indeed, the supervisors of the youth press are often sympathetic to the coverage of that press).

Before a given issue of a periodical was published, every publisher was required by law to send copies of the galley proofs to the Office of the State Prosecutor. This requirement applied to every periodical published in Yugoslavia regardless of its sponsorship, content, or intended audience.[3] The Prosecutor's Office was, however, understaffed and read comparatively little of the voluminous material which crossed its desk: amateur radio magazines, fashion magazines, sports magazines, and so forth were apt to be ignored, for instance, with greater attention paid to the mainline secular press (*Borba*, *Politika*, *Vjesnik*, etc.) and secondarily to the religious press. Partly for that reason there were few stories of pre-publication censorship in Yugoslavia.[4] More typically, if the communists found something amiss, the issue in question had not only

3. Interview with former editor of a religious periodical, Belgrade, July 1987; confirmed in interview with former editor of a youth periodical, Ljubljana, July 1987.

4. One exception concerns the front-page of an issue of the Croatian weekly, *Hrvatski Tjednik*, in late 1971, which its editors defiantly published with a blank

been printed but also distributed – and the article in question would no doubt have been read by many. The authorities would then reckon with the fact that suppression of the issue would inevitably heighten public interest in it. One informant recounted his experiences with the authorities:

> Our newspaper has been banned three times in all, three times over a span of 20 years. But the bad thing when they ban an issue is that they come to your office and they demand the addresses of all the subscribers and you must give all the addresses, and then they go to the churches and confiscate the unsold issues. And then, if they want to do so, they go to the subscribers and demand to have the issue surrendered. It's dreadful. The previous editor told me they received letters from old people saying please don't send the newspaper to us any more because the police came late in the night and said, 'You received an "enemy" newspaper. Give it to us.' So in a way it is better if an issue is banned *before* distribution.[5]

A ban could be issued by either federal or republican authorities, the latter exercising this prerogative more rarely than the former. A republican ban applies only within the borders of the republic, so that, for instance, if Croatian authorities were to ban an issue of *Mladost*, the very same issue might be freely and openly sold in Serbia, Bosnia, and elsewhere in Yugoslavia. Both the federal and republican bans may be challenged in court, and from time to time this has resulted in a ban being overturned.

The State Prosecutor's Office was concerned with the day-to-day routine, and had its eyes fixed, as it were, on the trees rather than on the forest. Other review agencies were responsible for monitoring the overall performance of the press, namely the Commission for Ideological Work and the Commission for Political-Propaganda Activity in Information, both attached to the Central Committee (CC) of the League of Communists of Yugoslavia (LCY), the Section for Information and Public Opinion of the Socialist Alliance of Working People of Yugoslavia (SAWPY), the Committee for Press, Radio and Television of the CC SAWPY, and republican branches of these bodies. These bodies were required to issue annual reports on the functioning of the press.[6] These reports, judging from reports in the press itself, tended to dwell on perceived

---

page and a brief notice that the material intended for that page had been administratively suppressed.
5. Interview, Belgrade, July 1987.
6. Interview with staff members of *Vjesnik*, Zagreb, July 1982.

shortcomings and problems.[7] In addition, the Association of Journalists of each given federal unit periodically reviewed the performance of its members.[8]

The State Secretariat for Information was the body authorized to announce news bans, but, in practice, news bans have been announced by others as well. In February 1986, for instance, the president of the Federal Assembly told the 60 Yugoslav journalists accredited to cover the assembly's deliberations that they were not to write about what irate Serbs from Kosovo were saying that day in the assembly. But since the ban was illegal and since it affected one of the most burning issues of the day, namely Serb–Albanian tensions in the province of Kosovo, journalists protested, some wrote sharp commentaries about the news 'embargo', and within a few days, several publications printed the substance of the meeting, the embargo notwithstanding.[9] Journalist Mihailo Rasić voiced the sentiment of many in the media in describing that ban as a 'semi-private action' imposed without proper authority.[10]

Other matters have also been subject to news bans in recent years. Perhaps the most controversial was the abortive attempt to limit news coverage of the April 1981 riots in Kosovo to official communiqués prepared by the government.[11] In another instance of an unsuccessful ban, authorities at first tried to prevent reportage of the 10 March 1986 session of the CC of the Croatian party, at which Milka Planinc and Jure Bilić failed to be nominated to represent Croatia in the Presidium of the CC LCY. Similarly, in October 1985, Yugoslav newspapers were not allowed to report that Palestinian terrorist Abu Abbas was in Belgrade,[12] while the Yugoslav press has recently become much more reticent than it had been up to the early 1980s in discussing Yugoslavia's foreign debt. Writing in the pages of the party weekly, *Komunist*, Zdravko Leković complained in June 1987 that one could legitimately speak of 'a censorship of information in a broad sense', adding that information about events in Kosovo was still being blocked and that the press

7. See *Oslobodjenje* (Sarajevo), 21 January 1982, p. 6; *Politika* (Belgrade), 16 January 1985, p. 6 and 25 December 1985, p. 6; *Komunist* (Belgrade edition), 20 December 1985, p. 17; *Borba* (Zagreb edition), 22–23 February 1986, p. 8 and 11 September 1987, p. 3; and *Vjesnik* (Zagreb), 9 July 1987, p. 3.
8. See, for example, *Politika*, 19 December 1985, p. 6.
9. *NIN* (Belgrade), No. 1836, 9 March 1986, p. 9.
10. *Večernje Novosti* (Belgrade), 14 March 1986.
11. Discussed in Stevan Nikšić, *Oslobodjenje Štampe* (Belgrade; Mladost, 1982).
12. TANJUG's director, Mihajlo Šaranović, later complained about this in a speech reported in *Vjesnik*, 14 March 1986.

had been unable to obtain basic statistics about many investments even though they were *not* secret.[13] There were other sundry specific proscriptions, as well as limits in the spheres of foreign policy, national mythology, religious policy, and nationalities policy,[14] though these limits changed somewhat over time and were, in any case, periodically tested by daring editors.

In addition to the political authorities themselves, the army also occasionally expresses its opinion about coverage of its activities in the press. In March 1985, for instance, the Ljubljana Army District Command prepared an analysis of the public information media in Slovenia and, while generally satisfied with the treatment it had been accorded in the press, found several articles in the Slovenian youth press 'unacceptable and extremely harmful . . . because they present a distorted picture of life and work in the Yugoslav National Army. The publishing of such texts', the statement continued, 'cannot be permitted any longer.'[15]

In general, when one abstracts the situation to a 'global' level, the Communists tended to believe that the press's basic assignment was to strengthen the values of socialist self-management and to support the policies of the LCY, assisting the politicians in finding and implementing 'necessary solutions'.[16] As recently as September 1985, *Komunist*, the organ of the LCY, described itself as aspiring 'to be the class weapon of the League of Communists [and] to contribute . . . to the strengthening of the unity in action and thought of the League of Communists'.[17] Accordingly, Yugoslav newspapers were apt to be criticized for failing to support (or even for being at variance with) party policy, for confronting the public with differing analyses, for 'confusing' the public, for overemphasis of negative phenomena in society, for loss of 'seriousness', even for 'neutrality' in the treatment of burning social issues.[18] Yugoslavia's 11,000 journalists – 90 per cent of whom are party members[19] –

13. *Komunist*, 26 June 1987, p. 12.
14. Detailed in Ramet, 'The Yugoslav Press in Flux', pp. 104–6.
15. *Politika*, 30 March 1985, p. 6.
16. TANJUG, 24 September 1986, translated in Foreign Broadcast Information Service (FBIS), *Daily Report* (Eastern Europe), 25 September 1986, p. I7; and *Večernji List* (Zagreb), 9 July 1987, p. 5.
17. *Komunist*, 13 September 1985, p. 8.
18. See, for example, *Politika*, 12 July 1984, p. 6; TANJUG, 9 December 1985, translated in Joint Publications Research Service (JPRS), *East Europe Report*, No. EER–86–008, 21 January 1986, p. 101; *Politika*, 25 December 1985, p. 6; and *Borba* (Zagreb edition), 16 September 1987, p. 4.
19. Dennison I. Rusinow, 'Yugoslavia 1983: Between "Continuity" and "Cri-

were expected to take their cues from the party. When they displayed too much independence, they were apt to be criticized for setting themselves up as independent judges of society or as 'some kind of arbiter or conscience of society'.[20] This, however, led to some strange dilemmas with circumspection and uncertainty leading to a situation where, as one Yugoslav journalist put it, 'many journalists, and the younger ones in particular, find it difficult to decide what their position is due to the fact that the LC is often late in taking necessary actions'.[21]

Nationalism and the Republicanization of the Press

The federalization of the Yugoslav political system was intended to defuse nationalism by granting nationality-based federal units wide-ranging autonomy. Instead of defusing nationalism, however, federalization transformed the nationalities factor by shifting the centre of gravity from the federal government to the republican governments and by arming those governments with the powers to seek 'national' objectives (e.g. Serbian and Montenegrin interest in the construction of the now-completed Belgrade–Bar railway).

In the years since Tito has died, it has become increasingly evident that the nationalities factor is far from being solved. First, in 1981, Kosovo erupted in ethnic violence and far from being able to bring this cauldron under control, authorities in desperation placed the province under federal protectorship in autumn 1987. The rise of Albanian nationalism associated with the Kosovo violence in turn triggered a second nationalist reawakening – among the Serbs, who viewed the shifting demographic balance in Kosovo and increased militance of the Albanians there with distress and resentment. Among the signs of the new Serbian nationalism have been a renewed interest in the Serbian Orthodox Church,[22] and the appearance of a number of openly nationalist books, such as the best-selling *Knjiga o Milutinu*.[23] By 1986, it was clear that Slovenes too were inflamed by a new cultural awareness sparked in part in reaction to other republics' resentment of Slovenia's relative

---

sis"', *University Field Staff International Reports* (1983), No. 3, p. 10; and *Vjesnik*, 7 February 1987, p. 3.

20. *Vjesnik*, 3 November 1992, p. 5.
21. TANJUG, 9 December 1985, footnote 18, p. 102.
22. Various interviews, Belgrade, July 1987.
23. Danko Popović, *Knjiga o Milutinu* (Belgrade, Niro Književne novine, 1986).

prosperity, in part by Slovenian fears of in-migration of non-Slovenes into Slovenia, and in part by the national soul-searching associated with the multi-media *Neue Slowenische Kunst* aesthetic current.[24]

In the initial months after the April 1981 riots, the Albanian-language press in Kosovo was subjected to stiff criticism, and some editors were replaced. Already in mid-June 1981, an extraordinary session of the Association of Kosovo Journalists was convened, in order to identify shortcomings which needed to be corrected. Yet, two years later, the Provincial Committee for Information found that reportage in the province's Albanian-language daily, *Rilindja*, differed rather substantially from what was offered in the local Serbo-Croatian daily, *Jedinstvo*. Subsequently, a session of the Information Commission of the LCY noted, in November 1987, that while *Jedinstvo* reported evidence of discrimination against Serbo-Croatian, reported that the emigration of Slavs from the province was rising, and adhered to the official line, *Rilindja* discounted any discrimination, reported that out-migration was declining, and talked of 'unacceptable' demands from Serbs and Montenegrins.[25] In late 1985, Kosovo's journalists were still being told to counter 'counterrevolutionary ideologies and action' and to find ways to discourage the emigration of Serbs and Montenegrins from the province.[26] Yet, as recently as August 1986, *Rilindja* was still said to be marred by 'superficiality, one-sidedness, lack of commitment, and . . . an excessive insistence on national elements that very often leads to the very brink of nationalism'.[27] *Jedinstvo* was simultaneously charged with having engaged in 'masquerades' designed to obscure the position of the journalist and the paper.[28]

The sector for public information of the Republic Committee for Information of SR Serbia carried out an analysis of the provincial press of Kosovo and Vojvodina, covering the period 14 September 1987–20 January 1988, and examining the following papers: *Dnevnik*, *Magyar Szo* and *Stav* from Vojvodina, and *Jedinstvo* and

24. See the short article in *Art Forum*, Vol. 26, No. 3, November 1987, pp. 151–2; and Pedro Ramet, 'Yugoslavia 1987: Stirrings from Below', *South Slav Journal*, Vol. 10, No. 3 (Autumn 1987).

25. TANJUG, 12 June 1981 and 6 June 1983, translated respectively in FBIS, *Daily Report* (Eastern Europe), 16 June 1981, pp. I13–I14 and 9 June 1983, p. I; and Louis Zanga, 'News Media Coverage of Events in Kosovo', *Radio Free Europe Research*, 20 November 1987, p. 2.

26. TANJUG, 7 October 1985, translated in FBIS, *Daily Report* (Eastern Europe), 17 October 1985, p. I3.

27. *Borba* (Belgrade edition), 22 August 1986, p. 3.

28. Ibid., 26 August 1986, p. 3.

Rilindja from Kosovo. The study found that the Hungarian-language *Magyar Szo* devoted more space than did the Serbo-Croatian-language *Dnevnik*, to commentary on the constitutional changes under discussion at the time, especially where measures affecting the position of the Hungarian minority were concerned. Of the three Vojvodinan papers, *Stav*, the organ of the provincial youth organization, was the most openly and explicitly critical of the proposed changes. In Kosovo, there were more fundamental differences in coverage: the Albanian-language daily, *Rilindja*, fiercely criticized the proposed changes, whereas the Serbo-Croatian daily, *Jedinstvo*, assumed a non-committal posture.[29] Later, however, *Rilindja*'s staff had switched to the offensive and had criticized the press from other republics for 'one-sidedness' in treatment of Kosovo.[30]

The chief culprit among these 'other republics' was surely Serbia, whose press was criticized for 'petit-bourgeois liberalism and nationalism' during a session of the Presidium of the CC LC Serbia in February 1983. Momčilo Baljak, who presented the opening report at that session, seemed particularly upset that:

> no editorial office is willing to criticize the texts to be found in the book, *Stvarno i moguće* [The Real and the Possible], by Dobrica Ćosić, which has just been published by Otokar Keršovani, the Rijeka publishing house. These texts are permeated with anxiety for the Serbian people, and in essence they reflect the socio-socialist and unitarist concept of our society.[31]

Two months later, Dragoljub Trailović resigned his post as chief editor of the influential Belgrade daily, *Politika*, amid charges of Serbian nationalism and complaints that he had failed to respond appropriately to the staging of a play inspired by Greater Serbian nationalist concepts.[32] This did not settle matters, however, and the same issue came up for discussion in September 1987, when Ivan Stojanović, director of the 'Politika' publishing house, and Živana Olbina, a member of

---

29. Dragana Roter-Crkvenjakov, 'Pokrajinska štampa o promenama ustava SR Srbije', *Novinarstvo*, Vol. 24, Nos. 1–2, 1988, pp. 59–60.
30. *Vjesnik*, 15 June 1987, p. 3.
31. Quoted in TANJUG, 7 February 1983, translated in FBIS, *Daily Report* (Eastern Europe), 8 February 1983, p. I16.
32. *Le Monde*, (Paris), 11 May 1983, p. 6, translated in FBIS, *Daily Report* (Eastern Europe), 11 May 1983, p. I9.

Politika's editorial staff, created a stir by accusing the newspaper of indulging in a nationalist obsession with Kosovo, and of sensationalizing nationalist causes.[33] At the end of a stormy session at which the staff by and large rejected her charge that *Politika* was sliding into 'anti-communism', Olbina resigned from the council. The following month Stojanović was himself forced to resign, amid charges that he had failed to exercise proper control over the periodicals being published by 'Politika'. The result, as his critics pointed out, was that the periodicals being published by 'Politika' frequently disagreed among themselves about facts or the interpretations of facts, even at times to the point of conducting polemics with each other.[34]

In late 1987, Slobodan Milošević edged aside his erstwhile patron, now rival, Ivan Stambolić, to establish himself as head of the Serbian party organization. He replaced the editors of publications at Belgrade's 'Politika' publishing house and a number of good writers were sent off to glorious exile as foreign correspondents. In this way, Milošević assured himself of the subservience and unanimity of viewpoint on the part of the Serbian press. Interestingly enough, the editor-in-chief of *Politika* had never been a political appointee until Milošević's arrival.[35] By contrast, Belgrade's 'Borba' publishing house, which publishes the daily papers, *Borba* and *Večernje Novosti*, remained independent, because all the Yugoslav republics enjoy influence in its operation.

Slovenia has similarly produced controversy in this area. In February 1987 the cultural monthly, *Nova Revija*, brought out its issue No. 57, devoted entirely to the Slovenian national question. The contributors to this issue, who included some of the leading Slovenian intellectuals, suggested that Slovenia had suffered by its incorporation into Yugoslavia, described the so-called National Liberation Struggle as a civil war punctuated by a struggle for power, and argued that the communist-controlled Anti-Fascist Council of 1943 had no legitimate basis for behaving as a government.[36] One of the contributors – Tine Hribar, in his article, 'Slovenian Statehood' – called the Socialist Republic of Slovenia an inadequate reflection of Slovenian sovereignty, while another writer

33. *Vjesnik*, 16 September 1987, p. 5.
34. Stojanović had only been in the job for nine months. See *Politika*, 13 October 1987, pp. 1, 5–7; and *Borba* (Zagreb edition), 13 October 1987, pp. 1, 3.
35. Interview with staff members of *Delo* (Ljubljana), 1 September 1989.
36. As summarized in *Vjesnik*, 21 February 1987, p. 3.

– Alenka Goljevšek – outlined a programme of virtual independence for Slovenia, in which the Slovenian government would dispose of its own armed forces.[37]

Jože Smole, president of the Republic Conference of SAWP Slovenia, called the views expressed in that issue 'unacceptable'.[38] The editor of *Nova Revija* was quickly fired. And various party bodies throughout Slovenia issued sharp condemnations of the journal.[39] The original 3,500 copies of the issue quickly sold out, but *Književne Novine* in Belgrade soon put out a special issue, setting forth all the essentials of the controversial issue, only now in Serbo-Croatian translation. The issue became a *cause célèbre*. Politicians and other public figures throughout Yugoslavia spoke out against *Nova Revija*, and there was talk of banning the issue. In March 1987, the executive council of the journal met and lent its full support to the editorial board of *Nova Revija*, while the journal's new editor underlined that he endorsed the controversial issue and intended to assert continuity in editorial policy. Ultimately, the Slovenian public prosecutor engaged in polemics with the federal prosecutor over the issue, and the journal found enough backers within the Slovenian leadership to ride out the storm.[40]

Slovenia, Serbia and Kosovo are the chief areas where nationalism in the press has become controversial. But they are not the only ones. In October 1986, for instance, the Macedonian party CC expressed discontent with its local press, finding that certain papers were giving undue attention to local troubles. CC member, Metodi Petrovski, mentioned, in particular, excessive coverage by Macedonian media of a brawl between Albanian and Macedonian youth. He urged more even reporting of news from other Yugoslav republics.[41]

Despite the old Titoist formula according to which party spokesmen should restrict themselves to criticizing nationalist phenomena in their own republics, the very opposite has become the case and the various newspapers have preferred to criticize nationalist excesses of *other* nationality groups.[42]

37. As summarized in *Politika*, 23 February 1987, p. 6.
38. *Vjesnik*, 21 February 1987, p.3.
39. *Politika*, 15 March 1987, p. 6.
40. Interviews, Ljubljana, July 1987. See also TANJUG, 11 March 1987, translated in FBIS, *Daily Report* (Eastern Europe), 6 April 1987, p. 18; *The Economist*, 11 April 1987, p. 50; and *Borba* (Zagreb edition), 11 September 1987, p. 3.
41. TANJUG, 30 October 1986, translated in FBIS, *Daily Report* (Eastern Europe), 6 November 1986, p. 15.

Sabrina P. Ramet

Explicit nationalism is not the only symptom of the republican-ization of the press, however. There is a kind of implicit national-ism, better described as *localism*, which some papers have been trying hard to steer clear of. *Borba* has long taken particular pains to assure the 'all-Yugoslav' character of its coverage,[43] and it may well be the only genuine *Yugoslav* newspaper among the major dailies. *Vjesnik* for a while looked beyond its Croatian horizons and aspired to a country-wide audience.[44] *Politika*, of course, looks back with pride to its long tradition as an independent paper and likes to think of itself as a paper for all Yugoslavia; in reality, however, its readership is limited to Serbs and Montenegrins, since most Croats do not bother to learn the Cyrillic alphabet.[45]

A New Law on the Press

Yugoslavs began talking about a new law concerning the press and public information in early 1979,[46] but due to the amount of controversy generated, it was not until May 1985 that the law was finally adopted. The chief purpose of the new legislation, as tire-lessly pointed out in the press itself, was to produce greater uni-formity in the press across republican boundaries. Beyond that, the law was also intended to strengthen the founding agencies' control over their publications, whether the agency concerned is one of SAWPY's branches, the LCY, or a socio-cultural organization.[47] Shortly after the passage of the new law, *Komunist* spoke optimisti-cally of 'the fact that with this law a unified regime for public information for all of Yugoslavia has been introduced'.[48] This optimism has proven illusory. Even when *Komunist* itself was con-cerned, there was not much unity among its various local editions. Indeed, *Mladost*, the magazine published by the Socialist Youth Federation, pointed out that nothing had changed almost a year and a half later. On the contrary, as *Mladost* observed: 'In the eight

42. See the report of the session of the CC Presidium's Commission for Infor-mation and Propaganda Activity in *Večernje Novosti* (Belgrade), 9 December 1986.
43. Discussed in *Večernji List*, 29 May 1987, p. 5.
44. See discussion in *Vjesnik*, 9 July 1987, p. 3.
45. *Borba* is published in both Cyrillic and Latin-alphabet editions.
46. Tanjug, 15 March 1979, translated in FBIS, *Daily Report* (Eastern Europe), 16 March 1979, p. I10.
47. See, for instance, *Borba* (Zagreb edition), 17 January 1986, p. 3; also *Komun-ist*, 19 June 1987, p. 6.
48. *Komunist*, 26 July 1985, p. 4.

editions of *Komunist*, whose mastheads differ only in reflecting the republic or provincial names, the Yugoslav portion has been melting away more and more, and has almost disappeared, because republic and provincial editorial boards have been carrying more and more articles in accordance with their republic and provincial top leaders' attitudes.'[49] And again, if the law had really succeeded in creating a 'unified information system', it should have been possible to avoid the dispute of December 1986. On that occasion, the Slovenian SAWP organization criticized the Croatian SAWP organization for allowing *Vjesnik* to publish a commentary which was alleged to be injurious to the interests of the Slovene minority community in Italy as well as to the wider Slovenian interests.[50]

Despite the shortcomings of the new law, with its passage there was some talk of 'the importance of coordinating the republican and provincial information media laws with the federal ones'.[51] Going one step further, and in harmony with more general aspirations in SR Serbia to erode some of the autonomy enjoyed by the autonomous provinces of Kosovo and Vojvodina (both administratively parts of SR Serbia), the Serbian Assembly proposed in 1987 that the two provinces agree to the passage of a unified republican law on public information. In effect, the proposal asked the provinces to decline to pass their own information laws and merely to accept the extension of the Serbian law into the areas of their jurisdiction. A few months later the Serbian League of Journalists proposed to revise the statute of the Yugoslav League of Journalists to give the provincial associations lesser representation in the presiding council of the Yugoslav organization. Not surprisingly, both provinces rejected these initiatives, and polemics ensued.[52]

By 1988–89, there was growing consensus among Yugoslav journalists that the Law on Press and Information was obsolete. For one thing, Yugoslav appeals courts were repeatedly overturning the temporary ban of specific papers. In March 1988, for example, a court ruled that there was no cause to ban an issue of *Mladina*, the youth paper of Slovenia. The issue in question had included an

49. *Mladost* (1986), as quoted in *Borba* (Belgrade edition), 3 October 1986, p. 11.
50. TANJUG, 9 December 1986, translated in FBIS, *Daily Report* (Eastern Europe), 10 December 1986, p. I4, referring to a commentary published in *Vjesnik* on 3 December 1986.
51. TANJUG, 9 December 1985, translated in JPRS, *East Europe Report*, No. EER–86–008, 21 January 1986, p. 103.
52. See *Borba* (Zagreb edition), 4 September 1987, p. 4; and ibid., 13 October 1987, p. 3.

article to the effect that Yugoslavia's leaders were responsible for leading the country into 'hopeless crisis'. The court, however, ruled that the article in question 'contained no untrue information which could disturb the public'.[53] Later, in August 1988, a decision by the Split public prosecutor to ban an issue of *Omladinska Iskra*, for having published the text of a speech by Milovan Djilas at a meeting in Maribor, was overturned by the Supreme Court of Croatia.[54] And that same month, the Split District Court overturned a ban of the 28 August issue of *Nedeljna Dalmacija*, which the public prosecutor had claimed had 'hostile' content.[55]

Yugoslav journalists were bridling at the rein. In October 1988, at its annual conference, the Union of Yugoslav Journalists 'called for an end to the "informal marriage" of political structures and mass media and demanded a greater measure of independence for their profession'.[56] 'The existing press law is obsolete and needs to be revised completely', a prominent Slovenian journalist told me in 1989. 'According to the letter of the law, we could be charged with infringements every day. But we just go ahead and publish what we want, and take our chances.'[57] In particular, federal law included an article (No. 139) relating to high treason, formulated so vaguely that people could be – and in the past, were – prosecuted for bad intentions. Another grievance had to do with the appointment of editors. Many prominent Yugoslav papers are the organs of the Socialist Alliance of Working People – including *Borba*, *Vjesnik*, and *Delo* – which means that the editor-in-chief, the managing editor and the director are all appointed by the Alliance, rather than being selected by the journalists themselves (as they would prefer).

The Youth Press

Various bits of evidence suggest that in certain concrete ways (e.g. coverage of Laibach), the party gives the youth press more latitude than enjoyed by the mainline daily press. At the same time, the recurrent testing of the limits by the youth press and the recurrent

53. Quoted in *Christian Science Monitor*, 23 March 1988, p. 2.
54. TANJUG Domestic Service, 15 August 1988, translated in FBIS, *Daily Report* (Eastern Europe), 16 August 1988, p. 24.
55. *Politika*, 31 August 1988, p. 11.
56. TANJUG, 28 October 1988, translated in FBIS, *Daily Report* (Eastern Europe), 31 October 1988, p. 71.
57. Interview, Ljubljana, 1 September 1989.

impulses, on the part of the authorities, to ban specific issues, suggest that part of this relatively greater latitude should be attributed to the greater daring and even recklessness of some journalists and editors in publications intended for young people.[58]

The most visible youth periodicals in Yugoslavia today are *Mladina* and *Katedra* from Slovenia, *Mladost* and *Studentski List* from Croatia, and *NIN*, *Student*, and *Vidik* from Serbia. Of these *Mladina* has probably been the most controversial in recent years. I propose to throw some light on the youth press by examining its case in some detail.

Mladina is officially the organ of the Socialist Youth Organization of Slovenia, which, in theory, picks the editor. In practice, the editorial board chooses the editor, subject to the approval of the youth organization. The editorial staff clashed with the authorities over editorial policy throughout the 1970s, but even when the authorities intervened more directly in the selection of the editor, *Mladina* remained defiantly independent. In fact, *Mladina* and Ljubljana's Radio Student played an important role in opening up the discussion of previously taboo subjects (like political prisoners) in the early 1980s.[59] A staff member of *Mladina* recalls that period:

> The first reaction of the authorities was to ban specific issues of *Mladina*. Then they would call the people of Radio Student to party headquarters and they would tell them that what they were doing was not right. They would threaten to kick them out of the party. But the party organization in Radio Student stood up for its people and defended them.[60]

Democratic centralism, thus, had proven fictitious.

In late 1984 the Yugoslav authorities decided to put half a dozen Serbian intellectuals on trial for 'dissent'. *Mladina*[61] defended them, resulting in a boom of *Mladina*'s circulation, which rose from 10,000 when the trial began to 18,000 by the time the trial was over, climbing subsequently to 28,000 by mid-1987. In October 1985, *Mladina* published a long interview with Vladimir Šeks, a lawyer from Osijek. Before taking up duties as an advocate, Šeks had been a public prosecutor, and in this capacity he had found out (in 1981) that the security police were routinely opening all

---

58. The examples I provided in 'The Yugoslav Press in Flux', pp. 111–12, in 1985 should be quite sufficient to justify this portrayal.
59. Interview with a staff member of *Mladina*, Ljubljana, July 1987.
60. Ibid.
61. And Radio Student.

foreign correspondence coming into Osijek. He decided to take the police to court, but, as a result, immediately lost his job and was himself taken to court on charges of Croatian nationalism. Šeks did not serve any time then, but after acting as the defence lawyer for the six Serbian intellectuals in 1984, the earlier sentence was revived and Šeks went to prison for six months.[62] His interview with *Mladina* was conducted shortly after his release from prison.

Slovenian authorities were dismayed and banned the issue. But the *Mladina* staff took the case to the Supreme Court of Slovenia, which overturned the ban, allowed *Mladina* to re-release the issue, certain that the abortive ban could only have excited wide interest in the issue. This stimulated a certain self-confidence among the staff of *Mladina*, who took to describing the incident as the 'last' time the magazine was banned. In late July 1987, however, the public prosecutor in Ljubljana imposed a temporary ban on a double-issue scheduled for release.[63]

Mladina started to play tricks on the authorities. Well aware that the galley proofs would be checked 'higher up', the staff on one occasion prepared a dirty poem about Tito without intending to publish it. When the magazine came out, the police were ready with an order to ban it, but the poem was not in the magazine.

There were new confrontations on 1986. In February, Mladina was preparing to publish an article criticizing Prime Minister Branko Mikulić for political trials in his native Bosnia. The article suggested that his record disqualified him as prime minister. The editorial staff was abruptly summoned before the Central Committee of the Slovenian party and threatened with imprisonment unless the article was withdrawn. The staff caved in, but the page on which the article had been scheduled to appear was left blank. Later, the article was published in the youth newspaper from Maribor, *Katedra*.[64]

The following month, *Mladina* featured an article about the elections, speculating that the Communist Party would 'probably' win and describing them as 'elections of the delegates of delegates of delegates of delegates'. Other satirical articles followed. By late summer, the Slovenian daily, *Delo*, reported that Pavlo Car, the Slovenian public prosecutor, was openly complaining of:

---

62. Interview with a staff member of *Mladina*, Ljubljana, July 1987.
63. *Borba* (Zagreb edition), 1–2 August 1987, p. 6.
64. Interview, Ljubljana, July 1987.

a mass sowing of bitterness, pessimism, carping, and political insinuations, that has been perpetrated by the press, radio and television, publishing houses, various tribunes, and round-table conferences . . . that 'craftily walk on the brink of the criminal zones.' . . . In Car's words, the specific culprits include three Slovenian newspapers, *Mladina*, *Nova revija*, and *Katedra*, and in addition to them the Commission for the Protection of Thought and Writing of the Writers Association of Slovenia.[65]

This complaint was subsequently amplified in *Borba*, which wrote sarcastically, in November 1986:

It is only when one has read the Ljubljana 'youth' newspaper *Mladina* that one 'realizes' that all our leaderships and organs (and especially the federal ones) not only are 'stupid' and 'incapable' but also intentionally work against the interests of the working class and the working people (so that they 'may continue to stay in power'). 'Only' the editors and correspondents of that newspaper know the efficacious recipe for quickly and successfully resolving all our problems and crises.

'Evidence' that our 'authorities' work against us may be found in every issue of *Mladina*, including the latest, in which the writer of the editorial, 'Backward into the Future', 'discloses' that the statement by the Presidency and the LCY Presidium of 20 October 'conceals a maneuver which recalls the dark ages of Stalinism', and one Janez Završnik 'warns' us that this is 'senseless paranoia,' and that it is 'high time that those in power should cease creating the internal enemy and should devote themselves to their work.' . . .

It only remains to us to recommend to the signatories of the republican social accord on [the] co-financing [of] *Mladina* to increase their subsidies so that *Mladina* may increase our joy by issuing a completely 'clear' and 'legitimate' outline and that it may inform us even more exhaustively about 'the fate' of 'political prisoners', 'civilian service in the Yugoslav People's Army', 'civilian society in a civilian state', and what cologne is used by the former responsible editor (who, as we learn in *Mladina*, is at [the] moment serving in the Army in Pančevo) and other socially involved editors and contributors (and not only what they do and at what time they go to bed).[66]

The editors of *Mladina*, *Katedra* and *Nova revija* joined the chairman of the Slovenian Commission for the Protection of Thought

65. *Delo* (Ljubljana), 19 September 1986, p. 6, translated in FBIS, *Daily Report* (Eastern Europe), 1 October 1986, p. 19.
66. *Borba* (Belgrade edition), 15–16 November 1986, p. 5, translated in FBIS, *Daily Report* (Eastern Europe), 9 December 1986, p. 18.

and Writing and the president of the Slovenian Writers' Association in signing a letter protesting Car's statements.[67] But Car refused to retract anything.[68]

Katedra, the organ of the students of the University of Maribor, has been increasingly visible since the mid-1980s, and has shown itself repeatedly ready to take risks. In January 1987, for instance, the newspaper published an interview with Serbian intellectual Kosta Čavoški, co-author of an important study of the Yugoslav Communist Party's consolidation of its power monopoly in the late 1940s.[69] In March the paper published an interview with Yugoslav dissident Milovan Djilas: the interview had originally been scheduled to appear in *Mladina*, but when authorities prevented *Mladina* from publishing it, the text was passed on to *Katedra*. It was the first time Djilas has been heard in his own country since his disgrace in 1954.[70] When *Katedra* returned less than three months later with an open letter from dissident Vojislav Šešelj, said to 'insult the representatives of the socio-political life of our country', authorities banned the issue.[71] When *Mladina* criticized Defence Minister Branko Mamula in February 1988 for his involvement in an arms sale to Ethiopia and for assigning a group of soldiers (among them Slovenes) to help build a villa for his use in Opatija, the federal prosecutor instructed the Slovenian prosecutor to initiate legal proceedings against *Mladina*'s editor, Franc Zavrl. Among other things, *Mladina* had called Mamula a 'merchant of death'. But the Slovenian prosecutor decided to arraign Zavrl not on the charge suggested by Belgrade – of 'offending the honor of Yugoslavia and of its army' – but on the minor charge of personal defamation, which carries a maximum penalty of three months in prison or a fine.[72]

Two months later, *Mladina* published materials showing that the army was preparing a plan to arrest politically 'undesirable' figures (including journalists) in Slovenia and quash the movement for democratization. A Slovenian human rights publication records that:

67. *Delo*, 19 September 1986, p. 6, translated in FBIS, *Daily Report* (Eastern Europe), 1 October 1986, pp. I9–I10.
68. *Delo*, 20 September 1986, p. 4, translated in FBIS, *Daily Report* (Eastern Europe), 1 October 1986, pp. I10–I11.
69. Translated in *South Slav Journal*, Vol. 10, No. 1, spring 1987, pp. 38–45.
70. *The Economist*, 11 April 1987, p. 50.
71. *Večernji List*, 2 July 1987, p. 4.
72. *Christian Science Monitor*, 9 March 1988, p. 2; *The Economist*, 19 March 1988, p. 48; and *New York Times*, 19 March 1988, p. 15.

At the meeting of the [Yugoslav] Military Council, the Commander of Ljubljana Army Region is given the duty to come to an agreement with the Slovene Ministry for Internal Affairs, concerning security measures in Slovenia on the basis of the opinions of the Military Council, [to] begin criminal prosecution of the writers of some of the army about the army, and [to] order imprisonments . . . if, as a result, there was public unrest.[73]

Orders were sent to stop publication of the offending issue, and three journalists and one enlisted man were put on trial. The trial electrified the Slovenian public and directly contributed to the proliferation of independent committees and parties in Slovenia.[74]

Mladina has remained in the forefront of the movement for democratization, publishing the results of a poll in December 1988, showing that 64 per cent of Slovenes considered it necessary to introduce a multi-party system, and that in free elections, the communists would obtain only 7.3 per cent of the vote (as compared with 26.9 per cent for the Social Democrats, 18.7 per cent for the Christian Democrats, and 14.2 per cent for the Greens).[75]

Among other youth publications, the Serbian youth-oriented publications *Student* and *Vidik* have likewise repeatedly come under critical scrutiny, have sometimes been chastened for lapsing into 'anti-Marxist' views,[76] and from time to time have had their wrists slapped – most recently in late September 1987, when the deputy editor and five members of the editorial staff of *Student* were forced to resign.[77] There have also been complaints about 'bourgeois' orientations in Croatia's youth press,[78] while the Albanian-language organ of the Kosovo Socialist Youth Federation, *Zeri i Rinis*, was criticized in 1986 for failing to take a forceful line against Albanian nationalism and irredentism.[79]

73. 'Slovenian Spring – Centralism or Democracy?', *Independent Voices from Slovenia*, Vol. 4, Special edition, October 1988, p. 6.
74. For a more detailed discussion of the effects of this trial, see Pedro Ramet, 'Yugoslavia's Troubled Times', *Global Affairs*, Vol. 5, No. 1, Winter 1990.
75. *Mladina* (Ljubljana), 9 December 1988, pp. 18–19, translated in FBIS, *Daily Report* (Eastern Europe), 16 December 1988, pp. 57–8.
76. *Die Presse* (Vienna), 22 January 1982, p. 2.
77. *Borba* (Zagreb edition), 1 October 1987, p. 3.
78. Zagreb Domestic Service, 8 December 1986, translated in FBIS, *Daily Report* (Eastern Europe), 10 December 1986, p. I1; and *Politika*, 11 December 1985, p. 6.
79. TANJUG, 9 October 1986, translated in FBIS, *Daily Report* (Eastern Europe), 15 October 1986, p. I7.

431

Life of a Journalist

A journalist's life, in Yugoslavia, is difficult – or as Austrians are supposed to be fond of saying, 'hopeless but not serious'. The 'average' Yugoslav journalist is male, 40 years old (as of 1989) and has less than 20 years to live – (54 per cent of Yugoslav journalists die before reaching retirement age). He has one child but is either divorced or about to be divorced. He smokes 40 cheap cigarettes a day, drinks brandy, suffers from recurrent stomach-aches, rents his apartment, and does not own his car. Of journalists surveyed in 1989, 81 per cent were members of the League of Communists, and 65 per cent had a university degree.[80] In Slovenia, journalists have been complaining that their incomes are low and their living standards in decline.[81] Stress is a constant occupational hazard.[82]

Journalists are cautioned to write 'responsibly'. If they are thought to have failed in this task, they may be subject to prosecution.[83] But where a journalist is fired not through her or his own fault, she or he is assured financial sustenance from the official 'solidarity fund' of the Journalists' Association. In the course of 1986, a group of Serbian journalists took the initiative in setting up an independent solidarity fund – the implication being that they could not rely on the official fund. Authorities quickly declared that the independent fund was 'unnecessary' and that its real purpose was to organize a forum for political opposition. At least two journalists have been expelled from the (Vojvodina) Journalists' Federation because of their affiliation with the independent solidarity fund.[84] But before the end of the year, a similar solidarity fund was set up in Slovenia.

Recently, Slovenian journalists have taken an initiative which seems to suggest their desire for ideological latitude. Specifically, in October 1986, the Slovenian Journalists' Association unanimously adopted a resolution to drop from its statutes a clause requiring members to be 'consciously loyal to the ideas of Marxism–Lenin-

80. *Muenchner Merkur* (Munich), 15–16 March 1986, p. 4; *Večernji List*, 14 September 1989, p. 5; and *Večernje Novosti*, 14 September 1989, p. 19. See also *NIN*, No. 1840, 6 April 1986, pp. 22–3.
81. *Borba* (Zagreb edition), 6 February 1986, p. 3; and *Borba* (Belgrade edition), 28 October 1986, p. 3.
82. *Politika*, 15 March 1986, p. 6.
83. See the report in Nova Hrvatska (London), 1 November 1987, p. 6.
84. TANJUG, 24 July 1986 and 2 April 1987, translated respectively in FBIS, *Daily Report* (Eastern Europe), 25 July 1986, p. I10 and 3 April 1987, p. I9; and *Politika*, 21 February 1987, p. 6 and 19 March 1987, p. 6.

ism' and promised to seek 'even more extensive changes to the Yugoslav journalists' charter'.[85] *Delo*, the Slovenian daily, carried an article defending the proposal that the affirmation of loyalty to Marxism–Leninism be dropped from the Yugoslav Journalists' Charter, while the Bosnian daily, *Oslobodjenje*, criticized the proposal. The latter, in its unattributed commentary, was certainly hostile to the Slovene proposal and argued that 'what is obviously offered and wished [for] is that our press should de jure open itself to all possible ideological and political orientations and in fact to legalize the breakthrough of authors of largely rightist or falsely leftist positions, a breakthrough that has been virtually realized in some newspapers'.[86] The subject was also taken up in *Politika*. But regardless of the press discussions, one may suspect that if the clause in question is dropped, some suitable substitute (e.g. loyalty to self-managing socialism) may be found.

A Critical Press

The Yugoslav press is famous for being critical. But, of course, it is critical in different ways. One may, perhaps, distinguish between criticism which is directed 'inward' and criticism which is directed 'outward'. By the former, I mean criticism of the government or the party, or of party policies, or of persons in the political establishment, or investigative reporting which probes issues of the day. By the latter, I mean criticism directed specifically against non-party sectors of society, such as rock musicians, dissidents and religious institutions.

Inward criticism is, of course, the more problematical from the authorities' point of view. The authorities are well aware that a critical/investigative approach contributes to making a publication interesting, and that in the absence of such an approach, a publication may adhere to party formulae and end up being boring and ineffective. The party organ, as has been repeatedly admitted, suffers from this problem and its influence today is correspondingly described as 'minimal'.[87] Still, it is understandable that those being

85. TANJUG, 10 October 1986, translated in FBIS, *Daily Report* (Eastern Europe), 22 October 1986, p. I13.
86. *Oslobodjenje*, as reprinted in *Borba* (Belgrade edition), 17 October 1986, p. 11, as summarized in FBIS, *Daily Report* (Eastern Europe), 13 November 1986, p. I6.
87. *Politika Ekspres* (Belgrade), 25 June 1987, p. 2.

criticized take umbrage at the fact: Tomislav Bardin, a delegate to the Serbian Assembly, objected when one bi-weekly Belgrade feature magazine, *Duga*, published an article critical of that body's discussion of language equality in Kosovo;[88] the veterans' organization in Zagreb raised a small clamour about how it was being portrayed in *Danas, Polet, NIN* and *Politika*;[89] even where the recent Agrokomerc scandal is concerned, there have been polemics about press coverage.[90]

NIN was in the forefront of investigative journalism in the early 1980s. More recently, *Duga*, with its feisty interviews, has become a magazine to watch. Illustrative of *Duga*'s bold journalism was an interview with Mišo Pavićević, a member of the Council of the Federation, published in October 1985. In this interview, Pavićević spoke of the older (partisan) generation 'losing its way' and noted that the present crisis in Yugoslavia can only be described as the result of 'a process which has been going on for over a decade and a half'. By this he meant above all the process of decentralization which had contributed to satisfying the autonomist aspirations among Yugoslavia's diverse nationality groups. The result, for Pavićević, is that Yugoslav policymaking is frequently deadlocked or strangled, and in his view, little time remains for Yugoslavia to find a solution, before it will be threatened with serious disintegration.[91] *Duga* has also been prepared to probe scandals and to allow public figures to vent their frustrations.

In September 1986, the republican conference of SAWP Serbia reviewed *Duga*'s performance and concluded that the magazine had 'published a number of articles whose content and message is, from an ideological and political standpoint, unacceptable. This relates, in particular, to certain interviews, letters, and features that, in a sensationalist way, sow distrust, stimulate nationalist sentiment, and provoke disputes.' The conference also complained of 'articles containing historical lies and which wrote in an unacceptable way about LCY cadres'.[92] The following year *Duga*'s editor (along with the editors of *NIN, Intervju* and *Svet*) was replaced, but even so, Serbian party chairman Slobodan Milošević declared: 'The situation

88. See *Duga* (Belgrade), 13–26 June 1987, p. 11.
89. *Večernji List*, 23 June 1987, p. 4.
90. *Borba* (Zagreb edition), 6 October 1987, p. 5.
91. *Duga*, 5–18 October 1987, as translated in *South Slav Journal*, Vol. 8, Nos. 3–4, autumn–winter 1985, pp. 81–8.
92. TANJUG, 19 September 1986, translated in FBIS, *Daily Report* (Eastern Europe), 22 September 1986, p. I4.

in *Duga* will not change until there are broader changes in the editorial staff of *Duga*.'[93]

Then there is the case of Ranka Čičak, an enterprising journalist, who, after uncovering a scam operation involving pig farmers and local politicians, was charged with having insulted Tito in a private conversation and with having justified both Croatian separatism and Albanian irredentism, imprisoned for six months, and later injured in a mysterious traffic accident.[94]

Again, when party authorities banned a professional meeting of the Philosophical Society of Serbia, which was to have discussed 'the possibilities of reform in socialist countries', *Književne novine* provided a forum in which the Society's president could register his protest.[95]

The authorities say they want criticism but such criticism must be 'progressive' and 'in line with self-management', and should not be contrary to LCY policy.[96] In a micro-example of this kind of thinking, the traditionally conservative *Borba*, upon cancelling publication of a pre-announced interview with drama director Ljubiša Ristić in 1984, wrote: 'The editors of this paper are not in agreement with some of Ristić's views and he did not consent to having them excluded. So, as a result, we are publishing another . . .discussion [instead].'[97]

And, finally, there is *outward* criticism, in the sense in which I have defined it. Outward criticism is not a feature in the entire secular press. The youth press contains very little, if any, outward criticism, at least not at the party's behest. Magazines like *Duga*, *Start* and *Reporter* likewise engage in little outward criticism, and for that matter, *Danas* and *NIN* also do not make much space for criticizing persons outside the party. The daily press, on the other hand, is a routine vehicle for outward criticism.

The churches are one target of outward criticism. Where the Catholic Church is concerned, such criticism has recently ranged from complaints about Cardinal Kuharić's annual defence of Cardinal

93. Quoted in *Danas*, No. 278, 16 June 1987, p. 8.
94. *Vjesnik*, 24 December 1982, p. 14, translated in FBIS, *Daily Report* (Eastern Europe), 3 January 1983, p. I7; *Los Angeles Times*, 3 April 1983, Pt I–A, pp. 8–9; and *Neue Zuercher Zeitung* (Zurich), 9 May 1984, p. 4.
95. *Književne Novine* (Belgrade), 1 September 1987, p. 3.
96. TANJUG, 7 November 1985, translated in FBIS, *Daily Report* (Eastern Europe), 8 November 1985, p. I7.
97. *Borba* (Belgrade edition), 15–16 September 1984, p. 9, translated in JPRS, *East Europe Report*, No. EPS–84 –127, 12 October 1984, p. 109 (punctuation altered slightly).

Stepinac (d. 1960), who was convicted, in a rather dubious trial in 1946, of collaboration with the fascists during the Second World War,[98] to charges that unnamed church circles were calling on believers 'to settle accounts with the communists, emphasizing that the communists are on the top of the list for liquidation, if another government takes over',[99] to insinuations that Pope John Paul II went to Chile to endorse the Pinochet regime when in fact the very opposite was the case,[100] to claims that the church weekly *Glas Koncila* called communism one of the 'most reactionary ideologies of the century'.[101] In September 1986, the Novi Sad daily, *Dnevnik*, published an article adorned with a caricature of a man in an Ustasha uniform, standing in front of a barbed wire fence and waving a copy of *Glas Koncila*:[102] the clear implication was that the paper – the official organ of the Zagreb archdiocese – was advocating fascistic ideas. Usually *Glas koncila* contents itself with expostulations on its editorial page. On this occasion, however, the editor took *Dnevnik* to court. The District Court refused to consider the case; so *Glas Koncila* took the case to the Higher Court in Novi Sad.[103] The court ultimately handed down a judgement in *Dnevnik*'s favour. The decision, signed by president of the Court, Mirjana Carić, explained that: 'the connection of part of the Catholic clergy in Croatia . . .with the Ustasha movement and its activity during the National Liberation War, *as well as later*, is not new or unknown, but falls into [the category of] historically established fact'.[104] Hence *Glas Koncila*, which was established only in the mid-1960s, could be 'legitimately' portrayed as pro-Ustasha. But *Dnevnik* and Belgrade's *Večernje Novosti* have been perhaps the most hostile toward the Catholic Church, while other papers have adopted a more balanced approach.

The Serbian Orthodox Church has likewise found that its treatment at the hands of the secular media has been uneven. Misleading and disparaging reports have surfaced most frequently in *Oslobodjenje*, the Bosnian daily, although these reports are sometimes reprinted in other newspapers.[105]

98. *Politika*, 18 February 1987, p. 6; and *Vjesnik*, 26 February 1987, p. 4.
99. *Novi List*, (Rijeka), 17 April 1987, as quoted in *Glas Koncila*, 26 April 1987, p. 2.
100. *Vjesnik*, 5 April 1987, as cited in *Glas Koncila*, 12 April 1987, p. 2.
101. *Danas*, No. 279, 23 June 1987, p. 25.
102. *Dnevnik* (Novi Sad), 8 September 1986, p. 5.
103. Interview, Zagreb, June 1987.
104. A copy of the decision (No. 132/87, dated 18 March 1987) is in the author's file.
105. Interview, Belgrade, July 1987.

Outward criticism – whether of religious leaders or dissident intellectuals or rock stars or other persons – sometimes portrays the persons concerned as engaged in illegal activity (though, usually, no one is arrested or brought to trial) or as morally degenerate or politically disloyal or as disseminating disinformation (which, typically, is challenged only in a polemical or sarcastic way). Outward criticism, thus, unlike inward criticism, has more to do with trying to cast a pall over the reputations of certain people and with signalling to the readership that these people are, at least for party members, 'off limits', than with any serious effort to raise and discuss issues. Outward criticism is a political tool of sectors of the political establishment; inward criticism is more usually a vehicle for persons (whether inside or outside the establishment) who are critical of the regime.

Conclusion

The republicanization of the press has been a basic fact of Yugoslav public life and is one of a number of factors which push in the direction of the disintegration of the country. People in Bosnia commonly say that local Muslims read the Bosnian republic press (*Oslobodjenje, AS*), local Croats read the Croatian republic press (chiefly *Vjesnik* and *Večernji List*), and Bosnian Serbs read the Serbian republic press (chiefly *Politika*, but also *Politika Ekspres*). In October 1989, the Belgrade daily, *Borba*, published the results of a public opinion poll in which 120 persons (20 per republic) were asked three questions: which papers they considered the most influential in the country; which they most respected and which they least respected; and which they read most frequently.[106] While the results for Slovenia and Macedonia are clearly affected by the fact that these republics speak different languages, it is clear that for all republics there is a close correlation between republic of residence and orientations toward the press.

Only Macedonians (8 per cent), for example, cited the Skopje daily, *Nova Makedonija*, as one of the most influential papers in the country, and only Slovenes cited Slovenian periodicals (*Delo* 18 per

---

106. The percentages cited in the following text are invariably larger than those given in Tables 14.1 and 14.2 because the analysis in the tables includes only responses relating to the principal publications.

Table 14.1 Which Periodical Do You Respect the Most?[a] (%–120 people, 1989)

	BOSNIA	CROATIA	MACEDONIA	MONTENEGRO	SERBIA	SLOVENIA
Serbian papers						
Politika	25		27	27	31	
NIN			13	7	5	
Duga					9	
TV Revija				7		
Croatian papers						
Vjesnik	4	10				
Start		14			14	
Slobodna						
Dalmacija		19				
Večernji list	7	5				
Slovenian papers						
Delo						23
Večer						14
Mladina						9
Other papers						
Borba		10				
Večernje novosti				10		
Nova Makedonija			6			
Oslobodjenje	11					
Pobjeda				10		
Women's						
magazines						23
None			19			9

[a] Figures are for principal publications only

Source: Borba, 2 October 1989, p. 7, translated in FBIS, Daily Report (Eastern Europe), 23 October 1989, pp. 58–9.

cent, *Mladina* 11 per cent, and *Večer* 7 per cent) among the most influential. Of Serbs, 54 per cent mentioned *Politika*, but only 8 per cent of Croats did so. Only Croats and Bosnians cited the Croatian press.[107]

Asked what periodicals they respected most (see Table 14.1), 54 per cent of Serbs cited a Serbian periodical, 58 per cent of Croats cited a Croatian periodical, and 58 per cent of Montenegrins cited either a Montenegrin or a Serbian publication. Results in the other republics were more mixed.

And in terms of readership (see Table 14.2), 56 per cent of

107. *Borba* (Belgrade), 2 October 1989, p. 7.

Table 14.2 Which Periodical Do You Read the Most Frequently?
(%–120 people, 1989)

	BOSNIA	CROATIA	MACEDONIA	MONTENEGRO	SERBIA	SLOVENIA
Serbian papers						
Politika	9		12	18	30	
NIN			8	7	6	
Croatian papers						
Vjesnik		15				
Start		7		6		
Slobodna Dalmacija		26				
Večernji list	9	19				
Danas				6		
Slovenian papers						
Delo						24
Večer						10
Mladina						5
Ljubljanski Dnevnik						10
Revija						20
Macedonian papers						
Nova Makedonija			33			
Politikin zabavnik			17			
Večer			6			
Other						
Večernje novosti	11	12	6	10	6	
Oslobodjenje	20					
Pobjeda				35		
Women's magazines	17					

Source: Borba, 2 October 1989, p. 7, translated in FBIS, *Daily Report* (Eastern Europe), 23 October 1989, pp. 59–60.

Note: The percentages cited in the text which follows are invariably longer than those given in Tables 14.1 and 14.2 because the analysis in the tables includes only responses relating to principal publications.

Macedonians rely chiefly on Macedonian periodicals, 42 per cent of Serbs rely chiefly on Serbian or Vojvodinan (*Dnevnik*) periodicals, 79 per cent of Croats rely chiefly on Croatian periodicals, 72 per cent of Slovenes on Slovenian periodicals, 68 per cent of Montenegrins on Montenegrin or Serbian periodicals, but only 26 per cent of Bosnians on Bosnian publications. Only in Bosnia did a large number of respondents (17 per cent) cite women's magazines as their major source of news and information.

Naturally, the influence any newspaper enjoys fluctuates over time. *Borba* and *Slobodna Dalmacija* were marginal papers ten years ago; today they are, together with *Delo*, arguably the most widely respected papers in the country. But neither *Slobodna Dalmacija* nor *Delo* can claim a wide readership outside their respective republics. Leaving aside ethnically mixed Bosnia, only the Serbian periodicals *Politika* and *NIN*, the Croatian weekly magazine *Danas* and fortnightly *Start*, and the Belgrade publications *Borba* and *Večernje Novosti* can claim a wide readership that extends beyond the boundaries of the republic in which they are published.[108]

The highest circulations are enjoyed by the evening tabloids (*Večernje Novosti*, *Večernji List* and *Politika Ekspres*), although *Komunist*, *Politika* and *AS* also have circulations over 200,000 (see table 14.3). Among church publications, only the Catholic papers, *Družina* and *Glas Koncila*, have circulations in excess of 100,000.

In January 1990, the League of Communists of Yugoslavia passed a resolution to introduce a multi-party system in the country. If carried out, this will necessarily have major ramifications for the functioning of all aspects of the system, including the press. As of February 1990, secession was being widely discussed in both Croatia and Slovenia, where the local party organization dissolved its connection with the federal party and redesignated itself the Democratic Party for Renewal. At this time of writing, it is far too early to be able to tell what shape the Yugoslav press will assume in the years to come.

I began this chapter by noting that the press reflects the more general chaos which characterizes Yugoslavia. I shall close by noting that this chaos – both at the systematic level and within the sphere of journalism specifically – is in part the deliberate design of the Tito era and serves certain functions, in part the product of the partially successful struggle of certain editorial staffs (especially of *Start*, *Duga*, *NIN* and the youth press) to broaden their latitude, in part the by-product of federalization, republicanization and devolution, and in part, a by-product of the gathering crisis and weakening of authority at the centre.

108. According to the data reported in Ibid.

Table 14.3 Yugoslav Newspapers with Circulations Larger Than 20,000 in Rank Order (1983)[a]

	Copies printed	Copies sold
Komunist (all editions)	550,000	n/a
Večernje Novosti (Belgrade)	379,921	339,859
Večernje List (Zagreb)	342,533	309,839
Politika Ekspres (Belgrade)	286,451	249,758
Politika (Belgrade)	278,101	243,826
AS (Sarajevo)	215,159	n/a
Sportske Novosti (Zagreb)	169,887	141,247
Sport (Belgrade)	127,712	106,781
Delo (Ljubljana)	105,042	99,840
Družina (Ljubljana, Catholic)	100,000[b]	n/a
Glas Koncila (Zagreb, Catholic)	100,000[b]	n/a
Vjesnik (Zagreb)	91,116	73,030
Oslobodjenje (Sarajevo)	83,331	71,557
Ognjišće (Koper, Catholic)	80,000[c]	n/a
Novi List – Glas Istre (Rijeka)	78,976	71,274
Slobodna Dalmacija (Split)	78,242	71,571
Večer (Maribor)	58,477	55,476
Dnevnik (Ljubljana)	53,497	50,723
Mali Koncil (Zagreb, Catholic)	50,000[c]	n/a
Rilindja (Pristina)	46,252	41,141
Večernje Novine	45,670	35,049
Borba (Belgrade)	42,563	30,976
Dnevnik (Novi Sad)	38,697	34,158
Večer (Skopje)	36,771	31,959
Magyar Szo (Novi Sad)	30,279	26,485
Preporod (Sarajevo, Islamic)	30,000	n/a
Nova Makedonija (Skopje)	29,124	25,089
Pobjeda (Titograd)	22,568	20,073
Pravoslavlje (Belgrade, Orthodox)	22,000[d]	n/a

[a] Figures are for principal publications only; [b] = 1987; [c] = 1973; [d] = 1982.

Sources: *Naša stampa*, (July–August 1983, pp. 9–10; *Naša stampa*, February 1984, p. 9; AKSA 20 May 1983); *NIN*, 22 May 1983, translated in FBIS, *Daily Report* (Eastern Europe), 1 June 1983; interviews, Belgrade and Zagreb, July 1982; and interviews, Zagreb and Ljubljana, June–July 1987.

PART III

Bibliographical Review

15

Frederick Bernard Singleton and Yugoslavia: A Bibliography of his Published Works

John J. Horton

Fred Singleton's writings were not confined to Yugoslav topics – he wrote two major books on Finland, one economic, the other historical, plus many articles on Finnish affairs. He also wrote two important books on the history of his native county of Yorkshire, one general, the other on the Industrial Revolution. This present volume, however, is a tribute to his Yugoslav profile, and the following list is thus confined to his writings on Yugoslavia, and to those on Eastern Europe where they have a bearing on Yugoslav studies. But it is important to have drawn attention to his other interests, because it is clear that his studies of Yorkshire and Finland afforded him a comparative experience and perspective (particularly of regional problems) which shows in his approach to the study of Yugoslavia.

For Fred Singleton was primarily a geographer, and one who successfully made the transition to the discipline of ' area studies'; he did not pretend to be a specialist historian or economist, but the combination of his vast store of knowledge, his ability to collate and interpret it in the context of Yugoslavia as a whole, and his skills as a communicator gained from his teaching in a variety of contexts (school, university, workers' education) meant that his books and other writings could always be appreciated by the informed general reader and often offer a new perspective to the hardened specialist. This ability to communicate was especially recognized in 1968 when he accepted a commission from BBC Television to present their six-part documentary series on Yugoslavia.

He differed from many Western writers and commentators on

John J. Horton

Yugoslav affairs who have too often been motivated either by preconceived commitment to the Yugoslav experiment or by personal hostility to the post-war developments. As a socialist Fred undoubtedly possessed great sympathy and goodwill for the Yugoslav way, but never allowed this to suppress his criticisms where he thought these should be expressed – his criticism, however, was of a constructive character, and for this objectivity he was widely respected in Yugoslav academic and diplomatic circles, as well as by his countless friends and colleagues in Yugoslavia.

In addition to the individual books, articles, and so on, listed below, Fred also served on the editorial boards of the Soviet and East European Studies Series for Cambridge University Press, and of the quarterly journal *Soviet Studies* plus its original offshoot *Abstracts for Soviet and East European Studies (ABSEES)*.

N.B. Items under each heading are arranged by date of publication.

Books as Author

Yugoslavia (with Muriel Heppell), London, Benn, 1961, 236pp
Background to Eastern Europe, Oxford, Pergamon Press, 1965, 226pp
Yugoslavia: The Country and Its People, London, Queen Anne Press, 1970, 138pp
Twentieth Century Yugoslavia, London, Macmillan, 1976, 346pp
The Economy of Yugoslavia (with Bernard Carter), London, Croom Helm, 1982, 279pp
A Short History of the Yugoslav Peoples, Cambridge, Cambridge University Press, 1985, 309pp

Volumes As Editor

Environmental Misuse in the Soviet Union, Papers from the International Slavic Conference, Banff, Alberta, 1974, New York, Praeger; London, Martin Robertson, 1976, 100pp
The Just Society (with Ken Coates) [Conference, University of Bradford, 1976], Nottingham, Spokesman Books and the Bertrand Russell Peace Foundation, European Socialist Thought Series, No. 10, 1977, 183pp

Environmental Problems in the Soviet Union and Eastern Europe, Papers from the 3rd World Congress for Soviet and East European Studies, Washington, DC, 1985, Boulder, Colo., Lynne Rienner, 1987, 208pp

Shorter Monographs

Workers' Control in Yugoslavia (with A.J. Topham), Fabian Research Series, No. 233, London, Fabian Society, 1963, 32pp

Geography, Politics and the Environment: A Study of Soviet and East European Practice, London, Centre for Environmental Studies, 1976, 28pp

Regional Economic Inequalities, Migration and Community Response, with Special Reference to Yugoslavia, Bradford Studies on Yugoslavia, No. 1, Postgraduate School of Yugoslav Studies, Bradford, University of Bradford, 1979, 28pp

Environmental Protection in Yugoslavia, Berlin, International Institute for Environment and Society, 1986, 18pp

Contributions to Volumes

The Annual Register: A Record of World Events, London, Longman [Section on Yugoslavia in the volumes from 1960 to 1987]

'Workers' Self-Management and the Role of Trade Unions in Yugoslavia', in *Trade Union Register*, edited by Ken Coates, A.J. Topham and Michael Barratt-Brown, London, Merlin Press, 1970, pp. 231–47

'Problems of Regional Economic Development: The Case of Yugoslavia', in *Yearbook of East European Economics*, Vol. 2, Munich; Vienna, Olzog, 1971, pp. 371–95

'The Economic Background to Tensions Between the Nationalities in Yugoslavia', in *Probleme des Industrialismus in Ost und West: Festschrift für Hans Raupach*, edited by Werner Gumpel and Dietmar Keese, Munich; Vienna, Olzog, 1973, pp. 281–304

'Yugoslavia's Foreign Economic Relations', in *Südosteuropa Handbuch*, Vol. 1, edited by Klaus-Detlev Grothusen, Göttingen, Vandenhoeck and Ruprecht, 1975, pp. 275–88

Mind Alive Encyclopaedia [Sections on the Balkans, USSR, etc.], London, Marshall Cavendish, 1977

John J. Horton

Encyclopaedia Britannica (macropaedia) 15th edn, 1979, entry on Belgrade (with Milorad Vasović), pp. 825–6; entry on Yugoslavia (with Vladimir Bakarić), pp. 1098–107.

'Socialist Federative Republic of Yugoslavia', in *Marxist Governments: A World Survey*, Vol. 3, edited by Bogdan Szajkowski, London, Macmillan, 1981, pp. 784–821

'Environmental Problems in Socialist Countries', in *The Just Society*, ed. Singleton and Coates, pp. 100–26

'Objectives and Methods of Economic Policies in Yugoslavia', in *The East European Economies in the 1970s*, edited by Alec Nove, Hans Hermann Höhmann and Gertraud Seidenstecher, London, Butterworth, 1982, pp. 280–314

'Yugoslavia's Foreign Trade and External Relations', in *Südosteuropa in Weltpolitik und Weltwirtschaft der achtziger Jahre*, edited by Roland Schönfeld, Oldenbourg, Südost-Institut, 1983, pp. 227–32

'Yugoslavia', in *The Party Statutes of the Communist World*, edited by W. B. Simons and S. White, The Hague, Nijhoff, 1984, pp. 479–533

'Environmental Problems in Eastern Europe [USSR and Yugoslavia]', *Proceedings of the Anglo-Bulgarian Symposium, 1982*, vol. 2, edited by L. Collins, London School of Slavonic and East European Studies, 1985, pp. 58–74

'Regionale ökonomischen Ungleicheiten in Jugoslawien', in *Jugoslawien am Ende der Ära Tito*, Vol. 2, *Innenpolitik*, edited by Klaus-Detlev Grothusen, Othmar Nikola Haberl and Wolfgang Höpken, Munich, Oldenbourg, 1986, pp. 143–57

'Czechoslovakia: Greens versus Reds', in *Environmental Problems in the Soviet Union and Eastern Europe*, ed. Singleton, pp. 169–82

'National Parks and Conservation of Nature in Yugoslavia', in *Environmental Problems in the Soviet Union and Eastern Europe*, ed. Singleton, pp. 183–98

'Mr Gladstone and the Eastern Question', in *Yugoslav–British Relations: Papers presented to the Round Table on Yugoslav–British Relations on the Occasion of the 150th Anniversary of the Arrival of the First British Consul to Serbia, held at Kragujevac from 23rd to 25th September 1987*, Belgrade: Institut za savremenu istoriju, 1988, pp. 39–50

'The British Youth Brigades in Yugoslavia', *Yugoslav–British Relations*, pp. 345–58

Articles in Periodicals

'The Jugoslav Economic Experiment', *Socialist Commentary*, August 1958, pp. 20–2

'Adult Education in Yugoslavia', *Adult Education*, Vol. 33, No. 2, July 1960, pp. 142–5

'Yugoslav Workers' Control: The Latest Phase' (with Tony Topham), *New Left Review*, No. 18, January–February 1963, pp. 73–84

'Yugoslav Academics and their Right to Reply', *Times Educational Supplement*, 30 September 1966, pp. 698

'Peace on a Re-drawn Frontier' [the Julian region], *Geographical Magazine*, Vol. 39, No. 10, February 1967, pp. 821–9

'Macedonia on the Move', *Geographical Magazine*, Vol. 40, No. 7, November 1967, pp. 537–47

'Young People's Republic', *The Listener*, Vol. 79, 4 January 1968, pp. 17–18

'Migrant Workers in the E.E.C.', *European Studies* (European Communities Information Service), No. 8 (1970), 4 pp

'Export Trade as Key to Economy', *The Times*, 14 April 1970, p. 16 [special report on Yugoslavia]

'Socialist Yugoslavia's first official strike?' *Spokesman*, No. 8, December 1970, pp. 14–15

'Blueprint for the Redistribution of Powers' and 'Concern over growing foreign payments deficit', *The Times*, 23 June 1971, p. 12 [special report on Yugoslavia]

'Belgrade Flirts with the Capitalists', *New Statesman*, Vol. 81, 25 June 1971, p. 870

'The New Yugoslav Constitution', *Journal of the British–Yugoslav Society*, Winter 1971, p. 3–5

'The Yugoslav Crisis', *Spokesman*, No. 19–20, December 1971–January 1972, pp. 23–32, 41

'Roots of Discord in Yugoslavia', *World Today*, Vol. 28, No. 4, April 1972, pp. 170–80

'Yugoslavia: From Crisis to Crisis', *New Society*, vol. 22, 23 November 1972, pp. 451–3

'Yugoslavia: Democratic Centralism and Market Socialism', *World Today*, Vol. 29, No. 4, April 1973, pp. 160–8

'Svolta in Jugoslavia', *Mercurio* (Rome), No. 2, February 1974, pp. 71–7

'Croatia' and 'Slovenia's Riches', *Financial Times*, 23 May 1975, pp. 41–2

'Yugoslavia: Move to Market Socialism', *The Times*, 25 June 1975, p. II [special report on mixed economies]

'Albania and her Neighbours: The End of Isolation', *World Today*, Vol. 31, No. 9, September 1975, pp. 383–90

'Problems of Environmental Misuse in Yugoslavia', *Spokesman*, No. 32, Summer 1976, pp. 96–103

'Worker–Management Debate Goes Back to Basics', *The Times*, 23 March 1977, p. II [special report on Yugoslavia]

'The Belgrade–Bar Railway' (with John H. R. Wilson), *Geography*, Vol. 62, No. 2, April 1977, pp. 121–5, with maps

'Tito's Road to Socialism', *Spectator*, Vol. 240, 11 March 1978, p. 11

'Yugoslavia', *Contemporary Review*, No. 234, June 1979, pp. 293–7

'Jugoslawiens Stellung in der Weltwirtschaft', *Osteuropa : Zeitschrift für Gegenwartsfragen des Ostens* (Stuttgart), Vol. 28, No. 7, July 1978, pp. 631–9

'Social Democracy and the Environment: A Study of Environmental Problems in Industrializing Countries, with Particular Reference to the U.S.S.R. and Yugoslavia', *Co-existence*, Vol. 15, No. 2, October 1978, pp. 152–69

'Jugoslawiens Aussenhandel, 1965–1977', *Osteuropa* Vol. 28, No. 12, December 1978, pp. 1094–102

'Yugoslavia takes Stock', *Critique: A Journal of Socialist Theory*, Nos. 10–11, Winter–Spring 1978–79, pp. 173–80

'How vulnerable is Yugoslavia?', *The Times*, 22 January 1980, p. 19

'Yugoslavia Will Maintain Tito's Non-alignment', *Middle East Economic Digest*, Vol. 24, No. 8, 22 February 1980, pp. 12–15

'Yugoslavia Faces the Future', *Contemporary Review*, No. 236, March 1980, pp. 118–22

'Yugoslavia without Tito', *World Today*, Vol. 36, No. 6, June 1980, pp. 204–8

'Yugoslavia: Economic Grievances and Cultural Nationalism', *World Today*, Vol. 39, No. 7–8, July–August 1983, pp. 284–90

'National Parks and the Conservation of Nature in Yugoslavia', *Journal of the British–Yugoslav Society*, Winter 1984, pp. 4–6

'Political Trials in Yugoslavia: Background to the Belgrade Proceedings', *Across Frontiers* (Berkeley, Calif.), Vol. 2, No. 1, Summer 1985, pp. 2–3

'Ecological Crisis in Eastern Europe: Do the Greens Threaten the Reds?', *Across Frontiers*, Vol. 2, No. 1, Summer 1985, pp. 5–10

'The Yugoslav Economic Crisis and the Future of Self-management', *Journal of the British–Yugoslav Society*, Winter 1985, pp. 4–6

'The 13th Congress of the League of Communists of Yugoslavia', *Journal of the British–Yugoslav Society*, Autumn 1986, pp. 4–8

'Attitudes to Environmental Problems in the U.S.S.R. and Eastern Europe' [The Dressler Lecture], *University of Leeds Review*, Vol. 30, 1987–88, pp. 223–36

'The Triglav National Park in the 1980s', *Slovene Studies*, Vol. 10, No. 1, 1988, pp. 39–49

Notes on the Contributors

John B. Allcock has taught at Leicester and Bradford Universities and was involved in the establishment of the Research Unit and subsequently the Postgraduate School of Yugoslav Studies at Bradford, of which he became Chairman in 1981. His research interests in sociology have covered a wide range, with published work in the history of sociology and political sociology, as well as in aspects of the study of Yugoslav society. In this last area, his major concerns have been with the study of Yugoslav rural society; the social and economic impact of tourism; and stratification and power in Yugoslavia. His published articles have appeared in British, Yugoslav, German, American, Hungarian and Polish publications. Dr Allcock is a member of the British National Committee of AIESEE (the Association International d'Etude du Sud–Est Européen) and an editor of *Bradford Studies on Yugoslavia*. His latest publication, co-edited with Marko Milivojević and Pierre Maurer, is *Yugoslavia's Security Dilemmas: Armed Forces, National Defence and Foreign Policy* (Oxford and New York, 1988).

Patrick Artisien is Lecturer in East European Economics at the University of Cardiff, UK, and Visiting Associate Professor at the European Institute of Public Administration, Maastricht, Netherlands. Dr Artisien obtained his MA in the Postgraduate School of Yugoslav Studies at Bradford University, under the supervision of Fred Singleton, for his thesis on Albanian–Yugoslav relations. He has taught at various levels in the UK, Yugoslavia, Canada, the United States, the Netherlands and Sweden, and acted as Consultant to the World Bank, *The Economist* and the International Labour Office. His recent books on Yugoslavia include *Joint Ventures in Yugoslav Industry, Yugoslavia to 1993: Back from the Brink?*, and *Yugoslav Multinationals Abroad*. Dr Artisien is a frequent visitor to Yugoslavia.

Will Bartlett, BA(Cambridge), MSc(London), PhD(Liverpool), has been a Research Associate in Economics since 1988 at the School for Advanced Urban Studies, University of Bristol. Previously, he lectured in economics at the Universities of Southampton (1978–81), Bristol (1981–82) and Bath (1986–88). In 1983–86, he was a Research Fellow at the European University Institute, Florence. His published work has appeared in a number of academic journals and collections of papers.

Alan Brown, M. Phil.(Glasgow), is a Research Assistant in International Business and a doctoral candidate at the University of Cardiff Business School.

Zagorka Golubović graduated in philosophy from Belgrade University, and after a year's research in socio-cultural anthropology at the University of Nottingham, she gained her doctorate from Belgrade University in 1962. Thereafter, she taught at the same university until her dismissal in 1975 for her membership of the *Praxis* group. From 1975 to 1981, Dr Golubović lectured at the Universities of Stockholm, Lund, Göteburg and Uppsala, and Bradford. Re-engaged by Belgrade University in 1981, she is presently in charge of the project, 'Comparative research into different conceptions of socialism', at the Institute of Social Sciences, University of Belgrade. She is also President of the Serb Philosophical Society. Her latest publication in Serbo-Croat is *The Identity Crisis of the Contemporary Yugoslav Society* (Belgrade, 1988).

John J. Horton is Deputy Librarian of the University of Bradford and current Chairman of the Board of Studies in Social Sciences at the university. He has taken a special interest in the work of its Postgraduate School of Yugoslav Studies since its inception in 1971 and is co-editor of its serial publication, *Bradford Studies on Yugoslavia*. He has been responsible for building up the Library's substantial stock of materials in Yugoslav Studies and for advising research students on the sources of information available on Yugoslav topics. He has made regular visits to Yugoslavia, including specialist tours for the British Council involving lectures to Yugoslav librarians and the establishment of agreements for exchange of library materials. He speaks Serbo-Croat and is a member of the British Yugoslav Society. He is the author of the volume on Yugoslavia in the World Bibliographical Series published by Clio Press (Oxford) and has recently completed the revised edition.

Barbara Jančar received her PhD from Columbia University and a Certificate from Columbia's Institute on East Central Europe. She is Professor of Political Science at the State University of New York at Brockport. From 1984–87, she was Co-director of the SUNY Paris Program in the Social Sciences, and in 1987 was a Fellow at the East European Program of the Wilson Center, Smithsonian Institution, Washington, D C. She has travelled and published widely on Soviet and East European domestic affairs, particularly as regards the status of women and environmental issues. She is a frequent traveller to Yugoslavia and was an IREX scholar there. Her most recent full-length monograph, *Environmental Management in the Soviet Union and Yugoslavia: Structure and Regulation in Federal Communist Systems*, received the 1989 Harold and Margaret Sprout Award given by the International Studies Association for the best book in international relations pertaining to the environment.

Ljubomir Madžar is Professor of Economics at the University of Belgrade, whose economic faculty he joined in 1970. He is also a Senior Research Associate at the Institute of Economic Studies, which he joined in 1963. He has acted as a consultant to the governments of Jordan and Guyana, and held a visiting professorship at the University of Addis Ababa. He has also held research fellowships at the Universities of California (Berkeley) and Chicago. A prolific author, his books include *Optimization in the Theory of Production and of Economic Growth* (1973), *Theory and Models of Aggregate Demand* (1982), and, as co-author, *Stabilization and Development* (1985). He is also a member of the editorial board of *Ekonomist*, the journal of the Yugoslav Economic Association, and editor-in-chief of *Ekonomska Misao*, the journal of the Economic Association of Serbia.

Milan Mesić graduated in sociology and history from Zagreb University (1973); later going on to gain an MA (1977) and a PhD (1979) at the same university. Thereafter, he taught at the University of Zagreb, becoming Director of its Institute for Migration and Nationalities in 1984, when he also became editor-in-chief of the academic journal, *Migration Themes*. Dr Mesić has published widely, including two books in Serbo-Croat: *October and Workers'*

Management (Zagreb, 1983), and *Labour and Management* (Zagreb, 1986).

Marko Milivojević is a freelance writer and consultant on Yugoslav affairs. In 1986, he became an Honorary Visiting Research Fellow in Yugoslav Studies at the Research Unit in Yugoslav Studies, University of Bradford. In 1988–89, he was a Research Associate at the International Institute for Strategic Studies, London, where his research topic was Yugoslavia and Western Security. In 1989, he became a member of the Advisory Council of The South Slav Research and Study Centre, London. Mr Milivojević is a member of the UK Study Group on Intelligence. His publications include *The Debt Rescheduling Process* (London and New York, 1985), *The Yugoslav Hard Currency Debt and the Process of Economic Reform Since 1948* (Bradford, 1985), *The Yugoslav People's Army: The Military Dimension* (Bradford, 1988), *The Yugoslav People's Army: The Political Dimension* (Bradford, 1988), *Tito's Sword and Shield: The Story of the Yugoslav Intelligence and Security Community* (London, 1989), *Descent Into Chaos: Yugoslavia's Worsening Crisis*, European Security Studies No. 7 (London, 1989), and, as co-editor, *Yugoslavia's Security Dilemmas: Armed Forces, National Defence and Foreign Policy* (Oxford and New York, 1988), and *Swiss Neutrality and Security: Armed Forces, National Defence and Foreign Policy* (Oxford and New York, 1990).

Donna Parmelee is currently a Program Associate at the Center for Russian and East European Studies, University of Michigan. She has also taught at Colgate University, Hamilton, New York, where she regularly offered courses on Yugoslavia and directed two semester-long study tours of undergraduate students throughout Yugoslavia. She has conducted extensive research on the Yugoslav health-care system under the auspices of International Research and Exchanges Board and Fulbright-Hays grants. She has served as a consultant for several joint Yugoslav–World Health Organization conferences in Yugoslavia. Her publications have appeared in *Social Science and Medicine* and in edited volumes on Yugoslav health care and comparative health systems.

Dijana Pleština is Assistant Professor of Political Science at The College of Wooster, in Wooster, Ohio. Born in Zagreb, she spent her childhood in Yugoslavia and Canada. She received her BA in French literature and MA in Comparative literature from Carleton University in Ottawa, Canada and her PhD in Political Science from the University of California, Berkeley, USA in 1987. She is currently finishing a book on regional development (Westview Press, forthcoming, 1992).

Thomas M. Poulsen is the Head of the Geography Department and past Director of the Central European Studies Center at Portland State University. He received his PhD degree in geography from the University of Wisconsin. He has been a Fulbright scholar in Yugoslavia and a Ford Foundation fellow at the Russian Research Center of Harvard University. He has also directed summer graduate student field seminars in Yugoslavia for the Association of American Geographers. He is particularly interested in political geography and the geography of tourism. Among his recent publications is co-authorship of *Europe in the 1990s. A Geographic Analysis*, edited by George W. Hoffman, Wiley, 1989.

Sabrina P. Ramet is currently an Assistant Professor at the University of Washington, Seattle. Prior to her present position she taught at the Universities of California (Santa Barbara) and UCLA. Her research interests have included: Soviet foreign policy in the Middle East (especially Egypt and Syria); religion and politics in the Soviet Union and Eastern Europe; the philosophies of Kant, Hegel and Marx; and all aspects of contemporary Yugoslavia. She has published articles on Yugoslavia in various publications on subjects as varied as politics, religion, nationalism, foreign policy, culture, journalism, feminism and the media. Dr Ramet is fluent in Serbo-Croat, and has lived in Yugoslavia for various periods of time over the years. Her publications include *Nationalism and Federalism in Yugoslavia, 1963–1983* (Bloomington, Ind., 1984), *Yugoslavia in the 1980s* (Boulder, Colo., 1985), *Cross and Commissar: The Politics of Religion in Eastern Europe and the Soviet Union* (Bloomington, Ind., 1987), *Religion and Nationalism in Soviet and East European Politics* (Durham, NC, 1984) and *Eastern Christianity and Politics in the Twentieth Century* (Durham, NC, 1988).

Tony Topham is currently Senior Research Officer at the Adult Education Department, University of Nottingham. Prior to his present position, which began in 1987, he was the North Yorkshire and Cleveland Organizing Tutor for the Workers' Educational Association (1954–62); and, Lecturer, Senior Lecturer, and head of the Industrial Studies Unit, at the Adult Education Department, University of Hull (1962–87). A lifelong member of the Labour Party, Mr Topham is also a founder member of the Institute for Workers' Control; a Director of the Bertrand Russell Peace Foundation and Secretary of the Trade Union Group in the European Nuclear Disarmament Conventions. His publications include (with Fred Singleton) *Workers' Control in Yugoslavia* (London, 1962), (with Ken Coates) *Industrial Democracy in Britain* (London and Nottingham, 1968, 1970 & 1975), *The Organized Worker* (London, 1975), (with Ken Coates) *Trade Unions in Britain* (Nottingham & London, 1980, 1981 & 1988), and (with Ken Coates) *Trade Unions and Politics* (Oxford, 1986).

Andrew M. Wood, MA(Cambridge), CMG(1986), was UK Ambassador to Yugoslavia from 1985–89. His career has included positions in Washington (1967), Belgrade (1976), and Moscow (1979), as well as positions in the Cabinet Office (1971) and the Foreign and Commonwealth Office (1970, 1973, 1982 and 1983) in London. While at the FCO in London, he has been head of its West European Department (1982) as well as of its Personnel Operations Department (1983). He is currently a minister with the UK Diplomatic Service in Washington.

Index